STREL

Dorset

Bournemouth and Poole

First published in 2002 by

Philip's, a division of
Octopus Publishing Group Ltd
2–4 Heron Quays, London E14 4JP

First colour edition 2002
Second impression with revisions 2003

ISBN 0-540-08121-3 (pocket)

© Philip's 2003

Ordnance Survey®

This product includes mapping data licensed
from Ordnance Survey® with the permission
of the Controller of Her Majesty's Stationery
Office. © Crown copyright 2003. All rights
reserved. Licence number 100011710.

Printed and bound in Spain
by Cayfosa-Quebecor

Contents

III	**Key to map symbols**
IV	**Key to map pages**
VI	**Route planning**
VIII	**Administrative and Postcode boundaries**
1	**Street maps** at 2½ inches to 1 mile
188	**Street maps** at 1¼ inches to 1 mile
212	**Street map** at 2½ inches to 1 mile
213	**Town map of** Salisbury
214	**Index** of towns and villages
217	**Index** of streets, hospitals, industrial estates, railway stations, schools, shopping centres, universities and places of interest

Digital Data

The exceptionally high-quality mapping found in this atlas is available as digital data in
TIFF format, which is easily convertible to other bitmapped (raster) image formats.

The index is also available in digital form as a standard database table. It contains all the
details found in the printed index together with the National Grid reference for the map
square in which each entry is named.

For further information and to discuss your requirements, please contact
Philip's on 020 7644 6932 or james.mann@philips-maps.co.uk

III

	Motorway with junction number	
	Primary route – dual/single carriageway	
	A road – dual/single carriageway	
	B road – dual/single carriageway	
	Minor road – dual/single carriageway	
	Other minor road – dual/single carriageway	
	Road under construction	
	Pedestrianised area	
DY7	**Postcode boundaries**	
	County and unitary authority boundaries	
	Railway	
	Railway under construction	
	Tramway, miniature railway	
	Rural track, private road or narrow road in urban area	
	Gate or obstruction to traffic (restrictions may not apply at all times or to all vehicles)	
	Path, bridleway, byway open to all traffic, road used as a public path	
	The representation in this atlas of a road, track or path is no evidence of the existence of a right of way	

⇥ Walsall	**Railway station**	
🚇	**Private railway station**	
➖	**Bus, coach station**	
◆	**Ambulance station**	
◆	**Coastguard station**	
◆	**Fire station**	
◆	**Police station**	
✚	**Accident and Emergency entrance to hospital**	
H	**Hospital**	
✚	**Place of worship**	
𝒊	**Information Centre** (open all year)	
P	**Parking**	
P&R	**Park and Ride**	
PO	**Post Office**	
X	**Camping site**	
🚐	**Caravan site**	
▶	**Golf course**	
✕	**Picnic site**	
Prim Sch	**Important buildings, schools, colleges, universities and hospitals**	
River Medway	**Water name**	
	River, stream	
	Lock, weir	
	Water	
	Tidal water	
	Woods	
	Houses	
Church	**Non-Roman antiquity**	
ROMAN FORT	**Roman antiquity**	

214

168

72

Adjoining page indicators
(The colour of the arrow indicates the scale of the adjoining page - see scales below)

217

The map area within the blue band is shown at a larger scale on the page, indicated by the blue block and arrow

Acad	**Academy**	Mkt	**Market**
Allot Gdns	**Allotments**	Meml	**Memorial**
Cemy	**Cemetery**	Mon	**Monument**
C Ctr	**Civic Centre**	Mus	**Museum**
CH	**Club House**	Obsy	**Observatory**
Coll	**College**	Pal	**Royal Palace**
Crem	**Crematorium**	PH	**Public House**
Ent	**Enterprise**	Recn Gd	**Recreation Ground**
Ex H	**Exhibition Hall**	Resr	**Reservoir**
Ind Est	**Industrial Estate**	Ret Pk	**Retail Park**
IRB Sta	**Inshore Rescue Boat Station**	Sch	**School**
		Sh Ctr	**Shopping Centre**
Inst	**Institute**	TH	**Town Hall/House**
Ct	**Law Court**	Trad Est	**Trading Estate**
L Ctr	**Leisure Centre**	Univ	**University**
LC	**Level Crossing**	Wks	**Works**
Liby	**Library**	YH	**Youth Hostel**

■ The small numbers around the edges of the maps identify the 1 kilometre National Grid lines ■ The dark grey border on the inside edge of some pages indicates that the mapping does not continue onto the adjacent page

he scale of the maps on the pages numbered in blue
3.92 cm to 1 km • 2½ inches to 1 mile • 1: 25344

0		¼		½		¾		1 mile
0	250m		500m		750m	1 kilometre		

he scale of the maps on pages numbered in green
1.96 cm to 1 km • 1¼ inches to 1 mile • 1: 50688

0	¼	½	¾	1 mile	
0	250m	500m	750m	1kilometre	

IV

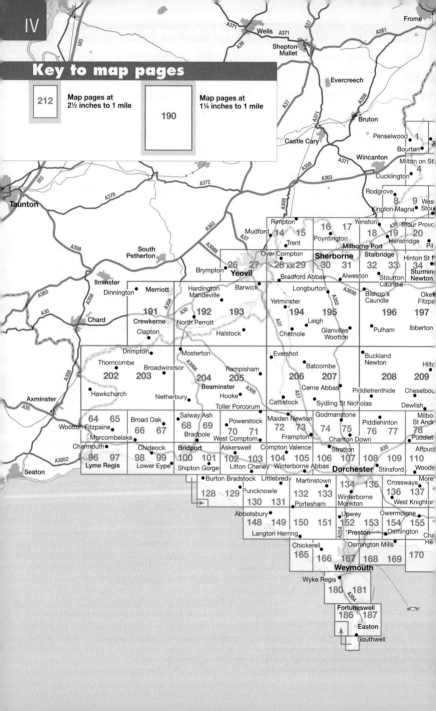

Key to map pages

| 212 | Map pages at 2½ inches to 1 mile |
| 190 | Map pages at 1¼ inches to 1 mile |

Frome

Wells

Shepton Mallet

Evercreech

Bruton

Penselwood   1

Bourton

Milton on St

Castle Cary

Wincanton   4

Cucklington

Rodgrove

Taunton   8   9   Wes Stou

Kington Magna

South Petherton

Rimpton   16   17   Yenston   18   19   20

Mudford   14   15   Poyntington   Henstridge   Pil

Ilminster

Trent   Milborne Port

Over Compton   Stalbridge   Hinton St I

Brympton   26   27   28   29   Sherborne   30   31   32   33   34   Sturminster Newton

Yeovil

Bradford Abbas   Alweston   Stourton Caundle

Dinnington   Merriott   Hardington Mandeville   Barwick   Longburton   Bishop's Caundle   Oke Fitzpa

Chard   191   192   193   Yetminster   194   195   196   197

Crewkerne   North Perrott   Leigh   Ibberton

Clapton   Halstock   Chetnole   Glanvilles Wootton   Pulham

Drimpton   Mosterton   Evershot   Buckland Newton   Hiltc

Thorncombe   Broadwindsor   Rampisham   Batcombe   208   209

202   203   204   205   206   207   Cheselbou

Hawkchurch   Netherbury   Beaminster   Cerne Abbas   Piddletrenthide   Dewlish

Axminster   Hooke   Cattistock   Sydling St Nicholas

Toller Porcorum

Salway Ash   Maiden Newton   Godmanstone   Milbo St Andr

64   65   Broad Oak   68   69   Powerstock   72   73   74   75   Piddlehinton   76   77   78   Puddlet

Wootton Fitzpaine   66   67   Bradpole   70   71   Frampton   Charlton Down

Morcombelake   West Compton

Charmouth   Chideock   Bridport   Askerswell   Compton Valence   Stratton   Affpuc

96   97   98   99   100   101   102   103   104   105   106   107   108   109   110   Woods

Seaton   Lyme Regis   Lower Eype   Shipton Gorge   Litton Cheney   Winterborne Abbas   Dorchester   Stinsford

Burton Bradstock   Littlebredy   Martinstown   134   135   Crossways   More

128   129   Puncknowle   132   133   Winterborne Monkton   136   137

130   131   Portesham   West Knighton

Abbotsbury   Upwey   Owermoigne

148   149   150   151   152   153   154   155   Cha

Langton Herring   Preston   Osmington   He

Chickerell   Osmington Mills

165   166   167   168   169   170

Weymouth

Wyke Regis

180   181

Fortuneswell

186   187

Easton

Southwell

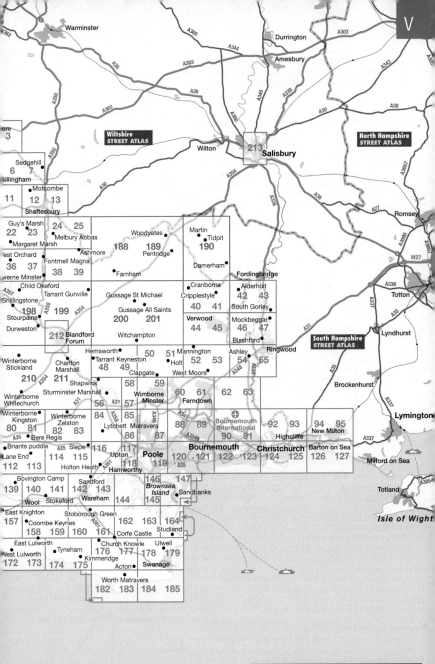

Warminster

A360

A303

Durrington
A344
Amesbury

A36

A303

A343

A303

A36

A345

A338

A30

A30

Romsey

Wiltshire
STREET ATLAS

Wilton

213 Salisbury

North Hampshire
STREET ATLAS

A354

A36

A3057

ere
3

Sedgehill
6 7

A350

A360

Totton

illingham

Motcombe
11 12 13
Shaftesbury

A30

A338

A27

M27

A336

A337

Guy's Marsh
22 23 24 25

Woodyates

Martin
Tidpit
190

Lyndhurst

Melbury Abbas
Margaret Marsh
Ashmore
188 189
Pentridge

Damerham

Fordingbridge

South Hampshire
STREET ATLAS

est Orchard
36 37
Fontmell Magna
38 39

Farnham

Cranborne
Cripplestyle
40 41

Alderholt
42 43
South Gorley

werne Minster

Child Okeford
Tarrant Gunville
Shillingstone

Gussage St Michael
Gussage All Saints
200 201

Verwood
44 45

Mockbeggar
46 47
Blashford

198 199
Stourpaine
Durweston

212 Blandford
Forum

Witchampton

Mannington
50 51 52 53
Holt

Ashley
54 55

Ringwood

Hemsworth
Tarrant Keyneston
48 49
Clapgate

West Moors

Brockenhurst

A348

A337

Winterborne
Stickland
210 211
Charlton
Marshall

Shapwick
58 59
Wimborne
Minster

60 61
Ferndown

62 63

Lymington

Winterborne
Whitechurch

Sturminster Marshall
56 57

Winterborne
Kingston
80 81
Winterborne
Zelston
82 83

Lytchett Matravers
84 85
86

88 89

Bournemouth
International

92 93
Highcliffe

94 95
New Milton

A337

Bere Regis

A35

A341

A3049

Barton on Sea
126 127

Briants puddle
Lane End
112 113
114 115
Slepe
116 117
Upton
118 119
Holton Heath
Hamworthy

Poole

120 121

BOURNEMOUTH

122 123

Christchurch
124 125

Milford on Sea

A35

Bovington Camp
139 140 141
Wool
Stokeford

Sandford
142 143
Wareham
144

146 147
Brownsea
Island
145
Sandbanks

Totland

Isle of Wight

East Knighton
157
Coombe Keynes
158 159 160

Stoborough Green
162 163 164
161
Corfe Castle
Studland

East Lulworth
West Lulworth
172 173
Tyneham
174 175
Kimmeridge
Acton

Church Knowle
176 177 178 179
Ulwell
Swanage

Worth Matravers
182 183 184 185

Scale				
0	5	10	15	20 km
0		5		10 miles

Route planning

Scale

| 0 | 5 | 10 | 15 | 20 km |

| 0 | 5 | 10 miles |

Administrative and Postcode boundaries

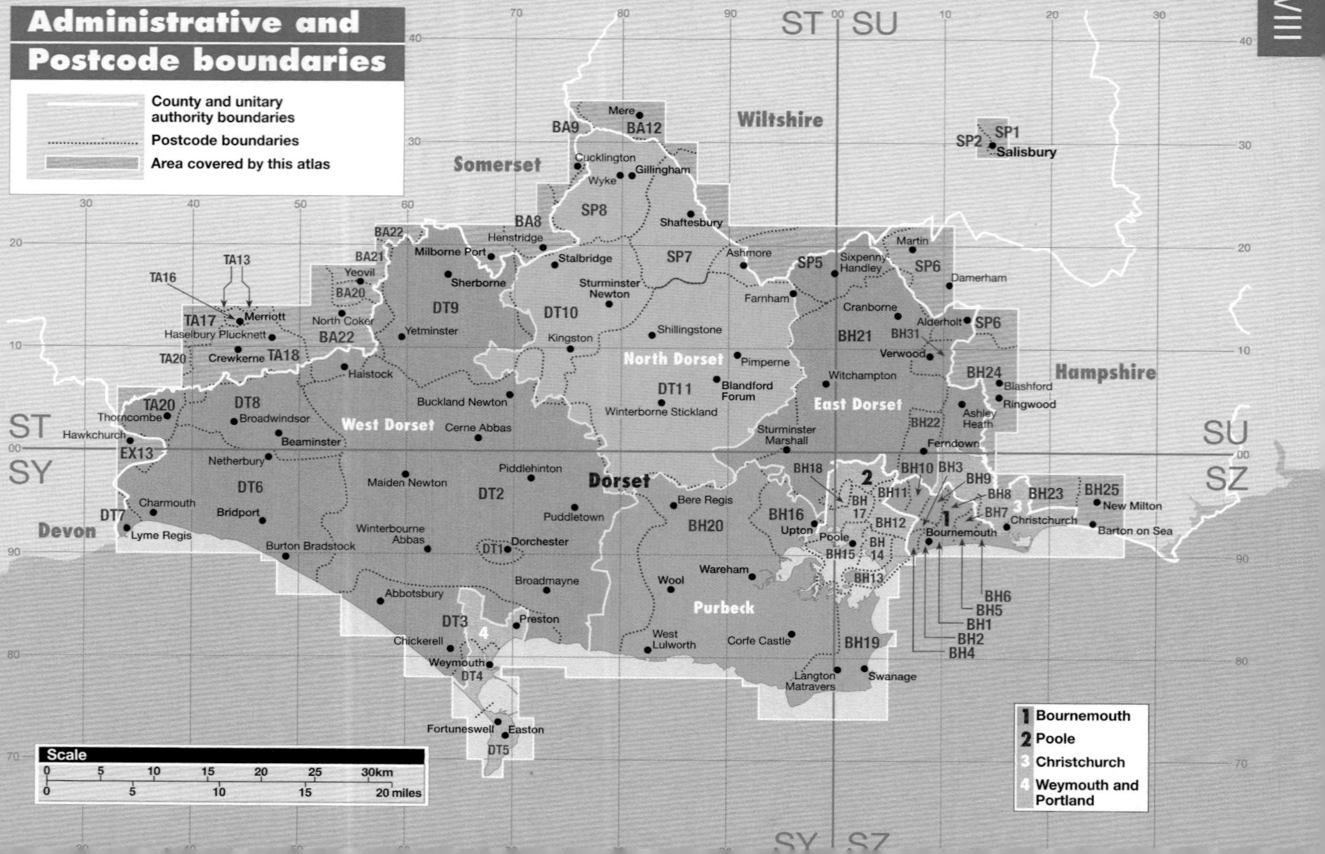

VIII

County and unitary authority boundaries

Postcode boundaries

Area covered by this atlas

1 Bournemouth
2 Poole
3 Christchurch
4 Weymouth and Portland

Scale

0	5	10	15	20	25	30km

0	5	10	15	20 miles

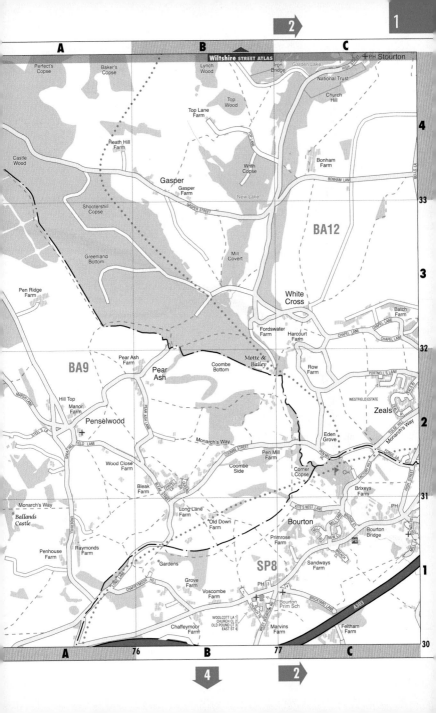

2

A **B** **C**

PH Stourton

Perfect's Copse

Baker's Copse

Lynch Wood

Iron Bridge

Garden Lake

National Trust

Church Hill

4

Top Wood

Top Lane Farm

Heath Hill Farm

Bonham Farm

Castle Wood

Gasper

Gasper Farm

Writh Copse

BONHAM LANE

33

Shootershill Copse

GASPER STREET

New Lake

BA12

Greenland Bottom

Mill Covert

3

Pen Ridge Farm

White Cross

Batch Farm

Fordswater Farm

Harcourt Farm

CHAPEL LANE

CHAPEL LANE

CHAPEL LANE

32

Pear Ash Farm

Pear Ash

Coombe Bottom

Motte & Bailey

Row Farm

PORTNELL'S LANE

BA9

Hill Top

Manor Farm

Penselwood

Monarch's Way

WESTFIELD ESTATE

Zeals

2

Eden Grove

Monarch's Way

Wood Close Farm

COOMBE STREET

Pen Mill Farm

Coombe Side

Corner Copse

CH

Bleak Farm

CHAPEL STREET

QUEENS

Brixeys Farm

PH

31

Monarch's Way

Long Lane Farm

Old Down Farm

KITE'S NEST LANE

Bourton

Bourton Bridge

Ballands Castle

UNDERHILL

Primrose Farm

MILL LA

NEW LA

PO

Penhouse Farm

Raymonds Farm

Gardens

Grove Farm

SP8

Sandways Farm

1

Voscombe Farm

PH 3

BRICKYARD LANE

A303

WOOLCOTT LA 1
CHURCH CL 2
OLD POUND CT 3
EAST ST 4

Bourton Prim Sch

Feltham Farm

Chaffeymoor Farm

Marvins Farm

30

A 76 **B** 77 **C**

4

2

A   **B**   **C**

Wiltshire STREET ATLAS

Cros
Dyke

Wood
Farm

4

Zeals
Knoll

33

Nor
Wood

MERE BY-PAS

BA12

A303

Cas
(site

Tumuli

Rec

Long
Hill

CADDY LA.
LONG HL.
UNDERHILL
FIELD
VALLEY

HILLSIDE CL.
PROSPECT PL.

3

B3095   CASTLE STRE

Quarry
Cottages

B3092

Long
Cross

Town
End

Greenhou

Lower
Zeals

32

St Martin
Farm

Manor
Farm

Zeals
First Sch

PH

Zeals
House

Castle Ground
Farm

ZEALS GN DR

Monarch's Way

2

Zeals

Wolverton

Zeals
Fish Farm

South
Lodge

B3092

Queen
Oak

31

Bagmore
Wood

Silton
Wood

Mapperton
Hill Farm

1

Fitz
Farm

SP8

Redmoor
Farm

MAPPERTON HILL

BULLEY LANE

Bagmore
Farm

Ridge
Hill Farm

30

78   **A**   **79**   **B**   **80**   **C**

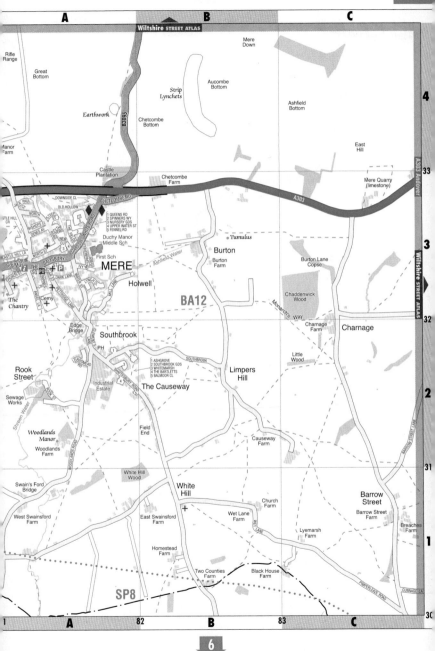

Mere
Down

Rifle
Range

Great
Bottom

Aucombe
Bottom

Strip
Lynchets

Ashfield
Bottom

Earthwork

Chetcombe
Bottom

Manor
Farm

Castle
Plantation

East
Hill

Mere Quarry
(limestone)

A303 Andover

Chetcombe
Farm

A303

33

DOWNSIDE CL
OLD HOLLOW

CHETCOMBE RD

1 QUEENS RD
2 SPINNERS WY
3 NURSERY GDS
4 UPPER WATER ST
5 FENNEL RD

Tumulus

Burton

Burton Lane
Copse

Duchy Manor
Middle Sch

First Sch

Ashfield Water

Burton
Farm

3

MERE

Chaddenwick
Wood

Holwell

BA12

Monarch's Way

Charnage
Farm

Charnage

32

The
Chantry

Cemy

Edge
Bridge

Southbrook

Little
Wood

Rook
Street

PH

SOUTHBROOK

1 ASHGROVE
2 SOUTHBROOK GDS
3 WHITEMARSH
4 THE BARTLETTS
5 BALMOOR CL

Limpers
Hill

Sewage
Works

Industrial
Estate

The Causeway

2

Shreen Water

Woodlands
Manor

Field
End

Causeway
Farm

Woodlands
Farm

31

Swain's Ford
Bridge

White Hill
Wood

White
Hill

Church
Farm

Barrow
Street

West Swainsford
Farm

East Swainsford
Farm

Wet Lane
Farm

WET LANE

Barrow Street
Farm

Breaches
Farm

Lyemarsh
Farm

1

Homestead
Farm

SP8

Two Counties
Farm

Black House
Farm

POMPELES LANE ROAD

CLINNAGE RD

30

A   82   B   83   C

A303 Honiton

A303

A   B   C

BROADOAK LANE

GRIMSEY LANE

MIDNEY LANE

4

Clapton
Farm

Manor
Farm

Iyletts
Farm

Blackwater
Farm

The Old Farm

West
Bourton

29

B3081

Slait Barn

3

Tinker's Hill

Cucklington
Wood

BA9

TINKER'S LANE

Depley
Farm

Broad Oak
Farm

Depley
Copse

28

SP8

Longhill Farm

Slait Farm

Ganges
Farm

Cucklington

BOWLE'S LANE

CROOKED
LANE

Church Farm
Dairy

WOODHOUSE
CROSS

2

Hale

Thorns Farm

Babwell
Farm

WITHYBED LANE

Bainley
Hill Farm

B3081 RD

Homers
Farm

Spear
Copse

SCHOOL HILL

27

Plaishbridge
Farm

Bainley
Bottom

Symphony
Farm

MACCLOSE LANE

Shanks
House

The
Belt

1

LONG LANE

Quarr
Farm

LANGHAM LA

Lower
Langham Farm

Clinger
Farm

Quarr

MOOR LANE

MOOR
LA

26

75   A   76   B   77   C

A   B   C

Huntingford

Sewage Works

Wyndham Farm

Slodbrook Farm

Higher Redmoor Farm

Rope Farm

4

Silton

Manor Farm

Redmoor

Spickett's Bridge

B3092

29

Whistley Coppice

River Stour

Spicketts Farm

Glendon Farm

Benjafields Farm

Hotel

Whistley Farm

Pierston Manor Farm

Gillingham Milton Prim Sch

Shreen Water

3

Little Marsh

Milton on Stour

SP8

Newlands Farm

Kendalls Farm

Milton Farm

The Kendalls

Colesbrook Farm

BURNS MILL LA

28

Woolfields Farm

Ford

FIELD LANE

Colesbook

North Dorset RFC

Peacemarsh

2

Longbury (Long Barrow)

WAVERING LANE

Stock Water

Stock House Farm

Stock Lane

Slaughtergate Farm

WAVERING LANE

WAVERING LANE

HYDE

27

Wyke Hall

Cerny

Gillingham CP Sch

Stock Hill (Hotel)

Wyke Farm

MILFORD COURT

ROLLS BR LANE

RIVER VIEW

KING EDMUND COURT

TURNERS LANE

Herons Wood

HAWTHORN AV

WYKE ROAD

B3081

1

Bramley Farm

Wyke CP Sch

Wyke

SYCAMORE WY

CHESTNUT WY

MAPLE WAY

THE OAKS

School Rd

Liby & Gillingham Museum

GILLINGHAM

B3081

HARRY LODGE'S LANE

CULVERS LANE

BRICKYARD LA

26

A   79   B   80   C

A1
1 BRICKYARD LA
2 PROSPECT CL
3 ROSE CT
4 RAILWAY TR
5 HAM LA
6 KINGSCOURT CL
7 ROOKERY CL

Park Pale

Higher Mere
Park

BA12

River Lodden

New Leaze
Farm

SP3

Snaggs
Farm

Lower
Park Farm

Forest
Oaks

Grove
Coppice

Westmarsh
Farm

PITTS LANE

Pitts
Farm

Sweetwell
Farm

Church
Farm

Sedgehill

Lower
House Farm

SP7

Cowridge
Copse

Withies
Farm

Earthwork

Berrybrook
Farm

STREET LANE

Hull
Copse

North End
Farm

Sedgehill
Manor

Hayes
Copse

North
End

Guests
Farm

Park
Farm

Butterstake
Farm

Culver House
Farm

Dewdown
Copse

Knapp Hill

Huggler's
Hole

Stile End

West
Toppleridge
Farm

PH

CORNER LANE

The
Corner

Elm Hill

Motcombe Grange
Preparatory Sch

North
Hayes Farm

Westley
Copse

Sewage
Works

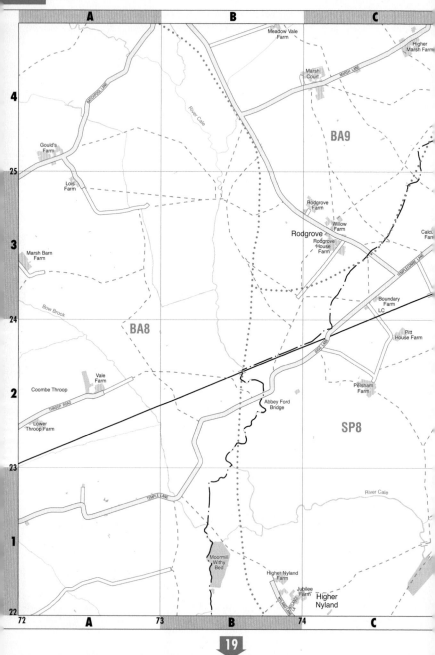

Meadow Vale Farm

Higher Marsh Farm

MARSH LANE

Marsh Court

BA9

River Cale

BALGROVE LANE

Gould's Farm

Lois Farm

Rodgrove Farm

Willow Farm

Rodgrove

Calcu Farm

Rodgrove House Farm

Marsh Barn Farm

TEMPLECOMBE LANE

Bow Brook

Boundary Farm LC

BA8

Pitt House Farm

Pelsham Farm

HIGH LANE

Vale Farm

Coombe Throop

Abbey Ford Bridge

THROOP ROAD

SP8

Lower Throop Farm

TEMPLE LANE

River Cale

Moormill Withy Bed

Higher Nyland Farm

Jubilee Farm

Higher Nyland

BRIDGE LANE

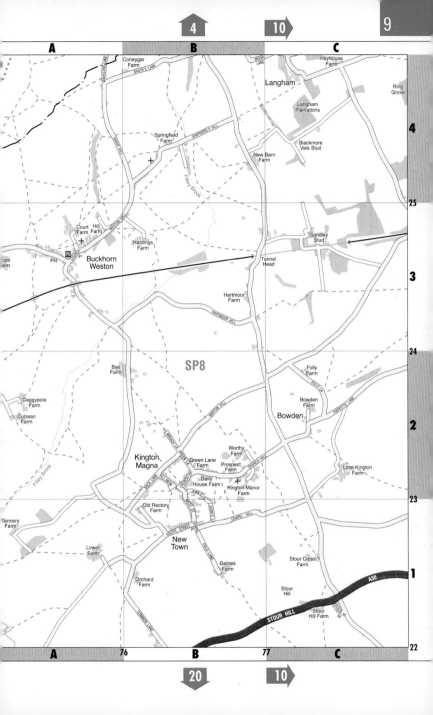

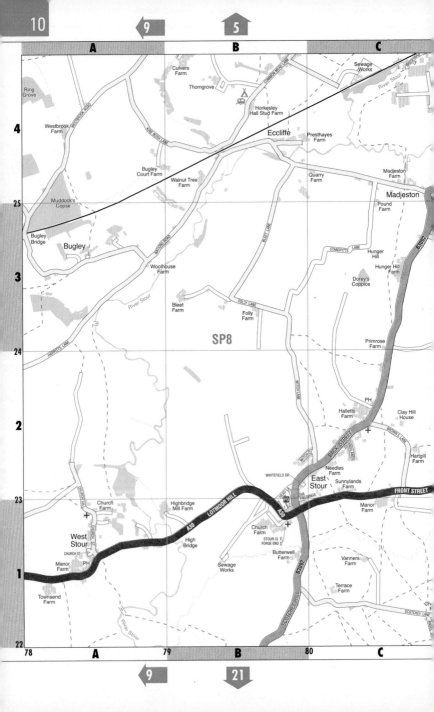

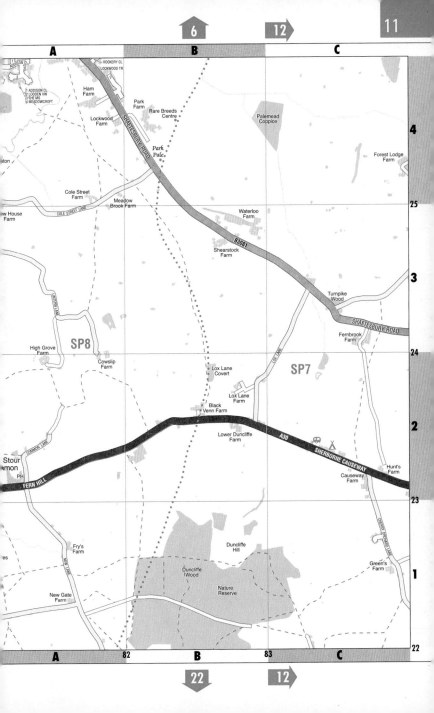

11
7

A   **B**   **C**

4

Shorts Green Farm

PH

NEW LANE

Valencia

SHORTS GREEN LANE

THE

Mole End

Motcombe

The Plantation

Kingsettle Wood

Nature Reserve

Shell Cop

Avenue Farm

Grant's Copse

P

Motcombe CE Sch

25

Church Farm

Little Grove

Bittles Green

Kingsettle Wood

PING LANE

Meaders Farm

Bittles Green Farm

Thanes Farm

North Heath

Manor Farm

3

Ryal's Plantation

Port Regis Sch

The Cliff

Motcombe House Plantations

Motcombe Park

Oates Plantation

MOTCOMBE ROAD

HOMEFIELD

B3081

SHAFTESBURY ROAD

24

Whitehouse Farm

SP7

Cowherd Shute Farm

LITTLEDOWN

A350

Hawkers Hill Farm

Old Brickyard Farm

Lady's Copse

Quoits Copse

GROSVENOR ROAD

2

SHAFTESBURY

NEW ROAD

LONG CROSS

LT CONDUIT LA

CHRISTY'S

THE VENN

LONGMEAD

Long Cross Farm

NETTLEBED NURSERY

NEW ROAD

Enmore Green

A30

SHERBORNE CAUSEWAY

CHURCH HILL

SALISBURY STREET

Lib

P

Barton Hill House Sch

BARTON HILL

HIGH ST

B3091

23

Woolcotts Farm

HORSEPONDS

i

PO

P

Football Club

BREACH LANE

UMBERS HILL
LANGFORDS LA
LAUNDRY LA

Abbey Mus

Mus

ST RUMB

BIMPORT

Westminster Memh

Mus

1

Grants Farm

LOVE LANE

Shaftesbury Upp Sch

ST JAMES'S ST

Alcester

Abbots Vale

St James

FRENCH MILL RI

Brinscombe

Cherry Orchard Farm

Edwards Farm

Church Farm

The Abbey CE First Sch

TOUT HILL

B3081

FRENCH MILL LANE

BRINSCOMBE LA

22

DENBY DR LANE

84   **A**   85   **B**   86   **C**

11
23

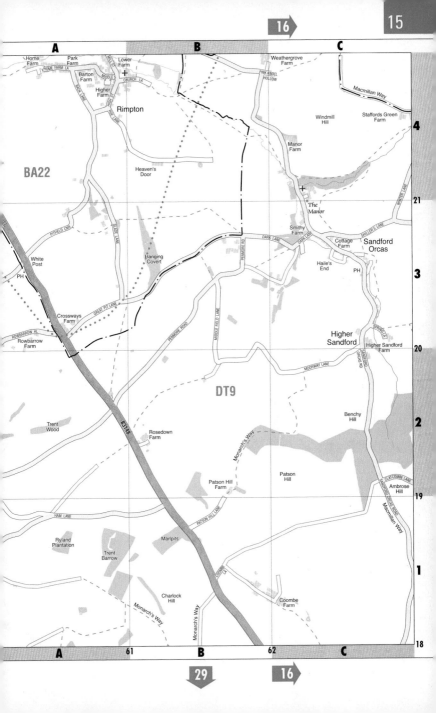

A   B   C

Wheat Sheaf Hill
Wheatsheaf Farm

Seven Wells Down

Seven Sisters Well (source of River Yeo)

Seven Wells Farm

Sleight Plantation

4 Stafford's Green

Macmillan Way

* Pillow Mounds

Milborne Down

Poyntington Down

West Down Farm

B3145

21

Holway Farm

Holway Hill

Poyntington Hill

3

Holway Ball Copse

Bickerley

Holway

Townsend Farm

Home Farm

Manor Farm

THE RIDGE

20

Macmillan Way

Holway Copse

DT9

RED POST

Hillside Farm

Poyntington

2

Higher Clatcombe Farm

Coll Farm

Higher Oborne

Dairy Farm

CH

CLATCOMBE LA

Sherborne Golf Club

B3145

Higher Oborne Farm

Vale View Farm

LOWER BURTON LANE

19

Ambrose Hill

BISHOP'S LANE

Oborne Wood

Mill Close Farm

Grange Farm

1

Oborne

Lower Oborne Farm

Laurels Farm

Macmillan Way

CASTLE TOWN WAY

Church Farm

18

63   64   65

A   B   C

B1
1 WHEATHILL CL
2 GLOVERS CL
3 LIMERICK CL
4 LWR GUNVILLE
5 HIGHER GUNVILLE
6 SANSOME'S HL
7 CHAPEL LA
8 CANNON CT MS
9 PUD BROOK
10 BAUNTONS CL
11 PLOVER CL
12 PRANKERDS RD
13 LAMBERT CL

Earthworks
Starve Acre
New Covert
Ridge Plantation
Bomer's Bridge
Laycock Farm
Bugle Farm
Bradley Head Spring
Manor Farm
Fort
Bowden Farm
Bradley Head Farm
Higher Farm
Milborne Wick
DT9
White House Farm
Everlanes Covert
Silverthorne Farm
Three Arch Bridge
Kingsbury Farm
Spurles Farm
Hen Wood
Coombe Hill Farm
Spurles Covert
Higher Coombe Farm
Kingsbury Regis
Wheathill Farm
East Hill Wood
Peaceville Farm
HIGHER KINGSBURY CL
Nurseries
Wynbrook Farm
New Town
GP Sch
Vartenham Hill
Milborne Port
Crendle Hill Wood
Crendle
Tapps Well
HIGH ST
Ven
Ilside Farm
CRACKMORE
Canons Court Farm
LONDON ROAD
Ven Farm
A30
Crackmore Wood
A30

MILLER'S HILL
WICK ROAD
SANDY ROAD
OLD BOWDEN WY
BOWDEN LANE
PROSPEROUS LANE
FURLONG LANE
COOMBE LANE
MANOR ROAD
BAUNTONS DR
WHEATHILL LANE
SPRING GDNS
GAINSBOROUGH
WEST ST
EAST STREET
SHERBORNE RD
GOLDINI'S LANE
BROOK ST
OXHILL ROAD

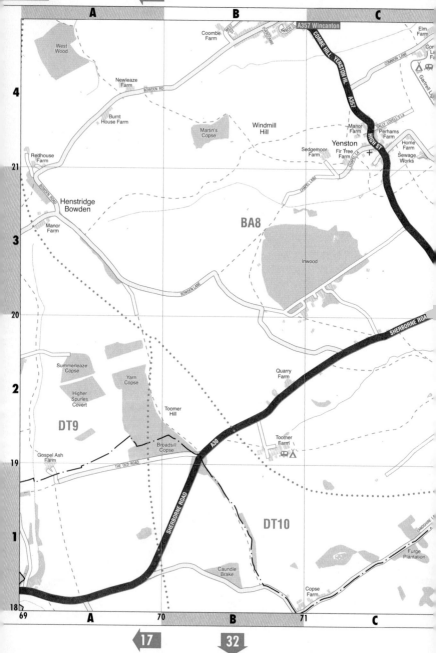

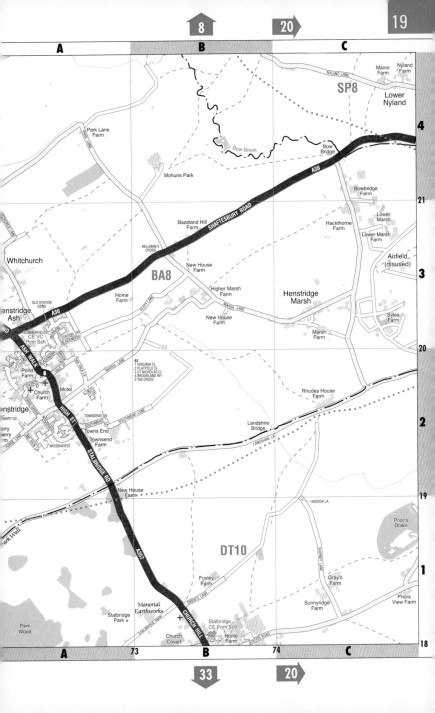

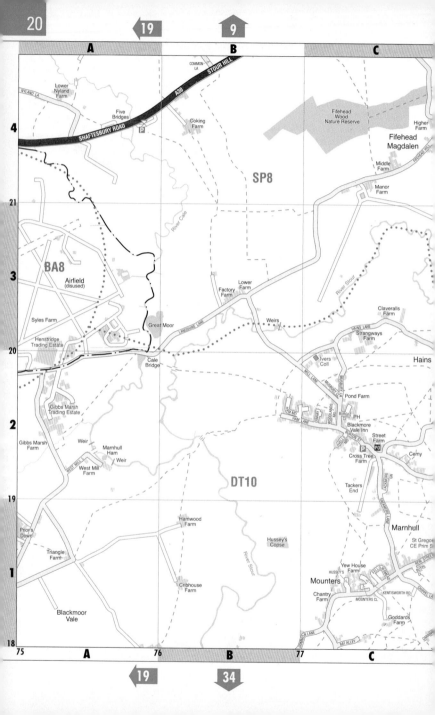

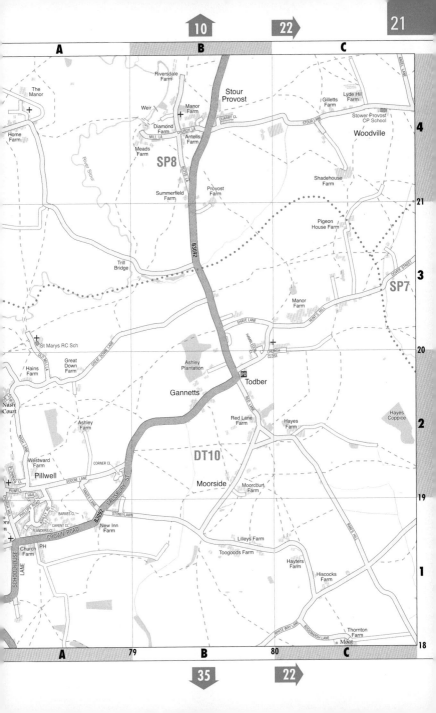

A B C

The Manor

Riversdale Farm

Stour Provost

Weir

Manor Farm

Diamond Farm

Gilletts Farm

Lyde Hill Farm

Stower Provost CP School

Home Farm

MILL LA

Antells Farm

CHURCH LA

QUARRY CL

STOUR LANE

Woodville

Meads Farm

SP8

4

River Stour

Summerfield Farm

Provost Farm

Shadehouse Farm

B3092

21

BUTTS CL

Pigeon House Farm

Trill Bridge

3

Manor Farm

DOVER STREET

SP7

SHAVE LANE

HUNT'S HILL

St Marys RC Sch

GREAT DOWN LANE

HAMM CL

CHURCH CLOSE

20

Hains Farm

Great Down Farm

Ashley Plantation

Gannetts

Todber

PO

RED LANE

Nash Court

Ashley Farm

Red Lane Farm

Hayes Farm

Hayes Coppice

2

Westward Farm

CORNER CL

SALISBURY ST

Pillwell

SODOM LANE

DANCEY LANE

DT10

Moorside

Moorcourt Farm

19

PILWELL

HAR...

BARNES CL

STONEYLAWN

PARK'S HILL

CARENT CL

PHILLIPS ROAD

FLANDERS CL

B3092

CROWN ROAD

New Inn Farm

Church Farm

PH

SCHOOL HOUSE LANE

Lilleys Farm

Toogoods Farm

Hayters Farm

Hiscocks Farm

1

Thornton Moat

WHITE WAY LANE

ROD MARSH LANE

18

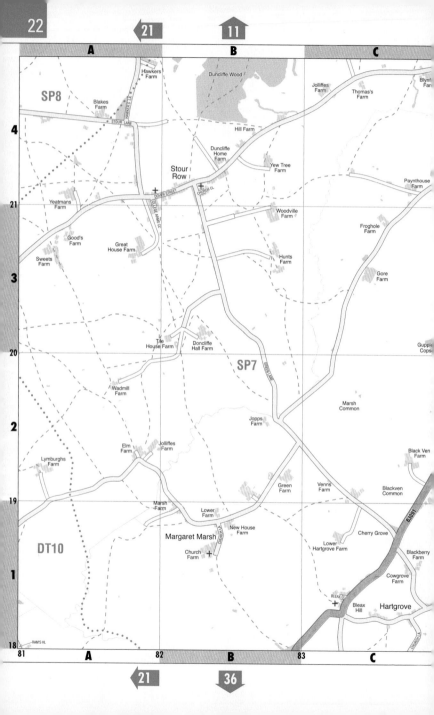

A B C

SP8

Hawkers
Farm

Duncliffe Wood

Jolliffes
Farm

Thomas's
Farm

Blynf
Far

Blakes
Farm

STOUR LANE

4

Hill Farm

Duncliffe
Home
Farm

Yew Tree
Farm

Stour
Row

CHURCH CL.

Paynthouse
Farm

21

Yeatmans
Farm

DOVER STREET

COLLIER ARMS CL.

Woodville
Farm

Froghole
Farm

Good's
Farm

Great
House Farm

Hunts
Farm

Gore
Farm

Sweets
Farm

3

Tile
House Farm

Doncliffe
Hall Farm

SP7

Gupple
Copse

20

Wadmill
Farm

Marsh
Common

BREEZE LANE

2

Jopps
Farm

Jolliffes
Farm

Elm
Farm

Black Ven
Farm

Lymburghs
Farm

Green
Farm

Venns
Farm

Blackven
Common

19

Marsh
Farm

Lower
Farm

New House
Farm

CHURCH LA.

B3091

DT10

Church
Farm

Margaret Marsh

Cherry Grove

Lower
Hartgrove Farm

Blackberry
Farm

Cowgrove
Farm

1

BLEAX CL.

Bleax
Hill

Hartgrove

CHURCH LA.

18

RAM'S HL.

81 A 82 B 83 C

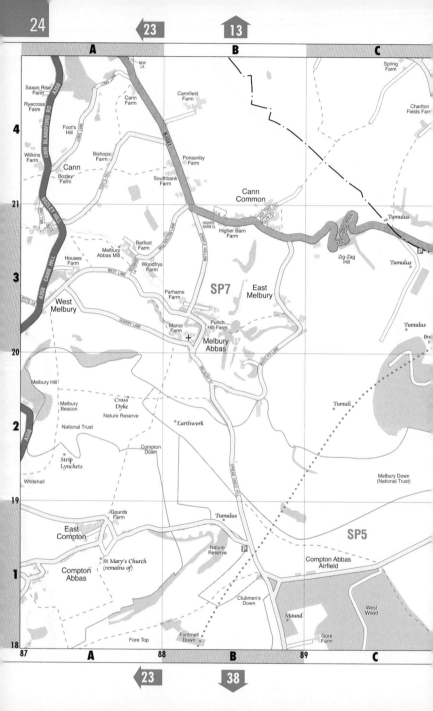

A   B   C

4

NEW LA

Saxon Rise
Farm

Ryecross
Farm

Foot's
Hill

Wilkins
Farm

Cann

Bozley
Farm

LONG LANE

Cann
Farm

Cannfield
Farm

A350

LWR BLANDFORD RD

Bishops
Farm

Ponsonby
Farm

Southbank
Farm

Cann
Common

21

BOZLEY HILL

MILL
LANE

MILL
LANE

A350 CANN HILL

PITTS LA

Barfoot
Farm

Melbury
Abbas Mill

Houses
Farm

Woodfrys
Farm

WEST LANE

MILTON DRIVE LANE

DRAFT HOLLOW

HIGHER
BARN CL

Higher Barn
Farm

FSS TREE LA

ZIG-ZAG HILL

ZIG

Tumulus

Zig-Zag
Hill

P

Tumulus

Spring
Farm

Charlton
Fields Farm

3

West
Melbury

QUARRY LANE

Parhams
Farm

Manor
Farm

+

SP7

Punch
Hill Farm

Melbury
Abbas

East
Melbury

WHITE PIT LANE

Tumulus

Bre

20

Melbury Hill

Melbury
Beacon

National Trust

Cross
Dyke

Nature Reserve

MELBURY ST

Earthwork

Tumuli

2

A350

Compton
Down

SPREAD EAGLE HILL

Melbury Down
(National Trust)

Strip
Lynchets

Whitehall

19

East
Compton

Gourds
Farm

Tumulus

P

SP5

Compton
Abbas

St Mary's Church
(remains of)

Nature
Reserve

Compton Abbas
Airfield

1

Clubmen's
Down

Mound

West
Wood

Gore
Farm

18

Fore Top

Fontmell
Down

A   B   C

Home Farm

Manor Farm

Wessex Ridgeway

SP7

Higher Berrycourt Farm

4

Beech Clump

21

Elliott's Shed

Charlton Down

Tumulus

Tumulus

National Trust

B3081

Win Green

3

Hawcombe Copse

Charlton Down

Cross Dyke

P

Melbury Wood

Win Green Plantation

Wessex Ridgeway

20

Quarry Bottom

Long Barrow

Nature Reserve

Melbury Down

SP5

2

Ashmore Down

POSSESSIONS CORNER

Abbot's Copse

19

Hatts Copse

Cross Dyke

NORTH ROAD

B3081

Ashgrove Farm

1

Woodley Down

Boyne Bottom

South Farm

Wessex Ridgeway

PO

18

A   91   B   92   C

B3
1 BRIGADIER CL
2 HOUNDSTONE CT
3 CELANDINE RD

C3
1 TRELLECH CT
2 THE REGENTS
3 DERWENT WY
4 HILLBORNE GDNS
5 THREE CORNER MD
6 BARLYNCH CT
7 MALVERN CT
8 NETLEY
9 TEWKESBURY

A   B   C

4

17

3

16

2

15

1

14

51   A   52   B   53   C

BA21

BA22

BA20

Thorne
Coffin

Manor
Farm

Mast

Oak
Farm

Lufton
Manor Coll

Lufton
Trading Estate

Yeovil
Coll

Yeovil Town
Football Club

Yeovil Coll

Houndstone

Manor
Farm

Lufton

High Leaze
Farm

Clarks
Close

Crematorium

Alvington

Alvington
Farm

Preston
Plucknett

Watercombe
Farm

Tithe
Barn

Preston City
Comp Sch

Cannington
Coll

Higher
Preston
Farm

DIY
Superstore

Lower
Odcombe

Bank Farm

Home
Farm

Brympton
House

Brympton
D'Evercy

Playing
Field

Lynx West
Trading
Estate

Lynx
Trading
Estate

Pye
Corner

Leaze
Cottages

Camp
Hill

Broadleaze Farm

Dry
Copse

Feebarrow

Sampson's
Wood

Ash
Copse

LYSANDER ROAD

WEST COKER RD

Nash
Farm

C1
1 DOWNLEAZE
2 WOODCOTE
3 THE BRIARS
4 OAKLEIGH
5 RIDGEMEAD
6 BIRCHDALE
7 THE SPINNEY
8 FOXCOTE
9 THE FURZE
10 THE CROFT

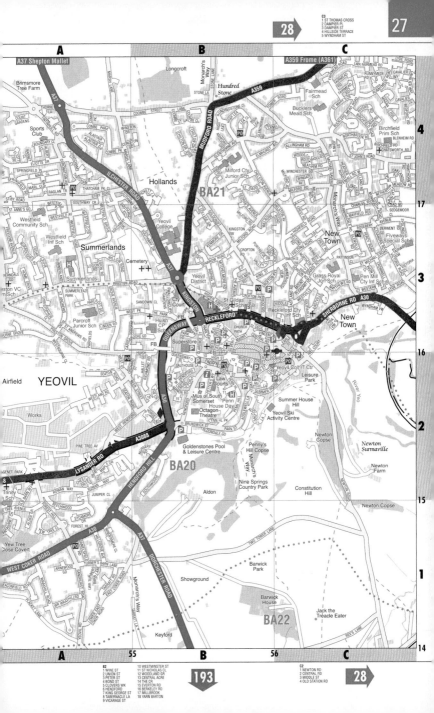

B2
1 WINE ST
2 UNION ST
3 PETER ST
4 BOND ST
5 CLOVERS WK
6 HENDFORD
7 KING GEORGE ST
8 TABERNACLE LA
9 VICARAGE ST
10 WESTMINSTER ST
11 ST NICHOLAS CL
12 WOODLAND GR
13 CENTRAL ACRE
14 THE CR
15 EVERTON RD
16 BERKELEY RD
17 MILLBROOK
18 YARN BARTON

C2
1 NEWTON RD
2 CENTRAL RD
3 MIDDLE ST
4 OLD STATION RD

193

28

A   **B**   **C**

1 CORTON CL
2 ADBER CL
3 COMPTON CL
4 SANDLEWOOD CL
5 ASHWOOD DR

Trent Brook

4

PO WY

HERTFORD

BLENHEIM RD

YEOVIL

ST JOHN'S RD

WELBECK RD

MONTROSE RD

PEMBROKE RD

MEADOW RD

BABYLON VIEW

Glebe Farm

Lower Dairy Farm

Net Com

PLUM ORCHARD

Plum Orchard Farm

Lower Farm

17

St MICHAELS

WESTERN ST

St Michels

WESTERN ST

Lower Farm

Over Compton

Compton Manor Farm

BELVEDERE RD

LYDE LA

VALE ROAD

Sewage Works

Higher Farm

Butterfly House

Pen Mill

Yeovil Coll

HERBLAY CL

BUCKLAND ROAD

Pen Mill Trading Estate

River Yeo

COMPTON ROAD

3

Sewage Works

BA21

LENNE LANE

Babylon Hill

BABYLON HILL

Noor Farm

Yeovil Pen Mill

SHERBORNE ROAD

A30

16

CH

Yeovil Golf Club

DT9

Tilly's Hill

LEAZE LANE

2

East Farm

15

UNDERDOWN HOLLOW

Coombe

Park House

BA20

River Yeo

Manor Farm

QUARRY LANE

FARM ROAD

PETTITTS CL

CROSS WY.

QUEENS RD

CROSS ROAD

AMBROSE LA

HIGHER WESTBURY

1

Bradford Abbas

PO

CHURCH RD

Yeovil Junction

BA22

Bradford Abbas Prim Sch

14

57   **A**   **58**   **B**   **59**   **C**

B1
1 BAKEHOUSE LA
2 THE CROSS

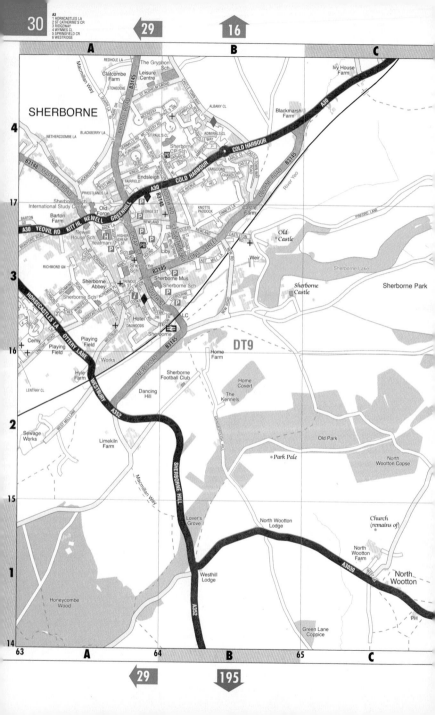

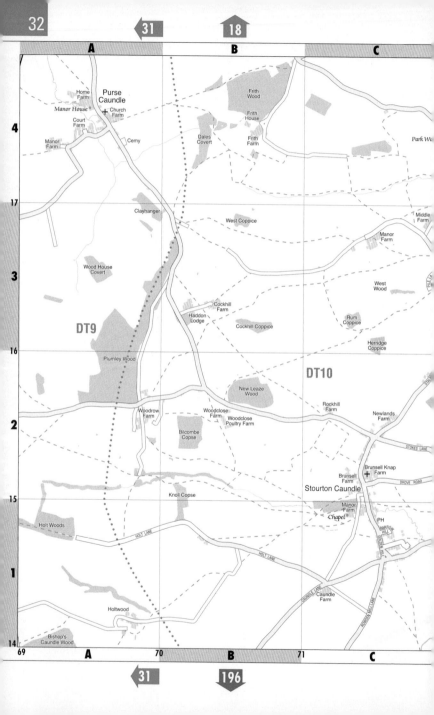

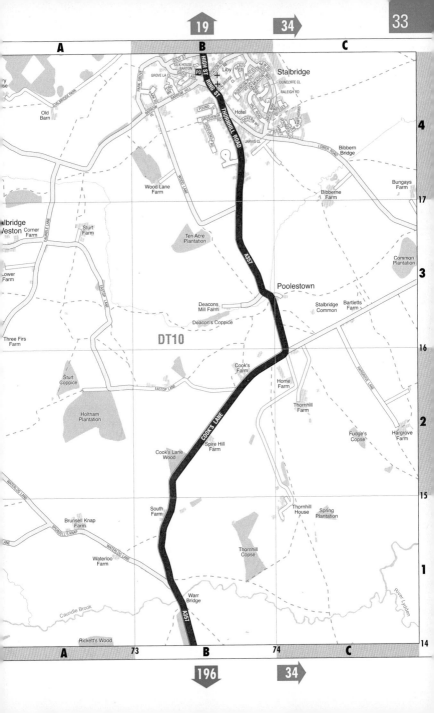

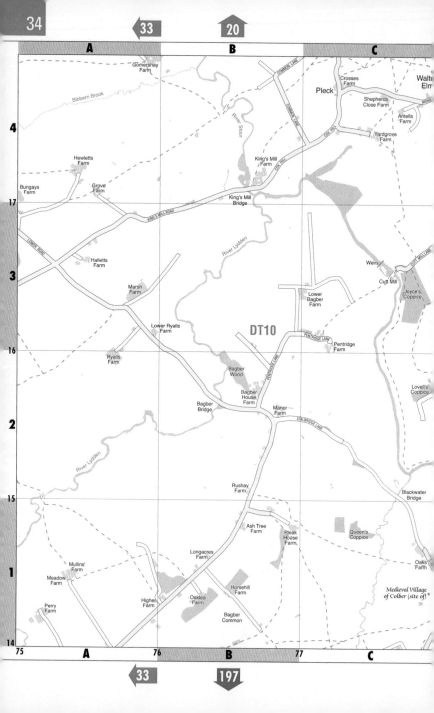

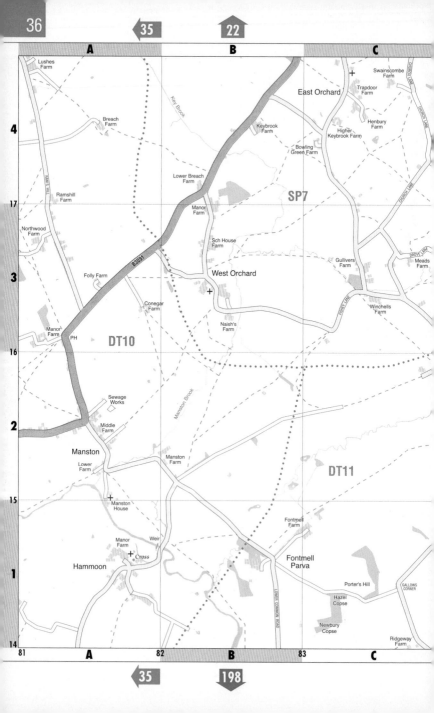

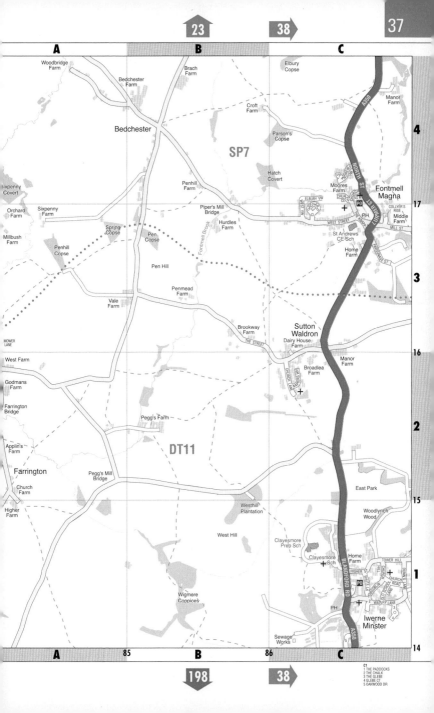

A
B
C

Shepherd's Bottom

Ashmore
Wessex Ridgeway
Tumulus

HIGH ST

HIGH ST

Wiltshire
Coppice

Hockley
Copse

Ashmore
Farm

SP5

4

17

Turkey
Plantation

Earthwork

Mudoak Wood

Gallops

Little Alderwood
Coppice

Well
Bottom

Tollard
Green

Great Alderwood
Coppice

Spring
Farm

3

Wessex Ridgeway

Tumuli

t Bench
ppice

Earthwork

Elederen
Coppice

shmore Wood

Tollard
Green Bottom

16

Deadman's
Coppice

Alner's
Coppice

Little Sedge
Oak Coppice

Bussey's
Down

Little Bench
Coppice

Stony
Bottom

Ashmore
Bottom

CAESAR'S CAMP
(Fort)

ne Down Coppice

Wagbush
Coppice

Upper Broadridge
Coppice

Ashmore Wood

Ashmore
Plantation

Manor
Hill

2

Hill Flower
Coppice

Crabtree
Coppice

Higher Downend
Coppice

DT11

15

Ball
Coppice

rchill's
ppice

Little Peakey
Coppice

Stubhampton
Bottom

Tumulus

Ashmore
Barn Farm

Bussey
Stool Farm

Hanging Coppice

Ashmore
Bottom

1

Bossleton Belt

Earl's Hill

Stubhampton Bottom

ASHMORE BOTTOM

ex Ridgeway

Tumuli

Dungrove
Hill

Bishop's Coppice

Stubhampton Down

A
91
B
92
C
14

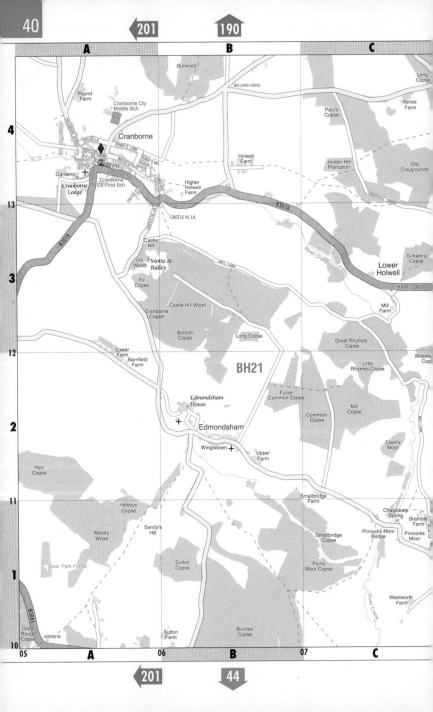

4

Pound Farm

Cranborne Cty Middle Sch

Burwood

BELLOWS CROSS

Long Copse

Ashes Farm

Paul's Copse

Cranborne

Holwell Farm

Jordan Hill Plantation

Old Claygrounds

Gardens

Cranborne Lodge

Cranborne CE First Sch

Higher Holwell Farm

B3078

13

CASTLE HL LA

Castle Hill

B3078

CASTLE HL LA

River Crane

Lower Holwell

HARE LANE

Gilham's Copse

Hill Wood

Motte & Bailey

Fir Copse

Cranborne Copse

Castle Hill Wood

MILL LANE

Mill Farm

3

Bottom Copse

Long Copse

Great Rhymes Copse

Lower Farm

Barnfield Farm

BH21

Little Rhymes Copse

Woodw Cop

12

Edmondsham House

Furze Common Copse

Common Copse

Mill Copse

Cook's Moor

2

Edmondsham

Wingsdown

Upper Farm

Pert Copse

Smallbridge Farm

Chalybeate Spring

Bramble Farm

11

Hobbys Copse

Sandy's Hill

Smallbridge Copse

Pinnocks Moor Bridge

Pinnocks Moor

Maldry Wood

Pinnocks C

Deer Park Ponds

Sutton Copse

Pains Moor Copse

1

B3081

Sutton Farm

Birches Copse

River Crane

Westworth Farm

Great Rough Copse

HORTON RD

10

A   B   C

Perry Copse

BONERWOOD ROAD

ASHFORD ROAD

Lake
Farm

Hill
Farm

Home
Farm

Manor
Farm

New
Farm

Midgham
Wood

Park
Farm
Alderholt
Park

Hill
Cottage
Farm

SANDLEHEATH ROAD

High
Wood

Salisbury
Arms
Farm

FORDINGBRIDGE ROAD

4

Cross
Farm

HILLBURY RD

Bonfire/
Hill

13

BOOTH

Wolvercraft
Spinney

Wolvercote
Copse

Hilbury
Wood

Camel
Green

High
Wood

Alderholt

CUPPERS CL

HATTERS

WINDSOR DRIV?

1 GREEN DR
2 SILVERDALE DR
3 CAMEL GN RD

Midgham
Farm

LIME TREE CL

STATION ROAD

St James
CE First
School

CAMEL GREEN RD

Hillbury
Wood

Midgh
Long C

3

DAGGONS ROAD

PH

STATION RD

ASH TREE

APPLE

ELDER DR

SOUTH BK

TUDOR

Hillbury
Farm

Midgh
Long C

PO

CHURCHILL C?

BLACKWATER

OLD ROAD

CHARING
CROSS

Charing
Cross

HAZEL DR

HAZEL
CL

WESTREE

BIRCHWOOD DR

WINDSOR

Alderholt
Sports Club

SP6

12

Cross Roads
Plantation

Sleepbrook
Farm

RINGWOOD ROAD

Marsh Lands

Oak Tree
Farm

Drove
End
Farm

NORTH END LANE

2

Warren
Park
Farm

HARBRIDGE DROVE

LOWER LA

Lomer
Copse

Alderholt
Common

Whitefield
Bottom

Bleak
Hill Farm

Braemoor

Bleak
Hill

Fern
Copse

Plumley
Wood

11

BH31

Sleep Brook

Sleep
Bottom

Whitefield
Bottom

Col
Wo

Plumley
Wood

1

North
Plumley Farm

BH24

Hamer
Copse

Col
Wo

Wiggs Copse

Kent Hill

Cootman's
Copse

10

A **B** **C**

King's Wood

Walnut Farm

Sutton Holms

Birches Copse

Sutton Hill Farm

B3081

Boys Wood

4

Romford Mill Farm

Ironmonger Copse

Romford East Farm

Romford

West Farm

Romford Bridge

B3081

STATION RD

PH

Gravel Pits Plantation

Jubilee Farm

Rainbow's End

Brook Farm

BROXF

CHURCH HILL

PARK LANE

09

Woodlands

Shirewood Farm

Whitmore

Hemmings Farm

HILLSIDE RD

BURGESS FIELD

CH

Crane Valley Golf Club

Dewlands Woods

WEST END

DEWLANDS

Woodlands Common

Ninney-cox Wood

Dewlands Common

STAGGWOOD

Brookfield Martins Farm

Martins Farm

Mount Pleasant Farm

Dewlands Farm

3

Cranborne Game Farm

River Crane

BH31

Apple Tree Farm

Woodlands Park

08

Wedgehill Farm

Bridge Farm

HORTON RIVER

Oakfield Farm

BH21

Knob's Crook

Ford

Tumulus

Tumulus

Holmes Wood

Redman's Hill

2

SLOUGH LANE

Tumulus

Tumuli

Earthworks

Riverside Farm

Tumulus

Monmouth Ash Farm

07

Ford

Monmouth's Ash

Bog Farm

SLOUGH LANE

Horton Wood

Harts Farm

Horton Heath Farm

Grixey Farm

HORTON LA

Hart's Bridge

Horton Common

1

Hart's Copse

Nettletree Farm

Horton Heath

Hope Lodge Farm

Bramble Farm

Clump Hill

Silverwood Farm

Holt Lodge Farm

Clump Hill Farm

CLUMP HILL

HORTON ROAD

06

Chapel Farm

Rose Cottage Farm

05

A **06** **B** **07** **C**

A B C

Cootman's
Copse

Hamer
Copse

Harbridge
Farm

Kent Hill
Plantation

Plumley
Wood

Wiggs
Copse

Harbridge
Sch
Turm

4

Ford

Harefield Plantation

Plumley
Farm

Lower
Turmer

09

Home
Farm

SHEPHERDS LANE

Reservoir
Cottage

SHEPHERDS HILL

CHESTNUT AVENUE

Home
Wood

Dog Kennel
Wood

3

ELLINGHAM DRIVE

New
Bridge

Ringwood
Forest

Nursery
Cottages

Somerley
Park

Somerley

08

BH24

Bluehaze

ELLINGHAM DR

Park
Cottage

2

Sunderton
Wood

07

Tumulus

B3081

DUNCOMBE DRIVE

ASHLEY LANE

Withybed
Copse

Tumuli

Sunderton
Wood

Ashley
Heath

VERWOOD ROAD

Duncombe
Lodge

1

Ashley
Farm

Moors Valley
Country Park

Baker's
Hanging

06

11 A 12 B 13 C

A B C

ROMAN
VILLA

Hemsworth

Zannies
Coppice

Hussey's
Coppice

Little
Coppice

Home
Covert

Bradford
Farm

4

River Allen

Old Lawn
Coppice

05

Bradford
Farm

Tumulus

Old Lawn
Farm

3

BH21

04

T11

The
Oaks

King Down
Farm

King
Down

2

KING DOWN DROVE

Tumuli

National Trust

Badbury
Rings

High
Wood

03

PITT'S DROVE

1

Chilbridge
Farm

P

Lodge
Farm

B3082

Marsh Copse

Lodge Down

P

02

A 97 B 98 C

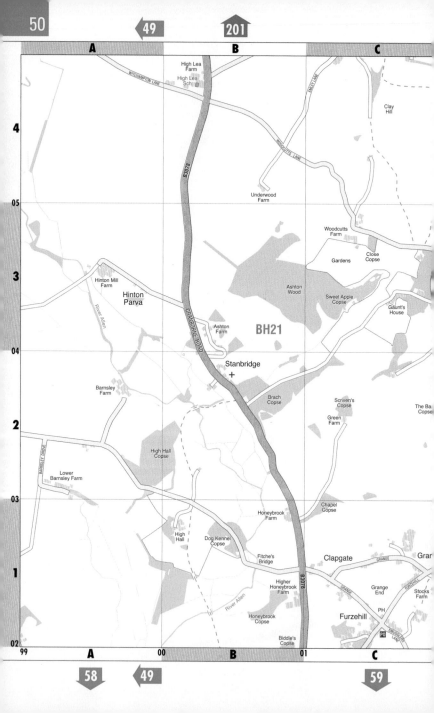

49

201

A **B** **C**

4

High Lea
Farm

High Lea
Sch.

WITCHAMPTON LANE

ELM'S LANE

Clay
Hill

WOODCUTTS LANE

B3078

Underwood
Farm

05

Woodcutts
Farm

Gardens

Close
Copse

3

Hinton Mill
Farm

Hinton
Parva

River Allen

Ashton
Wood

Sweet Apple
Copse

Gaunt's
House

CRANBORNE ROAD

Ashton
Farm

BH21

04

Stanbridge
+

Barnsley
Farm

Brach
Copse

Scriven's
Copse

The Ba
Cops

2

Green
Farm

BARNSLEY DROVE

High Hall
Copse

Lower
Barnsley Farm

03

Chapel
Copse

Honeybrook
Farm

High
Hall

Dog Kennel
Copse

Fitche's
Bridge

Clapgate

GRANGE

Grar

1

B3078

Higher
Honeybrook
Farm

GRANGE

Grange
End

Stocks
Farm

FURZEHILL

PH

Furzehill

SALISBURY LANE

River Allen

Honeybrook
Copse

Biddle's
Copse

PO

02

58

49

59

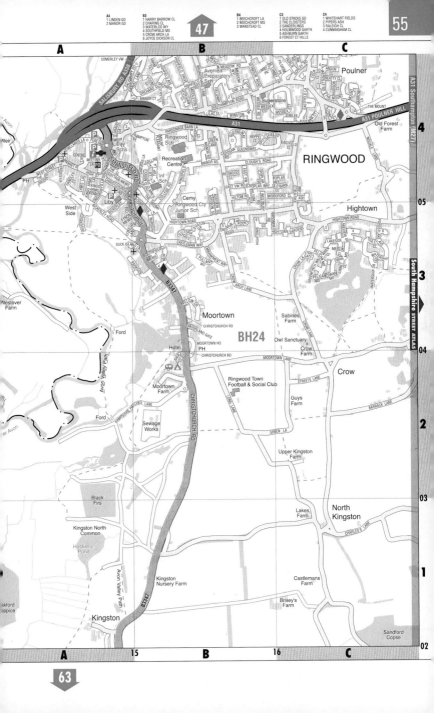

211
48

B2
1 CHARBOROUGH WY
2 HAYCOCK WY
3 PARKELEA
4 TATTERSHALL GD
5 SHERIDEN WY

A **B** **C**

Locust
Clump

Lodge
Down

B3082

Kingston
Plantation

BLANDFORD ROAD

PETTS DROVE

4

Ralph
Copse

Coneygar
Copse

Kingston Lacy Park

Kingston Lacy House
(National Trust)

Lodge

TADDON
COTTS

Obelisks

01

ABBOTT STREET

Manor
House

P

Kingston Lacy
Gardens

Kingston Lacy
Home Farm

3

Barford
Farm

Stour Valley Wlk

All Fools Lane

SANDY LANE

Holly Lane

Wynne Copse

Poplar
Farm

Firs
Farm

Higher
Dairy Farm

Cowgrove

00

Star Cottage
Garden

ROMAN WAY

BH21

COWGROVE ROAD

Cowgrove Common

Cowgrove
Farm

Lower
Barford Farm

Chaw Meadow

River Stour

2

River Stour

99

Weir

CANOIS LA.

A31

Weir

Coventry
Arms
(PH)

Court
House

MILL STREET

Court
Farm

Mill
Farm

Henbury
Manor

BRICKYARD LA.

KNOLL LA.

BRIDGE ST.

1

BLANDFORD ROAD

B3073

RECTORY AVE.

Spring
Coppice

Orchard
Coppice

Water
Works

SLEIGHT LA.

Sleight

98

A 97 **B** 98 **C**

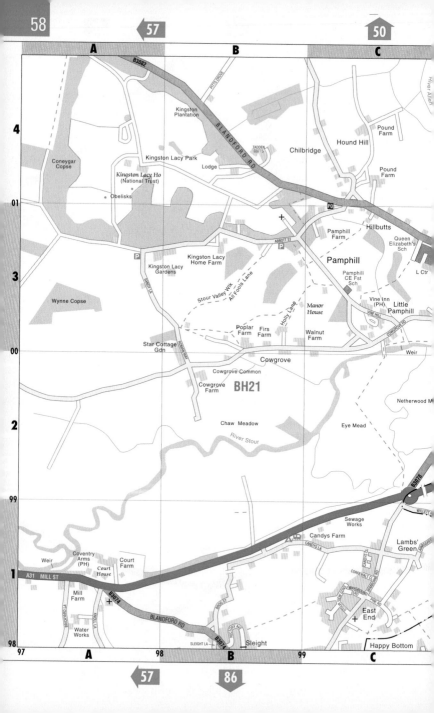

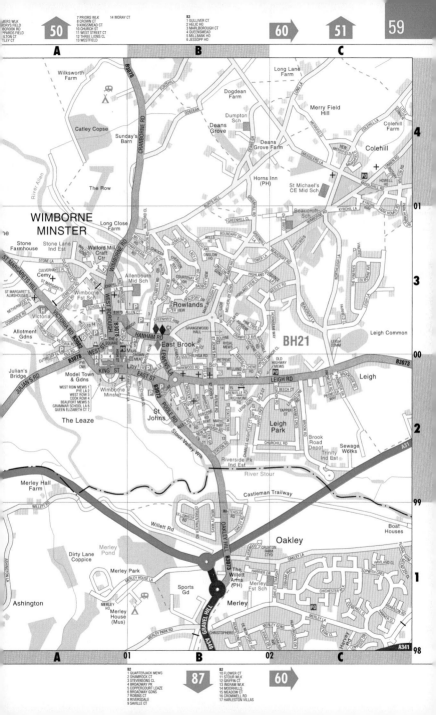

JERS WLK
7 PRIORS WLK
14 MORAY CT
VORYS FIELD
8 CROWN CT
BCROOK RD
9 KINGSMEAD CT
PPARDS FIELD
10 CHURCH ST
ILTON CT
11 WEST STREET CT
TLEY CT
12 THREE LIONS CL
13 WESTFIELD

50

B3
1 GULLIVER CT
2 HELIC HO
3 MARLBOROUGH CT
4 QUEENSMEAD
5 MILLBANK HO
6 JESSOPP HO

60   **51**

B2
1 QUARTERJACK MEWS
2 SHAMROCK CT
3 STEVENSONS CL
4 BROADWAY PK
5 COPPERCOURT LEAZE
6 BROADWAY GDNS
7 ROBINS CT
8 RIVERSDALE
9 SAVILLE CT

B2
10 FLOWER CT
11 STOUR WLK
12 GRIFFIN CT
13 INGRAM WLK
14 MOORHILLS
15 MEADOW CT
16 CROMWELL RD
17 HARLESTON VILLAS

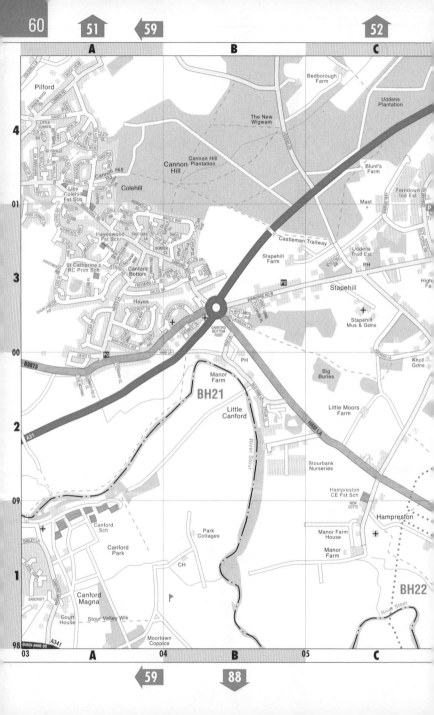

A   B   C

Pilford

Bedborough Farm

Uddens Plantation

4

The New Wigwam

Cannon Hill Plantation

Blunt's Farm

Cannon Hill

Cannon Hill

Ferndown Ind Est

Mast

Liby Colehill Fst Sch

Colehill

01

Castleman Trailway

Uddens Trad Est

PH

Park Homes Est

Hayeswood Fst Sch

Stapehill Farm

High Fa

St Catherine's RC Prim Sch

Canford Bottom

3

Stapehill

Hayes

Stapehill Mus & Gdns

Canford Bottom Rdbt

WIMBORNE RD W

WYELMANDS AVE

HAM LA

00

B3073

PH

Manor Farm

Big Buries

Knoll Gdns

BH21

Little Canford

River Stour

Little Moors Farm

2

A31

Stourbank Nurseries

09

Hampreston CE Fst Sch

NEW COTTS

Hampreston

Canford Sch

Park Cottages

Manor Farm House

Canford Park

OAKLEY LA

CH

Manor Farm

1

BH22

Canford Magna

SANCROFT

Court House

Stour Valley Wlk

River Stour

98

QUEEN ANNE DR   A341

Moortown Coppice

03   A   04   B   05   C

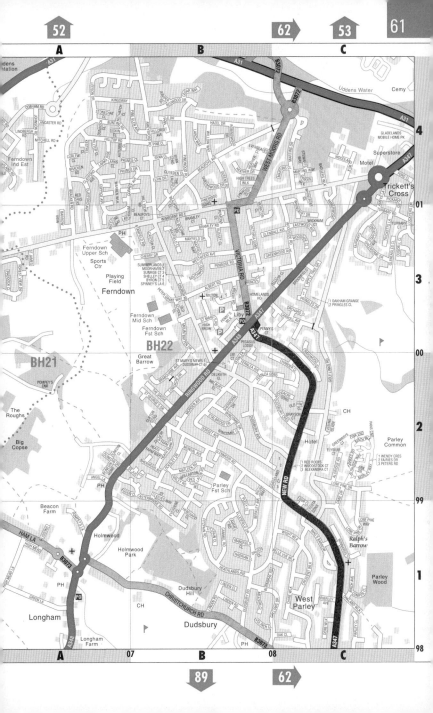

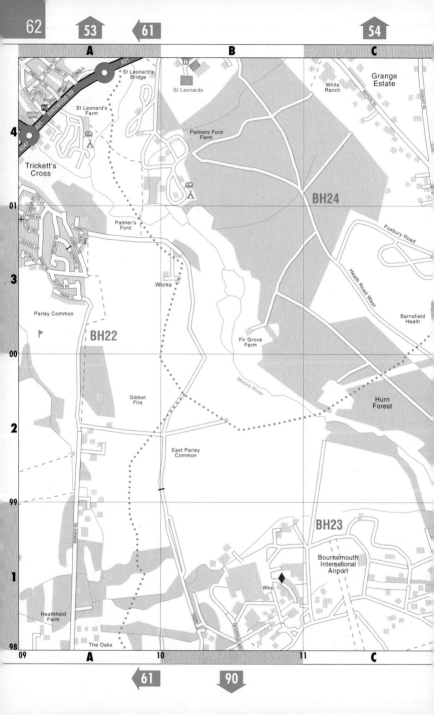

A
B
C

St Leonard's Bridge
H
St Leonards
White Ranch
Grange Estate

St Leonard's Farm
Palmers Ford Farm

PO
PRIORY RD

4
Trickett's Cross

BH24

Foxbury Road

01
Palmer's Ford

Heath Road West

Works

Barnsfield Heath

3
Parley Common

BH22

Fir Grove Farm

00
Moors River

Hurn Forest

Gibbet Firs

2
East Parley Common

99
BH23

Bournemouth International Airport

1
Wks
BARRACK RD

Heathfield Farm

98
The Oaks

09
A
10
11
C

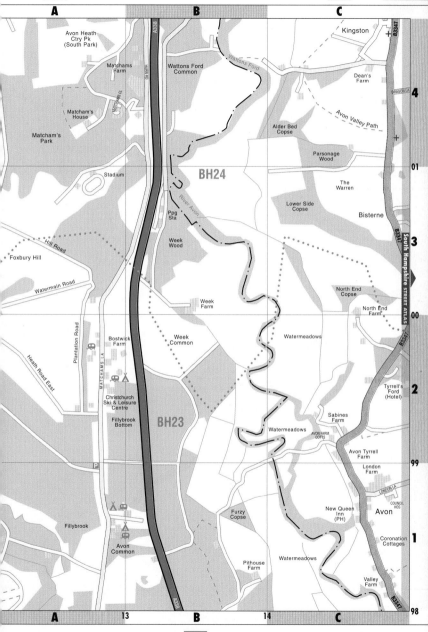

A   **B**   **C**

Avon Heath
Ctry Pk
(South Park)

Kingston

Matchams
Farm

Wattons Ford
Common

Wattons Ford

Dean's
Farm

Matcham's
House

MATCHAMS CL

Avon Valley Path

4

Matcham's
Park

Alder Bed
Copse

Parsonage
Wood

BH24

01

Stadium

The
Warren

River Avon

Lower Side
Copse

Bisterne

Ppg
Sta

Foxbury Hill

Hill Road

Week
Wood

3

Watermain Road

Week
Farm

North End
Copse

North End
Farm

00

Plantation Road

Bostwick
Farm

Week
Common

Watermeadows

MATCHAMS LA

Tyrrell's
Ford
(Hotel)

2

Heath Road East

Christchurch
Ski & Leisure
Centre

BH23

Sabines
Farm

AVON FARM
COTTS

Fillybrook
Bottom

Watermeadows

Avon Tyrrell
Farm

99

P

London
Farm

LONDON LA

Fillybrook

Furzy
Copse

New Queen
Inn
(PH)

COUNCIL
HOS

Avon

1

Avon
Common

Coronation
Cottages

Pithouse
Farm

Watermeadows

Valley
Farm

98

A   13   **B**   14   **C**

South Hampshire STREET ATLAS

A338

B3347

DRAGON LA

B3347

BOSLEY

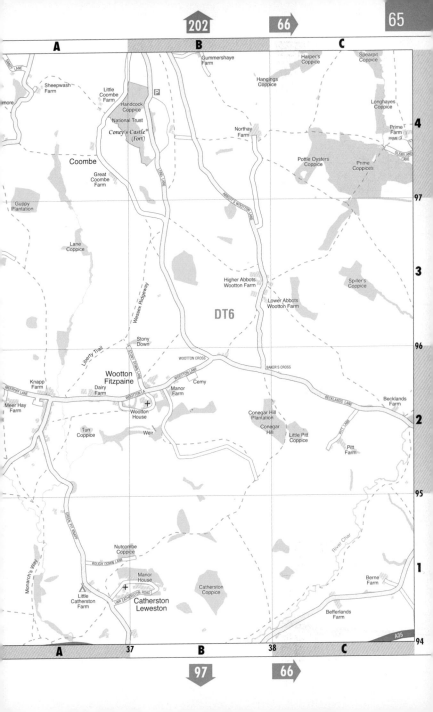

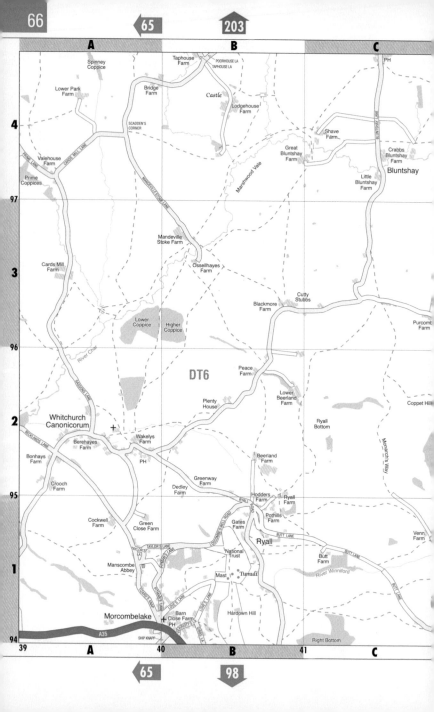

A B C

4

97

3

96

2

95

1

94

39 A 40 B 41 C

Spinney
Coppice

Taphouse
Farm

POORHOUSE LA
TAPHOUSE LA

PH

Lower Park
Farm

Bridge
Farm

Castle

Lodgehouse
Farm

Shave
Farm

BLUNTSHAY LANE

SCADDEN'S
CORNER

Crabbs
Bluntshay
Farm

Valehouse
Farm

PRIME LANE

CROSS MILL LANE

MARSHALLSEA LANE

Great
Bluntshay
Farm

Little
Bluntshay
Farm

Bluntshay

Prime
Coppices

Marshwood Vale

Mandeville
Stoke Farm

Ossellhayes
Farm

Cards Mill
Farm

Cutty
Stubbs

Blackmore
Farm

Purcomb
Farm

River Char

Lower
Coppice

Higher
Coppice

DT6

Peace
Farm

Coppet Hill

Lower
Beerland
Farm

Plenty
House

Ryall
Bottom

Whitchurch
Canonicorum

CASSON'S LANE

Wakelys
Farm

Monarch's Way

Berehayes
Farm

PH

Beerland
Farm

Bonhays
Farm

BUCKLAND LANE

Greenway
Farm

Crooch
Farm

Dedley
Farm

Hodders
Farm

Ryall
Farm

RYALL ROAD

Ryall

Cockwell
Farm

Green
Close Farm

Gates
Farm

Pothills
Farm

LOOSEMOOR WELL ROAD

BUTT LANE

Venn
Farm

Taylor's Lane

TAYLOR'S LANE

National
Trust

Butt
Farm

BUTT LANE

Manscombe
Abbey

Mast

Tumuli

River Winniford

BUTT LANE

EDDA'S WAY

WHANT'S LANE

LOVE'S LANE

LOVE'S LANE

Hardown Hill

Morcombelake

Barn
Close Farm

SEAHULL'S LANE

PH

A35

SHIP KNAPP

Right Bottom

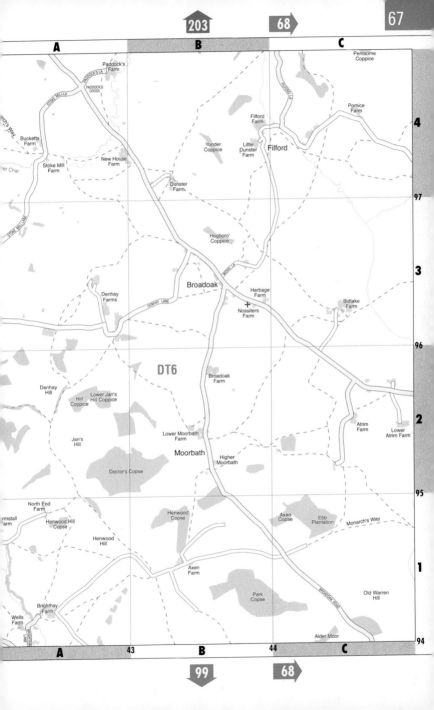

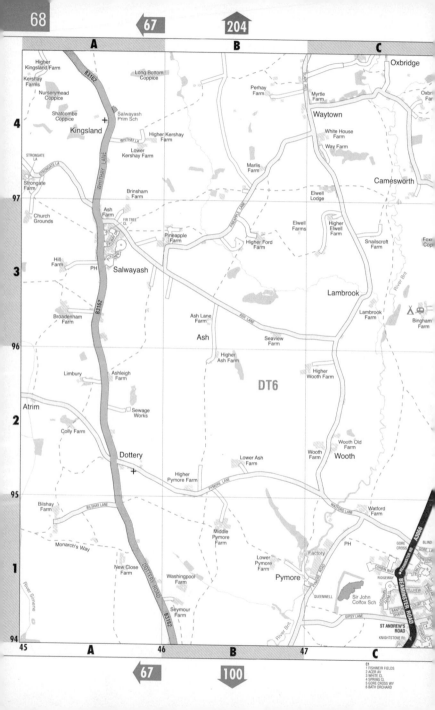

A **B** **C**

Higher Kingsland Farm

Kershay Farms

Nurserymead Coppice

Long Bottom Coppice

Oxbridge

B3162

Perhay Farm

Myrtle Farm

Oxbri Far

Shatcombe Coppice

Salwayash Prim Sch

Waytown

4

Kingsland

White House Farm

WHITHAY LA

Higher Kershay Farm

Way Farm

Lower Kershay Farm

Marlis Farm

Camesworth

STRONGATE LA

Brinsham Farm

Elwell Lodge

STRONGATE LA

97

Strongate Farm

Ash Farm

Elwell Farms

Higher Elwell Farm

Church Grounds

FIR TREE CL

Snailscroft Farm

Foxt Cop

Pineapple Farm

Higher Ford Farm

River Brit

Hill Farm

PH

WITCHI

Salwayash

3

Lambrook

Broadenham Farm

B3162

Ash Lane Farm

ASH LANE

Lambrook Farm

Bingham Farm

Ash

Seaview Farm

96

Higher Ash Farm

Limbury

Ashleigh Farm

Higher Wooth Farm

DT6

Atrim

Sewage Works

2

Colly Farm

Wooth Old Farm

Wooth Farm

Wooth

Dottery

Lower Ash Farm

BILSHAY LANE

Higher Pymore Farm

PYMORE LANE

95

Bilshay Farm

WATFORD LANE

Watford Farm

A3066

Monarch's Way

Middle Pymore Farm

PH

GORE CROSS

BLIND

BEAMINSTER RD

GORE LA

COBRIN WAY

1

New Close Farm

DOTTERY ROAD

Washingpool Farm

Lower Pymore Farm

Factory

PYMORE ROAD

Pymore

RIDGEWAY

BELLVIEW

Sir John Colfox Sch

River Simene

Queenwell

B3162

Seymour Farm

GIPSY LANE

ST ANDREW'S ROAD

River Brit

KNIGHTSTONE RD

94

45 **A** 46 **B** 47 **C**

C1
1 FISHWEIR FIELDS
2 ACER AV
3 WHITE CL
4 SPRING CL
5 GORE CROSS WY
6 BATH ORCHARD

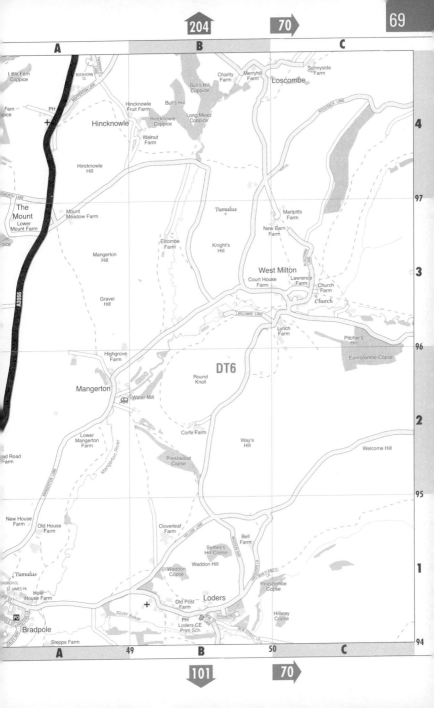

A B C

A 49 B 50 C

Little Fern Coppice

BUCKHORN CL

Fern pice

PH

Hincknowle

Hincknowle Fruit Farm

Bull's Hill

Bull's Hill Coppice

Charity Farm

Merryhill Farm

Loscombe

Sunnyside Farm

HORSEBACK LANE

Hincknowle Coppice

Long Mead Coppice

Walnut Farm

Hincknowle Hill

The Mount

Lower Mount Farm

Mount Meadow Farm

Elcombe Farm

Tumulus

Marlpitts Farm

New Barn Farm

97

Mangerton Hill

Knight's Hill

West Milton

Court House Farm

Lawrence Farm

Church Farm

3

Gravel Hill

LARCOMBE LANE

Church

Lynch Farm

Pitcher's Hill

96

Highgrove Farm

DT6

Earnscombe Copse

Mangerton

Water Mill

Round Knoll

2

Lower Mangerton Farm

Corfe Farm

Way's Hill

Welcome Hill

Mangerton River

Presswood Copse

95

New House Farm

Old House Farm

Cloverleaf Farm

YELLOW LANE

Bell Farm

WADDON WAY

Tumulus

CHURCH CL

ST JAMES PK

Hole House Farm

Symes's Hill Copse

Waddon Hill

Waddon Copse

Peascombe Copse

1

PO

Bradpole

River Asker

Old Post Farm

Loders

PH

Loders CE Prim Sch

HIGHACRES

Hillway Copse

Stepps Farm

94

A3066

MANGERTON LANE

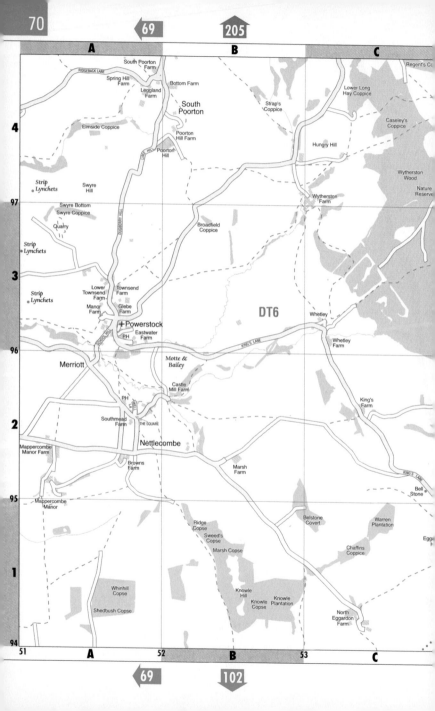

A   **B**   **C**

4

RIDGEBACK LANE

South Poorton
Farm

Spring Hill
Farm

Legland
Farm

Bottom Farm

South
Poorton

Strap's
Coppice

Lower Long
Hay Coppice

Regent's Co

Caseley's
Coppice

Elmside Coppice

Poorton
Hill Farm

Poorton
Hill

Hungry Hill

Wytherston
Wood

Nature
Reserve

97

Strip
Lynchets

Swyre
Hill

Swyre Bottom
Swyre Coppice

Quarry

Broadfield
Coppice

Wytherston
Farm

3

Strip
Lynchets

Strip
Lynchets

THE DOWER HOUSE

Lower
Townsend
Farm

Townsend
Farm

Manor
Farm

Glebe
Farm

DT6

Whetley

✚ **Powerstock**

Eastwater
Farm

PH

KING'S LANE

Whetley
Farm

96

Merriott

Motte &
Bailey

Castle
Mill Farm

King's
Farm

PH

Southmead
Farm

THE SQUARE

2

Nettlecombe

Mappercombe
Manor Farm

Browns
Farm

Marsh
Farm

KING'S LANE

Bell
Stone

95

Mappercombe
Manor

Ridge
Copse

Sweed's
Copse

Marsh Copse

Belstone
Covert

Warren
Plantation

Chaffins
Coppice

Egge
H

1

Whinhill
Copse

Shedbush Copse

Knowle
Hill

Knowle
Copse

Knowle
Plantation

North
Eggardon
Farm

94

51   **A**   **52**   **B**   **53**   **C**

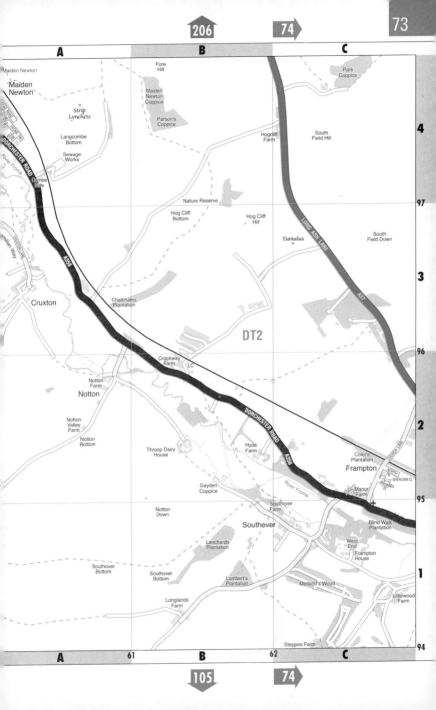

A   B   C

Maiden Newton

Fore Hill

Park Coppice

Maiden Newton

Strip Lynchets

Maiden Newton Coppice

Parson's Coppice

Langcombe Bottom

Sewage Works

Hogcliff Farm

South Field Hill

4

River Frome

DORCHESTER ROAD

Combe Elle

Nature Reserve

97

Hog Cliff Bottom

Hog Cliff Hill

South Field Down

Millman Way

A356

Tumulus

LONG ASH LANE

A37

3

Cruxton

Chalkhams Plantation

DT2

96

Crockway Farm

LC

Notton Farm

Notton

DORCHESTER ROAD

A356

2

Notton Valley Farm

Throop Dairy House

Hyde Farm

Coler's Plantation

CHURCH LANE

Frampton

Notton Bottom

SHERIDAN CL

Manor Farm

95

Gayden Coppice

River Frome

Southover Farm

Blind Walk Plantation

Notton Down

Southover

West End

Frampton House

Lanchards Plantation

1

Southover Bottom

Southover Bottom

Lambert's Plantation

Metland's Wood

Littlewood Farm

Longlands Farm

Steppes Farm

94

A   61   B   62   C

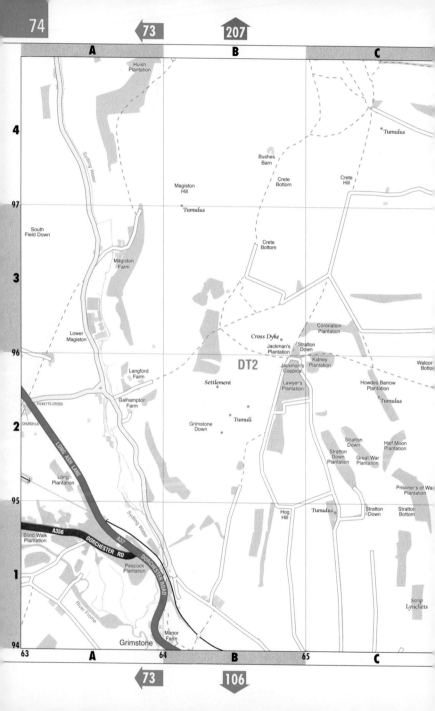

A   **B**   **C**

Huish
Plantation

Sydling Water

Tumulus

4

Bushes
Barn

Crete
Bottom

Crete
Hill

Magiston
Hill

97

Tumulus

South
Field Down

Crete
Bottom

Magiston
Farm

3

Lower
Magiston

Coronation
Plantation

Cross Dyke

Stratton
Down

Jackman's
Plantation

96

DT2

Langford
Farm

Jackman's
Coppice

Kidney
Plantation

Watcor
Botto

PICKETTS CROSS

Galhampton
Farm

Lawyer's
Plantation

Howdes Barrow
Plantation

Settlement

CHURCH LA

Tumulus

2

Grimstone
Down

Tumuli

Stratton
Down
Plantation

Half Moon
Plantation

LONG ASH LANE

Stratton
Down
Plantation

Great War
Plantation

Long
Plantation

Prisoner's of Wa
Plantation

95

Sydling Water

Hog
Hill

Tumulus

Stratton
Down

Stratton
Bottom

Blind Walk
Plantation

A356

DORCHESTER RD

A37

DORCHESTER ROAD

Peacock
Plantation

1

Strip
Lynchets

River Frome

Manor
Farm

Grimstone

94

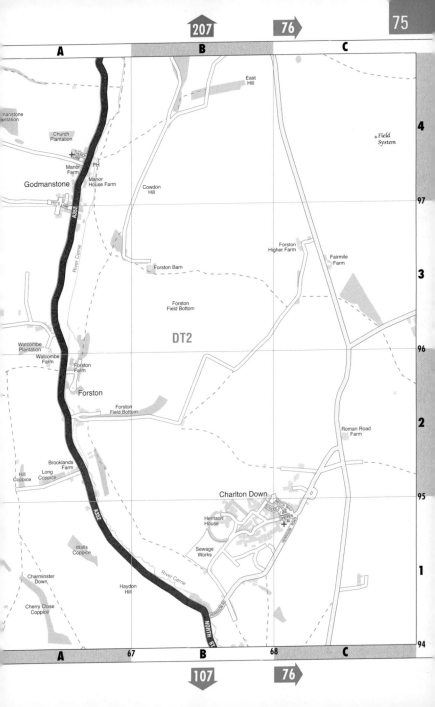

A   B   C

East
Hill

manstone
antation

Church
Plantation

Field
System

4

Manor
Farm

PH

Godmanstone

Manor
House Farm

Cowdon
Hill

97

FRY'S LANE A352

River Cerne

Forston
Higher Farm

Forston Barn

Fairmile
Farm

3

Forston
Field Bottom

DT2

Watcombe
Plantation

Watcombe
Farm

96

Forston
Farm

Forston

Forston
Field Bottom

2

Roman Road
Farm

Brooklands
Farm

Hill
Coppice

Long
Coppice

Charlton Down

95

A352

Herrison
House

MELCOMBE WAY
STROUDS AVE
STEEPEN LANE

HERRISON ROAD

Walls
Coppice

Sewage
Works

Charminster
Down

River Cerne

1

Haydon
Hill

Cherry Close
Coppice

HERRISON RD

NORTH ST

94

A 67 B 68 C

A   **B**   **C**

4

B3143

HIGH STREET

PH

Coombe
Plantation

Piddlehinto

Heave
Coppice

RECTORY RD

PH

CHURCH HILL

BYWAY

Heaves
Farm

97

Coombe Bottom

River Piddle or Trent

New
Buildings

Earthworks

3

Little Puddle Bottom

Little Puddle
Farm

Holcombe
Bottom

Little
Puddle
Coppice

96

DT2

• Tumuli

Little Puddle
Hill

Little Piddle Down

• Tumuli

2

Peak
Coppice

Charlton Higher Down

Wolfeton
Clump

95

• Tumulus

Laycock
Farm

Tumulus •

SILVER'S LANE

Lower
Covert

1

• Tumuli

Tum

B3143

Long
Coppice

94

69   **A**   **70**   **B**   **71**   **C**

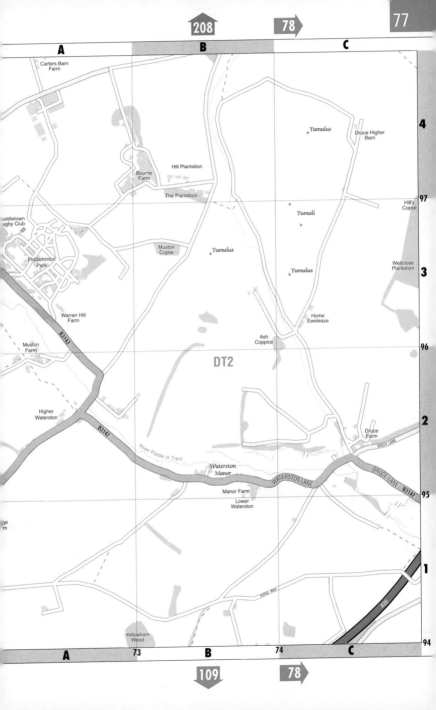

A   B   C

Carters Barn
Farm

Tumulus

Druce Higher
Barn

4

Hill Plantation

Bourne
Farm

The Plantation

97

Hill's
Copse

uddletown
ugby Club

Tumuli

Muston
Copse

Tumulus

Wellclose
Plantation

Piddlehinton
Park

Tumulus

3

Warren Hill
Farm

Home
Eweleaze

Muston
Farm

Ash
Coppice

96

DT2

Higher
Waterston

B3143

2

Druce
Farm

BIRCH LANE

River Piddle or Trent

B3142

Waterston
Manor

WATERSTON LANE

DRUCE LANE   B3142

Manor Farm

95

Lower
Waterston

ge
m

1

RIDGE WAY

A35

Yellowham
Wood

94

A   73   B   74   C

A1
1 BELLBURY CL
2 ASH TREE CL
3 WILLOUGHBY CL
4 BRYMER RD
5 WHITE HILL
6 CHAPEL VIEW

A   B   C

DT11

4

Foxpound

Tumulus

Long
Barrow

Jubilee Trail

Horse Close
Plantation

97

Tumulus

Haywards
Farm

BH20

3

Roke Barn

Millum
Head

BEE DOWN LANE

96

Roke Farm

Hollybush
Farm

BEE ROAD

Ashley
Barn

2

Roger's Hill
Farm

95

DT2

B3390

A35

Sitterton
Wood

Sitterton

Piddle Wood

DORCHESTER
RD

1

B3390

Double Barrow

Plantation

Jubilee Trail

Tumuli

Black
Hill

Southmoor
Farm

Tumuli

94

A   B   C

Hill Top

Middle
Farm

Muston
Farm

Ford

Manor
Farm

Anderson
Manor

Riverside
Farm

Rainbow
View Farm

4

Winterborne
Muston

Anderson

Winterborne
Tomson

River Winterborne

Willow
Farm

PH

Marsh
Farm

MARSH LANE

Kiddles
Farm

Winterbor
Zelston

97

RED POST

A31

Rectory
Farm

DT11

3

Tumulus

Tumuli

Botany Bay
Farm

Tum

Tumuli

Bloxworth
Down

96

Robinswood
Farm

Waterley
Wood

Poun
Woo

Hazel
Coppice

2

Kimberley
Wood

MORDEN LANE

BH20

95

Bloxworth
House

Newport

Brimland
Wood

2

Bere Wood

Bloxworth

NEWPORT LANE

Manor
Farm

1

Oak Coppice

East
Bloxworth

Longcutter
Coppice

Humber's
Coppice

East Coppice

Heron
Coppice

94

87   A   88   B   89   C

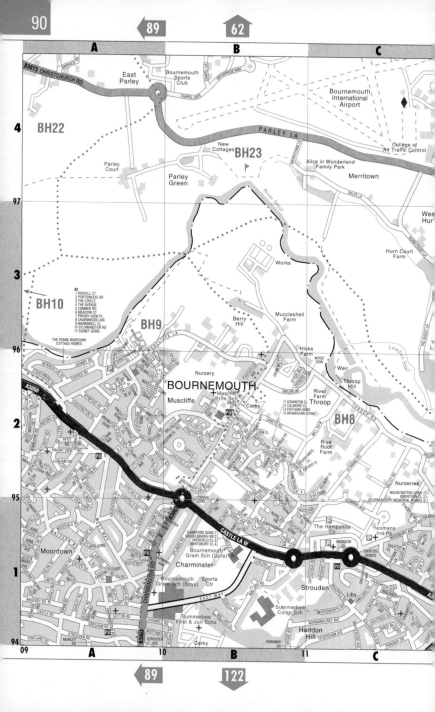

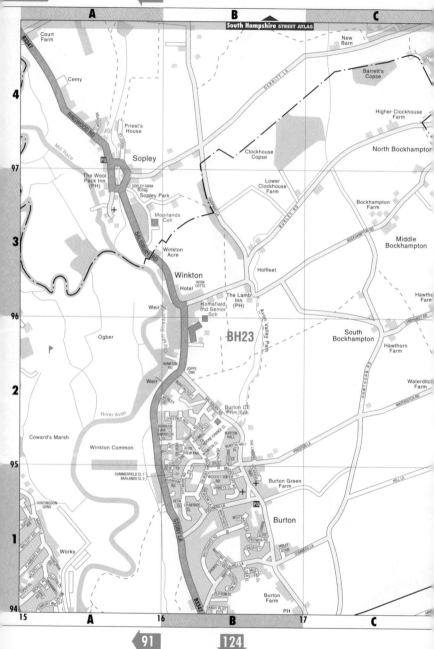

South Hampshire STREET ATLAS

A   B   C

Court
Farm

Cemy

RINGWOOD RD

Priest's
House

Sopley

PO

The Wool
Pack Inn
(PH)

SOPLEY FARM
BLDGS

Sopley Park

Moorlands
Coll

Winkton
Acre

Winkton

Hotel

AVON
COTTS

Homefield
Ind Senior
Sch

The Lamb
Inn
(PH)

Weir

BH23

Ogber

Winkton
RD

JOPPS
CNR

Weir

River Avon

Coward's Marsh

Winkton Common

Winkton Common

SUMMERFIELD CL 1
BARLANDS CL 2

HUNTINGDON
GDNS

Works

CHESTNUT
CL

Burton CE
Prim Sch

Burton
Hall

AVON
VIEW PARK

BURTON HALL
PL

THE LINDENS

Burton Green
Farm

PO

WOODSTOCK
RD

VINNEY'S CL

Burton

WHITE

HOLLY
GDNS

SUMMER LA

HILL LA

Burton
Farm

PH

New
Barn

Barrett's
Copse

Higher Clockhouse
Farm

North Bockhampton

Clockhouse
Copse

Lower
Clockhouse
Farm

Bockhampton
Farm

RURLEY RD

Middle
Bockhampton

BOCKHAMPTON RD

Holfleet

Avon Valley Path

South
Bockhampton

Hawthorn
Farm

Hawth
Farm

HAWTHORN RD

VINEHURST RD

Waterditch
Farm

PRESTON LA

WATERDITCH RD

HILL LA

Mill Race

SALISBURY RD

STONY LA

B3347

B3341

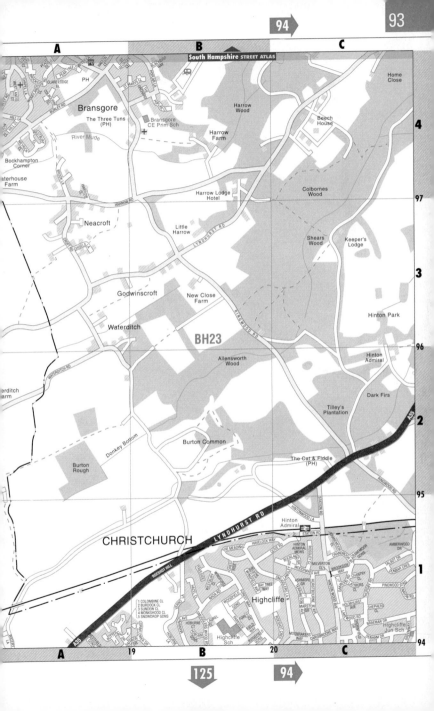

South Hampshire STREET ATLAS

A **B** **C**

Home Close

Bransgore

Harrow Wood

Beech House

4

The Three Tuns (PH)

Bransgore CE Prim Sch

Harrow Farm

River Mude

Bockhampton Corner

Colbornes Wood

97

Waterhouse Farm

Harrow Lodge Hotel

Neacroft

Little Harrow

Shears Wood

Keeper's Lodge

LYNDHURST RD

3

Godwinscroft

New Close Farm

Hinton Park

Waterditch

RINGWOOD RD

BH23

Allensworth Wood

Hinton Admiral

96

WATERDITCH RD

erditch arm

Dark Firs

Tilley's Plantation

A35

2

Donkey Bottom

Burton Common

The Cat & Fiddle (PH)

Burton Rough

95

HINTONWOOD LA

STATION RD

Hinton Admiral

RINGWOOD RD

CHRISTCHURCH

LYNDHURST RD

Hinton Admiral

HINTON ADMIRAL MEWS

AMBERWOOD DR

ROESHOT HILL

THE MEADWAY

HAVELOCK WAY

CLOVE

1

A35

BAY TREE CL

MILVERTON CL

CHANTRY CL

PINEWOOD CL

Highcliffe

MARSTON RD

SHEPHERD CL

1 COLOMBINE CL
2 BURDOCK CL
3 SUNDEW CL
4 MONKSHOOD GDNS
5 SNOWDROP GDNS

MOONRAKERS WAY

CARISBROOKE WAY

Highcliffe Jun Sch

Highcliffe Sch

BRAEMAR DR

94

A 19 **B** 20 **C**

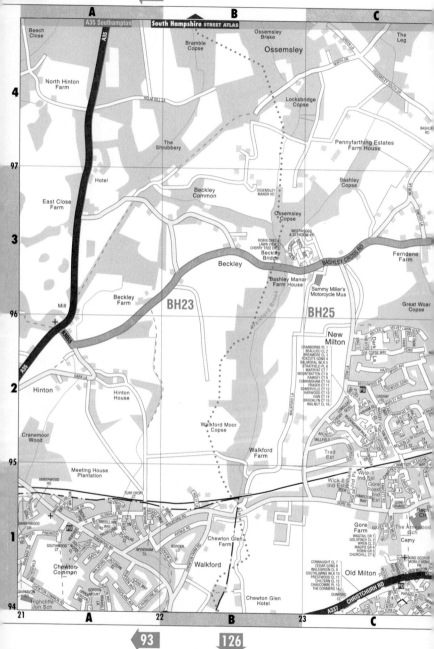

A35 Southampton

South Hampshire STREET ATLAS

Beech Close

North Hinton Farm

HOLM HILL LA

Bramble Copse

Ossemsley Brake

Ossemsley

The Leg

GREEN LA

NORTH DR

OSSEMSLEY SOUTH DR

Locksbridge Copse

BASHLEY RD

The Shrubbery

Pennyfarthing Estates Farm House

Hotel

East Close Farm

Beckley Common

OSSEMSLEY MANOR RD

Bashley Copse

MAIN RD

Ossemsley Copse

WESTWOODS & GLENDENE PK

Mill

Beckley Farm

Beckley

BH23

Beckley Bridge

ROBIN CRES 2
LAWN VIEW 2
CHERRY TREE DR 3

Bashley Manor Farm House

BASHLEY CROSS RD

Ferndene Farm

Sammy Miller's Motorcycle Mus

BH25

Great Woar Copse

Hinton

DARK LA

Hinton House

New Milton

DARK LA

CRANBORNE PL 1
BEAULIEU CL 2
BREAMORE CL 3
FOXCOTE GDNS 4
BALMORAL WLK 5
STRATFIELD PL 6
MARRYAT CT 7
MOUNTBATTEN CT 8
RAMSEY CT 9
CUNNINGHAM CT 10
FRASER CT 11
SOMERVILLE CT 12
HARWOOD CT 13
VIAN CT 14
BROOKLYN CT 15
WALNUT CL 16

Cranemoor Wood

Walkford Moor Copse

Walkford Farm

Meeting House Plantation

AMBERWOOD HO

TURF CROFT

Wick 2 Ind Est

Wick Ind Est

Gore Road Ind Est

Trad Est

AMBERWOOD DR

PINEWOOD

SOUTHWOOD CT

PO

GLENVILLE

TRESILLIAN WAY

CLINTON CL

DOUGLAS CL

WYNDHAM

BROAD LA

AVENUE RD

HEATH RD

WALKFORD RD

Chewton Glen Farm

BORDER LO

Walkford

Gore Farm

QUAVER WAY

The Arnewood Sch

Recn Gd

Cemy

KING GEORGE MOBILE HOME PK

Chewton Common

GORDON MOUNT

Highcliffe Jun Sch

CONNAUGHT CL 7
CEDAR GDNS 8
INGLESGREEN CL 9
SOUTHLAWNS WLK 10
PRESTWOOD CL 11
CHILTERN CL 12
CHAUCOMBE PL 13
THE DORMERS 14

Old Milton

DUNFORD CL

OLD MILTON RD

PO

Chewton Glen Hotel

CHRISTCHURCH RD

A337

South Hampshire **STREET ATLAS**

4

97

3

96

2

95

1

94

A 25 **B** 26 **C**

127

B3
1 ELIZABETH CL
2 DOLPHIN CL
3 SHERBOURNE LA
4 POOLE'S CT
5 MONMOUTH ST
6 BRIDGE ST

64

A   B   C

Rhode
Barton

Fern Hill
Coppice   Hotel

A3052

Sleech
Wood

Liberty Trail

Dragon's
Hill

A3052   Lyme Regis
Golf Club   Langmoor
Coppice   Lily
Farm

CH

4   DT6

GREENHAYES

East Devon Way   Sewage
Works   Pond
Coppice   South West Coast Path   Timber
Hill   CHARBERRY RI

BAY LANE

River Lim   DRAGONS HL   Rhodehorn
Plantation   Black
Ven

Middle Mill
Farm   National
Trust

DT7   OVERTON CL

93   Haye
Farm   PINE WOOD   The
Spittles   Canary
Ledges

Higher Netton
Farm   SPRINGHILL GD   CHARMOUTH CL

Liberty Trail   CHARMOUTH ROAD   SPITTLES LA

Woodroffe
Sch   Cemy   St. Michaels
VC Inf Sch)

SOMERHILL RD

ST MICHAELS

UPLYME ROAD

SOMERFIELDS   HALLET CT   A3052

3   ST ANDREWS RD   P

B3165   FERNDOWN RD

SILVER ST

Leisure   P

DINOSAUR
PORTLAND CT   Dinosaur
OLD VICARAGE RD   Liby   Land   P

LYME
REGIS

A3052 Sidmouth (A375)   SIDMOUTH ROAD   BROAD ST

CHURCH ST

LONG
ENTRY

92   A3052   POUND ST   P   Town
Mill   Lyme Regis
Philpot Mus

P

National
Trust   Cobb

2   P   Lyme   Bay

The
Cobb   Aquarium

Peke's Pool

91

1

90
33   A   34   B   35   C

A4
1 GARDENSIDE
2 KIDMORE CL
3 ORCHARD CL
4 OLD RECTORY CL

A   **B**   **C**

A35

Bellair

A35

Bellair
Farm

National Trust

Stonebarrow Hill

4

KIDCOMBE CL

Backlands
Farm

PH
Liby

PO

GEORGES CL

Dorset
Leisure Ctr

Motel

STONEBARROW LANE

DT6

National Trust

STONEBARROW LANE

National Trust

93

Monument
Coppice

LONG DOLES

MEADOW WY

Charmouth
C.P. Sch

THE LAWNS

Charmouth

National Trust

National
Trust

P

National
Trust

Westhay
Farm

National
Trust

P

Charmouth
Heritage
Coast Centre

South West Coast Path

Cain's
Folly

National
Trust

Monarch's Way

3

92

2

91

1

90

A   37   **B**   38   **C**

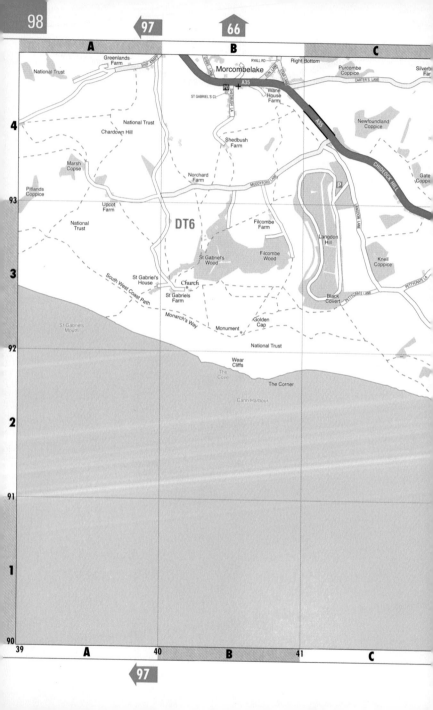

A   B   C

97

Greenlands Farm

National Trust

SHIP KNAPP

Morcombelake

RYALL RD

Right Bottom

Purcombe Coppice

Silverbi Far

ALBERT LANE

A35

CARTER'S LANE

RYALL LANE

ST GABRIEL'S CL

PO

Wane House Farm

National Trust

Chardown Hill

Shedbush Farm

A35

CHIDEOCK HILL

Newfoundland Coppice

4

Marsh Copse

Norchard Farm

MUDDYFORD LANE

Gate Coppice

Pitlands Coppice

Upcot Farm

P

93

National Trust

DT6

Filcombe Farm

Langdon Hill

LANGDON LANE

Knell Coppice

St Gabriel's Wood

Filcombe Wood

South West Coast Path

St Gabriel's House

Church

PETTICRATE LA

3

St Gabriels Farm

Black Covert

PETTICRATE LANE

St Gabriels Mouth

Monarch's Way

Monument

Golden Cap

National Trust

92

Wear Cliffs

The Cove

The Corner

Cann Harbour

2

91

1

90

39   A   40   B   41   C

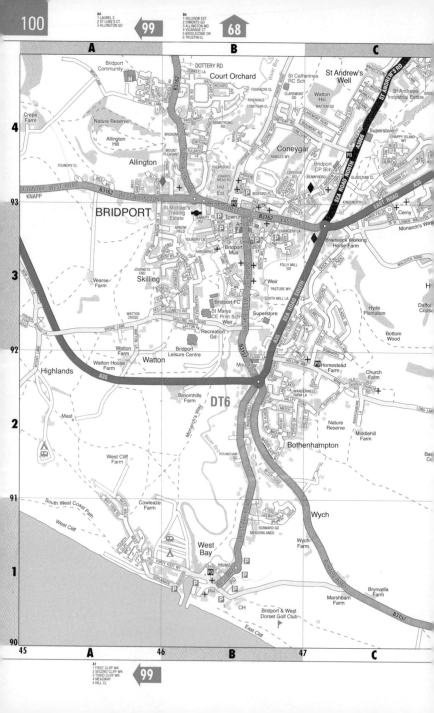

A   **B**   **C**

Lodersland Farm

4

Matravers Farm

Perwen Farm

Matravers

Spyway

SPYWAY ROAD

PH Maxemoor

93

Moens Farm

West Hembury Farm

Medway Farm

VINNEY CROSS

East Hembury Farm

Rocky Close Farm

Green Acres Farm

Askerswell

Ford

Rookhams Farm

Fir Tree Farm

Alexander Farm

DORCHESTER ROAD

PH

3

High Rigg

ICEN LA

PORTWAY

Church Farm

Down Farm

WALTERS LANE

WALTERS LA

Hill Copse

A35

Icen Farm

St Lukes Farm

CHILCOMBE LA

DT2

DORCHESTER ROAD

Askerswel Down

Higher Sturthill Farm

ICEN LANE

92

Lower Sturthill Farm

Chilcombe Hill (Fort)

Chilcombe Hill

DT6

Long Copse

Sturthill Copse

Tumuli

Stout's Copse

Long Copse

Hammiton Wood

Higher Coombe

2

Hammiton Farm

Tumulus

Chilcombe

Lower Coombe Farm

91

Eight Acre Copse

Chapel Copse

Chilcombe Farm

Lower Coombe

1

Rough Corner Copse

Berwick Copse

Rudge Farm

Hodder's Coppice

90

51   **A**   **52**   **B**   **53**   **C**

A
B
C

Eggardon
Copse

Mast

Tumuli

Mast

Burial
Chamber

New
Coppice

Tumulus

Two
Gates

Mast

Tumulus

4

Coombe
Bottom

Haydon
Down

93

Nallers
Farm

3

Ash Hill
Coppice

Stancombe
Farm

Cross Dykes

92

DORCHESTER ROAD

Tumulus

North Barn
Farm

A35

Earthwork

DT2

CHALK PIT LA

DORCHESTER ROAD

Tumuli

2

Bank Barrow

Strip
Lynchets

WHITE WAY

91

LONG BREDY HUT LANE

MANOR
FARM
CL

COOMBES
CL

mbefield
arm

Cross
Tree
Farm

Baglake
Farm

Dowerfield
Farm

Sands
Farm

CHALK PIT LANE

Charity
Farm

East Glebe

1

ins Knoll

Litton
Cheney

SCHOOL HOUSE LANE

COX'S LA

Thorners CE
Prim Sch

COW LANE

HINE'S MEAD LA

Rowden Farm

Long Bredy

Manor
Farm

PH

90

A
B
C

55
56

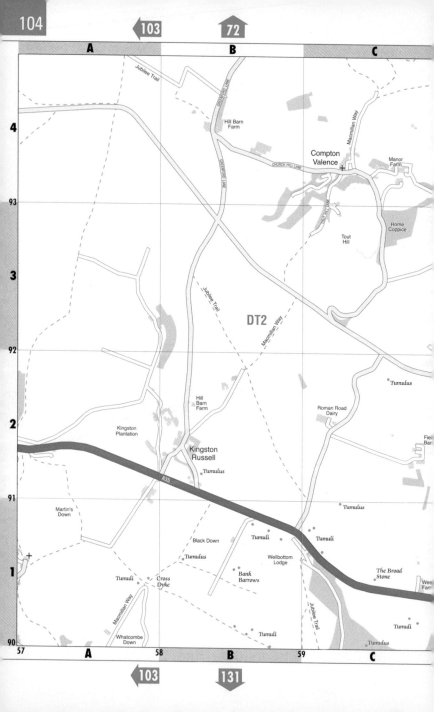

A   B   C

Jubilee Trail

Hill Barn
Farm

Compton
Valence

Manor
Farm

CHURCH HILL LANE

Home
Coppice

Tout
Hill

DT2

Jubilee Trail

Hill
Barn
Farm

Roman Road
Dairy

Tumulus

Fiel
Bar

Kingston
Plantation

Kingston
Russell

Tumulus

A35

Martin's
Down

Tumulus

Macmillan Way

Black Down

Tumulus

Tumuli

Wellbottom
Lodge

Tumuli

Tumulus

The Broad
Stone

Wes
Farr

Tumuli

Cross
Dyke

*Bank
Barrows*

Macmillan Way

Whatcombe
Down

Jubilee Trail

Tumuli

Tumulus

Tumulus

73 **106**

A B C

Compton Bottom

Tumuli

Long Bottom

West Hill Bottom

West Hill Bottom

Long Bottom Plantation

Town Hill Coppice

Town Hill Farm

Tumulus

Town Hill Slip Plantation

All Families Plantation

Tumulus

Hogleaze Farm

DT2

Field System

Tumulus

Tumuli

Cocked Hat Coppice

Barrow Plantation

New Littlewood Farm

Tumulus

Long Barrow

Tumulus

Tumulus

Tumuli

Midway Down

Midway Down Farm

Winterbourne Abbas

WEST WY

Glebe Farm

Little Glebe

BUTT FM

PH

Little Glebe Farm

Manor Farm

A35

BLACKSMITH'S PIECE

Nine Stones

English Heritage

Winterbourne Valley CE Fst Sch

Boxenhedge Farm

B3159

North Hill

Lodge Wood

Westfield Farm

Long Barrow

A B C

4

93

3

92

2

91

1

90

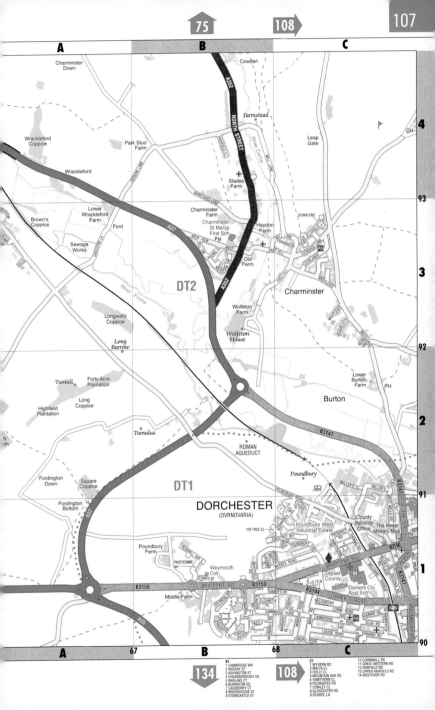

A B C

4

93

3

92

2

91

1

90

Charminster Down

Cowden

A352

NORTH STREET

Farmstead

River Cerne

MILL LANE

Leap Gate

CH

Wrackleford Coppice

Park Stud Farm

Slades Farm

WANCHARD LANE

DOWN END

Wrackleford

Lower Wrackleford Farm

Ford

GASCOYNE LA

Charminster Farm

Charminster St Marys First Sch PH

Haydon Farm

EAST HILL

Old Farm

DT2

A352

A31

WEIR VIEW

WEST

Charminster

Brown's Coppice

Sewage Works

Wolfeton Farm

Wolfeton House

River Frome

Longwalls Coppice

Long Barrow

Lower Burton Farm

PH

Tumuli

Forty Acre Plantation

Burton

Highfield Plantation

Long Coppice

Tumulus

B3147

ROMAN AQUEDUCT

Fordington Down

Square Coppice

DT1

Poundbury

MILLER'S

MILLER'S

County Hall

A35

Fordington Bottom

DORCHESTER (DVRNOVARIA)

POUNDBURY ROAD

County Records Office

The Keep Military Mus

B3150

THE GROVE

FIR TREE CL

Poundbury West Industrial Estate

Poundbury Farm

CHESTNUT WY

PROSPECT

POUNDBURY RD

B3147

Weymouth Coll

FESTHALL AVE

STOWEY ST

PACEYCOMBE WY

WHITFIELD RD

B3150

BRIDPORT RD

BRIDPORT RD

Dorset County

H

B3144

Damers Cty First Sch

MAUMBURY RD

Middle Farm

HOLME LA

DAMER'S RD

DAMERS ROAD

B3150

ELIZABETH PL

CAMBRIDGE ROAD

LORNE

DAGMAR RD

CASTLE ST

FLINTOCK ST

CAMBRIDGE

LOUISE RD

EDWARD RD

OLGA RD

COBURG ROAD

A B C

A B C

Hill Barn

Home Farm

Square Coppice

4

B3143

93

DT2

Limekiln Copse

Higher Burton Farm

Higher Kingston Farm

3

Badgers Copse

P

92

A35

Frome Whitfield Farm

Birkin House

Frome Whitfield

2

HOLLOW HILL

Coker's Frome

B3143

STINSFORD HILL

91

County Hall

Dorchester HM Prison

DT1

B3150

Stinsford

Kingston Maurward Agricultural Coll

Kingston Maurward Gardens & Animal Park

Kingston Maurward

Old Crown Ct & Cells

Dinosaur Mus

GREENINGS CT

LONDON RD

Greys Bridge

HIGH WEST

HIGH E ST

Mus

Tutankhamun Exhibition

P

DORCHESTER
(DVRNOVARIA)

Weir

River Frome

1

B3144

P

Dorchester Prep Sch

Stinsford VIEW

ST GEORGES ROAD

Louds Mill Sewage Treatment Works

PRINCE OF WALES ROAD

B3144

LANCASTER

P

STATION APP

Dorchester South

Sandringham Sports Ctr

A35

90

69 A 70 B 71 C

A1
1 NORTHERNWAY
2 NORTH SQ
3 THE BOW
4 ALINGTON ST
5 CHURCH ST
6 CHURCH CL
7 ACLAND RD
8 WEST WALKS RD
9 NEW ST
10 WEYMOUTH AVE
11 FAIRFIELD RD
12 UPR FAIRFIELD RD
13 CROMWELL RD
14 EARL CL
15 ATHELSTAN RD
16 FORDINGTON GD
17 SYDENHAM WAY
18 BARNES WAY
19 CULLIFORD RD NTH
20 LONDON CL
21 POUND LANE
22 CHURCH ACRE

111
80

A   **B**   **C**

4

Spring Garden Coppice

Tumulus

Sand a Gravel

Damerhill Coppice

Turners Puddle

Jubilee Trail

River Piddle or Trent

Turnerspuddle Farm

Throop

93

Briantspuddle

Bladen Plantations

Landshare Coppice

Throop Farm

THROOP HOLLOW

Brockhill Coppice

Brockhill Fish Farm

Cecily Bridge

Bryants Puddle Allotments Plantation

Battle Farm

Eweleaze Coppice

THE DROVE

DT2

Smokeham Bottom

3

Cull Peppers Dish

P

Tumuli

Tumulus

Tumuli

Longcroft Coppice

Tumuli

Bryants Puddle Heath

Rimsmoor Pond

Jubilee Trail

92

Oakers Wood

Throop Heath

Tumulus

Tumulus

Millicent's Plantation

Tumulus

2

Okers Wood House

Moreton Plantation

Tonerspuddle Heath

DANGER AREA

BH20

Chamberla Heath

East Plantation

Round Barrow

91

Clouds Hill

Lawrence of Arabia's Cottage NT

1

DORSET DRIVE

Moreton Plantation

P

Tank Training Area

90

A   82   **B**   83   **C**

81

A
B
C

Morden Mill

A35

QUARR HILL
PARK CORNER

Whitmoor Bottom

Bulbury Coppice
Bulbury Farm

CH

Bulbury Woods Golf Club

Sherford

A35

BH16

4

Slepe

Tumulus

CHITTEN HILL

Chitten Hill

Morden Park

B3075

93

Slepe Farm

Sherford Farm

Sherford River

3

Sherford Bridge

MORDEN ROAD

92

Old Decoy Pond

BH20

Gore Heath

National Nature Reserve

2

The Decoy

Decoy Heath

MORDEN ROAD

P

91

Memorial

1

B3075

Great Ovens Hill

Northport Heath

A
91
B
92
C
90

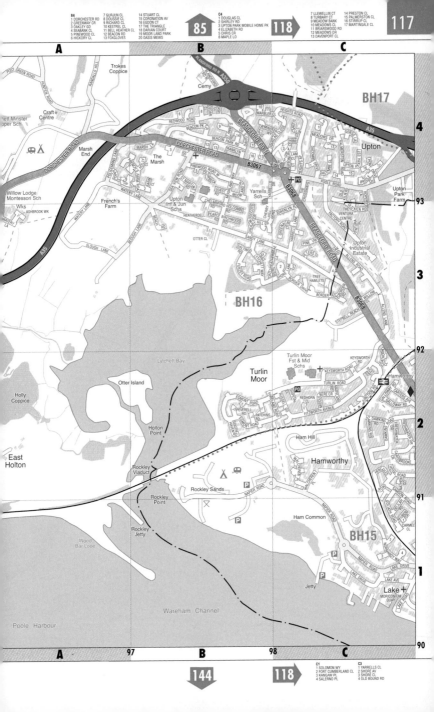

B4
1 DORCHESTER RD
2 GREENWAY CR
3 OAKLEY GD
4 SEABANK CL
5 PINEWOOD CL
6 HICKORY CL
7 GURJUN CL
8 DOUSSIE CL
9 RICHARD CL
10 KESTREL CL
11 BELL HEATHER CL
12 BEACON RD
13 FOXGLOVES
14 STUART CL
15 CORONATION AV
16 EGDON CT
17 THE TRIANGLE
18 DARIAN COURT
19 MOOR LAND PARK
20 OASIS MEWS

C4
1 DOUGLAS CL
2 SHIRLEY RD
3 UPTON PARK MOBILE HOME PK
4 ELIZABETH RD
5 CHRIS CR
6 MAPLE LO

7 LLEWELLIN CT
8 TURBARY CT
9 MEADOW BANK
10 MEADOWS CL
11 BRIARSWOOD RD
12 MEADOWS DR
13 DAVENPORT CL
14 PRESTON CL
15 PALMERSTON CL
16 STIRRUP CL
17 MARTINGALE CL

85   118   117

144   118

C1
1 SOLOMON WY
2 FORT CUMBERLAND CL
3 KANGAW PL
4 SALERNO PL

C3
1 YARRELLS CL
2 SHORE AV
3 SHORE CL
4 OLD BOUND RD

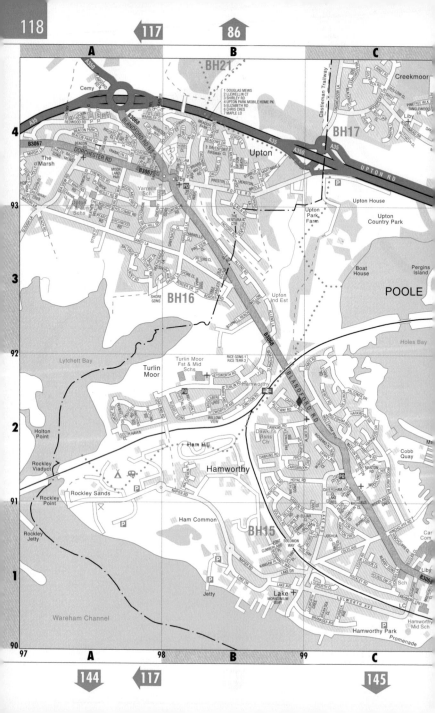

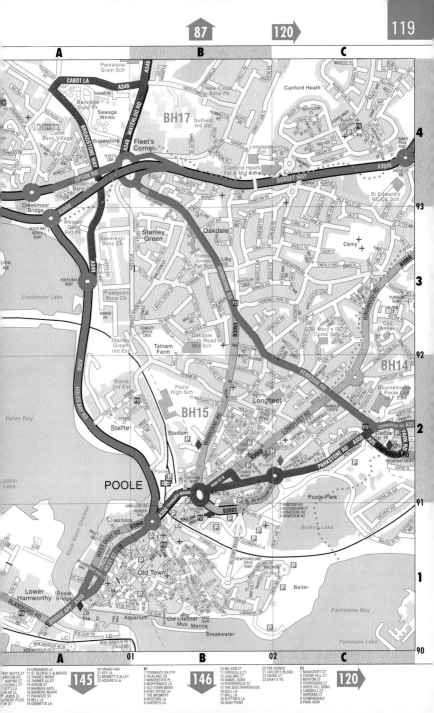

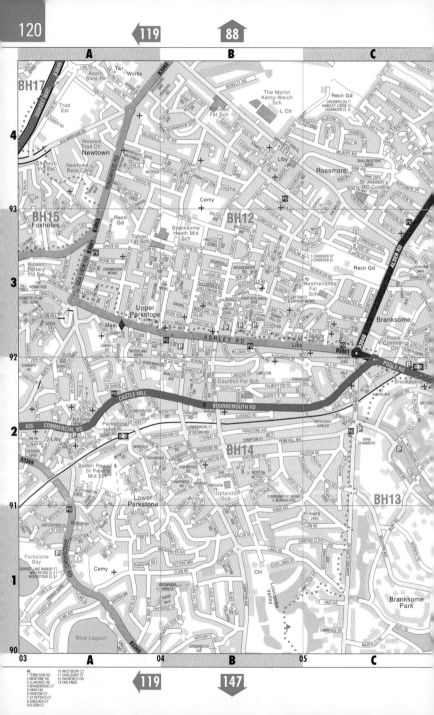

BOURNEMOUTH

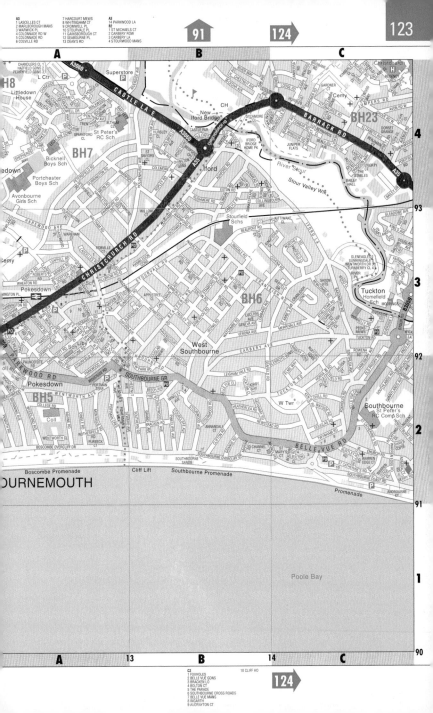

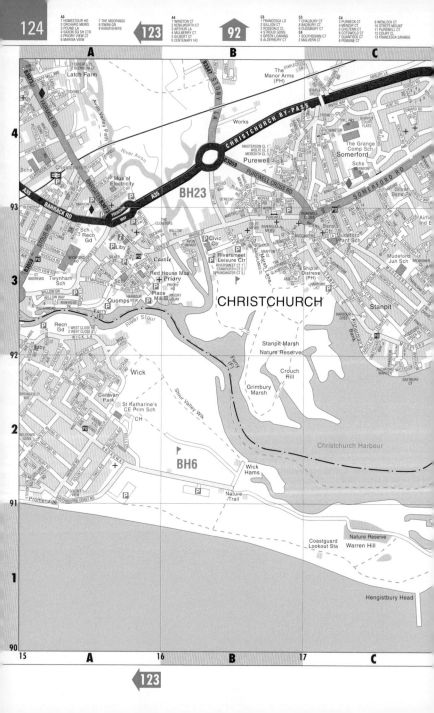

A **B** **C**

Superstore

Highcliffe

BH23

HIGHCLIFFE RD SHELLEY HILL

LYMINGTON RD

A337

4

Sea Vixen
Ind Est

Grange Road
Bsns Qtr

Somerford

High
Pines

SHELLEY
HAMLETS

Somerford
CH

Highcliffe
Castle

93

Friars
Cliff

Beaver
Ind
Est

Groynes

Groynes

3

CHRISTCHURCH

Mudeford

92

Sandhills

IRB
Sta
Little
Haven

Haven House
Inn
(PH)

2

Ferry (F)

91

BH6

Groynes

Valley Wlk

1

ngistbury
Head

A **B** **C**
19 20

90

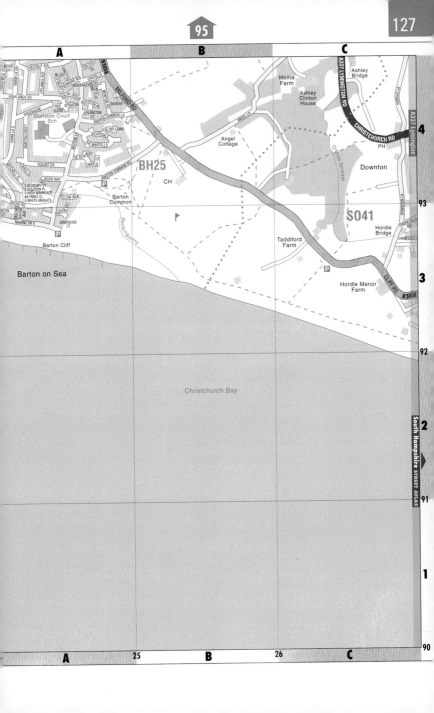

Home Farm

Ashley Bridge

Ashley Clinton House

A337 LYMINGTON RD

CHRISTCHURCH RD

A337 Lymington

PH

Downton

Angel Cottage

ANGEL LA

MILFORD RD

B3058

Durlston Court Sch

Durlston Court Sch

BH25

CH

Barton Common

BARTON COMMON RD

Barton Cliff

Becton Bunny

Barton on Sea

Oldos Stream

SO41

Hordle Bridge

SHOREFIELD RD

DANEHURST

Taddiford Farm

Hordle Manor Farm

CLIFF RD

B3058

Christchurch Bay

4

93

3

92

2

91

1

90

25

26

A

B

C

A4
1 HOWARTH CL
2 S ANWINGS
3 GROVE DR
4 ST LAWRENCE
5 DONKEY LA
6 DARBY LA

A　　　**B**　　　**C**

Burton Bradstock

BURTON ROAD
Shadrach
NORTH HL CL
Works
B3157
BARR LANE

CHARLES RD
BAGDUCKNE FIELD
GROVE ROAD
Magnolia
Farm

River Bride
Manor
Farm
PO
MILL
Church
Libby S
PH
Burton Bradstock
VC Prim Sch
HIGH ST

National
Trust
Southover
SOUTHOVER
Burton Cliff
Cliff Farm

4

Peacehaven Farm
Graston
Copse
Graston Farm
Bredy
Farm
BREDY LANE

BREDY ROAD

DT6
Tumulus

89

Burton Beach
South West Coast Path
National
Trust
P
COMMON LANE
BEACH ROAD
CROW ROAD
B3157
Bind
Barrow

Cogden
Farm

Old Coastguard House
B3157

Cliff End

P

3

88

47　　　　　**48**

DT6
East Cliff

89　　　　　　　　**89**

47　　　　　**48**

Cogden Beach
Burton
Mere

2

87

1

86

48　　**A**　　49　　**B**　　50　　**C**

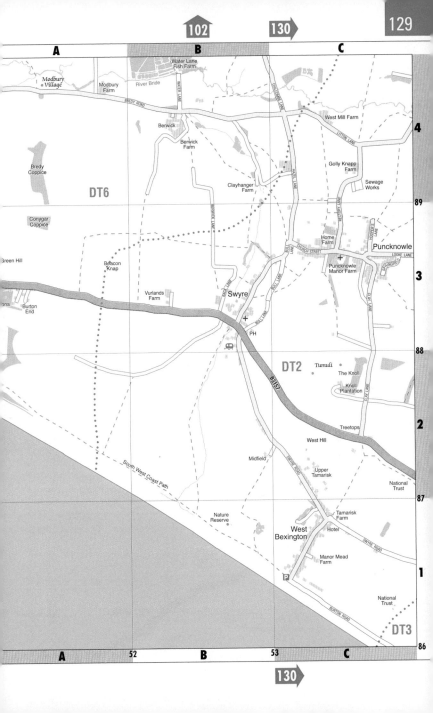

A
B
C

West End Farm
Four Meads Farm
LITTON LANE
YHA
COW LANE
COX'S LANE
River Bride
Middle Farm

Rowden Bridge

Lower Farm
Long Bredy Fa

4

PARK'S LANE
BRIDEBURY LANE

89

Tumulus
Parks Farm

Dantze Coppices

LOOKE LANE
Looke Farm
LOOKE LANE

DT2

Long Coppice

Ashley Chase Dairy

3

88

Chapel (rems. of)
Chapel Coppice

Look Wood
North Coppice

Nine Acre Coppice

Green Leaze

Ashley Chase House
Watergates Coppice
Pink Lake Coppice

2

Puncknowle Wood
Bexington Wood

Limekiln Coppice
DT3

87

Limekiln Hill
Tumuli
Mound
National Trust
South West Coast Path
B3157
Castle Coppice

Tumuli

Tumuli
Abbotsbury Castle (fort)
Wears Farm

1

SWYRE ROAD
Tulk's Hill
Labour in Vain Farm

Tumuli
Wears Hill
Tumuli
ABBOTSBURY HILL

86

Bexington Coppice

54
A
55
B
56
C

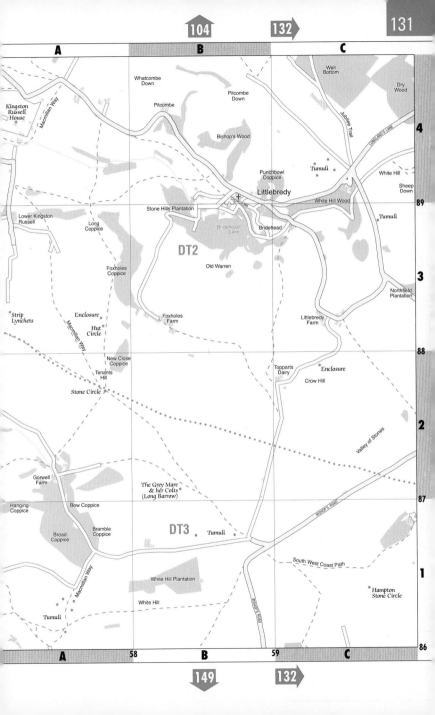

A B C

Longlands
Tumuli
Dry Wood
LONGLAND'S LANE
Big Wood
Tumulus
Coombe Farm
COOMBE ROAD
Strip Lynchets
Steepleton Farm
B3159
Great Whitwa
Manor Farm
Winterbourne Steepleton

4

Jubilee Trail
Loscombe Plantation
Loscombe Farm
Loscombe Down
Tumulus
Dairy

89

Sheep Down
COOMBE ROAD
Tumuli
Loscombe Wood
Tumulus

DT2

3

Long Barrow
Tumulus
Conygar Meadow Coppice
Jubilee Trail
Ballarat Farm
East Rew Farm

Enclosure
Tumulus
Goldcombe Farm

88

Tumuli
Black Down
Tumuli
South West Coast Path

2

Tumulus
BISHOP'S ROAD
Black Down Plantation
Hardy Coppice
P
Hardy Monument
National Trust
Tumuli
Tumuli
Bronkham Hill

Portesham Hill
Benecke Wood

87

South West Coast Path
Hell Stone (Long Barrow)
Wig Plantation
Jubilee Trail
Tumu

1

Tumuli
DT3
Hell Bottom Quarry (disused)
Bench
Hell Bottom

HAMPTON
FRONT ST
BACK
HELLSTONE
Portesham
Portesham Farm

86

60 A 61 B 62 C

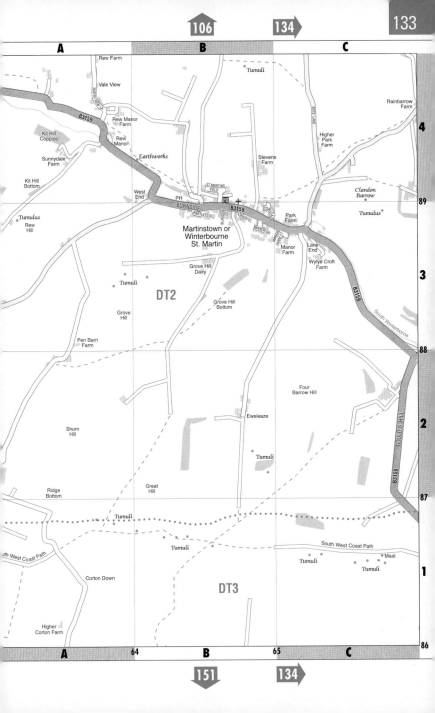

C4
1 AUGUSTAN CL
2 FARRINGDON CL
3 ELDRIDGE CL
4 D'URBERVILLE CL

A
B
C

Thomas Hardye Leisure Centre

Dorchester RFC

Sports Ground

City Middle Sch

Queen's Ave

Coburg Road

Maumbury Rd

Thomas Hardye Sch

Treves Rd

DORCHESTER
(DVRNOVARIA)

DT1

The Prince of Wales Sch

Garfield Ave

Mithras Cl

Hillfort

Thornhill Cl

Cunington

Castle Park

Maiden Castle Road

A354

David's Wk

Superstore

Rampant Wk

Sports Ground

Winterbourne

4

Cricket Ground

Weymouth

Weymouth Road

B3147

Road

Clandon

Cross Dyke

89

Maiden Castle Farm

P

Dorchester Town Football Club

Hog Hill

Maiden Castle

ROMAN TEMPLE
(Remains of)

DT2

Herringston Barrow

Winterborn Herringsto

3

Monkton Hill

Herringsto

88

Ashton Farm

West Field Plantation

Winterborne Monkton

A354

Herringston Farm

2

Tumuli

87

Tumuli

Tumuli

Bayard Barn

B3159

Gould's Hill

Tumuli

Came Dow Golf Club

1

Gould's Bottom

DT3

Came Down

CH

Da W

Dorchester Road

A354

Tumulus

Tumuli

86

Tumulus

66
67
68

A
B
C

108
136

A4
1 GABRIEL GN
2 EVERDENE RD
3 NONESUCH CL
4 ST ANDREWS CL
5 HIGHGROVE CL

B4
1 SANDRINGHAM CT
2 FRIARS CL
3 SMOKEY HOLE LA

St Marys Cath First Sch

Max Gate (NT)

Conquer Barrow

DT1

St Osmunds C E Mid Sch

Manor Park CE First Sch

A352

A352

A35

Henge

Tumulus

Frome Hill

North Plantation

Tumuli

North Plantation

Well Plantation

Bunker's Hill Plantation

Tumulus

Conygar Hill

Came Park

A352

Tumulus

Cole Hill Wood

Jubilee Trail

South Winterborne

Winterborne Came

Winterbourne Faringdon Village

Came House

Home Wood

DT2

Cole Hill Wood

Whitcombe

Jubilee Trail

Whitcombe Manor

Tumuli

Brick Hill Plantation

Tumulus

Higher Came Farm

South Plantation

Gallop

Tumuli

Down Wood

Cripton Cottage

Cripton Wood

Whitcombe Barn Plantation

Tumuli

Whitcombe Down

Tumulus

Tumulus

Cripton Spinney

Whitcombe Barn

Tumuli

South Drove Farm

Warren Barn

SOUTH DROVE

CHALKY RD

A B C

Stafford House

The Manor House

Lower Lewell Farm

Gould's Coppice

South Winterborne

PH

THE PADDOCK

RECTORY

BARTON CL

West Stafford

4

GLEBELAND CL

Knighton Wood

Parsonage Plantation

Sandy Barrow

HIGHGATE LANE

89

Bunker's Hill Plantation

Tumulus

Knigh Heath

Cook's Plantation

Stafford Farm

Lewell Lodge

3

West Knighton Pit

Huck Bar

Jubilee Trail

Lower Glebe Farm

88

DT2

PH

Salt Hill Plantation

Mayers Por Wood

Glebe Farm

Common Plantation

Empool Heath

Higher Lewell Farm

Empool Bottom

STAFFORD

2

South Loscombe Plantation

LEWELL WAY

West Knighton

Littlemayne Farm

Broadmayne Cty First Sch

Jubilee Trail

WATERGATES LANE

WATERGATES LANE

87

OLD BRICKFIELDS

Fryer Mayne Wood

Black Hill

BRAMBLE DV

MAIN STREET

ST MARTINS

BRAMBLE EDGE

CONWAY DRI

BROADMEAD

Broadmayne

1

CARTEL CL

LITTLEMEAD

High Trees

PH

Tumulus

Fryer Mayne

Beech Plantation

SOUTH DROVE

CRAWEY ROAD

CROSSTREE CL

WOODLANDS

OSMINGTON DV

A352

Friarmayne Farm

Beech Farm

Broadmayne House Farm

DOMINGTON DRIVE

Warmwell Wood

86

72 A 73 B 74 C

A B C

4

Higher
Woodsford

LC
LC
Moreton
LC
89

WOODSFORD CL
PAULS WY
CLYFFE VW
DICK O' TH'
BANKS CL
GREYSTONES
CL
DICK O' TH' BANKS ROAD
B3390
REDBRIDGE ROAD
BINGHAMS RD
BINGHAMS
RD
GREEN LANE
HEATHLAND
CLOSE
SKIPPET
Liby
Crossways
3
WARMWELL ROAD
MORETON ROAD
REDBRIDGE LANE
Heath
Farm
88

Warmwell
Quarry

DT2
Bowley's
Plantation
Tinker's
Barrow

Outer
Heath
Warmwell
Leisure
Resort
Skippet
Heath
Moigne
Combe Wood
Hotel
Tumulus
Nether
Moynton
Farm

Outer Heath
Halsdon
Farm
Skippet
Plantation
2

Stroud's Moor
Ploughman's
Coppice
Moigne
Combe Farm
Jubilee Trail
Moigne
Combe

Withy
Bed
Warmwell
Heath

B3390
Ryeclose
Mill House
Cider Mus
87

Warmwell
Heath
Hope
Wood
Holly
Farm

Lastridge
Wood
Knap
Farm
1

her
Farm
Misery
Farm
Gillard's
Coppice
MORETON ROAD
Ham
Coppice

B3390
Warmwell
Watercombe Heath
86

The Plantation

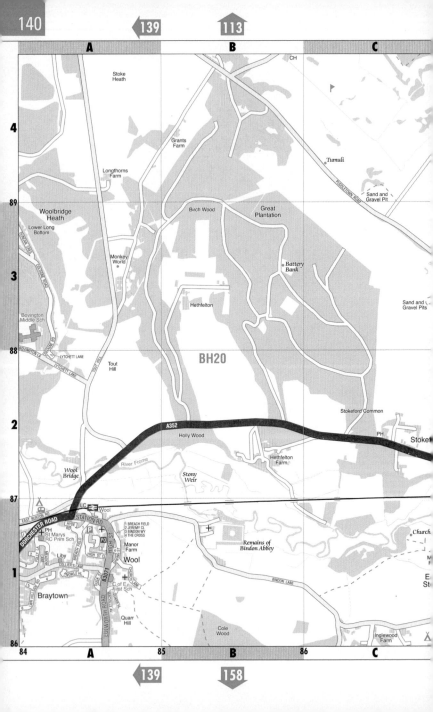

4

89

3

88

A

B

C

Stoke
Heath

CH

Grants
Farm

Tumuli

Longthorns
Farm

POOLE STATION ROAD

Sand and
Gravel Pit

Woolbridge
Heath

Birch Wood

Great
Plantation

Lower Long
Bottom

GORE HILL

GORE ROAD

Monkey
World

Battery
Bank

Sand and
Gravel Pits

Bovington
Middle Sch

Hethfelton

BOVINGTON LA

LYTCHETT LANE

LYTCHETT LANE

TOUT HILL

Tout
Hill

BH20

88

2

87

1

86

A352

Holly Wood

Stokeford Common

PH

Stoke

River Frome

Hethfelton
Farm

Wool
Bridge

Stony
Weir

EAST BURTON ROAD

DORCHESTER ROAD

LC

Wool

STATION RD

HYDE
RD

PH
St Marys
RC Prim Sch

1 BREACH FIELD
2 JEREMY CL
3 BINDON WY
4 THE CROSS

Manor
Farm

HIGH ST

Church

Remains of
Bindon Abbey

Liby

COLLIER'S LANE

Wool

B3071

KNOWLE HL

BRACK FIELD

HIGH ST CL

DUCK ST

CHURCH LA

C of E
First Sch

BINDON LANE

E
St

Braytown

LULWORTH ROAD

WOODROW RD

Quarr
Hill

Cole
Wood

Inglewood
Farm

86

84

A

85

B

86

C

C2
1 ST MARTIN'S CL
2 COOPER'S LA
3 DOLLIN'S LA
4 CARRION LA
5 KENNINGTON SQ
6 HEMSBACH CT
7 CHURCH GN
8 THE QUAY
9 ABBOTS QUAY
10 TANNER'S LA
11 ST MICHAEL'S RD
12 HILLARD CT
13 DALER CT
14 KNIGHTSTONE CT

4

St Martin
CE First
Sch

CHERRY CL
SYCAMORE CL

CHESTNUT CL

Birch
Wood

Jubilee
Wood

Willow
Wood

Keysworth
Farm

89

Sewage
Works

West Field
Coppice

Keysworth
Point

Poole
Harbour

3

Buck's Cove
Saltmarsh

BH20

88

Swineham
Farm

Swineham
Point

Gigger's
Island

Arne
Heath

2

River Frome

The Moors

87

Ridge
Wharf

The
Moors

Salterns
Copse

Club

1

Redcliffe
Farm

BARNDALE DR

Ridge
Farm

Ridge

ARNE ROAD

Mound

Slepe
Copse

BARNHILL RD

Slepe Heath

Broad
Marsh

Slepe
Heath

SOLDIERS ROAD

86

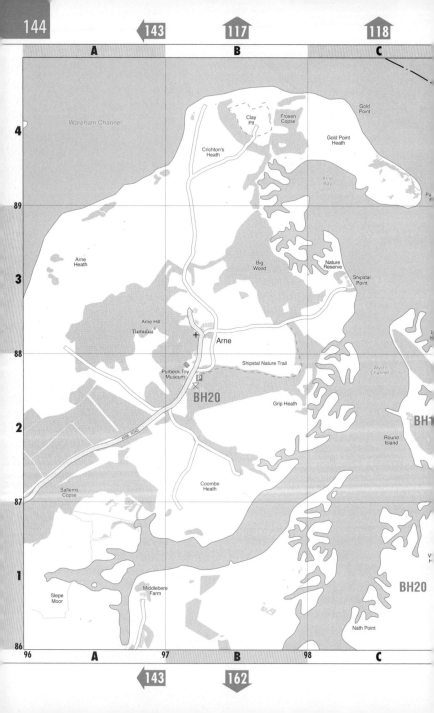

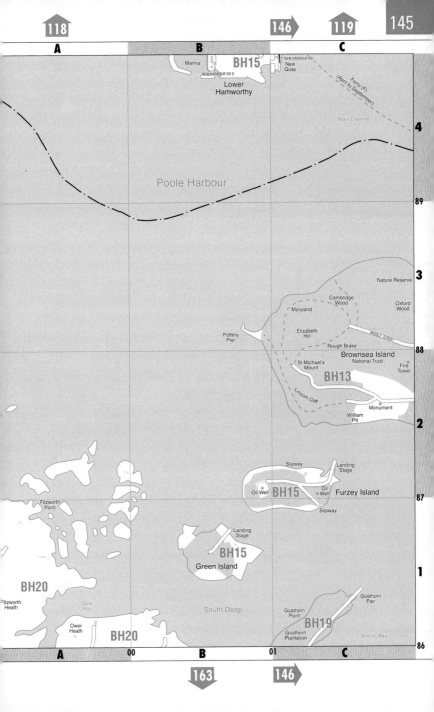

A   B   C

BH15

Marina

NEW HARBOUR RD

New Quay

NEW HARBOUR RD S

Lower
Hamworthy

Ferry (F)
(April to September)

Main Channel

4

Poole Harbour

89

3

Nature Reserve

Cambridge
Wood

Maryland

Oxford
Wood

Pottery
Pier

Elizabeth
Hill

MIDDLE STREET

Rough Brake

88

Brownsea Island
National Trust

St Michael's
Mount

Fire
Tower

BH13

Lincoln Cliff

Monument

William
Pit

2

Slipway

Landing
Stage

Oil Well

BH15

Oil
Well

Furzey Island

87

Slipway

Landing
Stage

BH15

Green Island

1

BH20

Fitzworth
Point

Fitzworth
Heath

Ower
Bay

South Deep

Goathorn
Point

Goathorn
Pier

BH19

Ower
Heath

BH20

Goathorn
Plantation

Brands Bay

86

A   00   B   01   C

145
119

A
B
C
Marina
BH15
NEW HARBOUR RD S
RD
NEW HARBOUR
New Quay
Main Channel
4
Ferry (F) (April to September)
Poole Harbour
89
3
Cambridge Wood
Nature Reserve
Oxford Wood
Maryland
The Villa
West Lake
East Lake
Elizabeth Hill
MIDDLE STREET
Pottery Pier
Rough Brake
88
Brownsea Island
National Trust
BH13
St Michael's Mount
Fire Twr
Harley Wood
Church Hill
Lincoln Cliff
Monument
William Pit
Farm Buildings
2
Harry Point
Landing Stage
Oil Well
BH15
Oil Well
Furzey Island
87
Slipway
Landing Stage
BH15
Green Island
1
Goathorn Pier
South Deep
Goathorn Point
BH19
Jerry's Point
BH20
Goathorn Plantation
Brand's Bay
BH19
86
00
A
01
B
02
C

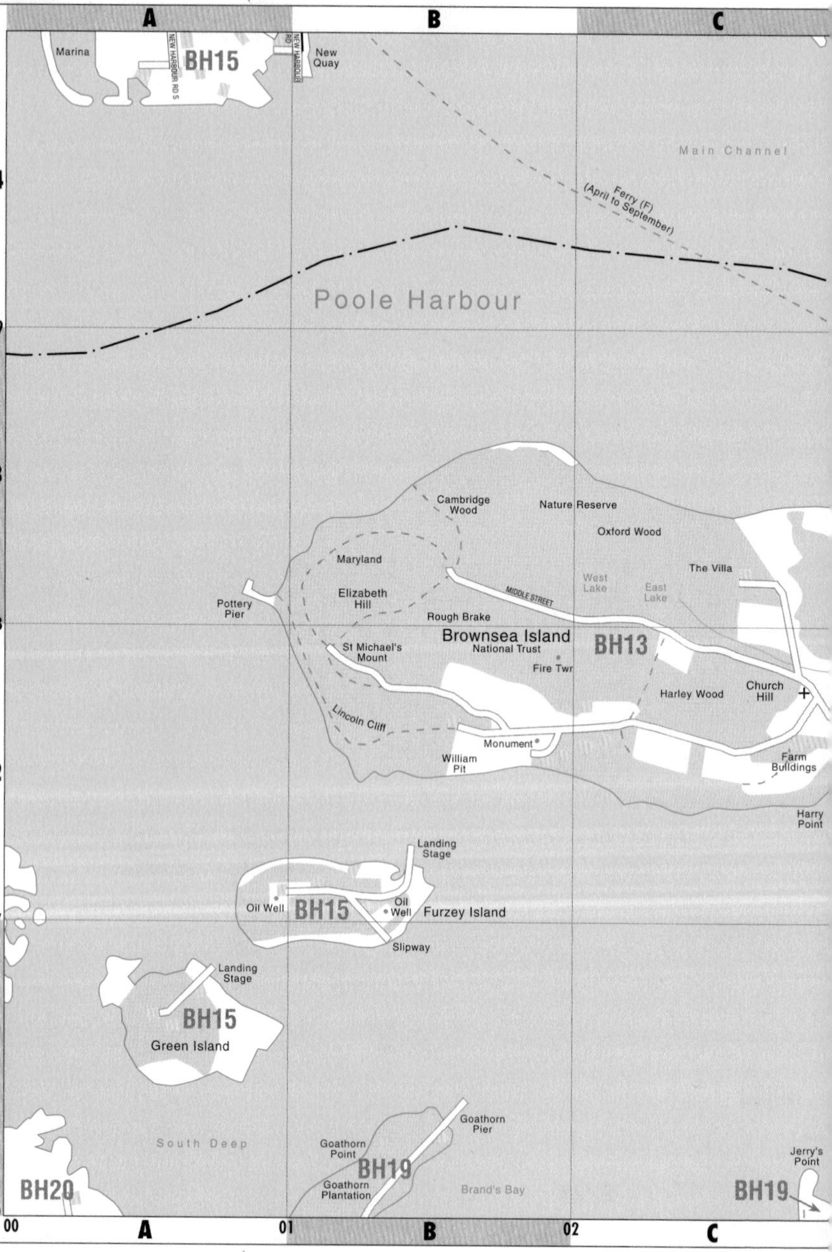

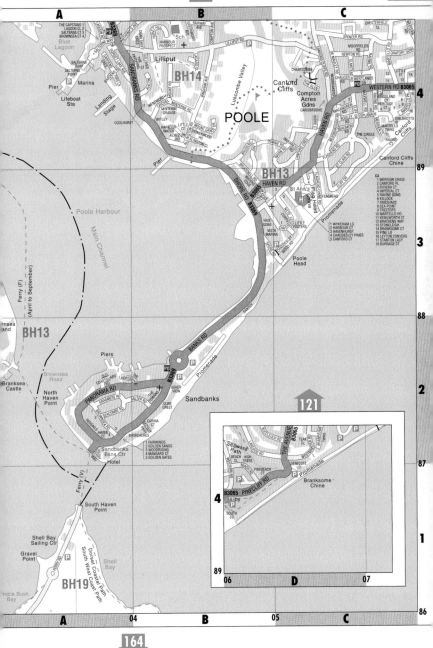

A

B

C

The Old
Coastguards

East
Bexington Farm

Bexington
Coppice

Ferny
Planta

East Bexington
Dairy House

ABBOTSBURY HILL

B3157

4

BURTON ROAD

Lawrence's
Cottage

DT3

Countess
Coppice

CLEVERLAWNS

P

Abbotsbury
Sub-Tropical Gardens

South West Coast Path

85

129

86

54

86

DT3

BURTON ROAD

54

BURTON ROAD

Peasons
Plantations

Stavordale
Wood

3

54

P

Strip Lynchets

84

Reeds
End

2

83

1

82

54

A

55

B

56

C

A
B
C

Friar Waddon

Hewish Farm

Windsbatch
Farm

Yules
Farm

Corton Hill

FRIAR WADDON
ROAD

4

Corton
Farm

Tumuli

Tumuli

Friar Waddon Hill

Jubilee Trail

85

Westbrook
Dairy

3

Pucksey Brook

Hewish
Farm

DT3

84

Dairy House
Coppice

Hewish
Hill

Square Coppice

2

Moor Coppice

Loscombe
Wood

Holwell Farm

Hyde Coppice

Higher Moor

83

on
use

NOTTINGTON LANE

East
Farm

North Farm

Buckland
House

Tatton Farm

Broad Coppice

atton
oppice

Middle Farm

The End

1

Buckland
Ripers

Coverwell
Coppice

Higher
Barn

82

A
64
B
65
C

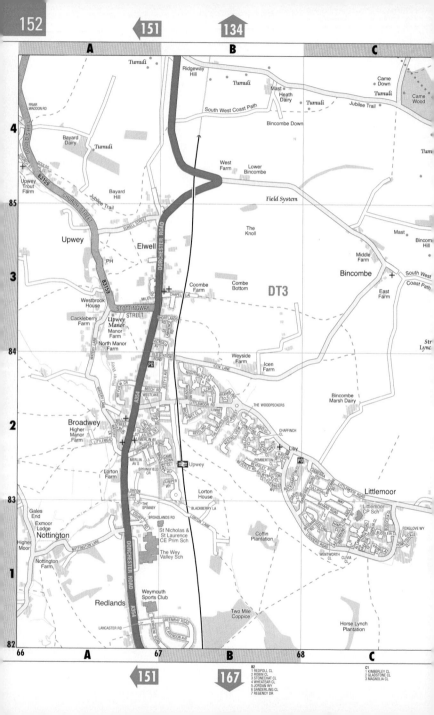

A B C

4

Tumuli

Ridgeway Hill

Tumuli

Came Down

Tumuli

Came Wood

FRIAR WADDON RD

Mast
Heath Dairy

Tumuli

Jubilee Trail

South West Coast Path

Bincombe Down

Bayard Dairy

Tumuli

West Farm

Lower Bincombe

85

Upwey Trout Farm

B3159

CHURCH STREET

Bayard Hill

Jubilee Trail

Field System

Mast

Bincombe Hill

ELWELL STREET

Upwey

Elwell

The Knoll

Middle Farm

3

DORCHESTER ROAD

Coombe Farm

Combe Bottom

DT3

Bincombe

South West Coast Path

PH

CHAPEL LA

East Farm

B3159

Westbrook House

STOTTINGWAY STREET

Cackleberry Farm

Upwey Manor

Manor Farm

North Manor Farm

SHORTLANDS

84

OLD STATION

PO

Weyside Farm

Icen Lane

Icen Farm

Bincombe Marsh Dairy

River Wey

A354

BEECH RD

WESTLAKE

NIGHTINGALE

LITTLEMOOR ROAD

THE WOODPECKERS

LINNET

Stri Lync

2

Broadway

Higher Manor Farm

LITTLEMEAD

MERLIN AV S

SPRINGFIELD ROAD

CHAFFINCH

PEMBERTON

BEVERLEY ROAD

PO

CAMEDOWN

Upwey

Littlemoor

Lorton Farm

MERLIN AV S

JUNIPER WY

Lorton House

Lorton Lane

Littlemoor CP Sch

83

Gales End

Exmoor Lodge

Nottington

THE SPINNEY

BROADLANDS RD

BLACKBERRY LA

BAYARD ROAD

FOXGLOVE WY

St Nicholas & St Laurence CE Prim Sch

Coffin Plantation

Higher Moor

NOTTINGTON LANE

LORTON LANE

Nottington Farm

The Wey Valley Sch

WENTWORTH

CLIVIA CL

1

Weymouth Sports Club

DORCHESTER ROAD

A354

Redlands

Two Mile Coppice

Horse Lynch Plantation

LANCASTER RD

GREENWAY ROAD

CLARENDON AVE

82

66 A 67 B 68 C

A
B
C

Warmwell House
Warmwell
B3390

Ower Wood

CASTLE LA
Moigne Court
Moat
Bartlett's Coppice

Owermoigne
CE Prim Sch

MONKTON RD
HOLLANDS MD AV
E FARM LA
POLLARDS LN
CHURCH LA
East Farm
GLEBEFORD CL
Orchard Coppice
Galton

4

WAREHAM ROAD
West Barn
Chilbury Plantation
CHILBURY Gd
WAREHAM ROAD
Manor Farm

Newgate Farm
A352

85

Glebe Farm

Watercombe
Watercombe Farm

GALTON HILL
East Farm

Hill Dairy

3

Owermoigne Down Barn

DT2

Lord's Barrow

Moigns Down Barn
Tumulus
Tumulus
84

Tumuli

Northground Dairy

2

Moigns Down

North Holworth Farm

South Holworth Farm
Clayland Coppice
Holworth Village

83

West Chaldon

Brimstone Bottom

1

muli
P
Falcon Barn
Brimstone Bottom Barn

Ringstead Farm
South Down Farm

82
A
76
B
77
C

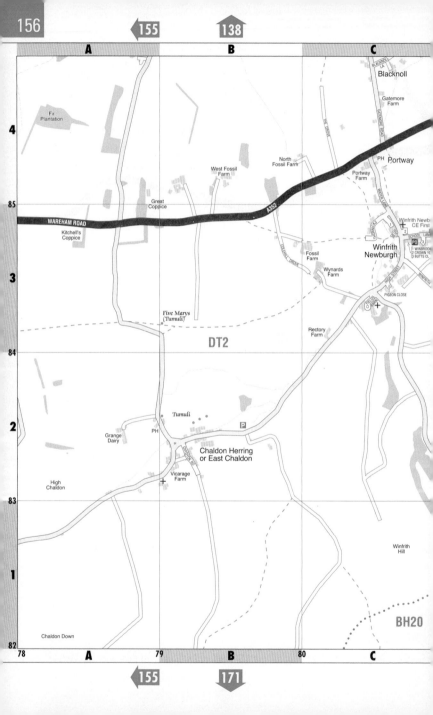

A B C

4

85

3

84

2

83

1

82

Blacknoll

BLACKNOLL LA

Gatemore Farm

THE DRIVE

GATEMORE ROAD

PH Portway

North Fossil Farm

Portway Farm

West Fossil Farm

A352

Fir Plantation

Great Coppice

WAREHAM ROAD

Kitchell's Coppice

COLLIERS DROVE

Fossil Farm

Winfrith Newb CE First

SCHOOL LAN

PO

1 WINBROOK
2 CROWN YE
3 BUTTS CL.

Winfrith Newburgh

MAIN STREET

WATER LANE

Wynards Farm

PIGEON CLOSE

Five Marys (Tumuli)

DT2

Rectory Farm

Tumuli

P

Grange Dairy

PH

CHALDON RD

Chaldon Herring or East Chaldon

High Chaldon

Vicarage Farm

Winfrith Hill

Chaldon Down

BH20

A B C

4

West Burton Farm

Home Farm

Longcutts Farm

PH

ast ghton

A352

North Wood

85

East Knighton Farm

EAST KNIGHTON LANE

Newburgh Farm

Claypits Farm

CLAYPITS LANE

Newburgh Dairy

Coombe Wood

3

B3071

NEWTOWN HILL

DT2

Fields Farm

84

Drove Dairy

2

Tumulus

BH20

Marley Bottom

Vine's Down Buildings

Lulworth Common

83

Belhuish House

B3071

Tumulus

ey d

Marley Wood House

Burngate Wood

1

Belhuish Coppice

A 82 B 83 C 82

Cole
Wood

Woodstreet
Farm

Barn
Coppice

Highwood
Wood

Highwood

Tumulus

Long
Coppice

Tumuli

New
Buildings

Woodman's
Cross

Dorset
Wood

Baylea
Farm

DANGER
AREA

4

Knap Coppice

85

Vicarage
Coppice

Haremere
Wood

Oak
Tree Farm

Coombe Heath

Kick Hill
Coppice

Kick Hill
Farm

3

Coombe
Keynes

West
Farm

Kimbert's
End

Coombe
Beacon

Tumuli

Church
Coppice

84

Vary
Coppice

Kennel
Wood

BH20

The
Lake

Lime Kiln
Dairy

Kennel
Farm

Bellevue
Plantation

Lake
Plantation

Lake Hill
Plantation

2

Lodge
Wood

Lime Kiln
Cottage

Shaggs

Park
Lodge

New Barn
Plantation

Home
Farm

Blac
Barro

83

Burngate
Wood

Botany
Plantations

1

Park
Wood

Bowling
Green Wood

Cemy

Botany
Farm

Botany
Wood

Botany
Farm

DANGER AREA

Whiteway

Lulworth Castle

Ball
Coppice

82

A B C

West Holme
Farm

French Grass
Coppice

East
Holme

Luckford
Lake Farm

West Holme

HOLME LANE

Heath
Range
DANGER AREA

4

New Barn
Farm

Highwood
Heath

Woodbury
Coppice

85

West Holme
Heath

B3070

Luckford Lake

3

Tumuli

Five
Barrow Hill

DANGER
AREA

Tumulus

Hurst
Mill

84

BH20

Lulworth
Heath

Tumuli

Pool
Pond

Mare
Pond

2

Povington
Heath

King's Standing

Tumuli

83

Earl's
Kitchen

North Hills
Plantation

West
Creech

1

DANGER AREA
(Tank Ranges)

West Creech
Farm

Grey's
Coppice

Povington
Barrow

Povington
Wood

82

A 88 B 89 C

4

NEW LANE

A351

B3075

OVAL GDT.
NEW ROAD
CORFE ROAD
TUCKERS
MILL LC.
THE
DROVE

Tumulus

King's
Barrow

Holme Lane
Plantation

HOLME LANE

Hotel

Doreys
Farm

Stocks
Wood

85

Stoborough
Heath

Battle
Plain

Rifle
Range

Three Lords'
Barrow

Tumulus

LC

3

Holme Heath

Tumuli

New Hall
Farm

Creech
Bottom

DANGER
AREA

Grange
Barn

84

BH20

Snug
Farm

Icen
Barrow

Creech Heath

Tumulus

GRANGE ROAD

Grange Heath

2

Haskells
Farm

Clay Pits

Tumulus

Creech

Smithys
Farm

Tumuli

Drinking
Barrow

DANGER
AREA

Breach
Plantation

83

John's
Plantation

Cotness

Great
Plantation

Mine

Whitehall

Mine (dis)

Alder
Moor

East
Creec

1

Creech Barrow
Hill

Little
Wood

Grange
Farm

Tumulus

Tumulus

Creech
Grange

GRANGE HILL

Tumulus

Stonehill
Down

82

Great Wood

Tumulus

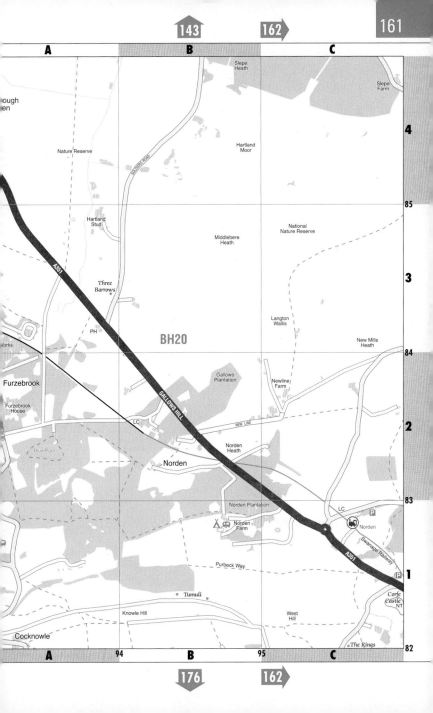

A   B   C

Slepe

Fitzworth
Heath

4

Wytch
Farm

Middlebere
Heath

Oil Wells

Oil
Well

Corfe River

Depot

85

Sharford
Bridge

Wytch
Heath

Wytch
Moor

Rempstone
Heath

3

Flashet
Plantation

84

Scotland
Farm

Thrasher's
Heath

BH20

Batrick's
Plantation

Meadus's
Plantation

• Tumulus

2

Bushey

THRASHER'S LANE

Lower
Bushey Farm

MEADUS'S LANE

Brenscombe
Heath

Sewage
Works

BUSHEY LANE

Higher
Bushey Farm

83

THRASHER'S LANE

Jack Green's
Copse

Keeper's
Copse

Rempstone
Farm

B3351

Ashey Copse

Rollington
Farm

1

NEW ROAD

East
Hill

Brenscombe
Farm

Bushey
Wood

Corfe Castle

1 THE SQ
2 WEST ST

EAST ST

SANDY HILL LANE

P

Rollington Hill

Brenscombe
Wood

Little
Wood

B3351

Rem
We

PO

Dairy House
Challow Farm
Hotel

82

96   A   97   B   98   C

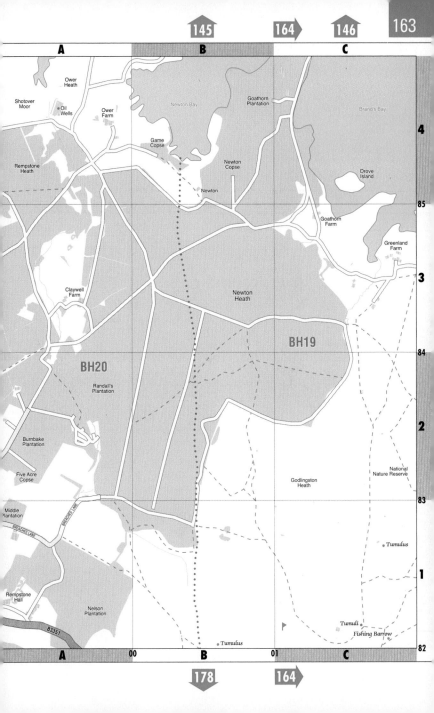

A   B   C

Redhorn
Quay

4

South West Coast Path

FERRY ROAD

85

Studland Heath

National Nature
Reserve

3

Little Sea

05

84

Studland Heath

BH19

Old Harry's
Wife
(NT)
Old
Harry

Studland
Wood

BH19

The Foreland or
Handfast Point

South West Coast Path

82

The Pinnacles

Sewage
Works

FERRY ROAD

2

P

Knoll House
Hotel

B3351

Studland Bay

179

179

05

Puckstone

National Nature
Reserve

Tumulus

WADMORE LANE

Tumulus

FERRY ROAD

83

Wadmore
Farm

P

Redend
Point

Agglestone

BLACK ROAD

FERRY ROAD

RECTORY LANE

MANOR ROAD

Hotel

Black Down

AGGLESTONE
ROAD

CHURCH ROAD

Cliff End

+

1

Manor
Farm

P

+

+

P

WATERY LANE

South West Coast Path

BEACH GREEN ROAD

Studland

WATERY LANE

West Wood

SWANAGE ROAD

B3351

The Warren
Wood

King Barrow

82

02   A   03   B   04   C

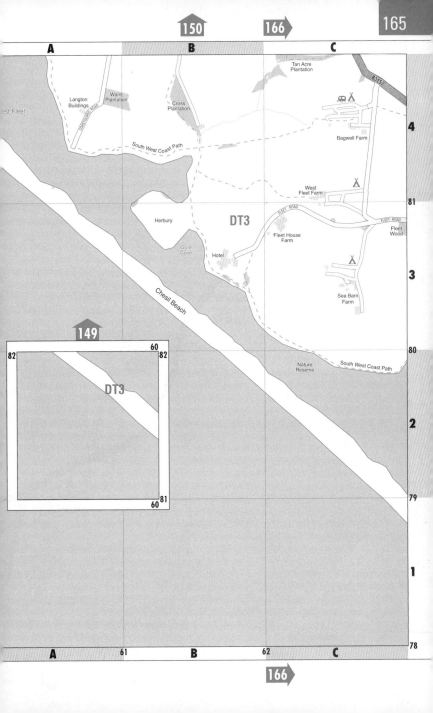

est Fleet

Langton
Buildings

Wans
Plantation

Cross
Plantation

Tan Acre
Plantation

B3157

South West Coast Path

Bagwell Farm

West
Fleet Farm

81

Herbury

DT3

FLEET ROAD

FLEET ROAD

Fleet
Wood

Gore
Cove

Fleet House
Farm

Hotel

3

Chesil Beach

Sea Barn
Farm

80

Nature
Reserve

South West Coast Path

149

82 | 60

82

DT3

2

60 | 81

60

79

1

78

166

165

151

B3
1 CURLEW CL
2 GREBE CL
3 HERON CL

165

180

C1
1 GORDON CR
2 LINCOLN RD
3 LIVERPOOL RD
4 TOLLERDOWN

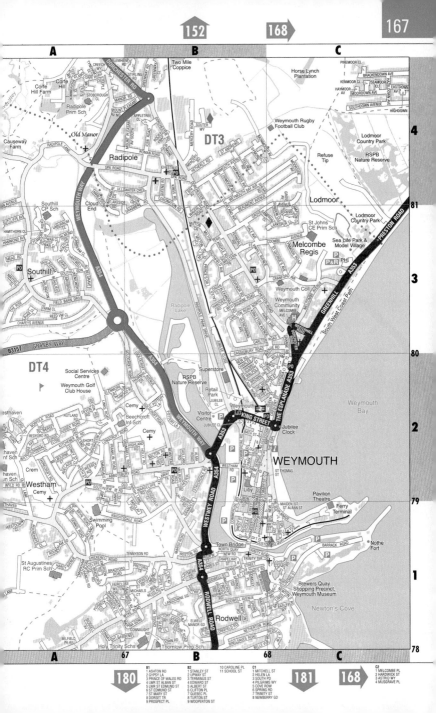

B1
1 ASHTON RD
2 GYPSY LA
3 PRINCE OF WALES RD
4 LWR ST ALBAN ST
5 LWR ST EDMUND ST
6 ST EDMUND ST
7 ST MARY ST
8 DORSET TR
9 PROSPECT PL

B2
1 STANLEY ST
2 UPWAY ST
3 TERMINUS ST
4 EDWARD ST
5 ALBERT ST
6 CLIFTON PL
7 QUEBEC PL
8 TURTON ST
9 WOOPERTON ST

10 CAROLINE PL
11 SCHOOL ST

C1
1 MITCHELL ST
2 HELEN LA
3 SOUTH PD
4 PILGRIMS WY
5 COVE ROW
6 SPRING RD
7 TRINITY ST
8 NEWBERRY GD

C2
1 MELCOMBE PL
2 HARDWICK ST
3 ASTRID WY
4 MUSGRAVE RD

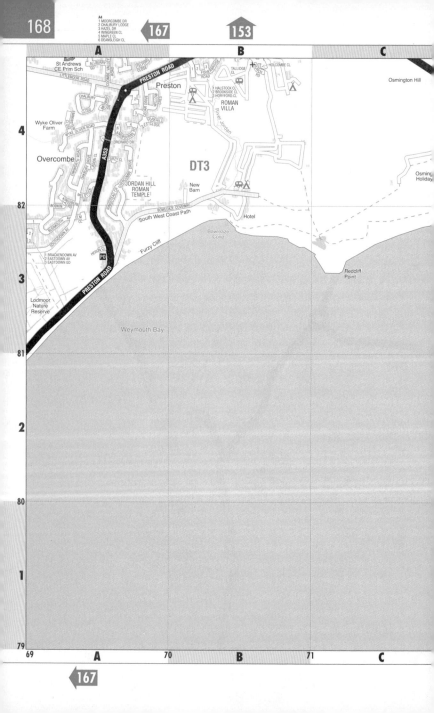

167
153

A4
1 MOORCOMBE DR
2 CHALBURY LODGE
3 HAZEL DR
4 WINGREEN CL
5 MAPLE CL
6 DEANSLEIGH CL

St Andrews
CE Prim Sch
LITTLEMOOR ROAD
ALBERRY
PRESTON ROAD
Preston

FISH
HOLCOMBE CL
TALLIDGE
CL

1 HALSTOCK CL
2 BROOKSIDE CL
3 HORYFORD CL

ROMAN
VILLA

Osmington Hill
Osmington Hill

Wyke Oliver
Farm

CHALBURY

WYKE OLIVER ROAD

ORCHARD DR

DT3

Overcombe

A353

JORDAN HILL
ROMAN
TEMPLE

New
Barn

River Jordan

Osming
Holiday

4

BODKIN

82

BOWLEAZE COVEWAY
South West Coast Path

Hotel

Bowleaze
Cove

1 BRACKENDOWN AV
2 EASTDOWN AV
3 EASTDOWN GD

PO

Furzy Cliff

Redcliff
Point

3

HERRINGS

PRESTON ROAD

Lodmoor
Nature
Reserve

81

Weymouth Bay

2

80

1

79
69   A   70   B   71   C

167

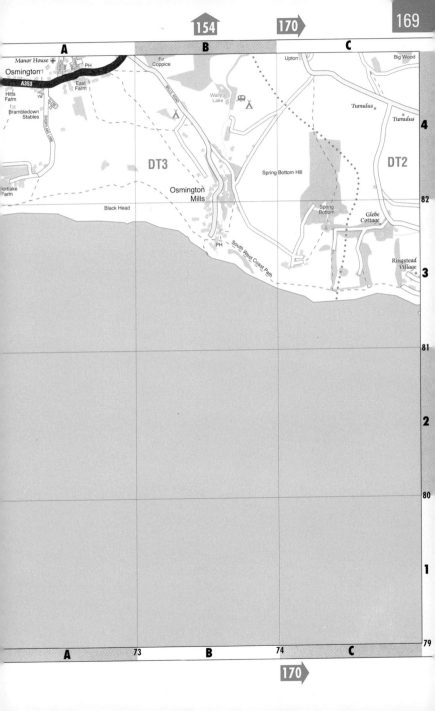

154

170

Manor House
Osmington
A353
Hitts Farm
East Farm
Brambledown Stables
PH

Fir Coppice

Upton

Big Wood

Wally's Lake

Tumulus

Tumulus

DT3

DT2

Osmington Mills

Spring Bottom Hill

82

Black Head

Spring Bottom

Glebe Cottage

ortlake Farm

PH

South West Coast Path

Ringstead Village

3

81

2

80

1

79

170

169

155

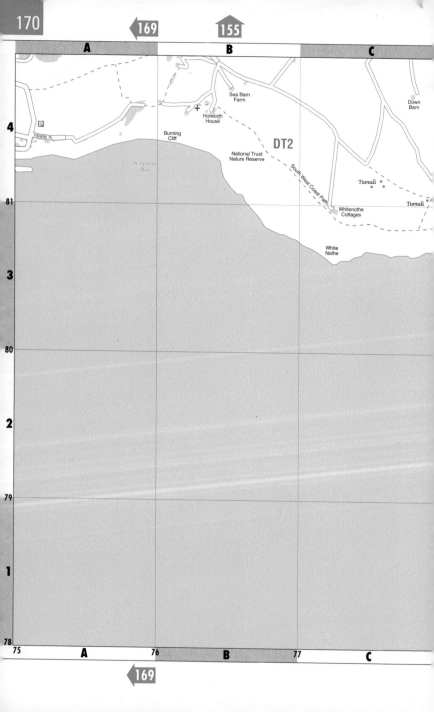

A

B

C

4

P

FISHERS PL

Burning
Cliff

Ringstead
Bay

Sea Barn
Farm

+

Holworth
House

National Trust
Nature Reserve

DT2

South West Coast Path

Down
Barn

Tumuli

Tumuli

Whitenothe
Cottages

White
Nothe

81

3

80

2

79

1

78

75

A

76

B

77

C

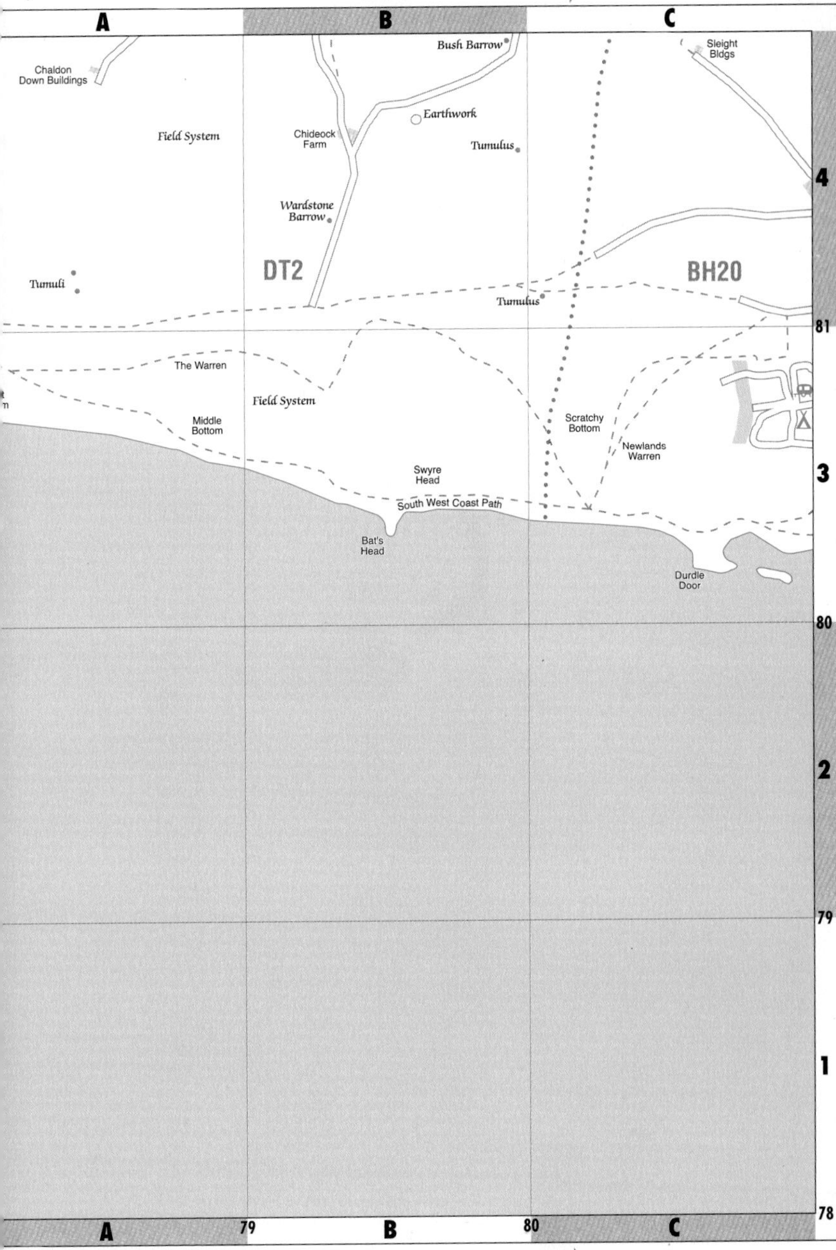

A B C

Chaldon
Down Buildings

Field System

Bush Barrow

Earthwork

Sleight
Bldgs

Chideock
Farm

Tumulus

Wardstone
Barrow

4

Tumuli

DT2

BH20

Tumulus

81

The Warren

Field System

Middle
Bottom

Scratchy
Bottom

Newlands
Warren

3

Swyre
Head

South West Coast Path

Bat's
Head

Durdle
Door

80

2

79

1

A 79 B 80 C

78

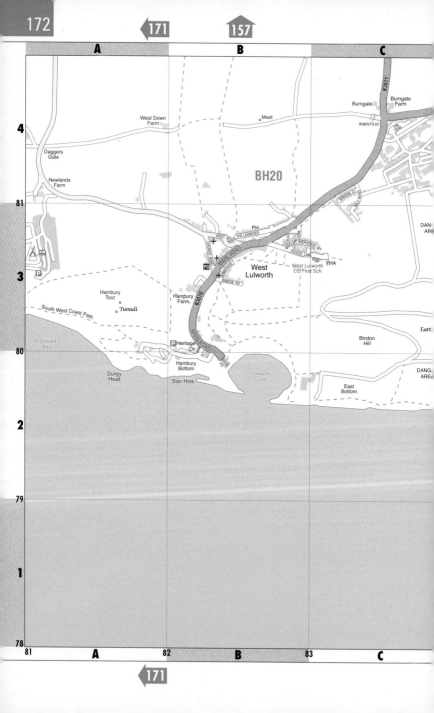

A

West Down Farm

Daggers Gate

Newlands Farm

4

Mast

Burngate

Burngate Farm

WINFRITH DV

THE JINNY

B3071

B

BH20

BINDON PL.

VALE ROAD

81

DAN. ARI

PH

WEST ROAD   THE LAUNCHES

CHURCH HILL

MAIN ROAD

BEACH CLOSE

THE GRANGE

SHEPHERDS WY

SCHOOL LANE

PO

West Lulworth

West Lulworth CE First Sch

YHA

3

Hambury Tout

Tumuli

South West Coast Path

Hambury Farm.

B3070

BINDON RD.

DANVIS DR.

St Oswald's Bay

Heritage Ctr

Hambury Bottom

Dungy Head

Stair Hole

MAIN ROAD

B3070

Bindon Hill

Lulworth Cove

East Bottom

Eart

DANG. AREA

80

79

2

1

78

Observation
Tower
P
B3070
East
Lulworth
PH
Water
Barrows
Ferny
Barrows
Milldown
DANGER AREA
DANGER
AREA
4
Broom's
Plantation
Tumuli
ulworth
Camp
Old Marl
Plantation
Bower's
Coppice
Tumulus
BH20
81
Monastery
Farm
Bindon
Range
Maiden
Plantation
Rings
Hill
Flower's
Barrow
(Hill Fort)
3
Tumuli
Halcombe
Vale
DANGER
AREA
Tumuli
80
Bindon
Plantation
South West Coast Path
Arish
Mell
Cockpit
Head
Worbarrow
Bay
Mupe Bay
Worbarrow
Tout
2
Mupe
Rocks
79
1
4
85
86
78
A
B
C

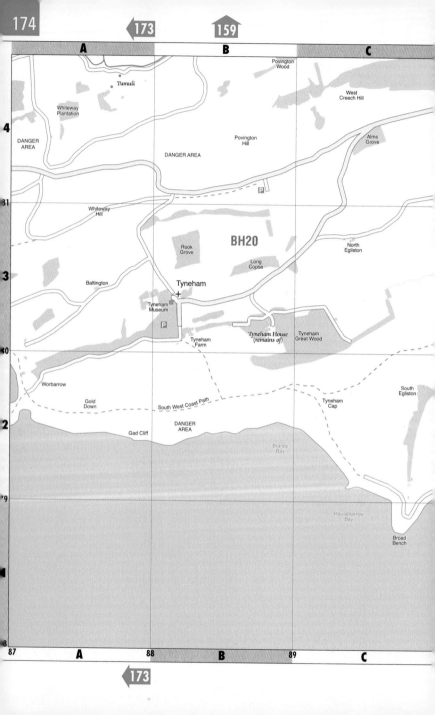

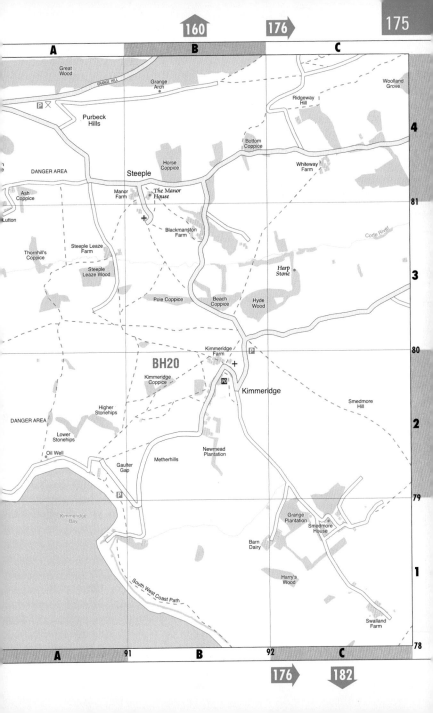

A
B
C

Great
Wood

GRANGE HILL

Grange
Arch

Woolland
Grove

P ✕

Purbeck
Hills

Ridgeway
Hill

4

Bottom
Coppice

DANGER AREA

Steeple

Horse
Coppice

Whiteway
Farm

Ash
Coppice

Manor
Farm

The Manor
House

Lutton

+

81

Blackmanston
Farm

Corfe River

Thornhill's
Coppice

Steeple Leaze
Farm

Harp
Stone

3

Steeple
Leaze Wood

Pole Coppice

Beach
Coppice

Hyde
Wood

BH20

Kimmeridge
Farm

P

+

80

Kimmeridge
Coppice

PO

Kimmeridge

Smedmore
Hill

Higher
Stonehips

2

DANGER AREA

Lower
Stonehips

Metherhills

Newmead
Plantation

Oil Well

Gaulter
Gap

P

79

Kimmeridge
Bay

Grange
Plantation

Smedmore
House

Barn
Dairy

1

South West Coast Path

Harry's
Wood

Swalland
Farm

78

A
91
B
92
C

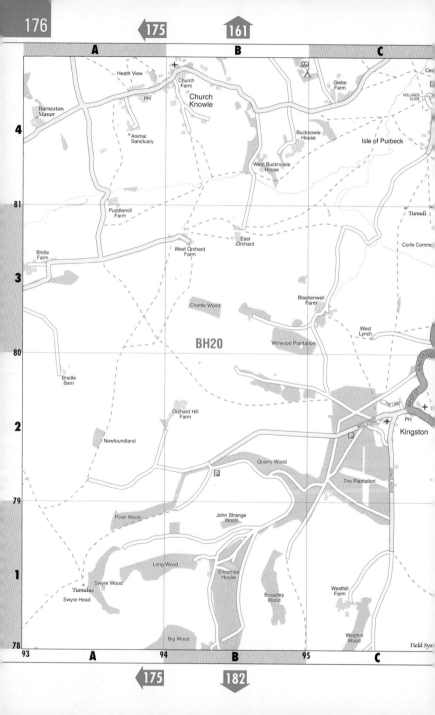

178

177 163

C1
1 VICTORIA AV
2 LEESON CL
3 GLOBE CL
4 ANVIL CL
5 ALDERBURY CL
6 KINGSWOOD CL
7 SHOTSFORD CL
8 BAY VIEW
9 CASTERBRIDGE CL
10 SHASTON CL
11 SANDBOURNE CL
12 QUARRY CL
13 PURBECK VW

A B C

Rempstone
Wood

Kingswood
Farm

Tumuli

Isle of Purbeck
Golf Club   CH

B3351

B3351

King's
Wood

Currendon
Farm

Dean
Hill

4

Purbeck Way

Ailwood
Farm

Godlingston
Hill

BH20

Oakwood
Farm

Nine
Barrow Down

Giant's
Grave Bottom

Tumuli

81

Lower
Grove

Knaveswell
Farm

Round
Down

Cow Leaze
Copse

Knitson
Farm

Strip
Lynchets

Godlingston
Wood

3

Rickett's
Copse

North Lease
Farm

Godlingston
Manor

Seekings
Farm

New
Buildings

Marsh
Copse

Cem'y

VALLEY ROAD

Greyseed
Farm

Herston
Yards Farm

30

LC

Alderbury
Copse

BH19

New
Barn

Square
Copse

Wilkswood
Farm

Quince
Hill Wood

Great Linnings
Copse

Victoria Avenue
Industrial Esta

2

Langton
West Wood

Talbot's Wood

Serrell's
Copse

Swanage Railway

A351

AUGBURTH
RD

VALLEY ROAD

Litchfield
Copse

ANCASTER
RD

Herston
Halt

Langton
Matravers

Farm
Wood

Langton
Matravers
Mus.

Swanage Cty
Middle Sch

Herston

HIGH STREET   A351

Superstore

Castle
View

Langton Matravers
Prim Sch

ST GEORGE'S

LWR
STEPPES

SERRELL'S MD

COOMBE HILL

HIGH ST

Herston
C E Sch

79

HIGH STREET

NORTH ST

B3069

EAST DROVE

Coombe
Farm

HOLMES RD

MARSH

PRIEST'S WY

CAPSTAN FIELD

GYPSHAYES

Putlake
Adventure Farm

Field Studies
Centre

HIGH ST

SYDENHAM RD

B DAY'S RD

1

Lighthouse

THE DROVE

Langton
House

Belle Vue
Farm

Blacklands

Verney
Farm

8

99   A   00   B   01   C

4

81

3

Obelisk Tumulus

Ballard Down

Purbeck Way

Tumuli

South West Coast Path

Ballard Cliff

Ballard Point

National Trust

Shepherds Farm

Ulwell Farm

National Trust

Ulwell

Whitecliff Farm

New Swanage

BH19

Swanage Farm

Duriston Farm

Swanage Town & Herston Football Club

80

1 HIGHCLIFFE RD
2 CLIFTON CL

Swanage Bay

WESSEX WY 1
ANGLEBURY AV 2
CAULDRON MS 3

Cauldron Barn Farm

Harrow House

Purbeck View Sch

Prospect Farm

VICTORIA AVENUE

A351

SWANAGE

79

Cemy

Pier Head

Swanage Sailing Club

Heritage Centre

Peveril Point

Tithe Barn Mus

Town Hall

St. Marys RC First Sch

Peveril Point

78

South West Coast Path

A1
1 STATION PL
2 NEWTON MANOR CL
3 WEST DR
4 NEWTON RI
5 HOWARD RD
6 GORDON RD
7 HANBURY RD
8 CHURCH HL
9 CHURCH CL
10 SPRINGFIELD RD
11 ELDON TR
12 FOXHILL CL
13 COWLEASE
14 MANWELL'S LA
15 DURNFORD PL
16 QUEENS MD

B1
1 COMMERCIAL RD
2 CORNWALL RD
3 MOUNT PLEASANT LA
4 EXETER RD
5 MARSHALL ROW
6 BURT'S PL
7 BELVEDERE RD
8 KNOLLSEA CL
9 SALISBURY RD

A   03   B   04   C

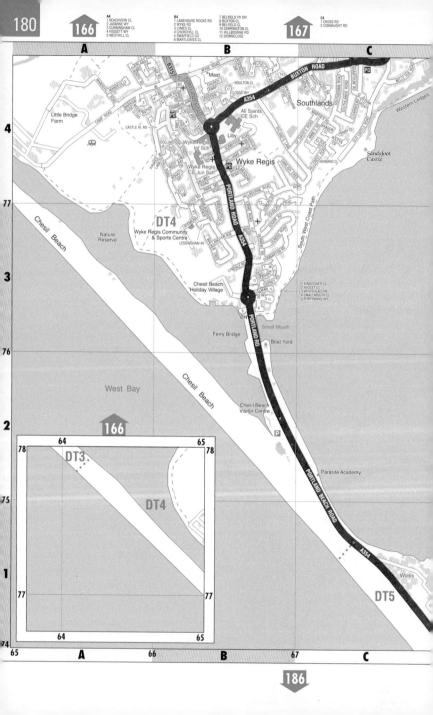

A

B

C

4

77

3

76

2

75

1

74

Breakwater

C Head

North Ship Channel

B Head

Breakwater

A Head

East Ship Channel

Portland Harbour

Breakwater

Weymouth &
Portland
Sailing Academy

Portland Oceaneering/
Breakwater Diving
Centre

ROCK ROAD

Portland Port

HM Prison Weare

CASTLETOWN

CASTLETOWN

ROTHERHAM RD

MAIN ROAD

OLD DEPOT RD

INNER BREAKWATER RD

D Head

South Ship
Channel

Portland
Castle

CASTLE ROAD

PO

Portland
Youth
Hostel

H

EAST WEAR RD

INCLINE ROAD

CANTEEN. RD

Balaclava
Bay

DT5

Castletown

Cemy

A

69

B

70

C

A1
1 LEET CL
2 BEEL CL
3 AMELIA CL

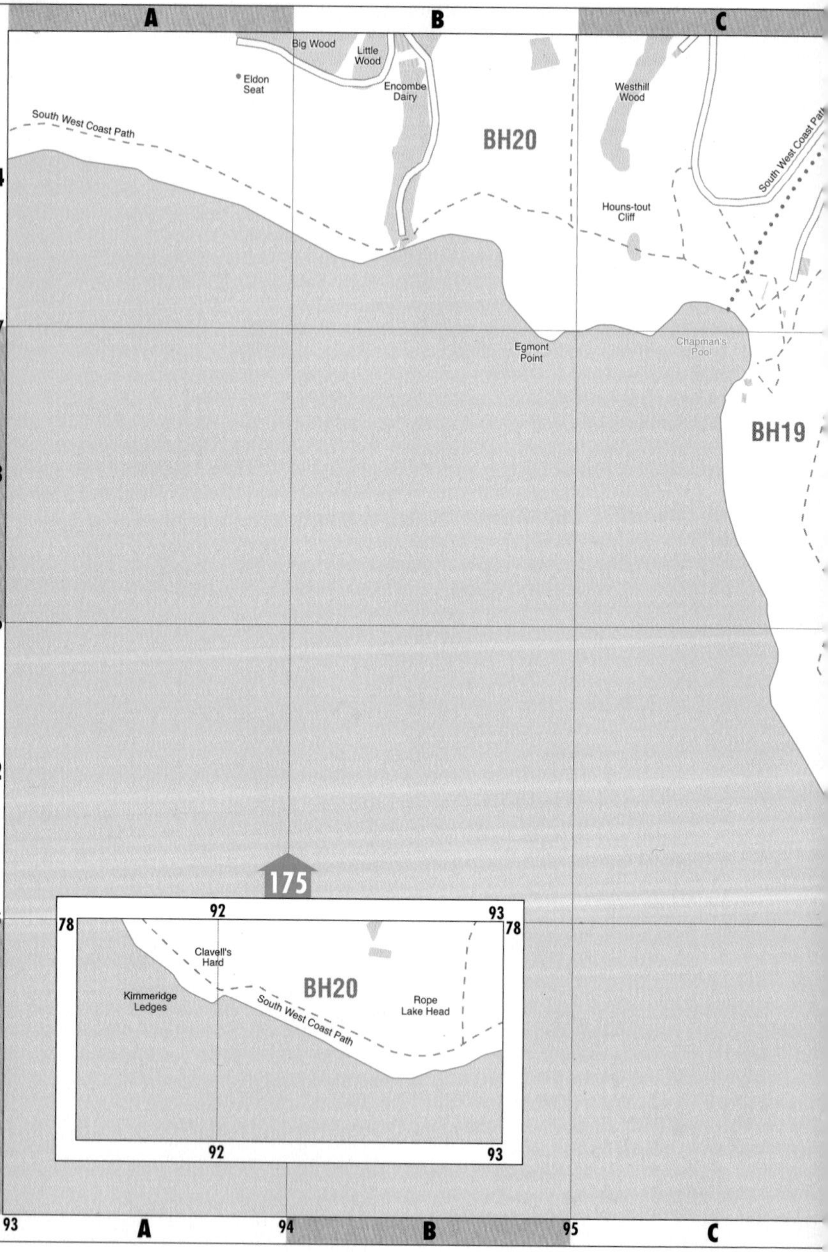

A   B   C

South West Coast Path

Big Wood
Little Wood

Eldon Seat

Encombe Dairy

Westhill Wood

BH20

South West Coast Path

Houns-tout Cliff

4

77

Egmont Point

Chapman's Pool

BH19

3

76

2

175

75

78   92   93   78

Clavell's Hard

Kimmeridge Ledges

BH20

Rope Lake Head

South West Coast Path

1

92   93

74

93   A   94   B   95   C

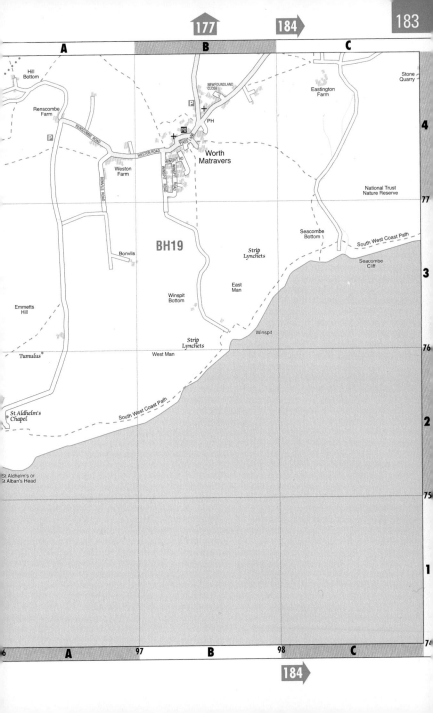

Hill
Bottom

Renscombe
Farm

RENSCOMBE ROAD

NEWFOUNDLAND
CLOSE

P

PH

PO

PIKES LANE

WESTON ROAD

WINSPIT RD

BONVILS ROAD

Weston
Farm

WINSPIT ROAD

Worth
Matravers

Eastington
Farm

Stone
Quarry

National Trust
Nature Reserve

Seacombe
Bottom

South West Coast Path

Seacombe
Cliff

BH19

Bonvils

Strip
Lynchets

East
Man

Winspit
Bottom

Winspit

Emmetts
Hill

Strip
Lynchets

West Man

South West Coast Path

Tumulus

St Aldhelm's
Chapel

St Aldhelm's or
St Alban's Head

South West Coast Path

4

77

3

76

2

75

1

74

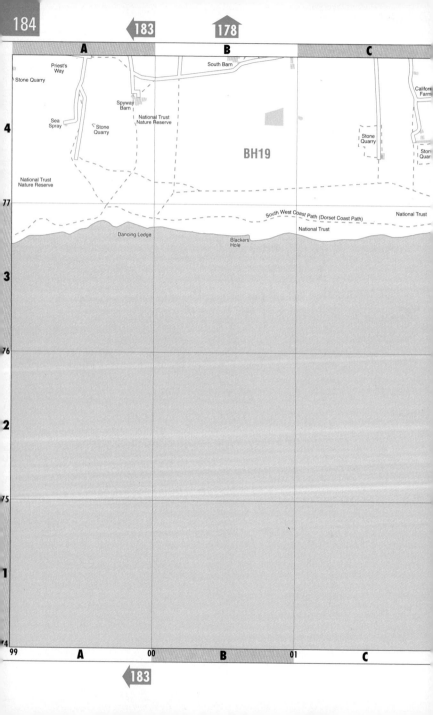

183
178

A
B
C

Priest's
Way

South Barn

Stone Quarry

California
Farm

Spyway
Barn

National Trust
Nature Reserve

Sea
Spray

Stone
Quarry

4

Stone
Quarry

BH19

Stone
Quarry

National Trust
Nature Reserve

77

South West Coast Path (Dorset Coast Path)

National Trust

Dancing Ledge

National Trust

Blackers
Hole

3

76

2

75

1

74

| A | B | C |

4

BH19

Stone
Quarry

Durlston
Bay

Durlston Country
Park

DURLSTON
RD

BOUNDARY
CL

Round Down

ST CATHARINE'S ROAD

Durlston
Head

77

Anvil Point
Lighthouse

Tilly Whim
Caves

3

Anvil
Point

76

2

75

1

| A | 03 | B | 04 | C |

74

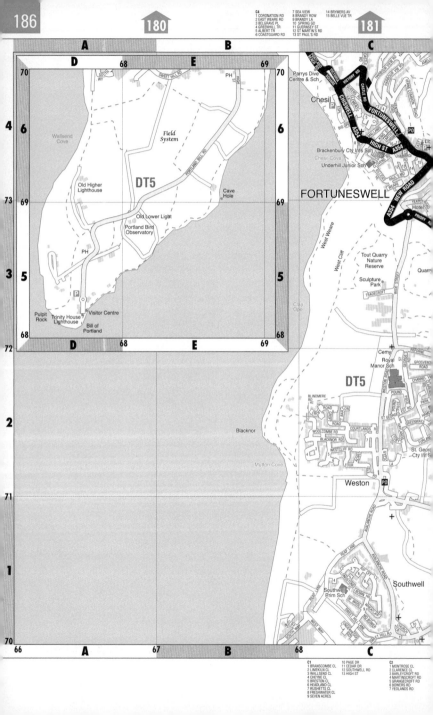

Parrys Dive
Centre & Sch

Chesil

Brackenbury Cty Infs Sch
Chesil Cove
Underhill Junior Sch

FORTUNESWELL

Hotel

West Weare

West Cliff

Tout Quarry
Nature
Reserve

Sculpture
Park

TRADECROFT

Quarry

Clay
Ope

Cemy

Royal
Manor Sch

DT5

GROSVENOR
ROAD

BLINDMERE
RD

WOOLLCOMBE RD
BLACKNOR RD
WESTCLIFF RD

COURTLANDS

GREENWAY

St. Geor
Cty Inf S

Blacknor

Multon Cove

Weston

Southwell

REAP LANE

Southwell
Prim Sch

Inset map (186 detail)

SOUTH
WY

SWELL HILL RD

PH

**Field
System**

Wallsend
Cove

Old Higher
Lighthouse

DT5

PORTLAND BILL RD

Cave
Hole

Old Lower Light

Portland Bird
Observatory

PH

Pulbit
Rock

Trinity House
Lighthouse

Visitor Centre

Bill of
Portland

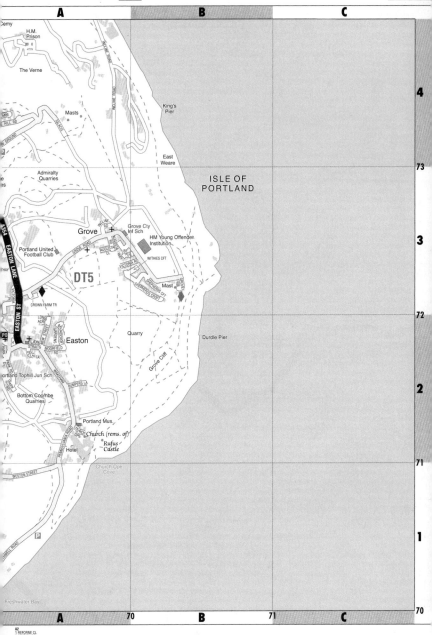

	A	B	C

4

Cemy

H.M. Prison

The Verne

King's Pier

Masts

East Weare

73

Admiralty Quarries

ISLE OF PORTLAND

3

Grove Cty Inf Sch

Grove

HM Young Offender Institution

Portland United Football Club

WITHIES CFT

DT5

Mast

CROWN FARM TR

72

LON ACRE

Quarry

Durdle Pier

Easton

Liby

STRAITS

MOORFIELD RD

Grove Cliff

Portland Tophill Jun Sch

BUMPERS LA

2

Bottom Coombe Quarries

Portland Mus.

Church (rems. of)

Hotel

Rufus Castle

Church Ope Cove

WESTON STREET

71

1

Freshwater Bay

70

A	70	B	71	C	70

A2
1 REFORNE CL
2 STATION RD
3 LADYMDCL
4 EASTON SQ

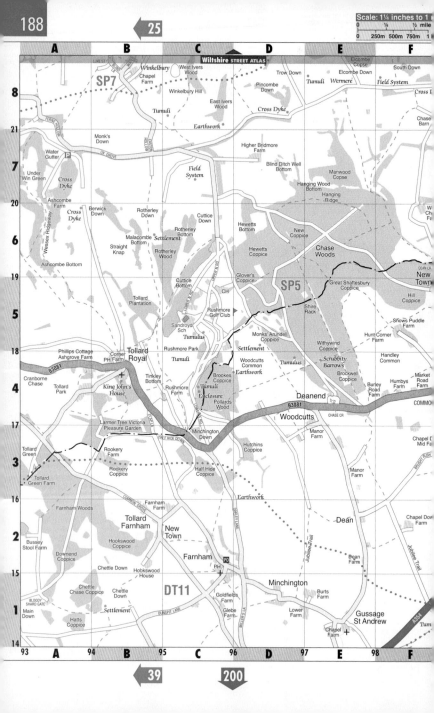

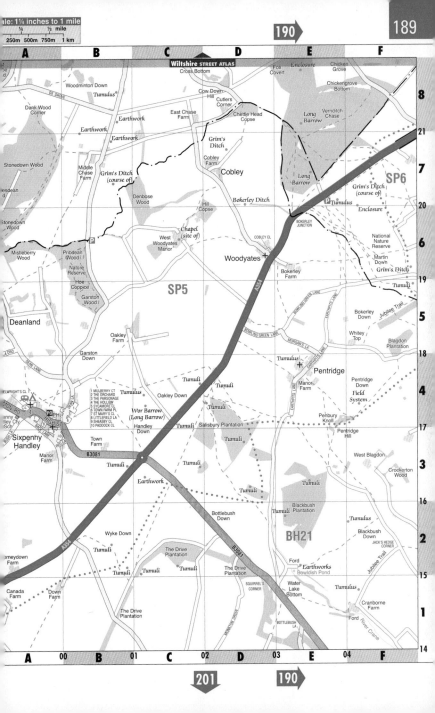

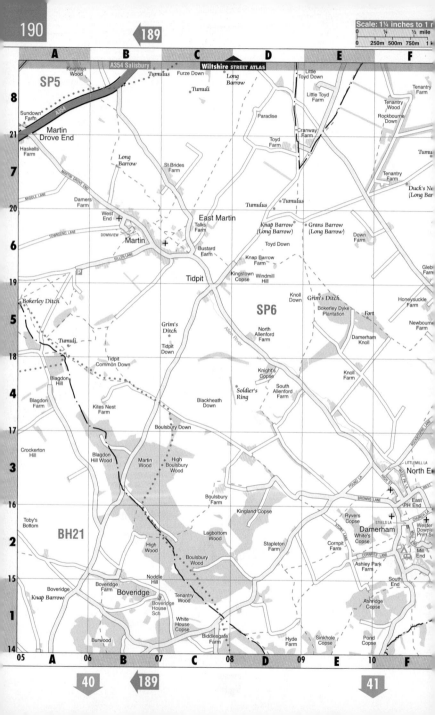

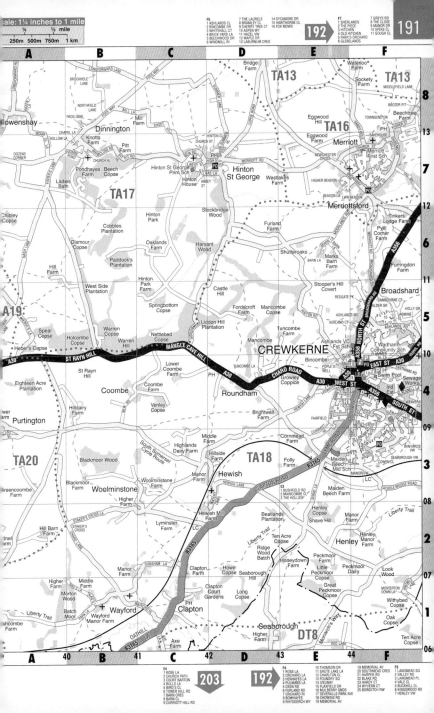

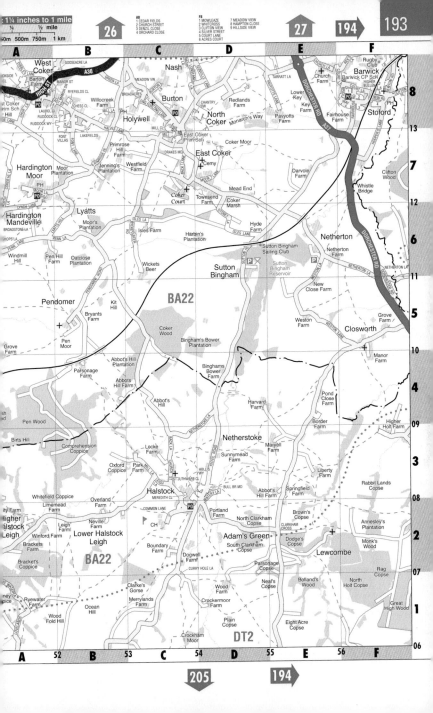

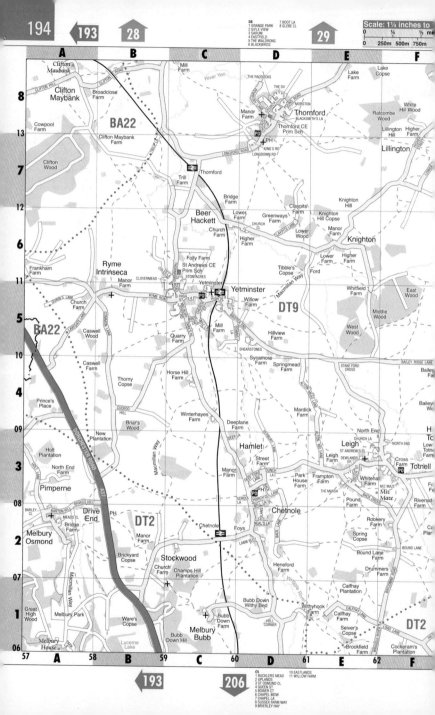

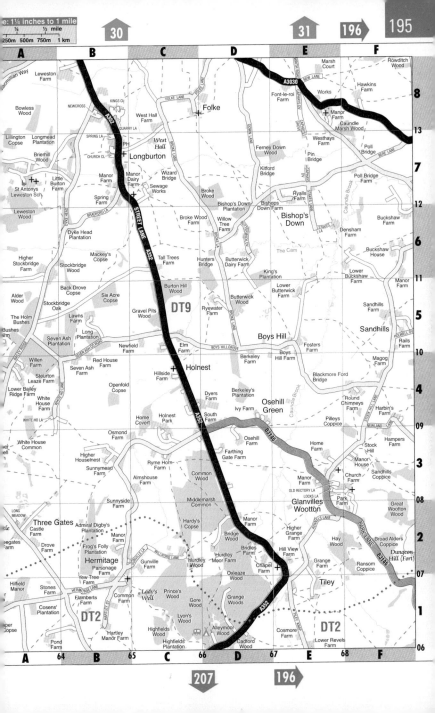

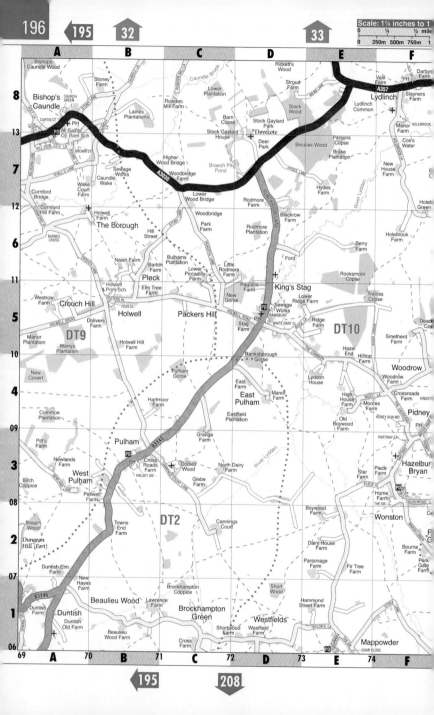

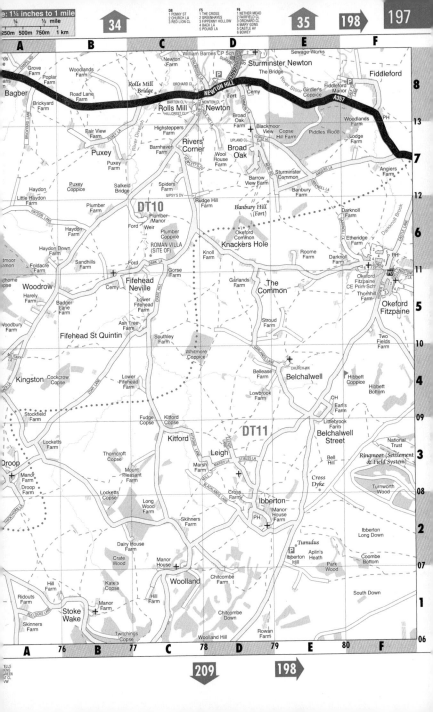

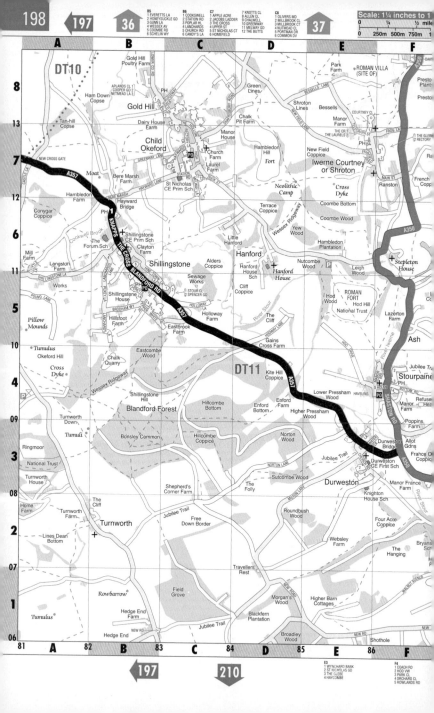

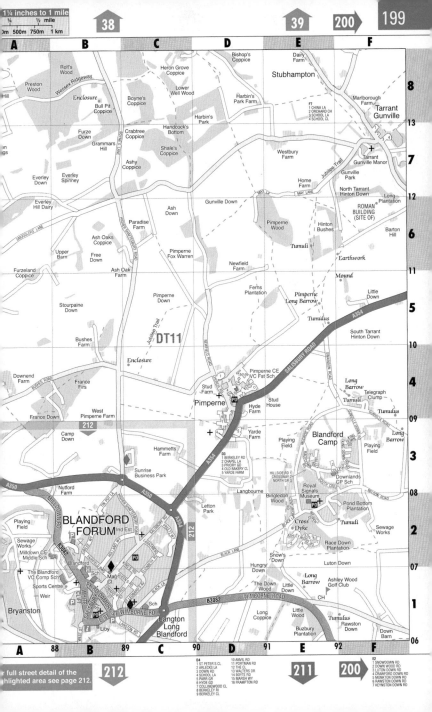

A   B   C   D   E   F

8
13
7
12
6
11
5
10
4
09
3
08
2
07
1
06

Preston Wood
Rolf's Wood
Hill
Enclosure
Wessex Ridgeway
Bull Pit Coppice
Boyne's Coppice
Heron Grove Coppice
Lower Well Wood
Harbin's Park Farm
Bishop's Coppice
Dairy Farm
Stubhampton
Marlborough Farm
Tarrant Gunville

Furze Down
Crabtree Coppice
Handcock's Bottom
Harbin's Park
Shale's Coppice
Grammars Hill
Ashy Coppice

F7
1 CHINA CH
2 ORCHARD CL
3 SCHOOL LA
4 SCHOOL CL

Westbury Farm
Tarrant Gunville Manor
Gunville Park

Everley Down   Everley Spinney
Ash Down
Gunville Down
Home Farm
North Tarrant Hinton Down
Long Plantation

MAY LANE
MAY LA

Everley Hill Dairy
Paradise Farm
Pimperne Wood
Hinton Bushes
ROMAN BUILDING (SITE OF)
Barton Hill

SMUGGLERS LANE
HIGHER SHAFTESBURY ROAD

Ash Oaks Coppice
Ash Down
Tumuli
Earthwork

Upper Barn   Free Down
Pimperne Fox Warren
Newfield Farm
Mound

Furzeland Coppice
Ash Oak Farm
Ferns Plantation
Pimperne Long Barrow
Little Down

Stourpaine Down
Pimperne Down
Tumulus
A354
South Tarrant Hinton Down

Bushes Farm
Jubilee Trail
DT11
SALISBURY ROAD
SWANLON ROAD
Long Barrow
Telegraph Clump
Tumuli

Enclosure
NEWFIELD ROAD
Pimperne CE VC Fst Sch
Stud Farm
Stud House
Tumulus
Long Barrow

Downend Farm
France Firs
West Pimperne Farm
Pimperne
PO
Hyde Farm
Blandford Camp
Playing Field

BUSHES ROAD
France Down
Camp Down
Yarde Farm
Playing Field
Downlands CP Sch

A350
Nutford Farm
Hammetts Farm
A354
D3
1 BERKELEY RD
2 CHAPEL LA
3 PRIORY GD
4 OLD BAKERY CL
5 YARDE FARM
Langbourne
HILLSIDE RD
CROSSWAY
NORTH DR
Royal Signals Museum
PO
Pond Bottom Plantation

Sunrise Business Park
212
Letton Park
Bingeldon Wood
Cross Dyke
Tumuli
Sewage Works

Playing Field
BLANDFORD FORUM Ind Est
A354
212
BLACK LANE
Snow's Down
Hungry Down
Race Down Plantation
Luton Down

Sewage Works
Milldown CE Middle Sch
B3082
Blandford VC Comp Sch
Mag Ct
PO
Sch
The Down Wood
Little Down
Long Barrow
Ashley Wood Golf Club
CH

The Blandford VC Comp Sch
Sports Centre
Weir
Sch
B3082
WIMBORNE ROAD
Luton Down

Bryanston
SALISBURY ST
WIMBORNE RD
Langton Long Blandford
Long Coppice
Little Wood
Buzbury Plantation
Tumulus
Rawston Down
Down Barn

Liby
LANGTON RD

A   B   C   D   E   F
88   89   90   91   92

r full street detail of the hlighted area see page 212.

D4
1 ST PETER'S CL
2 ARLECKS LA
3 DOWN RD
4 SCHOOL LA
5 PARK GR
6 HYDE GD
7 COLLINGWOOD LA
8 BERKELEY RI
9 BERKELEY CL
10 ANVIL RD
11 PORTMAN RD
12 THE CL
13 WALTERS DR
14 BOYTE RD
15 MARSH WY
16 FRAMPTON RD

E2
1 SNOWDOWN RD
2 DOWN WOOD RD
3 LUTON DOWN RD
4 CRAWFORD DOWN RD
5 MONKTON DOWN RD
6 RAWSTON DOWN RD
7 KEYNSTON DOWN RD

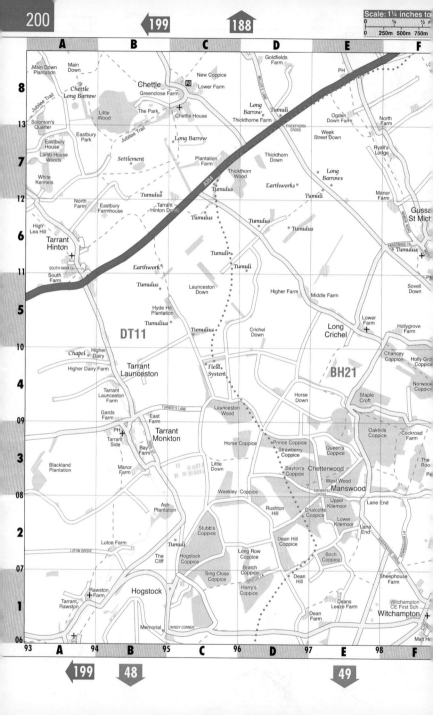

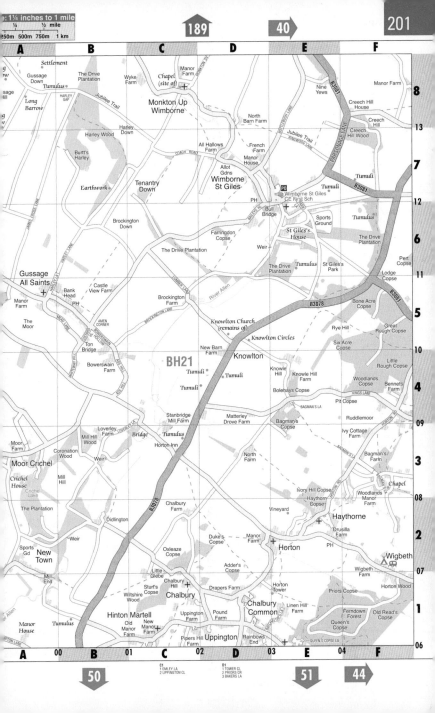

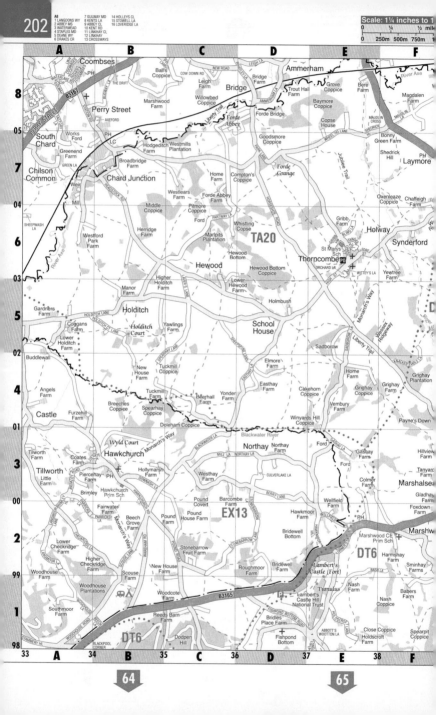

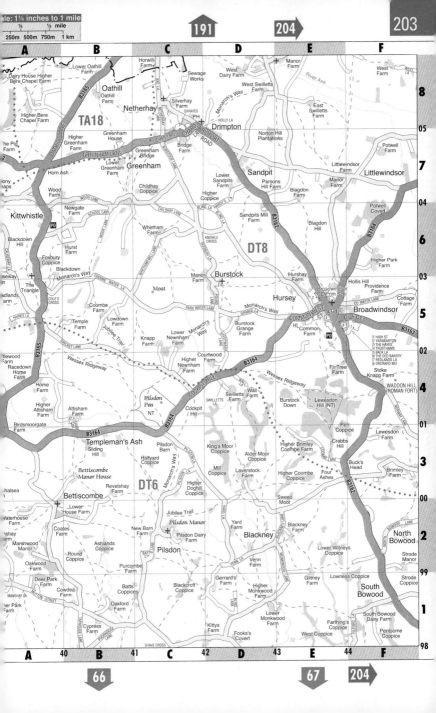

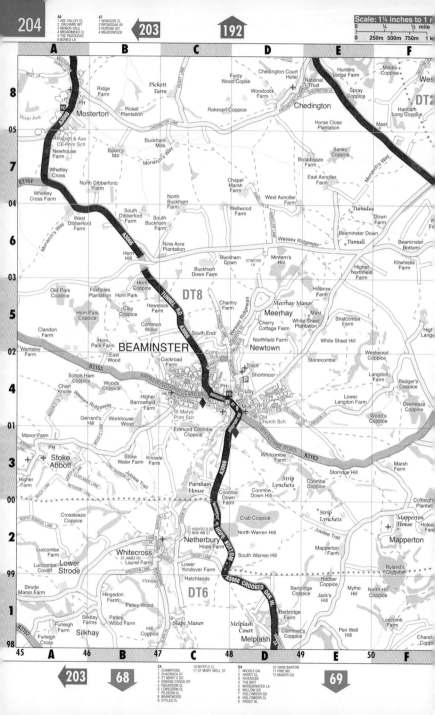

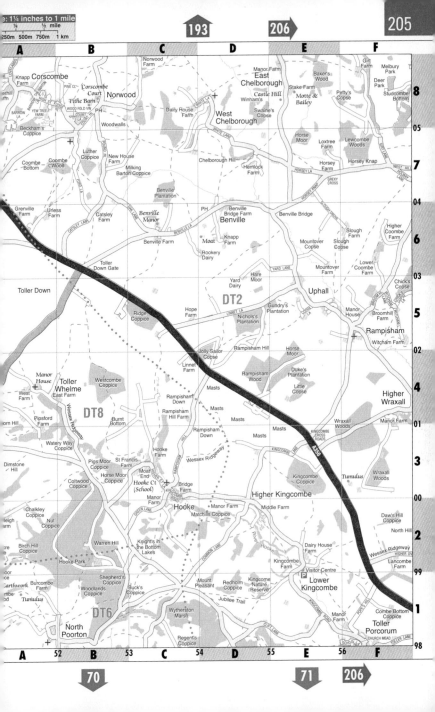

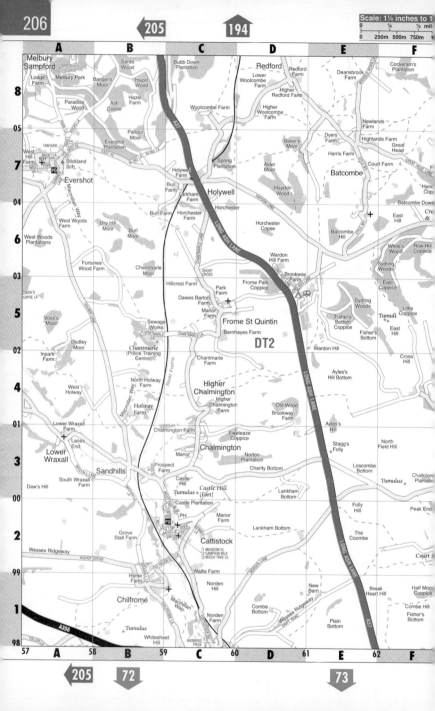

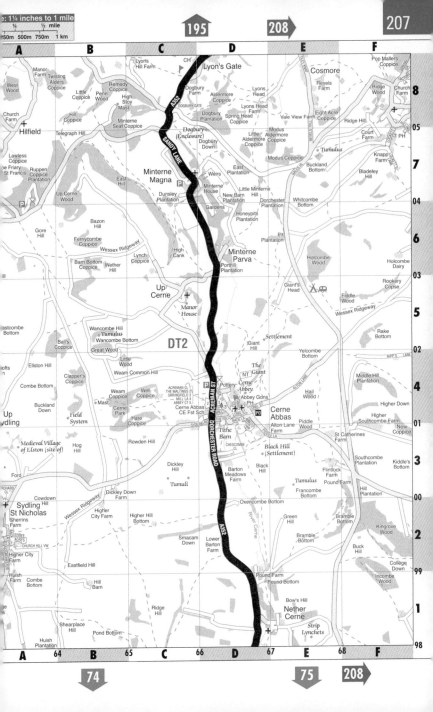

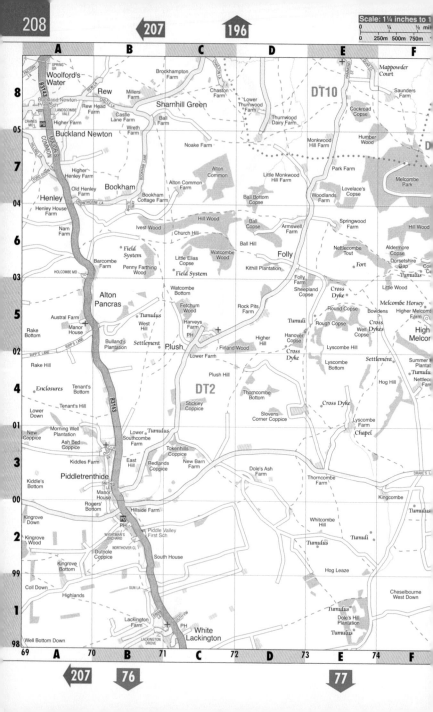

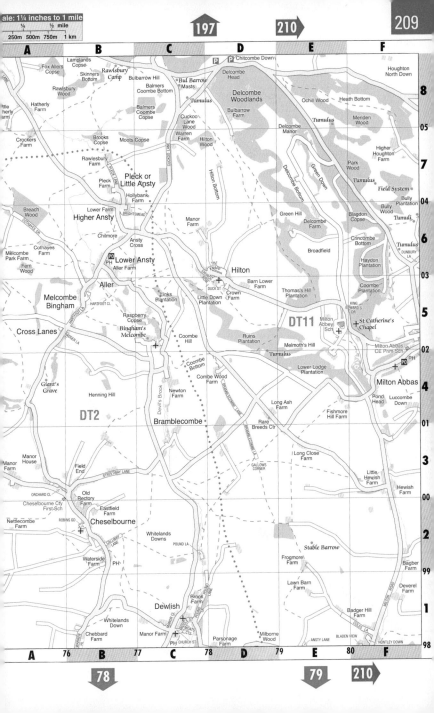

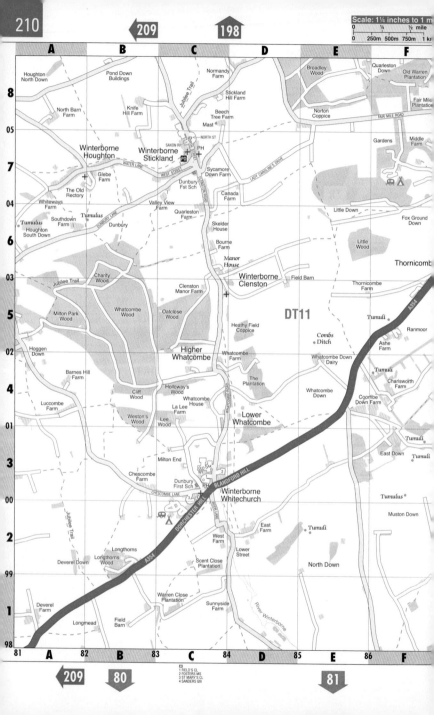

Scale: 1¼ inches to 1 m

A B C D E F

8

Houghton North Down
Pond Down Buildings
Normandy Farm
Broadley Wood
Quarleston Down
Old Warren Plantation

North Barn Farm
Knife Hill Farm
Stickland Hill Farm
Beech Tree Farm
Norton Coppice
Fair Mile Plantation

05

Mast
NORTH ST
FAIR MILE ROAD

Winterborne Houghton
SAXON RD
Winterborne Stickland
PH
PO
Gardens
Middle Farm

7

WATER LANE
WEST STREET
Sycamore Down Farm
LADY CAROLINE'S DRIVE

Glebe Farm
Dunbury Fst Sch

The Old Rectory
Valley View Farm
Canada Farm

04

Whiteways Farm
DUNBURY LANE
Quarleston Farm
Little Down
Fox Ground Down

Tumulus
Southdown Farm
Tumulus
Dunbury
Skelder House

Houghton South Down

6

Bourne Farm
Little Wood

Manor House
Thornicomb

03

Charity Wood
Winterborne Clenston
Field Barn
Thornicombe Farm

Jubilee Trail
Clenston Manor Farm

5

Milton Park Wood
Whatcombe Wood
Oatclose Wood
DT11
Tumuli
Ranmoor

A354

02

Hoggen Down
Heathy Field Coppice
Combs Ditch
Ashe Farm

Higher Whatcombe
Whatcombe Farm
Whatcombe Down Dairy
Tumuli
Charisworth Farm

4

Barnes Hill Farm
The Plantation
Whatcombe Down
Coombe Down Farm

Cliff Wood
Holloway's Wood

Luccombe Farm
Whatcombe House
La Lee Farm
Tumuli

01

Weston's Wood
Lee Wood
Lower Whatcombe
East Down
Tumuli

3

Milton End
OLD O4
WHATCOMBE ROAD
BLANDFORD HILL

Chescombe Farm
Dunbury First Sch
RH
Winterborne Whitechurch
Tumulus

00

CHESCOMBE LANE
Muston Down

Jubilee Trail
West Farm
East Farm

2

DORCHESTER HILL
Tumuli

Longthorns
Lower Street
North Down

Deverel Down
Longthorns Wood
A354
Scent Close Plantation

99

Warren Close Plantation

1

Deverel Farm
Sunnyside Farm
River Winterborne

Longmead
Field Barn

98

C3
1 FIELD'S CL
2 FOSTERS MS
3 ST MARY'S CL
4 SANDERS GN

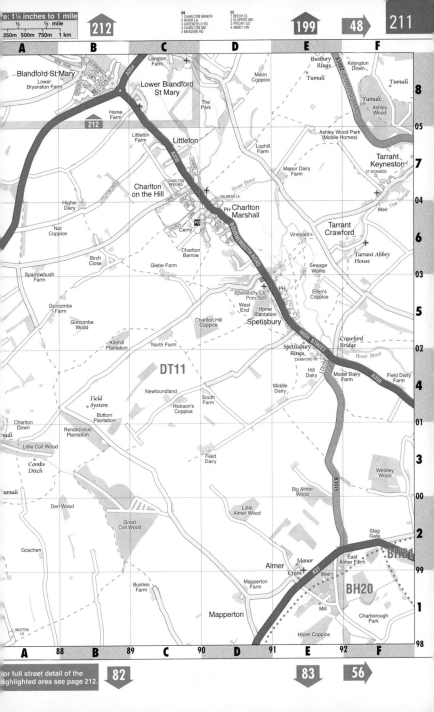

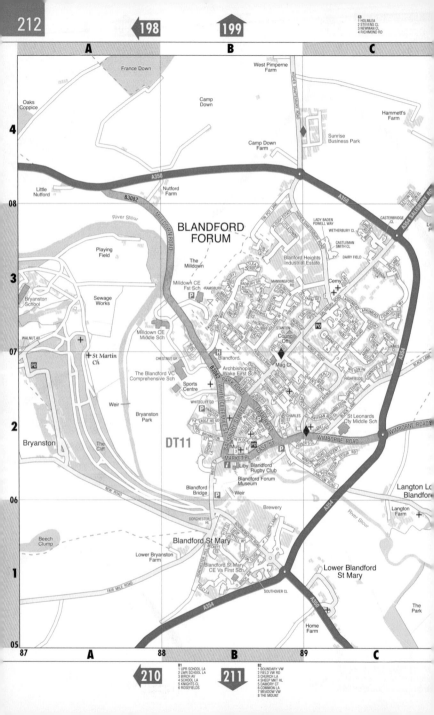

A3
1 CHANCERY CL
2 HIGHBURY CL
3 KENSINGTON RD
4 RICHMOND RD
5 JUBILEE CT
6 HAWTHORN CL
7 CHARLES ST
8 MEADOW RD
9 GEORGE ST (STH)
10 MEADOW RD (STH)
11 WINDSOR ST
12 WINDSOR RD
13 STATION TERR
14 SANDOWN PL
15 SOUTH ST

B3
1 THE VENTRY
2 VENTRY CLOSE
3 SWAYNES CL
4 BELLE VUE RD
5 CHAPEL PL
6 SUMMERLOCK APP
7 GRIFFINS CT
8 MALTHOUSE LA
9 PRIORY SQ
10 CHEESE MARKET
11 MINSTER ST
12 ROLLESTONE ST
13 ST EDMUNDS CHURCH ST
14 BROWN ST

A1
1 GRASMERE CL
2 HARVARD CL
3 CHRISTOPHER CL

A2
1 STEPHENS CL
2 TURNER CL
3 MUNKS CL

B1
1 BRITFORD LA WEST
2 SWALLOWMEAD
3 MARTINS CL
4 MAPLECROFT
5 HAWKSRIDGE
6 SWIFTDOWN
7 LYNNETSDENE
8 RAVENSCROFT
9 WRENSCROFT
10 OWLSWOOD
11 LONGHILL DR

B2
1 ROSEMARY LA
2 CULVER ST
3 HILL VIEW RD
4 BARNARD ST
5 PAYNE'S HILL
6 ST MARTIN'S CHURCH ST
7 GREEN'S CT
8 FRIAR'S ORCHARD
9 WHITEFRIARS RD

C2
1 METHUEN DR
2 ST MARGARET'S CL
3 COURTWOOD CL
4 BYWAYS CL
5 THE BEECHES
6 MILFORD HOLLOW
7 POLDEN RD
8 BOURNE CL
9 ST JOHN'S CL

Index

Church Rd **6** Beckenham BR2..........**53** C6

Place name	**Location number**	**Locality, town or village**	**Postcode district**	**Page and grid square**
May be abbreviated on the map	Present when a number indicates the place's position in a crowded area of mapping	Shown when more than one place has the same name	District for the indexed place	Page number and grid reference for the standard mapping

Public and commercial buildings are highlighted in magenta. Places of interest are highlighted in blue with a star★

Abbreviations used in the index

Acad	Academy	Comm	Common	Gd	Ground	L	Leisure	Prom	Promenade
App	Approach	Cott	Cottage	Gdn	Garden	La	Lane	Rd	Road
Arc	Arcade	Cres	Crescent	Gn	Green	Liby	Library	Recn	Recreation
Ave	Avenue	Cswy	Causeway	Gr	Grove	Mdw	Meadow	Ret	Retail
Bglw	Bungalow	Ct	Court	H	Hall	Meml	Memorial	Sh	Shopping
Bldg	Building	Ctr	Centre	Ho	House	Mkt	Market	Sq	Square
Bsns, Bus	Business	Ctry	Country	Hospl	Hospital	Mus	Museum	St	Street
Bvd	Boulevard	Cty	County	HQ	Headquarters	Orch	Orchard	Sta	Station
Cath	Cathedral	Dr	Drive	Hts	Heights	Pal	Palace	Terr	Terrace
Cir	Circus	Dro	Drove	Ind	Industrial	Par	Parade	TH	Town Hall
Cl	Close	Ed	Education	Inst	Institute	Pas	Passage	Univ	University
Cnr	Corner	Emb	Embankment	Int	International	Pk	Park	Wk, Wlk	Walk
Coll	College	Est	Estate	Intc	Interchange	Pl	Place	Wr	Water
Com	Community	Ex	Exhibition	Junc	Junction	Prec	Precinct	Yd	Yard

Index of localities, towns and villages

A

Abbotsbury 149 A4
Acton 177 C1
Adam's Green 193 D2
Adber 14 C3
Affpuddle 111 C4
Alcester 12 B1
Alderholt 42 A3
Alderney 88 B1
Aller 209 B5
Allington 100 A4
Allowenshay 191 A8
Almer 211 E2
Alton Pancras 208 B5
Alvington 26 B2
Alweston 31 A1
Ameysford 52 C1
Ammerham 202 D8
Anderson 82 A4
Arne 144 B3
Ash 68 B3
Ash 198 F5
Ashington 59 A1
Ashley 54 C3
Ashley 95 B2
Ashley Heath 53 C3
Ashmore 39 B4
Askerswell 102 B3
Athelhampton 78 C1
Atrim 68 A2
Avon 63 C1

B

Bagber 197 A8
Barrow Hill 84 C2
Barrow Street 3 C1
Barton on Sea 126 A4
Barwick 193 F8
Bashley 95 A4

Batcombe 206 E7
Bay 6 A1
Beaminster 204 B5
Bear Cross 88 C3
Bearwood 88 C3
Beaulieu Wood 196 B1
Beckley 94 B3
Bedchester 37 B4
Beer Hackett 194 C6
Belchalwell 197 E4
Belchalwell Street ...197 E3
Benville 205 D6
Bere Regis 81 A1
Bettiscombe 203 B3
Bickton 43 A3
Bincombe 152 C3
Binnegar 141 A2
Bishop's Caundle 196 A8
Bishop's Down 195 E6
Bishopdown 213 C4
Bisterne 63 C3
Bittles Green 12 B4
Blackney 203 D2
Blacknoll 156 C4
Blackwater 91 B2
Blandford Camp 199 E3
Blandford Forum 212 B3
Blandford St Mary 212 B1
Blandford 47 B1
Bleak Hill 42 C2
Bloxworth 82 A1
Bluntshay 66 C4
Bookham 208 B7
Boscombe 122 C2
Bothenhampton 100 C2
Bournemouth 123 A2
Bourton 1 C1
Boveridge 209 B1
Bovington Camp 139 B3
Bowden 9 C2
Bowridge Hill 6 A2
Boys Hill 195 E5
Bradford Abbas 28 B1

Bradford Peverell 106 C3
Bradpole 69 A1
Bramblecombe 209 C4
Branksome 120 C3
Branksome Park 120 C1
Bransgore 93 A2
Braytown 139 C1
Briantspuddle 112 A4
Bridge 202 D8
Bridport 100 A3
Broad Oak 197 D7
Broadmayne 136 A1
Broadoak 67 B3
Broadshard 191 F5
Broadstone 87 A1
Broadway 152 A2
Broadwindsor 203 F5
Brockhampton Green ...196 C1
Broom Hill 51 B1
Bryanston 212 B2
Brympton D'Evercy 26 A2
Buckhorn Weston 9 A3
Buckland Newton 208 A7
Buckland Ripers 151 B1
Bugley 10 A3
Burleston 78 C1
Burstock 203 D6
Burton 3 B3
Burton 92 B1
Burton 107 C2
Burton 193 C8
Burton Bradstock 101 A1
Bushey 162 B2

C

Camel Green 42 B3
Camesworth 68 C4
Canford Cliffs 147 C4
Canford Heath 87 C1
Canford Magna 60 A1
Cann 24 A4

Cann Common 24 B4
Carey 142 A3
Castle 202 A4
Castle Park 134 B4
Castletown 181 B1
Catherston Leweston ..65 B1
Cattistock 206 C2
Cerne Abbas 207 E4
Chalbury 201 C1
Chalbury Common 201 D1
Chaldon Herring 156 B2
Chalmington 206 C3
Chard Junction 202 B7
Charing Cross 42 A3
Charlestown 166 C1
Charlton Down 75 B2
Charlton Marshall 211 D6
Charlton on the Hill ..211 C7
Charminster 107 C3
Charminster 90 B1
Charmouth 97 A4
Charnage 3 C2
Chedington 204 E8
Cheselbourne 209 B2
Chesil 186 C4
Chetnole 194 D2
Chettle 200 B8
Chickerell 166 B3
Chideock 99 A3
Chilbridge 58 C4
Chilcombe 102 B2
Child Okeford 198 B7
Chilfrome 206 B1
Chilson Common 202 A7
Chilton Cantelo 14 A4
Christchurch 124 A3
Church Knowle 176 B4
Clapgate 50 C1
Clapton 191 C1
Clifton Maybank 194 A8
Closworth 193 F5
Cobb 96 A2
Cobley 189 D7

Cocknowle 161 A1
Cold Harbour 142 A4
Coldharbour 166 C4
Colehill 60 A4
Colesbook 5 C2
Combe Almer 84 B4
Compton Abbas 24 A1
Compton Valence 104 C4
Coneygar 100 B4
Coombe 13 C1
Coombe 65 A4
Coombe 191 B4
Coombe 158 A3
Coombe Keynes 158 A3
Coombess 202 B8
Corfe Castle 162 A1
Corfe Mullen 86 A1
Corscombe 205 A8
Coryates 150 C4
Cosmore 207 E8
Court Orchard 100 B4
Crab Orchard 45 A1
Cranborne 40 A4
Creech 160 B2
Crendell 41 A4
Crewkerne 191 E5
Cripplestyle 41 A3
Crooked Withies 52 A4
Cross Lanes 209 A5
Crossways 137 C3
Crouch Hill 196 A5
Crow 55 C2
Cruxton 73 A3
Cucklington 4 C1

D

Daggons 41 C3
Damerham 209 F2
Dean 188 C4
Deanend 188 E4
Deanland 189 A5
Dewlands Common 44 C3

...wlish ...209 C1
...nington ...191 B8
...chester ...107 B1
...tery ...68 A2
...ynton ...127 C4
...mpton ...203 D8
...ve End Farm ...194 A2
...op ...197 A3
...lsbury ...61 B1
...ntish ...196 A1
...weston ...198 E3

...st Bloxworth ...82 C1
...st Brook ...59 B3
...st Burton ...139 C1
...st Chaldon ...156 B2
...st Cheborough ...205 D8
...st Chinnock ...192 E8
...st Coker ...193 D7
...st Compton ...22 C1
...st Creech ...160 C1
...st End ...58 C1
...st Fleet ...166 A3
...st Holme ...159 C4
...st Holton ...117 A2
...st Howe ...89 B2
...t Knighton ...157 A4
...st Lulworth ...173 B4
...st Martin ...209 C6
...st Melbury ...24 B3
...st Morden ...83 B2
...st Orchard ...36 C4
...st Parley ...90 A4
...st Pulham ...196 D4
...st Stoke ...140 C1
...st Stour ...10 C2
...st Stour Common ...11 A2
...ston ...187 A2
...olake ...45 C2
...cliffe ...10 B4
...mondsham ...80 B2
...ampton ...47 A3
...'s Hill ...7 A1
...vell ...152 A3
...bury ...89 C3
...more Green ...12 B2
...sbury Park ...89 B1
...ershot ...206 A7

...rmile ...91 C1
...rnham ...188 C2
...rrington ...37 A2
...rndown ...61 B3
...ddleford ...197 F8
...ehead Magdalen ...20 C4
...ehead Neville ...197 C5
...ehead St Quintin ...197 B5
...ford ...67 C4
...eet ...166 A3
...ike ...195 D8
...ply ...208 D6
...ntmell Magna ...37 C4
...ntmell Parva ...36 B1
...rdingbridge ...43 A4
...rston ...75 A2
...rtuneswell ...186 C4
...xholes ...120 A3
...ampton ...73 C2
...ars Cliff ...125 B4
...ampton ...43 C4
...ome St Quintin ...206 D5
...rzebrook ...161 A2
...rzehill ...50 C1

...nnetts ...21 B2
...sper ...5 B4
...unt's Common ...51 A4
...ddy Green ...139 C1
...lingham ...5 C1
...anvilles Wootton ...195 E2
...athill ...31 B4
...d's Blessing Green ...51 B2
...dmanstone ...75 A4
...dwinscroft ...93 A3
...ld Hill ...198 B8
...re ...14 C2
...tham ...41 A2
...ange ...50 C1
...ange Estate ...62 C4
...eenham ...203 C7
...imstone ...74 A1
...ove ...187 A3
...assage All Saints ...201 A5
...assage St Andrew ...188 E1

Gussage St Michael ...200 F6
Guy's Marsh ...23 A3

H

Hains ...20 C2
Hale ...4 A2
Halstock ...193 C3
Ham Common ...6 A1
Hamlet ...194 D3
Hammoon ...36 A1
Hampreston ...60 C1
Hamworthy ...118 B2
Hanford ...198 D6
Harbridge ...43 A1
Harbridge Green ...43 A1
Harcombe Bottom ...64 A2
Hardington Mandeville ...193 A6
Hardington Moor ...193 A7
Harman's Cross ...177 C3
Harnham ...213 A1
Hartgrove ...22 C1
Haselbury Plucknett ...192 C6
Hawkchurch ...202 B3
Haydon ...31 B2
Haythorne ...201 F2
Hazelbury Bryan ...196 F3
Hemsworth ...49 A4
Henbury ...56 C1
Henley ...191 E2
Henley ...208 A7
Henstridge ...19 A2
Henstridge Ash ...19 A3
Henstridge Bowden ...18 A3
Henstridge Marsh ...19 C3
Hermitage ...195 B2
Herston ...178 C2
Hewood ...193 D3
Hewood ...202 C6
Highcliffe ...125 C4
Higher Ansty ...209 B6
Higher Bockhampton ...109 A3
Higher Chalmington ...204 C6
Higher Eype ...99 C3
Higher Halstock Leigh ...193 B4
Higher Kingcombe ...205 E3
Higher Melcombe ...208 F5
Higher Nyland ...8 A2
Higher Row ...51 C3
Higher Sandford ...15 C3
Higher Totnell ...194 F4
Higher Whatcombe ...210 C5
Higher Woodsford ...137 B4
Higher Wraxall ...205 F4
Highlands ...100 A2
Hightown ...55 C3
Highwood ...158 C4
Hilfield ...207 A7
Hillbourne ...87 A1
Hillbutts ...58 C3
Hilton ...209 D6
Hincknowle ...69 A4
Hinton ...14 A3
Hinton ...94 A2
Hinton Martell ...201 B1
Hinton Parva ...50 A3
Hinton St George ...191 D7
Hinton St Mary ...35 A2
Hogstock ...200 B1
Holdenhurst ...91 A2
Holditch ...202 B5
Hollands ...27 B4
Hollow Oak ...113 A4
Holmebridge ...141 C1
Holnest ...195 C4
Holt ...51 A2
Holt Heath ...52 B3
Holt Wood ...51 B4
Holton Heath ...116 A3
Holway ...16 A3
Holway ...202 E6
Holwell ...3 A3
Holwell ...196 B5
Holywell ...193 C8
Holywell ...206 C7
Hooke ...205 C2
Hordle ...95 C2
Horton ...201 E2
Horton Common ...44 B1
Horton Heath ...44 B1
Hound Hill ...58 C4
Houndstone ...26 B3
Hummer ...14 B2
Hungerford ...43 C4
Huntingford ...5 C4
Hurn ...91 A3
Hursey ...203 E5
Hurst ...111 B1
Hyde ...43 C3
Hyde ...100 C3

I

Ibberton ...197 D2
Ibsley ...47 B4
Iford ...123 B4
Ivy Cross ...13 A2
Iwerne Courtney ...198 E7
Iwerne Minster ...37 C1

K

Kimmeridge ...175 B2
King's Stag ...196 D5
Kingsbury Regis ...17 B2
Kingsland ...68 A4
Kingston ...55 A1
Kingston ...63 C4
Kingston ...176 C2
Kingston ...197 A4
Kingston Maurward ...108 C1
Kingston Russell ...104 B2
Kington Magna ...9 B2
Kinson ...89 A3
Kit Hill ...23 A2
Kitford ...197 C3
Kittwhistle ...203 A6
Knackers Hole ...197 D6
Knapp Hill ...7 B1
Knighton ...194 E6
Knob's Crook ...44 A2
Knowlton ...201 D4

L

Lake ...117 C1
Lambrook ...68 C3
Lambs' Green ...58 C1
Lane End ...113 B3
Lanehouse ...166 C1
Langham ...9 C4
Langton Herring ...150 B1
Langton Long Blandford ...212 C2
Langton Matravers ...178 A2
Laymore ...202 F7
Leigh ...194 E3
Leigh ...197 D3
Leigh ...59 C2
Leigh Park ...59 C2
Lewcombe ...193 E2
Lillington ...194 F7
Lilliput ...147 B4
Limpers Hill ...3 B2
Little Canford ...60 B2
Little Pamphill ...58 C3
Little Woolgarston ...177 B4
Littlebredy ...131 B4
Littledown ...123 A4
Littlemoor ...152 C2
Littleton ...211 C7
Littlewindsor ...203 F7
Litton Cheney ...103 B1
Loders ...69 B1
Lodmoor ...167 C4
Long Bredy ...103 C1
Long Crichel ...200 E3
Long Cross ...2 B3
Longburton ...195 C7
Longfleet ...119 B2
Longham ...61 A1
Loscombe ...69 C4
Lower Ansty ...209 B6
Lower Blandford St Mary ...212 C1
Lower Bockhampton ...109 A3
Lower Daggons ...41 B4
Lower Eype ...99 C2
Lower Halstock Leigh ...193 B2
Lower Hamworthy ...119 A1
Lower Holwell ...40 C3
Lower Kingcombe ...205 E1
Lower Mannington ...52 B4
Lower Nyland ...9 C4
Lower Odcombe ...26 A2
Lower Parkstone ...120 A2
Lower Row ...51 C4
Lower Stroke ...204 D5
Lower Turmer ...46 C4
Lower Whatcombe ...210 D4
Lower Wraxall ...206 A3
Lower Zeals ...2 B3
Lufton ...26 A3
Lulworth Camp ...173 A4
Lyatts ...193 B6
Lydlinch ...196 F8
Lyme Regis ...96 B3
Lyon's Gate ...207 D8
Lytchett Matravers ...84 B2
Lytchett Minster ...116 C4

M

Madjeston ...10 C4
Maiden Newton ...73 A4
Mangerton ...69 A2
Mannington ...52 B4
Manston ...36 A2
Manswood ...200 E3
Mapperton ...204 F2
Mapperton ...211 D1
Mappowder ...196 F1
Margaret Marsh ...22 B1
Marnhull ...20 C1
Marshalsea ...202 F3
Marshwood ...202 F2
Martin ...209 B6
Martin Drove End ...209 A8
Martinstown or Winterborne
  St Martin ...133 B3
Meerhay ...204 D5
Melbury Abbas ...24 B3
Melbury Bubb ...194 C1
Melbury Osmond ...194 A2
Melbury Sampford ...206 A8
Melcombe Bingham ...209 A5
Melcombe Regis ...167 B3
Melplash ...204 D1
Mere ...3 A3
Merley ...59 B1
Merriott ...70 A2
Merriott ...191 C7
Merriottsford ...191 E7
Merritown ...90 C4
Middle Bockhampton ...92 C3
Middle Chinnock ...192 C8
Milborne Port ...17 B1
Milborne St Andrew ...79 C4
Milborne Wick ...17 A3
Miles Cross ...99 C4
Milford ...213 C3
Milton Abbas ...209 F4
Milton on Stour ...5 B3
Minchington ...188 D1
Minterne Magna ...207 C2
Minterne Parva ...207 D6
Misterton ...192 A2
Mockbeggar ...47 C4
Monkton Up Wimborne ...201 C8
Monkton Wyld ...64 A3
Moor Crichel ...201 A3
Moorbath ...67 B2
Moordown ...90 A1
Moorside ...21 B2
Moortown ...55 B3
Morcombelake ...98 B4
Moreton ...138 C4
Mosterton ...204 A8
Motcombe ...12 A3
Mount Pleasant ...86 C4
Mounters ...20 C1
Muckleford ...106 A4
Mudeford ...125 A3
Mudford ...14 A2
Muscliffe ...90 B2

N

Nash ...193 D8
Neacroft ...93 A3
Nether Cerne ...207 E1
Nether Compton ...204 C2
Nethercott ...203 C8
Netherstoke ...193 D3
Netherton ...193 E6
Nettlecombe ...70 A2
New Milton ...94 C1
New Swanage ...179 A3
New Town ...9 B1
New Town ...17 A1
New Town ...27 C3
New Town ...188 C2
New Town ...188 F6
New Town ...201 A2
New Town ...120 A4
Newport ...82 B1
Newton ...197 D8
Newton ...204 D5
Newton Peveril ...56 A2
Newtown ...204 D5
Norden ...161 B2
North Bockhampton ...92 C3
North Bowood ...203 F2
North Chideock ...67 A4
North Coker ...193 D8
North End ...7 A2
North Gorley ...43 B2
North Kingston ...90 A1
North Perrott ...192 C4
North Poorton ...205 B1
North Poulner ...47 C1
North Wootton ...30 C1

Northay ...202 D3
Northbourne ...89 C2
Northbrook ...78 A1
Northport ...142 C3
Norwood ...205 B8
Nottington ...152 A1
Notton ...73 A2

O

Oakdale ...119 B3
Oakley ...59 C1
Oathill ...203 B8
Oborne ...16 C1
Okeford Fitzpaine ...197 F5
Old Milton ...94 C1
Organford ...116 A3
Osehill Green ...195 E4
Osmington ...169 A4
Osmington Mills ...169 B4
Over Compton ...28 C4
Overcombe ...168 A4
Owermoigne ...155 B4
Oxbridge ...68 C4

P

Packers Hill ...196 C5
Pallington ...111 B2
Pamphill ...58 A3
Park Gate ...196 F2
Parkstone ...120 A2
Parkway ...14 C4
Parley Green ...90 B4
Peacemarsh ...5 C2
Pear Ash ...1 B2
Pen Mill ...28 A3
Pendomer ...193 B5
Penn ...64 B2
Penselwood ...1 A2
Pentridge ...189 E4
Perry Street ...202 B8
Piddlehinton ...76 C4
Piddletrenthide ...208 A3
Pidney ...196 F4
Pig Oak ...51 A2
Pilford ...60 A4
Pillwell ...21 A2
Pilsdon ...203 C2
Pimperne ...194 A3
Pimperne ...199 D4
Pleck ...34 C4
Pleck ...196 B6
Pleck or Little Ansty ...209 C7
Plush ...208 C5
Pokesdown ...123 A2
Poole ...119 A1
Poolestown ...33 C3
Portesham ...132 A1
Portway ...156 C4
Post Green ...118 C4
Poulner ...47 C1
Powerstock ...70 A3
Poxwell ...154 C3
Poyntington ...16 C2
Preston ...168 A4
Preston Plucknett ...26 C2
Puddle Town ...192 B5
Puddletown ...78 A1
Pulham ...196 B3
Puncknowle ...129 C3
Purewell ...124 B4
Purse Caundle ...32 A4
Purtington ...191 A4
Putton ...166 C3
Puxey ...197 B7
Pymore ...68 B1

Q

Queen Oak ...2 A2

R

Radipole ...167 A4
Rampisham ...205 F5
Red Hill ...89 C3
Redbridge ...138 A3
Redford ...206 D8
Redlands ...152 A1
Rew ...208 B8
Ridge ...143 A1
Rimpton ...15 A4
Ringwood ...47 B1
Rivers' Corner ...197 C7
Rixon ...35 B1
Rockford ...47 C2
Rodden ...150 B3
Rodgrove ...8 C3

Rodwell 167 B1
Rolls Mill 197 C8
Romford 44 C4
Rook Street 3 A4
Rossmore 120 C4
Roundham 191 D4
Rowlands 59 B3
Rushton 141 A1
Ryall 66 B1
Ryme Intrinseca 194 B6

S

St Andrew's Well 100 C4
St Ives 54 B3
St James 12 C1
St Johns 59 B2
St Leonards 54 A1
Salisbury 213 B1
Salwayash 68 A3
Sandbanks 147 B2
Sandford 142 C4
Sandford Orcas 15 C3
Sandhills 195 F5
Sandhills 206 B3
Sandpit 203 D7
School House 202 D5
Seaborough 191 D1
Seatown 99 A2
Sedgehill 7 C3
Shaftesbury 12 C2
Shaggs 158 B2
Shapwick 56 B4
Sharnhill Green 208 C8
Sherborne 30 A4
Sherford 115 B4
Shillingstone 198 C6
Shipton Gorge 101 B2
Shroton 198 E7
Silkhay 204 A1
Silton 5 A4
Sitterton 80 C2
Sixpenny Handley ..189 A3
Skilling 100 A3
Slepe 115 C4
Somerford 124 C4
Sopley 92 A3
South Bockhampton ..92 C2
South Bowood 203 F1
South Chard 202 A7
South Gorley 43 C1
South Perrott 192 C2
South Poorton 70 B4
Southbourne 123 C2
Southbrook 3 A5
Southill 167 A3
Southlands 180 C4
Southover 73 B1
Southover 128 A4

T

Tadnoll 138 B1
Talbot Village 89 B1
Tarrant Crawford ...211 E6
Tarrant Gunville 199 F8
Tarrant Hinton 200 A6
Tarrant Keyneston ...48 A3
Tarrant Launceston ..200 B4
Tarrant Monkton ...200 B3
Tarrant Rushton 48 A4
Templeman's Ash ...203 B3
The Borough 196 B6

Southwell 186 C1
Spetisbury 211 D5
Springbourne 122 B3
Spyway 102 B4
Stafford's Green 16 A4
Stalbridge 33 C4
Stalbridge Weston ..33 A3
Stallen 29 A3
Stanbridge 50 B2
Stanley Green 119 B3
Stanpit 124 C3
Stapehill 60 C3
Steeple 175 B4
Sterte 119 A2
Stinsford 108 C2
Stoborough 142 C1
Stoborough Green ..161 A4
Stockwood 194 C2
Stoford 193 F8
Stoke Abbott 204 A3
Stoke Wake 197 B1
Stokeford 140 C2
Stone 101 A4
Stone 59 A3
Stour Provost 21 B4
Stour Row 22 B4
Stourpaine 198 F4
Stourton Caundle ..32 C2
Stratton 106 C4
Strouden 90 C1
Stubhampton 199 E8
Stuckton 43 C4
Studland 164 B1
Sturminster Marshall ..56 C2
Sturminster Newton ..35 A1
Summerlands 27 A3
Sutton Bingham ..193 D6
Sutton Holms 44 A4
Sutton Poyntz 153 B2
Sutton Waldron ...37 C3
Swanage 179 B2
Swyre 129 B3
Sydling St Nicholas ..207 A2
Symondsbury 99 C4
Synderford 202 F6

The Causeway 3 B2
The Common 197 D5
The Mount 69 A3
Thorncombe 202 E6
Thorne Coffin 26 B4
Thornford 194 D8
Thornicombe 210 F6
Three Gates 195 A2
Three Legged Cross ..45 A1
Throop 112 B4
Throop 90 C2
Tidpit 209 C6
Tiley 195 E1
Tillworth 202 A3
Tincleton 110 B2
Tiptoe 95 B4
Todber 21 B2
Tollard Farnham ..188 B2
Tollard Royal 188 B4
Toller Fratrum 72 B4
Toller Porcorum ...71 C4
Toller Whelme 205 B4
Tollerford 72 C4
Tolpuddle 79 B1
Totnell 194 F3
Town's End 81 B2
Trent 14 C1
Trickett's Cross ...61 C4
Tuckton 123 C3
Turlin Moor 117 B2
Turmer 46 C4
Turners Puddle ...112 B4
Turnworth 198 B2
Twyford 23 B1
Tyneham 174 B3

U

Ulwell 179 A3
Up Cerne 207 C5
Up Mudford 14 A1
Up Sydling 207 A4
Uphall 205 E5
Uploders 101 C4
Upper Parkstone ..120 A3
Uppington 201 D1
Upton 118 B4
Upwey 152 A3

V

Verwood 45 A3

W

Walditch 101 A3
Walkford 94 B1

Wallisdown 89 A1
Walton Elm 34 C4
Wareham 142 C3
Warmwell 137 A1
Warren 113 B2
Waterditch 93 A3
Waterloo 87 A1
Watton 100 A2
Wayford 191 B1
Waytown 68 C4
Well Bottom 39 B3
West Bay 100 B1
West Bexington ..129 C1
West Bourton 4 B4
West Chaldon 155 C1
West Chelborough ..205 D8
West Chinnock 192 B8
West Cliff 121 B1
West Coker 193 A8
West Compton 71 C1
West End 29 C3
West Holme 159 B4
West Howe 88 C2
West Hurn 90 C3
West Knighton ...136 B2
West Lulworth ...172 B3
West Melbury 24 A3
West Milton 69 C3
West Moors 53 A1
West Morden 83 A2
West Orchard 36 B3
West Parley 89 F4
West Pulham 196 A3
West Southbourne ..123 B3
West Stafford 136 A4
West Stour 10 A1
Westbourne 121 B2
Westfields 196 D1
Westham 167 A2
Weston 186 C2
Weston 204 F8
Weymouth 167 C2
Whitchurch 19 A3
Whitchurch
  Canonicorum ...66 A2
Whitcombe 135 C3
White Cross 1 C3
White Hill 3 B1
White Lackington ..208 C1
Whitecross 204 B2
Whitefield 83 A1
Whitmore 44 A3
Wick 124 A2
Wigbeth 201 F2
Wimborne Minster ..59 A3
Wimborne St Giles ..201 D7
Winfrith Newburgh ..156 C3
Winkton 92 B1
Winterborne Came ..135 B3
Winterborne Clenston ..210 D6

Winterborne
  Herrington ....134 ▪
Winterborne Houghton ..210 ▪
Winterborne Kingston ...81 ▪
Winterborne Monkton ..134 ▪
Winterborne Muston ...82 ▪
Winterborne Stickland ..210 ▪
Winterborne Tomson ...82 ▪
Winterborne
  Whitchurch ....210 ▪
Winterborne Zelston ...82 ▪
Winterbourne Abbas ..105 ▪
Winterbourne
  Steepleton ....132 ▪
Winton ....121 ▪
Winyard's Gap .....192 ▪
Witchampton ......200 ▪
Wolverton ....2 ▪
Wonston ....196 ▪
Woodbridge ....23 ▪
Woodcutts ....188 ▪
Woodlands ....44 ▪
Woodlands Common ..44 ▪
Woodrow ....196 ▪
Woodsford ....110 ▪
Woodville ....21 ▪
Woodyates ......189 ▪
Wool ....140 ▪
Woolbridge Heath ..140 ▪
Woolford's Water ..208 ▪
Woolgarston .....177 ▪
Woolland ....197 ▪
Woolminstone ...191 ▪
Woolsbridge ....53 ▪
Wooth ....68 ▪
Wootton ....95 ▪
Wootton Fitzpaine ..65 ▪
Worgret ....142 ▪
Worth Matravers ..183 ▪
Wych ....100 ▪
Wyke ....5 ▪
Wyke Regis ....180 ▪
Wynford Eagle .....72 ▪

Y

Yenston ....18 ▪
Yeovil ....27 ▪
Yetminster ....194 ▪
Yondover ....101 ▪

Z

Zeals ....1 C

8th August Rd BH20 ....139 C4

A

Aaron Cl BH17 ....119 C3
Abbey Barn* DT3 ....149 A4
Abbey CE VC Prim Sch The
DT9 ....29 C2
Abbey CE Voluntary Aided
Fst Sch The DT9 ....12 B1
Abbey Cl DT9 ....202 A8
Abbey Ct DT2 ....207 D4
Abbey Gdns*
Cerne Abbas DT2 ......207 D4
Ferndown BH21 ....60 B3
Abbey House* BH21 .....201 A1
Abbey Mews DT9 ....30 A3
Abbey Mus* DT9 ....12 C1
Abbey Sherborne DT9 ....30 A3
West Moors BH22 ....62 A4
Yeovil BA21 ....26 C3
Abbey St
Cerne Abbas DT2 ....207 D4
Crewkerne TA18 ....191 E4
Hinton St George TA17 .191 C7
Abbey Wlk 4 DT11 ......211 E5
Abbey Wlk SP7 ....12 C1
Abbot Rd SP1 ....213 C4
Abbots Cl BH23 ....125 C4
Abbots Meade BA20 ......26 C1
Abbots Quay 9 BH20 ...142 C2
Abbots Way
Sherborne DT9 ....29 C3
Yeovil BA21 ....26 C4
Abbots Wlk DT2 ....207 D4
Abbotsbury Castle (Fort)*
DT3 ....130 B1
Abbotsbury Hill DT3 ...130 B1
Abbotsbury La DT3 .....130 C4
Abbotsbury Rd
Broadstone BH18 ....86 C3
Weymouth DT3 ....167 A2
Abbotsbury Swannery*
DT3 ....149 A3
Abbott Cl BH9 ....122 A4
Abbott Rd BH9 ....122 A4
Abbott St BH20 ....58 B3
Abbott's Way DT9 ....5 C2
Abbott's Wootton La
Marshwood DT6 ....202 E1
Whitechurch Canonicorum
DT6 ....65 B4
Abbotts Mdw BH16 ......84 B2
Abbotts Way BH22 ......62 A4
Abber Cross DT9 ....14 C2
Abels La DT9 ....14 C1
Aberdare Rd BH10 ....89 C2
Abingdon Dr BH23 .....126 B4
Abingdon Rd BH17 .....119 B4
Abinger Rd BH7 ....123 A3
Abney Rd BH10 ....89 B2
Acacia Ave BH31 ....45 C2
Acacia Cl DT4 ....167 A3
Acacia Rd SO41 ....95 C2
Acer Ave 7 Bridport DT6 ..68 C1
Acer Dr BH21 ....26 C4
Ackerman Rd DT1 ......108 B1
Acland Rd
Bournemouth BH9 ......122 A4
7 Dorchester DT1 ......108 A1
Acorn Bsns Pk BH12 ...120 A4
Acorn Ct
Christchurch BH23 .....123 C4
New Milton BH25 ....95 B2
St.Leonards BH24 ....54 A2
Acorn Way BH21 ....45 B3
Acorns The BH21 ....60 A2
Acreman Cl DT2 ....30 A3
Acreman Pl
Cerne Abbas DT2 ......207 D4
Sherborne DT9 ....30 A3
Acreman St
Cerne Abbas DT2 ......207 D4
Sherborne DT9 ....30 A3
Acres Ct 4 BA22 ....193 F8
Acres Rd BH11 ....89 A1
Acton Rd BH10 ....89 A1
Ad Astra Fst Sch BH17 ...87 C1
Adamsfield Gdns BH10 ...89 B1
Adastral Rd BH17 ......119 C4
Adastral Sq BH17 ......119 C4
Adber Cl BA21 ....28 A4
Addington Pl BH23 .....124 B3
Addiscombe Rd BH23 ...124 A4
Addison Cl SP9 ....6 A1
Addison Sq BH4 ....55 B4
Addlewell La BA20 ......27 B2
Adelaide Cl BH23 ......123 C4
Adelaide Cres DT4 .....167 A2
Adeline Rd BH5 ....122 C2
Adelaide Rd DT9 ....30 B4
Admirals Cl DT9 ....30 B4
Admirals Way BH20 ....142 C3
Admirals Wlk BH21 ....121 B1
Aggis Farm Rd BH31 ....45 A3
Agglestone Rd BH19 ...164 A1
Aigburth Rd BH14 .....178 C2
Airetons Cl BH18 ....87 B2
Airfield Cl DT3 ....137 B3
Airfield Ind Est BH23 .124 C3
Airfield Rd BH23 ......124 C3
Airfield Way BH23 .....124 C4
Airspeed Rd BH23 .....125 A4
Akeshill Cl BH25 ....95 A3

Alamein Rd BH20 ....139 C3
Alan Ct 10 BH23 ......126 A4
Alastair Cl BA21 ....27 A4
Alastair Dr BA21 ....27 A4
Albany BH1 ....122 B2
Albany Cl
Barton on Sea BH25 .....94 C1
Sherborne DT9 ....30 B4
Albany Dr Horton BH21 ..52 C4
Three Legged Cross BH21 ..45 A1
Albany Gdns BH15 .....118 C1
Albany Pk BH17 ....119 A4
Albany Rd
Salisbury SP1 ....213 B3
Weymouth DT4 ....166 C2
Albemarle Rd BH3 .....121 C4
Albert Cl BA21 ....27 A4
Albert Rd
Bournemouth BH1 ......121 C2
Corfe Mullen BH21 ......86 B3
Dorchester DT1 ....107 C1
Ferndown BH22 ....61 B3
New Milton BH25 ....94 C1
Poole BH12 ....120 B3
Albert St
Blandford Forum DT11 .212 B2
6 Radipole DT4 ....167 B2
Albert Terr 5 DT5 .....186 C4
Albion Cl BH12 ....120 A4
Albion Rd BH21 ....91 C1
Albion Way BH31 ....44 C3
Alby Rd BH12 ....120 B3
Alcester Rd BH12 ......120 B3
Aldabrand Cl DT11 ....199 B8
Aldbury Ct BH25 ....127 A4
Alder Cl Burton BH23 ...92 B1
3 Sandford BH20 ......116 A1
Sturminster Newton DT10 ..35 B1
Alder Cres DT3 ....42 A3
Alder Dr SP6 ....42 A3
Alder Rd
Crewkerne TA18 ....191 F5
Yeovil BA20 ....27 A4
Alder Hills BH12 ......120 C3
Alder Hills Ind Est
BH12 ....121 A4
Alder Rd Poole BH12 ..120 C3
Sturminster Newton DT10 ..35 B1
Alderbury Cl 5 BH19 ..178 C1
Alderbury Cl BH25 ......95 A2
Alderholt Pk* SP6 ......42 A4
Alderley Rd BH10 ....89 C2
Alderney Mid Sch
BH11 ....88 B1
Alderney Ave BH11 .....88 B1
Alderney Hospl BH12 ...88 B1
Aldis Gdns BH11 ......118 C1
Aldondale Gdns BA20 ...27 B2
Aldridge Rd
Bournemouth BH10 ......89 B3
Ferndown BH22 ....61 C2
Aldridge Way BH22 .....61 C2
Alexander Cl BH23 ....124 C3
Alexandra Ct BH25 ....100 B3
Alexandra Lodge 6
BH1 ....122 A2
Alexandra Rd
Bournemouth BH6 ......123 B3
Bridport DT6 ....100 B3
Dorchester DT1 ....108 A1
Poole BH14 ....120 C2
Radipole DT4 ....167 B3
Weymouth DT4 ....166 C2
Yeovil BA21 ....27 C3
Alexandra St DT11 .....212 B2
Alexandra Ch BH22 .....61 C2
Alford Rd BH3 ....121 B4
Alfred Pl DT1 ....108 A1
Alfred Rd DT11 ....212 B2
Alfred St DT11 ....212 B2
Alice in Wonderland Family
Pk* BH23 ....90 C4
Alice Rd DT1 ....107 C1
Alington Ave DT1 .....135 B4
Alington Cl BH14 .....147 B4
Alington House BH14 .147 B4
Alington Rd
Bournemouth BH3 .....122 A3
Dorchester DT1 ....108 A1
Poole BH14 ....147 B3
Weymouth DT4 ....166 C2
Yeovil BA20 ....27 C3
Alipore Cl BH14 ......120 B2
Alipore Hts BH14 .....120 B2
Alisons The BH20 .....139 C1
All Saints CE Prim Sch
DT9 ....196 A8
All Saints CE Sch DT14 .180 B4
All Saints' Rd
Dorchester DT1 ....108 A1
Weymouth DT4 ....180 B4
Allamanda Rd DT3 ....152 C1
Allberry Gdns DT3 ....168 A4
Allen Cl BH21 ....198 C7
Allen Ct BH21 ....59 B3
Allen Rd BH21 ....59 B2
Allenbourn Mid Sch
BH21 ....59 B3
Allenby Rd BH17 ......87 A1
Allenby Rd BH17 ......87 A1
Allens La BH16 ....118 B3
Allens Rd BH16 ....118 B3
Allenview Rd BH21 .....59 A3
Allingham Rd BA21 ....27 C4
Allington Gdns 8 BH19 ..178 C1
Allington Mead 3 DT6 .100 B4
Allington Pk BH14 ....100 A4
Allington Rd BH14 ....147 B4

Alma Rd
Bournemouth BH9 .....122 A4
Weymouth DT4 ....167 B2
Almer Rd BH15 ....118 C2
Almond Gr Poole BH12 .120 B4
Radipole DT4 ....167 A3
Almshouses BH10 ....89 B1
Alpha Ctr The BH17 ...119 A4
Alpine Rd BH24 ....54 C1
Alton La DT7 ....203 C5
Alton Mead La DT9 ....194 E4
Alton Rd
Bournemouth BH10 ......89 A1
Poole BH10 E BH14 ....120 B3
Alum Chine Rd BH4 ...121 A2
Alumdale Rd BH4 .....121 A1
Alvandi Gdns 4 BH25 ..95 A2
Alverton Ave BH15 ....119 C2
Alverton Hall BH14 ...120 C2
Alvington La BA22 .....26 B2
Ambassador Cl BH23 ..125 C3
Ambassador Ind Est
............................125 A3
Amber Rd BH21 ....126 A4
Amberley Cl BH23 ....125 C4
Amberley Ct BH22 .....61 C2
Amberwood BH21 ....61 C3
Amberwood Dr BH23 ...93 C1
Amberwood Gdns
............................94 A1
Amberwood House
BH23 ....94 A1
Ambleside
Christchurch BH23 ......91 C2
Radipole DT4 ....167 A3
Ambrose Cl DT9 ....28 B1
Ambury La BH21 ......124 C4
Amelia Cl 3 BH5 ......181 A1
Amen Cnr BH21 ....201 B5
Amesbury Rd BH6 ....123 B3
Amethyst Rd BH23 ....125 C4
Ameys La BH22 ....61 C4
Ameysford Rd BH22 ...52 B1
Amiens Rd BH20 ....139 C4
Amira Ct 9 BH2 ....121 C1
Ammerham La BA22 ..202 D8
Ampfield Rd BH8 ......90 B2
Amsterdam Sq BH23 ..124 B3
Ancaster Rd BH19 ....178 C2
Anchor Cl
Bournemouth BH11 .....88 C3
Christchurch BH23 ....125 A3
Anchor Rd BH11 ....88 C3
Ancrum Lodge BH4 ...121 A2
Andbourne Ct BH6 ...123 C2
Anderson Manor*
DT11 ....82 B4
Anderson Rd BH23 ....125 C4
Andover Cl BH23 .....125 A4
Andover Gn BH20 .....139 B3
Andree Ct BH21 ....91 A3
Andover La DT11 ......212 C3
Andover La BH25 ....95 B1
Andrews Cl BH11 ......89 A2
Andrews Way SP2 ....213 A1
Angel Cl DT3 ....150 B1
Angel La
Barton on Sea BH25 ..127 B4
Ferndown BH22 ....61 A2
Langton Herring DT3 ..150 B1
Mere BA12 ....3 A3
Shaftesbury SP7 ....12 C2
Stour Provost SP8 .....10 C1
Angeline Cl BH23 .....125 C4
Angers La BH24 ....79 E7
Anglebury Ave BH19 ..179 A2
Anglewood Mans 9
BH1 ....121 B2
Anglo-European Coll of
Chiropractic BH5 .....123 A2
Angus Cl BH11 ....88 B3
Anjou Cl BH11 ....88 B3
Annandale Ct BH14 ...123 B2
Anncott Cl BH16 ....84 B2
Anne Cl
Blandford Forum DT11 .212 C2
Christchurch BH23 ......92 A1
Annerley Rd BH1 ......122 B3
Annet Cl BH15 ....118 C1
Anning Rd DT6 ....96 B3
Ansty La DT6 ....101 C1
Anson Cl
Christchurch BH23 ....124 C3
Ringwood BH24 ....54 C4
Anstey Cl BH11 ....89 A3
Anstey Rd BH11 ....89 A3
Ansty La DT11 ....79 B4
Antell's Way SP6 ....42 B3
Antelope Wlk DT1 .....108 A1
Anthony's Ave BH14 ..120 B1
Antler Dr BH25 ....94 C2
Anvil Cl 4 BH19 ......178 C1
Anvil Cres BH18 ....86 C3
Anvil Rd 10 DT11 .....199 D4
Aplands Cl DT11 ......198 B8
Apollo Cl
Dorchester DT1 ....134 C4
Poole BH12 ....120 A3
Apple Acre 1 DT11 ...198 C7
Apple Cl BH12 ....121 A2
Apple Gr DT4 ....167 A4
Apple Tree Gr BH22 ....61 C3
Apple Tree Rd SP6 .....42 A3
Apple Trees La DT3 .....99 A3
Appleslade Way BH25 ..95 A3

Appletree Cl
Bournemouth BH6 .....123 B3
New Milton BH25 ....95 A1
Radipole DT3 ....167 B4
Approach Rd BH14 ....120 A2
April Ct BH11 ....89 A2
Apsley Cres BH17 ....87 B1
Apsley Ct 2 BH8 ......122 A3
Aragon Ct DT1 ....180 C4
Aragon Way BH9 ....90 A2
Arbutus Cl DT1 ....108 A1
Arcade Ave BH8 ......121 A2
Arcade The 37 BH1 ...121 B2
Arcadia Ave BH8 ......122 A4
Arcadia Rd BH23 ....91 C1
Archbishop Wake Fst Sch
DT11 ....212 B2
Archdale Cl BH10 ....89 B1
Archway Rd BH14 ....120 A2
Arden Rd BH9 ....89 C2
Arden Wlk BH25 ....95 A1
Ardmore Rd BH14 ....120 B2
Argyle Rd
Christchurch BH23 ....124 C3
Radipole DT4 ....167 B3
Swanage BH19 ....179 A1
Argyll Mans 11 BH5 ..122 C2
Argyll Rd
Bournemouth BH5 .....122 C2
Poole BH12 ....120 B3
Ariel Cl BH24 ....124 A2
Ariel Dr BH6 ....124 A2
Ark Dr BH22 ....61 C2
Arlecks La 8 DT11 ....199 D4
Arley Rd BH14 ....120 A1
Arlington
Christchurch BH23 ......91 C2
Radipole DT4 ....167 A3
Arlington Cl BA21 ......26 C4
Arlington Ct BH25 ....127 A4
Armada Way DT1 .....135 B4
Armoury Rd BA22 ......26 B3
Arne Ave BH12 ....120 C4
Arne Cres BH12 ....120 C4
Arne Rd BH20 ....143 B1
Arnewood Ct BH2 ....121 C1
Arnewood Gdns BA20 ..27 A1
Arnewood Rd BH6 ....124 A2
Arnewood Sch The
BH25 ....94 C1
Arnold Cl DT3 ....153 A2
Arnold Rd BH20 ....53 A2
Arnolds Cl BH25 ....95 A4
Arran Way BH23 ....94 A1
Arras Cres DT4 ....139 B4
Arras Rd BH20 ....139 B4
Arrow Field DT6 ....100 B3
Arrowfield DT6 ....107 B2
Arrowsmith Cl BH21 ...87 C4
Arrowsmith La BH21 ...87 C4
Arrowsmith Rd BH21 ..87 C4
Arthur Cl BH12 ....121 A3
Arthur La 3 BH23 ....124 A3
Arthur Rd BH23 ......124 A4
Artillery Rd BA22 ......26 B3
Artist Row DT5 ....186 C4
Arts Inst of Bournemouth
The 121 B4
Arun Cl 4 SP8 ....5 C2
Arundel Cl BH23 ....94 C2
Arundel Rd BA21 ....28 A3
Arundel Way BH23 ....125 A4
Ascham Rd BH8 ......122 A4
Ascot Rd BH18 ....86 C3
Ash Ave BH20 ....116 A2
Ash Cl Alderholt SP6 ...42 B3
Sandford BH20 ....143 A4
Shaftesbury SP7 ....13 A2
Swanage BH19 ....179 C1
Upton BH16 ....118 A4
Ash End BH24 ....19 A3
Ash Gr BH24 ....54 C2
Ash Hill DT2 ....106 C4
Ash La DT6 ....68 B3
Ash Tree Cl DT2 ......206 A1
Ash Tree La SP7 ....24 B3
Ashbourne Cl 1 BH1 ...122 C3
Ashbourne Rd BH5 ...123 A3
Ashbrook Wlk BH11 ...89 A2
Ashburn Garth 6 BH23 .55 C3
Ashburton Gdns BH10 ..89 B1
Ashcombe La DT9 ......31 B2
Ashdene Cl BH21 ....59 B3
Ashdown DT11 ....199 D4
Ashdown Cl BH17 ......87 C1
Ashdown Sch BH17 ....87 C1
Ashdown Wlk BH25 ....95 B1
Ashfield Rd SP2 ......213 A3
Ashfield Trad Est SP2 ..213 A3
Ashford Gr BA21 ....27 B4
Ashford Rd
Bournemouth BH6 .....123 B3
Fordingbridge SP6 .....42 C4
Ashgrove BA12 ....3 A2
Ashington Gdns BH21 .86 C4
Ashington La BA21 .....59 A1
Ashington Pk BH25 ....95 A1
Ashington St 3 DT1 ..107 B1
Ashland Cl 1 BH21 ...134 C4
Ashlands Cl TA18 .....191 E5
Ashlands Mdw TA18 ...191 E5
Ashlands Rd TA18 ....191 F5
Ashlands VC Fst Sch
TA18 ....191 E5
Ashleigh Ave DT2 ......72 C4
Ashleigh Rise BH10 ....89 B1
Ashlet Gdns BH25 .....95 B2

Ashley Arnewood Ct 9
BH25 ....95 A1
Ashley Cl
Bournemouth BH1 .....122 C3
Ringwood BH24 ....55 C3
Ashley Comm Sch BH25 .95 B2
Ashley Ct BH22 ....62 C4
Ashley Dr BH24 ....40 A1
Ashley Dr N BH24 ......54 A3
Ashley Dr S BH24 ......54 A3
Ashley Dr W BH24 ......54 A3
Ashley Inf Sch BH25 ...95 B2
Ashley Jun Sch BH25 ...95 C2
Ashley La SO41 ....95 C2
Ashley Meads BH25 ....95 B2
Ashley Pk BH24 ....54 B3
Ashley Rd
Bournemouth BH1 .....122 C3
Dorchester DT1 ....135 A4
Marnhull DT10 ....21 A1
New Milton BH25 ....95 B2
Poole BH14 ....120 B3
Salisbury SP1 ....213 A3
Ashley Wood Golf Club
............................199 E1
Ashley Wood Pk DT11 .211 E2
Ashley Wood Rd DT11 .199 E2
Ashling Cl DT1 ....122 B4
Ashling Cres BH8 .....122 A4
Ashmead BA20 ....26 C1
Ashmeads Cl BH21 .....60 A3
Ashmeads Way BH21 ...60 A3
Ashmede BH4 ....121 B1
Ashmore BH21 ....159 B2
Ashmore Ave
Barton on Sea BH25 ...127 C4
Hamworthy BH15 ......118 C1
Ashmore Bottom DT11 ..39 B1
Ashmore Cl DT11 ......159 C2
Ashmore Cres BH15 ..118 C1
Ashmore Gr BH23 ....93 C1
Ashridge Ave 4 BH10 ..89 B3
Ashridge Gdns BH10 ...89 B3
Ashridge Par 8 BH10 ...89 B3
Ashton Cr
New Milton BH25 ....95 A2
Poole BH13 ....121 A1
Ashton Rd
Bournemouth BH9 ......89 C1
Weymouth DT4 ....167 B1
Ashurst Rd
Bournemouth BH8 ......90 B2
Ferndown BH22 ....53 A2
Ashwell Cr BH23 ....91 C1
Ashwood Dr
Broadstone BH18 ....87 B2
Yeovil Without BA21 ...28 A4
Asker Gdns DT6 ......100 B3
Askwith Cl DT9 ....29 C3
Aspen Dr BH31 ....45 B3
Aspen Gdns BH12 ....120 C4
Aspen Pl BH25 ....95 A1
Aspen Rd BH12 ....120 C4
Aspen Way
10 Crewkerne TA18 ..191 F5
Poole BH12 ....120 C4
Asquith Cl BH23 ......124 B3
Ass Hill BH21 ....201 B4
Assisi Rd SP1 ....213 B3
Astbury Ave BH12 .....89 A1
Aster Cl SP1 ....213 B4
Aston Mead
Christchurch BH23 ......91 C2
Athelhampton House*
DT2 ....78 C1
Athelhampton Rd DT2 ..78 C1
Athelney Ct 18 BH1 ..122 A2
Athelney Way BA21 ...26 C3
Athelstan Rd
Bournemouth BH6 .....123 C3
10 Dorchester DT1 ...108 A1
Atlantic Rd BH19 .....179 A1
Attisham La DT6 ......203 B4
Attwood Cl BH6 ....123 B3
Attwood Rd SP1 ......213 B4
Auburn Garth 6 BH23 .55 C3
Auckland Rd BH23 ....124 C3
Audemer Ct BA22 ......55 C4
Audrayton Ct 9 BH6 ..123 C1
Augusta Cl DT5 ....187 A3
Augusta Rd DT5 ......187 A3
Augustan Cl 1 DT1 ...134 C4
Austen Ave BH10 ......89 C3
Auster Cl BH23 ....125 A4
Austin Ave BH14 .....120 A1
Austin Cl BH1 ....122 C3
Australia Rd DT3 .....166 B2
Autumn Cl DT2 ....61 A4
Autumn Copse BH25 ...95 B1
Autumn Rd BH11 ....88 B2
Avalanche Rd DT5 ....186 C1
Avalon BH14 ....147 B4
Avebury Ave BH10 .....89 C3
Avenue Ct BH13 ......121 A2
Avenue La 10 BH2 ...121 C2
Avenue Rd
Bournemouth BH2 ....121 C2
Christchurch BH23 ......94 B1
Lyme Regis DT7 ....96 A3
New Milton BH25 ....95 A2
Radipole DT4 ....167 B2
Wimborne Minster BH21 .59 B2
Avenue Shopping Ctr The 2
BH2 ....121 C2

Avenue The
Bournemouth BH9 89 C2
6 Crewkerne TA18 192 A3
Ferndown BH22 53 A2
Poole BH13 121 A1
Salisbury SP1 213 C3
Sherborne DT9 30 B4
Yeovil BA21 27 B3
Avocet Cl DT4 180 B3
Avon Approach SP2 213 B3
Avon Ave BH24 54 C2
Avon Bldgs BH23 124 A4
Avon Castle* BH24 54 C2
Avon Castle Dr BH24 54 C2
Avon Cl
Bournemouth BH8 122 B3
Weymouth DT4 166 C2
Yeovil BA21 27 C3
Avon Cotts BH23 92 B3
Avon Cswy BH23 91 B4
Avon Ct BH23 124 B3
Avon Dr BH20 142 C3
Avon Farm Cotts BH23 63 C2
Avon Heath Ctry Pk* BH24 54 B2
Avon Heath Ctry Pk (South Pk)* BH24 63 A4
Avon House BH2 121 C1
Avon Mews BH8 122 B3
Avon Pk BH24 54 C3
Avon Rd
Bournemouth BH8 122 B3
Ferndown BH22 53 A1
Avon Rd E BH23 124 A4
Avon Rd W BH23 123 C4
Avon Run Cl BH23 125 A3
Avon Run Rd BH23 125 A3
Avon Terr SP2 213 A3
Avon View Par BH23 92 B2
Avon View Rd BH23 92 B2
Avon Wharf BH23 124 B3
Avonbourne Girls Sch BH7 123 A4
Avoncliffe Rd BH6 123 C2
Avondale Gdns SP8 5 C2
Avonlea Prep Sch BH24 55 B4
Award Rd BH21 60 C3
Axe La
Broadwindsor DT8 203 C8
West Crewkerne TA18 191 C1
Axe Valley Cl 1 DT8 204 A8
Axeford TA20 202 B8
Axford Cl BH8 90 B2
Axminster Rd DT6 96 C4
Axnoller La DT8 204 D6
Aylesbury Rd BH1 122 C2
Ayleswade Rd SP2 213 B1
Aysha Cl BH25 95 A1
Azalea Cl BH24 54 B3
Azura Cl BH21 53 B3

B

Babwell Rd BA9 4 A2
Babylon Hill DT9 28 B3
Babylon View BA21 28 A4
Back Dro DT9 194 E3
Back La Bere Regis BH20 81 A2
Bradford Abbas DT9 28 B1
Broadwindsor DT8 203 E5
Cerne Abbas DT2 207 D4
Chetnole DT9 194 D3
East Chinnock BA22 192 E8
East Coker BA22 193 C7
Evershot DT2 206 A7
Frome Vauchurch DT2 72 C4
Gillingham SP8 5 B3
Halstock BA22 193 C3
Hazelbury Bryan DT10 197 A4
Kington Magna SP8 9 B2
North Perrott TA18 192 C4
4 Okeford Fitzpaine DT11 197 F5
Rimpton BA22 15 A4
Sherborne DT9 30 A3
Sixpenny Handley SP5 189 A4
Sturminster Marshall BH21 56 B3
Swyre DT2 129 B3
Sydling St Nicholas DT2 207 A2
Back St Abbotsbury DT3 149 A4
East Stour SP8 10 C2
Portesham DT3 132 A1
Badbury Cl BH18 87 B2
Badbury Ct 8 BH23 124 C3
Badbury Dr DT11 212 B3
Badbury Rings (Hill Fort)* DT11 49 A2
Badbury View BH21 59 B3
Badbury View Rd BH21 86 B4
Baden Cl BH25 95 A1
Baden Powell & St Peter's Mid Sch BH14 120 A2
Bader Rd BH17 119 C4
Badger Hts BA22 26 B3
Badger La DT2 209 A5
Badger Way BH31 45 A3
Badgers Cl BH24 54 A3
Badgers Copse BH25 95 B3
Badgers Way DT10 35 A1
Badgers Wlk BH22 61 C4
Baglake DT2 103 B1
Bagman's La BH21 201 E3
Bagwood Rd 8 DT11 81 C4
Bailey Cl BH25 95 B2
Bailey Cres BH15 119 B4
Bailey Dr BH23 123 C4
Bailey Gate Ind Est BH21 56 C2
Bailey Hall BH23 123 C4
Bailey Ridge DT9 195 A4
Bailey Ridge La DT9 194 F4
Bailey's Dro BH20 139 C1
Baileys Hill BH21 201 D6
Baiter Gdns BH15 119 B1
Bakehouse TA16 191 F7
Bakehouse La 1 DT9 28 B1
Baker Rd BH11 89 A3
Baker's Cross DT6 65 B2
Bakers Farm Rd BH31 45 A4
Bakers La 3 BH21 201 D1
Bakers Paddock DT2 136 B1
Balaclava Rd
Bovington Camp BH20 139 C4
Fortuneswell DT5 181 B1
Balcombe Rd BH13 121 A2
Baldwin Cl BH23 124 B3
Balena Cl BH17 119 A4
Balfour Cl BH23 125 B4
Balfour Rd BH9 89 C1
Ball La 17 BH15 119 B1
Ballam Cl BH16 118 B4
Ballands Castle* BA9 1 A1
Ballard Cl
Lytchett Matravers BH16 84 B2
New Milton BH25 95 A2
Poole BH15 119 B1
Ballard Coll BH25 95 A2
Ballard Lee BH19 179 B3
Ballard Rd Poole BH15 119 B1
Swanage BH19 179 B3
Ballard Sch BH25 95 A2
Ballard Way BH19 179 B3
Ball's Hill BA22 26 A4
Ball's La BH21 56 B3
Balmoor Cl BA12 3 A2
Balmoral Ave BH8 90 C1
Balmoral Cres DT1 135 B4
Balmoral Ct 7 BH23 126 A4
Balmoral House BH2 121 B2
Balmoral Rd
Poole BH14 120 B2
Salisbury SP1 213 B4
Yeovil BA21 28 A3
Balmoral Wlk BH25 94 C2
Balston Rd BH14 120 A3
Balston Terr BH15 119 A1
Banbury Hill (Fort)* DT10 197 D6
Banbury Rd BH17 119 B4
Bank Chambers BH14 120 C2
Bank Cl BH23 124 A3
Banks Rd BH13 147 B2
Bankside Rd BH9 90 A2
Banocroft Ct 1 BH15 119 C2
Banstead Rd BH18 87 A3
Banton Shard DT6 68 C1
Barberry Way BH31 45 C3
Barbers Gate 15 BH15 119 A1
Barbers Piles 8 BH15 119 A1
Barbers Wharf 16 BH15 119 A1
Barclay Mans BH2 121 C3
Barclay Rd DT4 167 B2
Bardolfeston Village* DT2 78 B1
Bargates BH23 124 A4
Barges Cl DT2 103 B1
Baring Rd BH6 124 A2
Barlake Ct 5 DT1 107 B1
Barlands Cl BH23 92 B1
Barley Cl DT2 194 A2
Barley Way DT4 167 C1
Barleycroft Rd 3 DT5 186 C2
Barleyfields 10 SP8 5 C2
Barlynch Ct 6 BA21 26 C3
Barn Cl
8 Crewkerne TA18 191 E4
Upton BH16 118 A4
Barn Cres 7 TA18 191 E4
Barn La TA18 191 E6
Barn Rd BH18 87 A2
Barn St TA18 191 E4
Barnaby Mead SP8 5 C1
Barnard St 4 SP1 213 B2
Barndale Dr BH20 143 A1
Barnes Cl
Blandford Forum DT11 212 C3
Bournemouth BH10 89 B2
Marnhull DT10 21 A1
Sturminster Newton DT10 35 A1
Barnes Cres
Bournemouth BH10 89 B2
Wimborne Minster BH21 59 C2
Barnes Cross DT9 196 A6
Barnes La DT8 204 C4
Barnes Pl BA12 3 A3
Barnes Rd
Bournemouth BH10 89 B2
Wareham Town BH20 142 B1
Barnes Way 18 DT1 108 A1
Barneston Manor* BH20 176 A4
Barnet Cl BA21 27 A4
Barney's Cl DT6 97 A4
Barnfield BH23 125 B4
Barnhaven Cl DT4 167 A1
Barnhill Rd BH20 143 A1
Barns Rd BH22 62 A3
Barnsfield Rd BH24 54 B1
Barnsley Dro BH21 50 A2
Barons Ct 8 BH12 121 A2
Barons Rd BH11 88 B3
Barr La DT6 101 B2
Barrack La BH24 55 C2
Barrack Rd
Christchurch BH23 123 C4
Ferndown BH22 62 A1
Weymouth DT4 167 C1
Barrack St DT6 100 B4
Barr's La DT6 97 A4
Barrie Rd BH9 89 C2
Barrington Rd SP1 213 C4
Barrow Cl DT1 134 C4
Barrow Dr BH8 90 C1
Barrow Hill
Bere Regis BH20 81 A2
Stalbridge DT10 33 B4
Stourton Caundle DT10 32 C1
Barrow La DT2 205 A8
Barrow Rd BH8 90 C1
Barrow Rise DT4 180 A4
Barrow St La BA12 3 C2
Barrow View BH22 61 A3
Barrow Way BH8 90 C1
Barrowfield Cl DT6 128 A4
Barrowgate Rd BH8 90 B2
Barrowgate Way BH8 90 B2
Barrowland La DT2 71 A3
Barrs Ave BH25 95 A2
Barrs Wood Dr BH25 95 A2
Barrs Wood Rd BH25 95 A2
Barry Gdns BH18 86 C3
Barry La BA22 192 F6
Barters La
Broadstone BH18 86 C2
Donhead St Mary SP7 25 A4
Bartlets Cl DT2 133 B3
Bartlett Dr BH7 123 A4
Bartlett Rd SP1 213 B4
Bartletts The BA12 3 A2
Bartley Ct 6 BH21 59 A3
Bartom's La BH16 84 A1
Barton Cl
Sturminster Newton DT10 197 C8
Toller Porcorum DT2 71 B4
West Stafford DT2 136 A4
Barton Comm La BH25 127 A4
Barton Comm Rd BH25 127 A4
Barton Croft BH25 127 A4
Barton Ct BH25 127 A3
Barton Ct Ave BH25 127 A4
Barton Ct Rd BH25 95 A1
Barton Dr
Barton on Sea BH25 126 C4
Overcombe/Preston DT3 153 A2
Barton Gdns DT9 29 C3
Barton Gn BH25 127 A3
Barton Heritage Collection* SP2 213 A3
Barton Hill
Kington Magna SP8 9 B2
Melbury Osmond DT2 194 A2
Shaftesbury SP7 12 C2
Barton Hill House Sch SP7 12 C2
Barton House BH25 126 C4
Barton La
Barton on Sea BH25 126 C4
Mere BA12 3 A3
Barton Lodge BH12 120 A3
Barton The DT2 205 A8
Barton Way BH25 126 C4
Barton Wood Rd BH25 126 C4
Bartonside Rd BH25 126 B4
Barwick CP Sch BA22 193 F8
Bascott Cl BH11 89 A1
Bascott Rd BH11 89 A1
Bashley Comm Rd BH25 95 A4
Bashley Cross Rd BH25 94 C3
Bashley Dr BH25 95 A3
Bashley Rd BH25 95 A3
Bassett Rd BH12 120 A3
Bastone Way BH22 61 A3
Bat Alley DT10 20 C1
Batchelor Cres BH11 88 C2
Batchelor Rd BH11 88 C2
Batchelor's La BH21 201 D1
Batchpool La BA8 8 A4
Batcombe Cl BH11 88 C2
Batcombe Rd DT9 194 F1
Bath Hill Ct 9 BH1 122 A2
Bath Orch 6 DT6 68 C1
Bath Rd
Bournemouth BH1 122 A2
Sturminster Newton DT10 35 A1
Bath St DT4 167 B2
Bathwell La DT9 17 B1
Bats La DT2 106 C1
Batten Cl BH23 124 B4
Batterley Dro BH21 41 A2
Battle Mead
Corfe Castle BH20 177 A4
Swanage BH19 179 A2
Batts La DT6 203 C2
Baunton's Orch DT9 17 B1
Bauntons Cl 10 DT9 17 B1
Baverstock Rd BH12 121 A4
Bay Cl Swanage BH19 179 B3
Three Legged Cross BH21 53 A4
Upton BH16 118 A3
Bay Cres BH19 179 A3
Bay Hog La BH15 119 A1
Bay La SP8 6 A1
Bay Rd SP8 5 C1
Bay Tree Way BH23 93 B1
Bay View 8 BH19 178 C1
Bayard Rd DT3 152 C1
Baycliffe Rd DT4 167 A1
Baydon Cl DT3 153 A2
Bayfran Way DT11 212 C2
Baynard's Rd DT1 107 B1
Bayview Rd DT7 96 A3
Beach Ave BH25 126 C4
Beach Cl BH13 147 D4
Beach Gdns BH19 179 A2
Beach Rd
Burton Bradstock DT6 128 B4
Poole BH13 147 D4
Studland BH19 164 B1
Upton BH16 118 A3
Beach View BH13 147 B2
Beachcroft BH13 121 A2
Beachview Cl 1 DT4 180 A4
Beacon Ct BH23 125 C4
Beacon Dr BH23 125 C4
Beacon Gdns BH18 86 C2
Beacon Hill La BH21 86 A2
Beacon Pk Cres BH16 118 A4
Beacon Pk Rd BH16 118 A4
Beacon Rd
Bournemouth BH2 121 C1
Broadstone BH18 86 C2
Upton BH16 118 A4
Beacon Way BH18 86 C2
Beaconfield Rd BA20 27 A1
Beaconsfield Rd
Christchurch BH23 124 A4
Poole BH12 120 B3
Beadon La TA16 191 E7
Beaminster Mus* DT8 204 D4
Beaminster Rd DT6 68 C1
Beaminster VC Comp Sch DT8 204 C4
Beamish Rd BH17 119 C4
Bear Cross Ave BH11 88 C3
Bearwood Prim Sch BH11 88 B3
Beatrice Rd SP1 213 B4
Beatty Cl BH24 55 C4
Beatty Rd BH9 90 A1
Beau Ct
31 Bournemouth BH4 121 B2
9 New Milton BH25 95 A2
Beauchamps Gdns BH7 123 A4
Beaucroft La BH21 59 C3
Beaucroft Rd BH21 59 C3
Beaucroft Sch BH21 59 C3
Beaufort Cl BH23 125 A4
Beaufort Dr BH21 59 B3
Beaufort Mews BH21 59 A2
Beaufort Rd BH6 123 B3
Beaufoy Cl SP7 13 A2
Beaufoys Ave BH22 61 B4
Beaufoys Cl BH22 61 B4
Beaufoys Ct BH22 61 B3
Beaulieu DT4 167 A3
Beaulieu Ave BH23 123 C4
Beaulieu Cl BH25 94 C2
Beaulieu Dr BA21 26 C3
Beaulieu Rd
Bournemouth BH4 121 A1
Christchurch BH23 123 C4
Beaumont Ave
Bridport DT6 100 B4
Radipole DT4 167 B3
Beaumont Rd BH13 147 C4
Beaver Ind Est BH23 125 A3
Beccles Cl BH15 118 C1
Becher Rd BH14 120 C2
Becket Way SP1 213 C3
Beckett Cl DT11 212 B1
Beckhampton Rd BH15 118 C2
Becklands La DT6 65 C2
Beckley Copse BH23 94 A1
Becton La BH25 127 A4
Becton Mead BH25 95 A1
Bedale Way BH15 119 C3
Bedford Cres BH7 123 B4
Bedford Pl DT6 100 B4
Bedford Rd
Salisbury SP2 213 A3
Weymouth DT4 167 A2
Yeovil BA21 27 C4
Bedford Rd N BH12 88 B1
Bedford Rd S BH12 88 B1
Bedford Terr DT6 100 B4
Bedwin St SP1 213 B3
Beech Ave
Bournemouth BH6 123 B2
Holton Heath BH20 116 A2
Beech Cl Alderholt SP6 42 B3
Broadmayne DT2 136 A1
Broadstone BH18 86 C2
1 Spetisbury DT11 211 E5
Verwood BH31 45 A3
West Lulworth BH20 172 B3
Beech Ct BH21 59 C2
Beech La
Hawkchurch EX13 202 B1
Netherbury DT8 204 A3
St.Leonards BH24 54 A1
Beech Rd
Puddletown DT2 78 A1
Radipole DT3 152 A2
Beech Tree Cl DT2 206 C2
Beech Wood Cl BH18 87 A2
Beechbank Ave BH17 86 C1
Beechcroft BH1 122 A3
Beechcroft Inf Sch DT4 167 B2
Beechcroft La 1 BH24 55 B
Beechcroft Mews 2 BH24 55 B
Beechcroft Rd SP1 213 C
Beeches The
Beaminster DT8 204 C
Bournemouth BH7 123 A
5 Salisbury SP1 213 C
1 Shaftesbury SP7 12 C
Wareham St Martin BH20 143 A
Beechey Ct 6 BH8 122 A
Beechey Rd BH8 122 A
Beechfield 30 BH4 121 B
Beechwood BA20 27 A
Beechwood Ave
Bournemouth BH5 122 C
New Milton BH25 94 C
Beechwood Ct BH2 121 C
Beechwood Dr 5 TA18 191 F
Beechwood Gdns BH5 123 A
Beechwood Rd BH22 53 A
Beel Cl 2 DT5 181 A
Beer St BA20 27 A
Belben Cl BH12 88 B
Belben Rd BH12 88 B
Belfield Pk Ave DT4 167 A
Belfield Rd BH6 124 A
Belgrave DT4 167 A
Belgrave Ct BH1 122 B
Belgrave Pl 3 DT5 186 C
Belgrave Rd BH13 121 A
Bell Heather Cl BH16 118 A
Bell La 18 BH15 119 A
Bell St Shaftesbury SP7 12 C
Swanage BH19 178 C
Bellamy La SP1 213 B3
Bell's Orch La BH20 142 C
Bellbury Cl 1 DT2 78 A1
Belle Vue DT4 167 C1
Belle Vue Cl BH6 123 B2
Belle Vue Cres BH6 123 C2
Belle Vue Gdns 2 BH6 123 C2
Belle Vue Gr BH22 53 A1
Belle Vue Mans 7 BH6 123 C2
Belle Vue Rd
Bournemouth BH6 123 C2
Poole BH14 120 B2
4 Salisbury SP1 213 B3
Swanage BH19 179 B1
Weymouth DT4 167 B1
Belle Vue Terr 15 DT5 186 C4
Belle Vue Wlk BH22 61 C1
Bellflower Cl BH23 125 A4
Bellman's Cross BA8 19 B3
Bellows Cross BH21 40 B4
Bells House BH21 59 B3
Bells La BA12 1 C4
Belmont Ave BH8 90 B1
Belmont Cl
Shaftesbury SP7 12 C1
Verwood BH31 45 B3
Belmont Rd
New Milton BH25 95 B2
Poole BH14 120 B3
Belmour Lodge 26 BH4 121 B2
Belvedere Rd
Bournemouth BH3 122 A3
Christchurch BH23 124 A4
7 Swanage BH19 179 B1
Yeovil BA21 28 A3
Bembury La DT9 194 D8
Bemister Rd BH9 122 A4
Ben Nevis Rd DT4 167 B1
Benbow Cres BH12 88 C1
Benbridge Ave BH11 88 C3
Bendigo Rd BH23 123 C4
Benellen Ave BH4 121 B2
Benellen Gdns BH4 121 B2
Benellen Rd BH4 121 B3
Benellen Twrs BH4 121 B2
Bengal Rd BH9 121 C4
Benjamin Ct BH23 123 C4
Benjamin Rd BH15 118 C1
Benlease Way BH19 178 C1
Benmoor Rd BH17 119 A4
Benmore Cl BH25 95 B1
Benmore Rd BH9 90 A1
Bennett House 11 BH4 121 B2
Bennett Rd BH8 122 B3
Bennett's Alley 22 BH15 119 A1
Bennetts Hill La DT6 101 B1
Bennion Rd BH10 89 B2
Benridge Cl BH18 87 A2
Benson Rd BH17 119 B4
Bentley Rd BH9 89 C2
Benville La DT2 205 C6
Benville Manor* DT2 205 C6
Benville Rd DT4 166 C1
Bere Cl BH17 87 B1
Bere Down La BH20 80 C3
Bere La DT9 195 F7
Bere Marsh DT11 198 B7
Bere Rd
Northport BH20 142 B3
Winterborne Kingston DT11 81 C4
Bere Regis Cty Fst Sch BH20 81 A1
Bere Regis Sports Club BH20 81 B2
Beresford Cl BH12 120 B3
Beresford Gdns BH23 124 C3
Beresford Rd
Bournemouth BH6 123 A2
Poole BH12 120 B3
Berkeley Ave BH12 120 B4

Berkeley Cl
9 Pimperne DT11 ...199 D4
Verwood BH31 ...45 A4
Berkeley Ct DT6 ...100 B3
Berkeley Rd
Bournemouth BH3 ...121 C4
Berkeley Rise 8 DT11 ...199 D4
Berkley Ave BH21 ...61 B1
Berkshire Rd SP2 ...213 A2
Bermuda Ct 9 BH21 ...126 A4
Bernards Ct BH23 ...123 C4
Berne Ct 11 BH1 ...122 A2
Beron Ct BH15 ...119 C2
Berrans Ave BH11 ...89 A3
Berrans Ct BH11 ...89 A3
Berry La EX13 ...202 D3
Bertram Rd BH25 ...95 B2
Berwick La DT6 ...129 B3
Berwick Rd BH1 ...87 A2
Berwyn Ct BH18 ...87 A2
Bessborough Rd
BH13 ...147 C4
Bessells La DT11 ...198 D8
Bessemer Ct BH31 ...45 C2
Bestwall Cres BH20 ...142 C2
Bestwall Rd BH20 ...142 C2
Beswick Ave BH10 ...89 B1
Bethany Ct BH12 ...121 A4
Bethany House BH1 ...122 B3
Bethany Jun CE Sch
BH1 ...122 B3
Bethia Cl BH8 ...122 B3
Bethia Rd BH8 ...122 B3
Bettiscombe Manor House*
DT6 ...203 B3
Beverley Gdns BH10 ...89 B2
Beverley Grange 25
BH4 ...121 B2
Beverley Rd DT3 ...152 B2
Bexington Cl BH11 ...88 C2
Bickerley Gdns BH24 ...55 A3
Bickerley Rd BH24 ...55 A3
Bicknell Boys Sch
BH7 ...123 A4
Bicknell Cl 10 BH4 ...121 B2
Bicknell Gdns BA21 ...27 B4
Bicton Rd BH10 ...89 A2
Biddlecombe Orch 5
DT6 ...100 B4
Big Ope DT5 ...186 C4
Bilshay La DT6 ...68 A1
Bimport SP7 ...12 B1
Bincleaves Rd DT4 ...167 B1
Bincombe Dr 2 TA18 ...191 F5
Bincombe Rise DT3 ...152 C2
Bindbarrow Rd DT6 ...128 B3
Bindells The DT3 ...166 B3
Bindon Abbey (rems of)*
BH20 ...140 B1
Bindon Cl Poole BH12 ...120 C4
West Lulworth BH20 ...172 C4
Bindon La BH20 ...140 B1
Bindon Rd BH20 ...172 B3
Bindon Way BH20 ...140 A1
Bingham Ave BH14 ...147 B4
Bingham Cl
Christchurch BH23 ...124 C4
Verwood BH31 ...45 B2
Bingham Dr BH31 ...45 B2
Bingham Rd
Bournemouth BH9 ...122 A4
Christchurch BH23 ...124 C4
Salisbury SP1 ...213 C4
Westward BH31 ...45 B2
Binghams Rd DT2 ...137 B3
Binnegar La BH20 ...141 B2
Binnie Rd BH12 ...120 C3
Birch Ave
3 Blandford St Mary
DT11 ...212 B1
Burton BH23 ...92 B2
Ferndown BH22 ...61 C1
Holton Heath BH20 ...116 A2
New Milton BH25 ...94 B3
Birch Cl
Corfe Mullen BH21 ...86 B3
Poole BH14 ...120 C2
St.Leonards BH24 ...53 C2
Birch Dr BH8 ...91 A1
Birch Gr Ferndown BH22 ...52 C1
New Milton BH25 ...95 A1
Birch La Puddletown DT2 ...77 C2
Yetminster DT9 ...194 C5
Birch Rd BH24 ...54 B2
Birchdale 6 BA20 ...26 C1
Birchdale Rd BH23 ...59 B3
Birchfield Prim Sch
BA21 ...27 C4
Birchfield Rd BA21 ...27 C4
Birchwood Cl BH23 ...125 C4
Birchwood Dr SP6 ...42 B3
Birchwood Mews
BH14 ...120 B2
Birchwood Rd
Poole BH14 ...120 B2
Upton BH16 ...118 A3
Bird's Cl 5 BH18 ...191 E4
Bird's Hill Rd BH15 ...119 C2
Birds Hill Gdns 5 BH15 ...119 C2
Birkdale Ct BH18 ...87 A3
Birkdale Rd BH18 ...87 A3
Bishop Cl BH12 ...121 B4
Bishop Ct BH24 ...55 B4
Bishop Rd BH9 ...122 A4

Bishop Wordsworths Sch
SP1 ...213 B2
Bishop's La DT9 ...28 B1
Bishop's Palace* SP1 ...213 B2
Bishop's Rd
Abbotsbury DT3 ...149 B4
Portesham DT3 ...131 B1
Bishopdown Rd SP1 ...213 B4
Bishops Cl
Abbotsbury DT3 ...149 B4
Bournemouth BH7 ...122 C4
Mere BA12 ...3 A3
Bishops Dr SP2 ...213 A1
Bishops La BA12 ...193 A6
Bitchams Mead BH20 ...81 A1
Bitterne Way BH31 ...45 B3
Black Hill BH31 ...45 B3
Black La DT11 ...212 C2
Black Lawn SP8 ...5 C2
Black Mere BA12 ...26 B3
Black Moor Rd BH31 ...45 C2
Blackberry La
Christchurch BH23 ...124 C3
Radipole DT3 ...152 B1
Sherborne DT9 ...30 A4
Blackbird Cl BH17 ...118 C4
Blackbird Way BH23 ...93 B4
Blackbirds 6 DT9 ...194 D8
Blackbird Way BH21 ...120 A3
Blackers Hole (Cave)*
BH19 ...184 B3
Blackfield La BH22 ...53 A2
Blackfield Rd BH8 ...90 B2
Blackfriars Way SP1 ...213 B2
Blackhill Rd BH16 ...116 B2
Blackhill Rd W BH16 ...116 B1
Blacklands La DT11 ...197 D3
Blackmoor BA8 ...19 A3
Blackmoor La BA8 ...19 A2
Blackmore Rd
Shaftesbury SP7 ...13 A2
Stalbridge DT10 ...33 B4
Blacknell La TA18 ...191 F4
Blackney La DT6 ...203 C2
Blacksmith Cl DT2 ...135 C1
Blacknor Rd DT5 ...186 C2
Blackpool Cnr DT6 ...202 B1
Blackrow La DT10 ...196 D7
Blacksmith Cl BH21 ...86 B3
Blacksmith's Piece
DT2 ...105 B1
Blackthorn Way
New Milton BH25 ...95 B2
Verwood BH31 ...45 B3
Blackwater Dr BH21 ...87 B4
Blackwater Gr SP6 ...42 A3
Blackwater La EX13 ...202 C3
Bladen View DT1 ...79 C4
Bladon Cl BH21 ...121 A3
Blagdon Rd DT1 ...107 B1
Blair Ave BH14 ...120 B2
Blair Cl BH25 ...94 C2
Blake Dene Rd BH14 ...120 A1
Blake Hill Ave BH14 ...120 B1
Blake Hill Cres BH14 ...120 B1
Blake 22 TA18 ...191 F4
Blakey Rd SP1 ...213 C2
Blandford Cl BH15 ...118 C1
Blandford Hill
Milborne St Andrew DT11 ...79 C4
Winterborne Whitechurch
DT11 ...210 C3
Blandford Hospl DT11 ...212 B2
Blandford Rd
Corfe Mullen BH21 ...86 B4
Hamworthy BH15 ...118 B2
Iwerne Minster DT11 ...37 C1
Pamphill DT11 ...58 B4
Shapwick DT11 ...48 C1
Shillingstone DT11 ...198 B6
Sturminster Marshall
BH21 ...56 B2
Blandford Rd N
Lytchett Minster & Upton
BH16 ...85 A1
Upton BH16 ...118 A4
Blandford Sports Ctr
DT11 ...212 B2
Blandford St Mary CE VA Fst
Sch DT11 ...212 B1
Blandford VC Comp Sch The
DT11 ...212 B2
Blaney Way DT11 ...86 B3
Blanford Hts Ind Est
DT11 ...212 B3
Bleak St BA9 ...1 B2
Bleax Cl SP7 ...22 C1
Bleet La SP8 ...10 B3
Blemheim Rd DT3 ...152 A1
Blenheim Cres SO41 ...95 C2
Blenheim Ct
25 Bournemouth BH4 ...121 B2
Blenheim Dr BH23 ...124 A4
Blenheim Rd BA21 ...27 C4
Blind La
Berwick St John SP7 ...188 B8
Elsingham Harbridge & Ibsley
SP6 ...43 C1
Evershot DT2 ...206 B7
Marshwood DT6 ...203 D1
Thorncombe TA20 ...202 E6

Blind La continued
Wimborne Minster BH21 ...59 A3
Blind La Ct DT6 ...68 C1
Blind St BH20 ...81 A1
Blindmere Rd DT5 ...186 C2
Blissford Hill SP6 ...43 C3
Bloody Shard Gate
DT11 ...188 A1
Bloomfield Ave BH1 ...89 C1
Bloomfield Pl BH1 ...89 C1
Bloxworth Rd BH12 ...120 C4
Blue Boar Row SP1 ...213 B3
Bluebell Cl BH18 ...87 C3
Bluebell La BA22 ...26 B3
Bluntshay La DT6 ...66 C4
Blyth Cl SP1 ...213 B2
Blyth Way SP1 ...213 C4
Blythe Rd BH21 ...86 C1
Blythswood Ct BH25 ...126 C4
Boar St BA12 ...3 A3
Bob Hann Cl SP6 ...42 B3
Bockhampton Cross
DT2 ...109 A2
Bockhampton La DT2 ...109 A2
Bockhampton Rd DT2 ...92 C3
Bodkin La DT3 ...168 A3
Bodley Rd BH13 ...147 C4
Bodorgan Rd BH2 ...121 C2
Bodowen Cl BH23 ...92 B1
Bodowen Rd BH23 ...92 B1
Bodsmarsh La DT10 ...21 C1
Bognor Rd BH18 ...86 C2
Bohay's Dr DT4 ...180 A4
Bokerley Ditch* SP6 ...190 A5
Boldre Cl
Barton on Sea BH25 ...126 B4
Poole BH12 ...120 B4
Boleyn Cl BH9 ...90 A2
Boley Cres DT4 ...180 C4
Bolton Cl BH6 ...123 C2
Bolton Cres BH22 ...62 A3
Bolton Ct 4 BH2 ...123 C2
Bolton Rd BH6 ...123 C2
Bon Accord Rd BH19 ...179 A1
Bond Ave BH22 ...52 C2
Bond Rd BH15 ...119 C3
Bond St Radipole DT4 ...167 B2
4 Yeovil BA20 ...27 B2
Boney Rd BH20 ...108 A1
Bonfields Ave BH19 ...179 A2
Bonham La BA12 ...1 C1
Bonham Rd BH21 ...121 C4
Bonhole La DT6 ...101 C2
Bonington Cl BH23 ...124 C2
Bonnington Cl BH23 ...142 C2
Bonscombe La DT6 ...101 B3
Bonvils Rd BH19 ...183 A4
Bonham La DT2 ...208 B7
Boot La 7 DT9 ...194 D8
Boozer Pit TA16 ...191 F8
Border Dr BH16 ...118 B3
Border Lodge ...94 B1
Border Rd BH16 ...118 B3
Boreham Rd BH23 ...123 B3
Borley Rd BH17 ...119 A4
Borthwick Rd BH1 ...122 C3
Boscombe Cliff Rd
BH5 ...122 C2
Boscombe Gr Rd BH1 ...122 B3
Boscombe Overcliff Dr
BH5 ...123 A2
Boscombe Spa Rd
BH5 ...122 B2
Bosley Cl BH23 ...91 C1
Bosley Way BH23 ...91 C1
Boston Lodge 22 BH4 ...121 B2
Boswell's Ct BH20 ...81 A2
Bosworth Mews BH9 ...90 A2
Botham Dr BH9 ...100 C3
Bottlebush La DT11 ...190 B2
Bottom Dr BH14 ...120 C2
Bouchers Way SP2 ...213 B1
Boulnois Ave BH14 ...120 C2
Boulton Cl DT4 ...180 B4
Bound La DT9 ...194 F2
Boundary Ave BA22 ...26 B4
Boundary Cl
Swanage BH19 ...185 B4
Yeovil BA21 ...27 A4
Boundary Dr DT11 ...59 B3
Boundary La BH24 ...53 C1
Boundary Rd
Bournemouth BH10 ...89 C1
Salisbury SP2 ...213 C2
Yeovil BA22 ...26 B3
Boundary View 1 DT11 ...212 B2
Bountys La BH12 ...120 C3
Bourne Ave
Bournemouth BH2 ...121 C2
Salisbury SP1 ...213 C3
Bourne Cl
24 Bournemouth BH2 ...121 C2
Wimborne Minster DT11 ...59 B3
Bourne Dr BH21 ...59 B3
Bourne Pit DT10 ...76 C3
Bourne Hill SP1 ...213 B3
Bourne Pines 3 BH1 ...121 C2
Bourne Valley Rd
BH12 ...121 A3
Bourne Way
Gillingham SP8 ...5 C2
Salisbury SP1 ...213 C3
Bournemouth & Poole Coll of
F Ed BH21 ...119 C2

Bournemouth & Poole Coll
The BH1 ...122 A2
Bournemouth Aquarium*
BH2 ...121 C1
Bournemouth Aviation Mus*
BH23 ...91 A1
Bournemouth Central Bsns
Pk BH1 ...122 B3
Bournemouth Crown & City
Cts* BH7 ...91 B1
Bournemouth Gram Sch
(Boys) BH8 ...90 B1
Bournemouth Gram Sch
(Girls) BH8 ...90 B1
Bournemouth Int Airport
...90 C4
Bournemouth Int Ctr*
BH2 ...90 C4
Bournemouth Rd
Blandford St Mary DT11 ...212 B1
Charlton Marshall DT11 ...211 D6
Poole BH14 ...120 B2
Bournemouth Sta
BH1 ...122 A2
Bournemouth Univ
BH12 ...121 B4
Bournewood Dr BH4 ...121 B2
Bourton Gdns BH7 ...123 A4
Bourton Prim Sch SP8 ...1 C1
Bouverie Ave SP2 ...213 B1
Bouverie Ave S SP2 ...213 A1
Bouverie Cl
22 Barton on Sea BH25 ...95 A1
Salisbury SP2 ...213 A1
Boveridge Gdns BH9 ...90 A2
Boveridge House Sch
BH21 ...190 B1
Bovington Cl BH17 ...87 C1
Bovington Fst Sch
BH20 ...139 B3
Bovington La BH20 ...139 C3
Bovington Mid Sch
BH20 ...139 B3
Bow The 3 DT1 ...108 A1
Bowden La BA8 ...18 B3
Bowden Rd
Abbas & Templecombe
BA8 ...18 A4
Poole BH12 ...88 B1
Bowditch Row 22 TA18 ...191 F4
Bowdowns DT6 ...68 B2
Bower Cl 6 DT9 ...194 C5
Bower Gdns SP1 ...213 C2
Bower Hill Rd SP1 ...213 C3
Bower Rd BH8 ...122 B4
Bowers Rd 6 DT5 ...186 C4
Bowerswain Hollow
BH21 ...201 B5
Bowerwood Rd SP6 ...42 C4
Bowes La 6 DT9 ...204 A8
Bowey 8 DT11 ...197 F6
Bowgrove Rd DT8 ...200 D5
Bowhayes Bridport DT6 ...100 C3
6 Crewkerne TA18 ...191 F4
Bowland Rise BH25 ...95 B1
Bowleaze BA21 ...26 C3
Bowleaze Coveway
DT3 ...168 A3
Bowling Gn La SP5 ...189 D5
Bown Hill DT5 ...186 C1
Box Cl BH17 ...119 A4
Box Rd BH12 ...120 C3
Boyle Cl DT10 ...33 B4
Boyne's La
Iwerne Stepleton DT11 ...38 B1
Iwerne Stepleton DT11 ...199 B7
Boys Hill Dro DT9 ...195 B8
Boyte Rd 10 DT11 ...199 D4
Bozley Hill SP7 ...24 A4
Brabazon Dr BH23 ...125 A4
Brabazon Rd BH21 ...59 C1
Brabourne Ave BH7 ...62 A2
Bracken Cl BH22 ...53 C2
Bracken Glen BH15 ...119 C3
Bracken Lodge 3 BH6 ...123 C2
Bracken Rd
Bournemouth BH6 ...123 B2
Ferndown BH22 ...61 A4
Bracken Way BH23 ...94 A1
Brackenbury Cty Infs Sch
DT5 ...186 C4
Brackendale Cl BH21 ...52 C4
Brackendale Rd BH8 ...122 B4
Brackendown Ave
DT3 ...167 C4
Brackenhill BH13 ...121 A1
Brackenhill Rd BH21 ...60 A4
Brackens Way 8 BH13 ...147 C4
Brackley Ct BH23 ...91 A4
Bradbourne Rd BH2 ...121 C2
Bradford Abbas Prim Sch
DT9 ...29 B1
Bradford La DT9 ...195 B6
Bradford Rd
3 Bournemouth BH9 ...90 B2
6 Crewkerne TA18 ...192 A3
Sherborne DT9 ...29 C3
Weymouth DT4 ...167 A1
Bradpole Rd BH8 ...122 B4
Bradstock Cl DT4 ...120 C4
Braemar Ave BH6 ...124 A2
Braemar Cl BH6 ...124 A2
Braemar Dr BH23 ...93 C1
Braemar Rd DT1 ...135 B4

Braemar Rise SP1 ...213 B4
Braeside Rd
Ferndown BH22 ...53 A2
St.Leonards BH24 ...54 A2
Braidley Rd BH2 ...121 C2
Brailswood Rd BH15 ...119 C2
Braishfield Gdns BH8 ...90 B1
Brakes Hill DT2 ...194 A4
Bramar Ct BH4 ...121 B1
Bramble Cl SP6 ...62 B2
Bramble Ct BH22 ...53 A1
Bramble Dro DT6 ...100 B1
Bramble Dro DT2 ...136 A1
Bramble Edge DT2 ...136 A1
Bramble La
Christchurch BH23 ...94 A1
Haselbury Plucknett
TA18 ...192 C5
Bramblecombe La
DT11 ...209 D2
Brambles The SP1 ...213 C3
Brambling Cl DT3 ...152 B2
Bramdon Cl 6 DT3 ...150 A4
Bramdon La DT3 ...150 B3
Bramley Cl 8 TA18 ...191 F5
Bramley Ct BH22 ...61 B3
Bramley Hill
Bridport DT6 ...100 C3
Mere BA12 ...2 C3
Bramley Rd
Bournemouth BH10 ...89 B3
Ferndown BH22 ...61 B3
Brampton Rd BH15 ...119 B3
Bramshaw Gdns BH8 ...90 B2
Bramshaw Way BH25 ...126 B4
Branders Cl BH6 ...124 A3
Branders La BH6 ...124 A3
Brandwood Ct 4 BH14 ...120 A2
Brandy Row 8 DT5 ...186 C4
Branksea Ave BH15 ...118 C1
Branksea Cl BH15 ...118 C1
Branksome Cl BH25 ...95 A1
Branksome Ct 18 BH13 ...147 C4
Branksome Dene Rd
BH4 ...121 A1
Branksome Heath Mid Sch
BH12 ...120 B3
Branksome Hill Rd
BH4 ...121 A3
Branksome Sta BH12 ...120 C2
Branksome Twrs
BH13 ...147 D4
Branksome Wood Gdns
BH12 ...121 B2
Branksome Wood Rd
BH12 ...121 B2
Branscombe Cl 1 BH6 ...186 C1
Bransgore CE Prim Sch
BH23 ...93 B4
Brantwood 8 DT8 ...204 C4
Branwell Cl BH23 ...92 A1
Brassey Cl BH9 ...90 A2
Brassey Rd BH9 ...90 A1
Brassey Terr BH9 ...89 C1
Bratch La DT11 ...200 D1
Breach Cl SP8 ...1 C1
Breach Field BH20 ...140 A1
Breach La
Kington Magna SP8 ...9 B2
Shaftesbury SP7 ...12 B1
Breaches La BH20 ...163 A1
Bready Cl BH25 ...94 C2
Brearley Ct BH23 ...126 A4
Brecon Cl
Bournemouth BH10 ...89 C3
New Milton BH25 ...95 B1
Bredy Cl BH17 ...87 C1
Bredy Ct BH12 ...101 C1
Bredy Rd DT6 ...128 B1
Bremble Cl BH12 ...88 B1
Brendon Cl BH8 ...90 C1
Breston Cl 5 DT5 ...186 C1
Brian Cl BH23 ...143 C4
Briar Cl
Christchurch BH23 ...124 C3
Gillingham SP8 ...5 C1
Mudford BA21 ...27 A4
Poole BH15 ...119 C3
Radipole DT4 ...167 A3
Briar Way DT11 ...60 A3
Briarfield 28 BH4 ...121 B2
Briars End DT2 ...137 C3
Briars La 3 BA20 ...26 C1
Briarswood Rd BH16 ...118 B4
Brick Yd La 4 TA18 ...191 F5
Brickyard La Bourton SP8 ...1 C1
Broadstone BH21 ...58 A1
6 Gillingham SP8 ...6 A1
1 Gillingham SP8 ...5 C1
Silton SP8 ...10 C4
Sturminster Newton
DT10 ...197 A7
Swanage BH19 ...179 A3
Bridewell La SP7 ...7 A2
Bridge App BH15 ...119 C1
Bridge Cl SP8 ...5 B2
Bridge Inn La DT3 ...153 B2
Bridge Pl BH10 ...89 B4
Bridge Rd DT6 ...97 A4
Bridge St Bourton SP8 ...1 C1
Christchurch BH23 ...124 B3
6 Lyme Regis DT7 ...96 B3
Netherbury DT6 ...204 C2

Bridge St continued
Salisbury SP2 ....213 B2
Sturminster Marshall
BH21 ....56 B2
Sturminster Newton
DT10 ....197 D8
Bridges Cl BH22 ....53 A2
Bridges The BH24 ....55 A4
Bridgewater Rd BH12 ....120 B3
Bridle Cl BH16 ....118 B4
Bridle Cres BH7 ....123 B4
Bridle Way
Stofold BA22 ....193 F8
Wimborne Minster BH21 ...60 B3
Bridlebank Way DT3 ......152 A2
Bridmans Rd BH31 ....45 A3
Bridport & W Dorset Golf
Club DT6 ....100 B1
Bridport Com Hospl
DT6 ....100 A4
Bridport CP Sch DT6 .....100 C4
Bridport Leisure Ctr
DT6 ....100 B3
Bridport Rd
Beaminster DT8 ....204 D3
Broadwindsor DT8 ....203 C8
Dorchester DT1 ....107 B1
Poole BH12 ....120 C4
Verwood BH31 ....45 A3
Brierley Ave BH22 ....61 C1
Brierley Cl BH7 ....89 C3
Brierley Hay █ DT9 ......194 C5
Brierley Rd BH10 ....89 C2
Brigadier Cl BA22 ....26 B3
Bright Rd BH15 ....119 B3
Brighthay La DT6 ....67 A1
Brightlands Ave BH6 ....123 C3
Brightsmead DT2 ....209 B6
Brimclose Rd TA17 ....191 B7
Brimley Hill EX13 ....202 A2
Brimley Rd EX13 ....202 A3
Brimscombe La █ SP7 .....13 A1
Brinsley Cl DT10 ....35 A1
Brinsons Cl BH23 ....92 B2
Brionne Way SP7 ....13 A2
Brisbane Rd
Christchurch BH23 ....91 C1
Radipole DT3 ....152 C1
Brister End DT9 ....194 C5
Bristol Rd DT9 ....30 A4
Brit The █ DT8 ....204 D4
Brit View Rd DT6 ....100 A1
Britannia Cl BH12 ....120 A4
Britannia Rd BH14 ....120 A2
Britannia Way
Christchurch BH23 ....125 A4
Dorchester DT1 ....134 C4
Britford La SP2 ....213 B1
Britford La W █ SP2 .....213 B1
Britford Prim Sch
SPS 213 C1
Britmore La SP7 ....13 C4
Brixey Cl BH12 ....120 B4
Brixey Rd BH12 ....120 B4
Brixey's La BH20 ....142 C2
Broad Ave BH8 ....122 B4
Broad Cl BH17 ....81 C4
Broad Hill BA22 ....192 D7
Broad La Bridport DT6 ...100 A3
East Chinnock BA22 ......192 E7
Broad Mead Rd BH21 ......45 A1
Broad Rd BH19 ....179 B1
Broad Robin █ SP8 ....5 C1
Broad St DT7 ....96 B3
Broad Stone The*
DT2 ....104 C1
Broadacres
East Coker BA22 ....193 C8
Gillingham SP8 ....5 C2
Broadcroft Gdns DT5 .....187 A2
Broadhill La SP6 ....43 C4
Broadhurst Ave BH10 .....89 C2
Broadlands Ave BH6 .....123 C2
Broadlands Cl
Bournemouth BH8 ....90 B2
Christchurch BH23 ....94 A1
Broadlands Rd DT3 ....152 A1
Broadleaze BA21 ....26 C3
Broadmayne Cty Fst Sch
DT2 ....136 B2
Broadmayne Rd BH12 .....121 A4
Broadmead DT2 ....136 A1
Broadmere Ave DT6 ......100 B4
Broadmead Cl █ DT8 .....204 A8
Broadmeadow Rd
DT4 ....180 B4
Broadmoor Rd BH21 ......204 A7
Broadoak Ave █ DT8 .....204 A7
Broadoak Rd DT6 ....67 C1
Broads The BH21 ....58 C3
Broadshard La BH24 ......47 B1
Broadshard Rd TA18 .....191 F5
Broadstone Fst Sch
BH18 ....87 A2
Broadstone La
Hardington Mandeville
BA22 ....193 A6
West Chinnock TA18 ......192 C8
Broadstone Mid Sch
BH18 ....86 C1
Broadstone Rd BH18 .....86 C1
Broadwater Ave BH14 ....120 B1
Broadway
Bournemouth BH6 ....124 A2

Broadway continued
Merriott TA16 ....191 E7
Broadway Ct BH12 ....121 A3
Broadway Gables
BH14 ....120 C2
Broadway Gdns █ SP1 .....59 B2
Broadway La
Bournemouth BH6 ....90 B2
West Chinnock BA22 ......192 D8
Broadway Mews BH14 ....119 C2
Broadway Pk █ BH12 ......59 B2
Broadway The BH10 ......89 B3
Broadwey Cl DT3 ....152 B2
Broadwindsor CE Prim Sch
DT8 ....203 E5
Broadwindsor Craft & Design
Ctr* DT8 ....203 E5
Broadwindsor Rd DT8 ....204 B4
Brockenhurst Rd BH7 ....90 A1
Brockhills La BH25 ......93 B3
Brockhole La TA17 ......191 B8
Brockington La BH21 ....201 C5
Brockley Rd BH10 ....89 C2
Brocks Pine DT4 ....54 A2
Brodham Way DT11 ......198 B5
Brog St BH21 ....58 B1
Broke La DT9 ....195 B6
Brombys The █ BH15 .....119 C3
Bromley House BH21 .....121 A3
Bronte Ave BH23 ....92 A2
Brook Ave BH25 ....95 A2
Brook Dr BH31 ....45 B2
Brook Cl BH10 ....89 B2
Brook La
Bransgore BH23 ....93 A4
Corfe Mullen BH21 ....86 B3
Henstridge BA8 ....19 A2
Woodlands BH21 ....44 A4
Brook Rd
Bournemouth BH10 ....89 B2
Poole BH12 ....120 B3
Wimborne Minster BH21 ..59 C2
Brook St
Milborne Port DT9 ....17 B1
Shipton Gorge DT6 ......101 B2
Brook Terr SP6 ....43 A4
Brook Way BH23 ....125 B4
Brookdale Cl BH17 ....87 A2
Brookdale Farm BH18 ....87 A2
Brookhouse St █ DT1 ...107 B1
Brookland Way █ BA8 ....19 A2
Brooklands BH21 ....121 A2
Brooklyn Ct BH25 ....94 C2
Brookmead Cl DT3 ......153 B2
Brooks Cl BH24 ....55 B3
Brookside
Ellingham Harbridge & Ibsley
SP6 ....43 C1
█ Gillingham SP8 ....5 C2
Milborne Port DT9 ......129 B3
West Coker BA22 ....193 A8
Brookside Cl DT3 ....168 B4
Brookside Pk Homes
BH21 ....86 A2
Brookside Rd
Bransgore BH23 ....93 A4
Wimborne Minster BH21 ..59 C2
Brookside Way BH23 .....93 C1
Broom Hill DT2 ....205 F5
Broom Rd BH12 ....88 B1
Broomfield Cl BH22 .....61 C3
Broomfield Dr SP6 ....82 B3
Broughton Ave BH10 .....89 C2
Broughton Cl BH10 ......89 C2
Broughton Cres DT1 ....180 B4
Broughtons Dr █ TA18 ...192 A3
Brown St
Bishop's Caundle DT9 ...196 A7
█ Salisbury SP1 ....213 B3
Brown's Cres DT3 ....166 C3
Brown's La SP8 ....10 C2
Brownen Rd BH9 ....122 A4
Brownes Pl DT2 ....73 C2
Browning Ave BH5 ......123 A2
Browning Rd BH12 ......120 B3
Brownlow Ct █ BH44 ....121 B2
Brownlow St DT4 ....167 B2
Browns La SP6 ....190 E3
Brownsea Ave BH23 ......86 B3
Brownsea Cl BH25 ....94 C2
Brownsea Island (NT)*
BH15 ....147 A4
Brownsea Rd BH13 ......147 A2
Brownsea View Ave
BH14 ....120 B1
Brownsea View Cl
BH14 ....120 B1
Brudenell Ave BH13 ....147 B4
Brudenell Rd BH13 .....147 B3
Brune Way BH22 ....61 B2
Brunel Cl BH31 ....45 C2
Brunel Dr DT3 ....153 A2
Brunsell's Knap DT10 ...33 A1
Brunstead Pl BH12 .....121 A2
Brunstead Rd BH12 .....121 A2
Brunswick St BA20 ......27 B2
Brushy Bush La SP5 .....188 F3
Brutus Cl DT1 ....134 C4
Bryanston Pk* DT11 ....212 A2
Bryanston Sch DT11 ....212 A3
Bryanston St DT11 .....212 B2
Bryanstone Rd BH3 .....121 C4
Bryant Rd BH12 ....121 A4
Bryants La DT4 ....180 A4
Brymer Rd
█ Puddletown DT2 ....78 A1

Brymer Rd continued
Puddletown DT2 ....110 A4
Brymers Ave █ DT5 ......186 C4
Brympton Ave BA22 ......26 A2
Brympton Way BA22 .....26 C2
Bryn Rd Sandford BH20 ..143 A4
Weymouth DT4 ....167 A1
Bryony Cl BH18 ....86 C2
Bryony Gdns SP8 ....5 B1
Bub La BH23 ....124 C3
Buccaneers Cl BH23 ....124 C3
Buccleuch Rd BH13 .....121 A1
Bucehayes Cl BH23 .....126 A4
Buchanan Ave BH7 ......122 C3
Buckhill Ct █ TA18 .....191 F3
Buckhorn Cl DT6 ....69 A4
Buckingham Ct
█ Christchurch BH23 ....126 A4
Poole BH15 ....119 B2
Buckingham Mans █
BH1 ....122 A2
Buckingham Rd
Gillingham SP8 ....5 C1
Poole BH12 ....120 B3
Buckingham Way DT1 ...133 B4
Buckingham Wlk BH25 ...94 C2
Buckland Gr BH21 ....93 C1
Buckland Newton Prim Sch
DT2 ....208 A8
Buckland Rd
Poole BH12 ....120 B3
Yeovil BA21 ....28 A3
Buckland Terr DT2 ......120 B3
Buckle Pl DT2 ....54 A2
Bucklers Mead █ DT9 ...194 C5
Bucklers Mead Rd
BA21 ....27 C4
Bucklers Mead Sch
BA21 ....27 C4
Bucklers Way BH8 ....90 B2
Buckthorn Cl DT4 ....167 A1
Buddens La SP7 ....23 C2
Buddle Hill SP6 ....43 C2
Buddleia Cl DT3 ....152 C1
Budmouth Ave DT3 ......168 A3
Budmouth Sch DT4 ......168 C4
Buffalo Mews BH15 .....119 A1
Buffetts Rd DT10 ....35 A1
Bugdens La BH31 ....45 B3
Bugway La TA20 ....202 B8
Bulbury Woods Golf Club
BH16 ....115 C4
Bull Bridge Mead
BA22 ....193 D3
Bull Cl DT2 ....106 C4
Bull Gd La DT10 ....35 B1
Bull La
Maiden Newton DT2 ......72 C4
█ Poole BH15 ....119 B1
Pucknowle DT2 ....129 B3
Bull's Way BH8 ....90 A2
Buller's Way DT2 ....148 C3
Bullfinch Cl BH17 ....86 C1
Bullocks La DT11 ......197 A1
Bulls La █ TA18 ....191 E4
Bumpers La DT5 ....187 A2
Bunford La BA20 ....26 C2
Bunting Rd BH22 ....61 A4
Burbidge Cl BH16 ......84 B1
Burbitt La DT2 ....101 B2
Burbridge Cl BH17 .....119 C4
Burcombe Rd BH10 .....89 B3
Burdens █ DT12 ....197 A4
Burdock Cl BH23 ....93 A1
Bure Cl BH23 ....125 A3
Bure Haven Dr BH23 ....125 A3
Bure Homage Gdns
BH23 ....125 A3
Bure Homage La
BH23 ....125 A3
Bure La BH23 ....125 A3
Bure Pk BH23 ....125 A3
Bure Rd BH23 ....125 A3
Burford Ave SP2 ....213 B1
Burford Cl BH23 ....91 B1
Burford Ct █ BH11 ......122 A2
Burford Rd SP2 ....213 B1
Burges Cl DT10 ....20 C2
Burgess Cl BH11 ....88 C2
Burgess Field BH21 .....44 B3
Burgess Gn SP2 ....213 C4
Burleigh Rd BH6 ....123 B3
Burlestone Dro DT2 .....78 C1
Burley Cl
Barton on Sea BH25 ....126 B4
Verwood BH31 ....45 A3
Burley Rd
Bransgore BH23 ....93 A4
Burton BH23 ....92 B3
Burling Terr █ BH12 ....121 A2
Burlington Arc █ BH1 ...121 C2
Burlington Rd BH19 ....179 B2
Burn Cl BH31 ....45 C2
Burn View DT1 ....107 C3
Burnaby Cl BH4 ....121 B1
Burnaby Rd BH4 ....121 B1
Burnage Ct █ BH13 .....147 C4
Burnbake Rd BH21 ......60 B1
Burnbrae Rd BH22 ....61 B1
Burnet Way SP1 ....213 C4
Burnett Ave BH23 ......124 C4
Burnett Rd BH23 ....124 C4
Burngate Rd BH15 .....119 A2
Burnham Dr BH8 ....90 B1
Burnham Rd BH23 ......124 B4
Burnham's La BH19 ....178 B3
Burnleigh Gdns BH25 ...95 B2

Burns Rd
Bournemouth BH6 ....123 B4
Northport BH20 ....142 B3
Burnside
Christchurch BH23 .....125 B4
Winterborne St Martin
DT2 ....133 B3
Burraton Sq █ DT1 ......107 B1
Burroughes Ave DT2 ....27 A3
Burrows La BH31 ....41 A1
Burrywells DT2 ....102 B3
Burstock La DT8 ....203 C7
Burt's La Holt BH21 ....52 B4
Horton BH21 ....44 B1
Burt's Pl █ BH19 ....179 B1
Burtley Rd BH6 ....124 A3
Burton Bradstock VC Prim
Sch DT6 ....128 A4
Burton CE Prim Sch
BH23 ....92 B3
Burton Cl Burton BH23 ..92 B1
Shaftesbury SP7 ....13 A2
St.Leonards BH24 ......53 C3
Wool BH20 ....139 C1
Burton Cross BH20 .....139 C1
Burton Hall BH23 ....92 B2
Burton Hall Pl BH23 ....92 B2
Burton La BA22 ....193 C8
Burton Rd
Abbotsbury DT3 ....148 A4
Bournemouth DT6 ......100 C1
Burton Bradstock DT6 ..128 A4
Christchurch BH23 .....124 C4
Poole BH15 ....121 A2
Puncknowle DT2 ....129 C1
Wool BH20 ....139 C1
Burton St BH10 ....90 A2
Burton Wood BH20 .....139 C1
Burtoncroft BH23 ....92 B2
Burts Hill BH21 ....59 B3
Bury Rd BH13 ....120 C1
Bush Pk DT11 ....41 A1
Bushell Rd BH15 ....119 B4
Bushells Farm BH25 ....43 A4
Bushes Hill SP8 ....5 A4
Bushes Rd DT11 ....199 A4
Bushey La BH20 ....120 A1
Bushey Rd BH8 ....90 B1
Bushfield Rd █ TA18 ...191 E3
Bushmead Dr BH24 ......54 A3
Bute Dr BH23 ....126 A4
Butler Cl SP2 ....213 B1
Butlers La BH24 ....47 C1
Butt Cl DT2 ....78 A1
Butt Farm Cl DT11 ......105 B1
Butt La Bere Regis BH20 ..81 A2
Chideock DT6 ....66 C2
Butt La Hollow BH20 ....81 A2
Buttercup Cl █ SP8 ......5 B1
Buttercup Cl BH23 ......93 A1
Buttercup Way DT6 .....100 B1
Butterwick Dro DT9 ....195 D6
Buttery The BH23 ......124 C4
Button's La █ BH15 ....119 B1
Butts Cl Marnhull DT10 ..20 C1
Winfrith Newburgh DT2 ..156 C3
Butts La SP6 ....21 B4
Butts Mead █ SP7 ....21 A4
Butts Quarry La TA18 ...192 A4
Butts Rd SP7 ....213 B3
Butts Terr SP2 ....213 B3
Butts The
█ Child Okeford DT11 ...198 C7
Shaftesbury SP7 ....12 B2
Buxton Cl █ DT4 ....180 B4
Buxton Rd DT4 ....180 B4
Buzbury Rings* DT11 ...211 E8
Byard Rd BH20 ....26 B2
Byron Cl BH22 ....61 B3
Byron House █ BH25 ....95 A1
Byways Cl █ SP1 ....213 C2

C

Cabot Bsns Village
BH17 ....119 A4
Cabot La BH17 ....119 A4
Cabot Way BH25 ....94 C2
Cachy Rd BH20 ....139 C4
Cadhay Cl BA22 ....94 C2
Cadley Cl DT11 ....212 B3
Cadnam Way BH8 ....90 B2
Cadogan Rd BA24 ....55 B4
Caesar's Way BH18 .....86 C2
Caird Ave BH25 ....95 B1
Cairns Cl BH23 ....123 C4
Caister Cl BH23 ....61 B3
Calcraft Rd BH20 ......177 A4
Calder Rd BH17 ....119 C4
Caledon Rd BH14 ......120 C2
Caledonian Cl
Christchurch BH23 .....125 A4
Radipole DT3 ....167 B3
Caley Way DT6 ....69 A1
Calf Cl La DT10 ....197 F8
Calfhay La DT9 ....194 E1
Calkin Cl BH23 ....92 A1
Calluna Rd BH12 ......120 A4
Callway La DT2 ....209 B2
Calmore Cl BH8 ....90 B2
Calves La SP7 ....12 A2
Calvin Rd BH9 ....121 C4
Camborne Pl BA21 ......28 A3

Camborne St BA20 ....28 A1
Cambridge Cl BA20 ......26 C1
Cambridge Gdns BH23 ...91 C1
Cambridge Rd
Bournemouth BH2 ......121 B2
Dorchester DT1 ....107 B1
Salisbury SP1 ....213 B4
Weymouth DT4 ....166 C2
Cambridge Wlk █ DT1 ...107 B1
Camden Cl BH9 ....90 A1
Camden Way DT1 ....134 C4
Came Down Cl DT3 .....152 B2
Came Down Golf Club
DT2 ....134 C3
Came House* DT2 ....135 B3
Came View Cl DT3 ......135 B4
Came View Rd DT1 .....135 B4
Camel Gn Rd SP6 ....42 B3
Camellia Cl BH21 ....45 A1
Camellia Gdns BH25 ....95 A3
Camelot Way SP8 ....5 B1
Cameron Rd BH23 ......124 B4
Camesworth La DT6 .....69 A4
Cammel Rd BA22 ....61 B1
Camp Rd
Chickerell DT4 ....180 A4
West Coker BA22 ....26 B3
Campbell Rd
Bournemouth BH1 ......122 C3
Burton BH23 ....92 B2
Salisbury SP1 ....213 B3
Campion Cl
█ Gillingham SP8 ....5 B1
Radipole DT4 ....167 C4
Campion Dr BA22 ....26 B3
Campion Gr BH23 ......124 C3
Canberra Cres DT3 .....152 C2
Canberra Rd
Christchurch BH23 ......91 C1
Radipole DT3 ....152 C1
Candy's La █ DT11 .....198 B6
Candys Cl BH21 ....58 C1
Candys La BH21 ....58 C1
Canford Ave BH11 ....89 A1
Canford Bottom BH21 ...60 B3
Canford Cliffs Ave
BH14 ....120 C1
Canford Cliffs Rd
BH13 ....120 C1
Canford Cres BH13 ....147 C4
Canford Ct BH13 ....147 C3
Canford Gdns BH11 ....89 A1
Canford Heath Fst & Mid
Schs BH17 ....119 B4
Canford Heath Nature
Reserve* BH17 ....88 A2
Canford Heath Rd
BH17 ....87 C1
Canford Magna BH21 ...60 A1
Canford Pl █ BH13 ....147 C4
Canford Rd
Bournemouth BH11 ......89 A1
Poole BH15 ....119 B2
Canford Sch BH21 ....60 A1
Canford View Dr BH21 ..60 A3
Canford Way BH12 ....88 B1
Cann Hill SP7 ....24 A3
Cannings Ct La DT2 ...196 C3
Cannington Coll BA20 ..26 C3
Cannon Cl BH18 ....87 A1
Cannon Ct Mews █ DT9 ..17 B1
Cannon Hill Gdns BH21 ..60 A4
Cannon Hill La BH21 ...60 A4
Canteen Rd DT5 ....181 B1
Canterbury Cl
Ferndown BH22 ....53 A1
Weymouth DT4 ....166 C2
Capella Ct BH2 ....121 B2
Capesthorne BH23 .....125 A3
Caphays Dro DT9 ....195 E7
Capitol Cl DT1 ....134 C4
Capper Rd █ BH20 .....139 C3
Capper Rd W BH20 .....139 C3
Capstan Field BH17 ....178 A1
Capstans The BH14 ....147 A4
Capstone Pl BH8 ....122 B3
Capstone Rd BH8 ....122 A3
Capulet Rd SP1 ....213 A4
Carbery Ave BH6 ....123 C3
Carbery Gdns BH6 .....123 C3
Carbery La █ BH6 ......123 B3
Carbery Row █ BH6 ....123 B2
Cardigan Rd
Bournemouth BH9 ......121 C4
Poole BH12 ....120 C2
Cards Mill La DT10 ....66 A4
Carent Cl DT10 ....21 A1
Carey App BH20 ....142 B3
Carey Rd BH20 ....142 B3
Carey Cl
Bournemouth BH9 ....89 C2
Northport BH20 ....142 B3
Careys Rd BH8 ....90 B2
Carina Cl BH13 ....147 B2
Carisbrook Cres BH15 ..118 B2
Carisbrooke
Poole BH13 ....147 C4
Radipole DT4 ....167 A3
Carisbrooke Ct
Christchurch BH23 .....126 A4
New Milton BH25 ....94 C2
Carisbrooke Gdns
BA20 ....27 A3
Carisbrooke Rd BH21 ...93 C1
Carisbrooke █ BH5 .....122 C2
Carlton Ave BH25 ......126 C4
Carlton Gr BH12 ....120 B3
Carlton Rd BH1 ....122 B2

Ilton Rd N DT4 ......167 B3
Ilton Rd S DT4 ......167 B3
Iyle Rd BH6 ......123 B3
Imel Cl BH15 ......118 B1
Imelite Way SP1 ......213 B2
narvon Rd 4 BH1 ......122 C2
negie Cl BH14 ......120 B3
oline Ave BH23 ......123 C4
oline Pl BH14 ......167 B2
oline Rd BH11 ......89 A2
penters Cl DT2 ......106 C4
radale BH23 ......125 A4
raway La DT10 ......20 C1
rbridge Cl BH3 ......121 B4
rbridge Gdns BH3 ......121 B4
rbridge Rd BH3 ......121 B4
rick Cl DT1 ......135 B4
rick Way 95 B1
rrington Cl 10 DT4 ......180 B4
rrion La 4 BH20 ......142 C2
roll Ave 61 C3
roll Cl 61 C3
sworth Way BH17 ......88 A1
ter Cl DT11 ......212 C3
ter Com Sch BH15 ......119 B1
ter's La Chideock DT6 ......98 C4
ters Ave BH15 ......119 B1
ters La BH22 ......118 B2
ters La BA22 ......192 E8
tref Cl BH15 ......45 A3
twright Cl BH10 ......89 B2
vers La BH24 ......55 B4
ysfort Rd BH22 ......122 B2
seberry Cl 7 DT1 ......107 B1
shmoor Cl BH12 ......120 C4
slake Cl DT25 ......94 C1
ssel Ave BH13 ......121 A1
sselles Cl 13 BH25 ......95 A1
ssisbury Rd DT4 ......167 B2
sterbidge Cl
 andford Forum DT11 ......212 C3
 2 Swanage BH19 ......178 C1
sterbridge Rd
 orchester DT1 ......135 B4
 nerborn BH22 ......61 B2
tle Ave
 ournemouth BH9 ......90 A1
 tunewell DT5 ......181 A1
 salisbury SP1 ......213 B4
 herborne DT9 ......30 B4
tle Sq DT6 ......100 B3
tle St
 le Sq BH23 ......124 B3
 ranborne BH21 ......40 A4
 ere BA12 ......2 C3
 ole BH15 ......119 B1
 salisbury SP1 ......213 B4
tle Town Way DT9 ......16 A1
tle La E BH1 ......123 B4
tle La W BH8 ......90 B1
tle Par BH1 ......123 B4
tle Rd
 ournemouth BH1 ......90 A1
 tuneswell DT5 ......181 A1
 alisbury SP1 ......213 B4
 herborne DT9 ......30 B4
tlestown DT5 ......181 A1
stlewood DT4 ......54 C3
tle La DT10 ......33 A1
talina Cl BH23 ......125 A3
talina Dr BH15 ......119 C1
ters Pl DT1 ......108 A1
thedral Sch SP1 ......213 B2
therine St SP1 ......213 B2
therine Wheel Gdns
 SP23 ......91 C2
thole Bridge Rd
 A18 ......191 F3
ton Cl DT12 ......121 A4
nsley La DT2 ......205 B6
ttistock Rd
 ournemouth BH8 ......90 C1
uldon Ave BH19 ......72 C4
uldon Barn Rd
 19 ......179 A2
uldron Cres BH19 ......179 A2
uldron Mdws BH19 ......179 A2
undle La
 alfbridge DT10 ......33 A3

Caundle La continued
 Stourton Caundle DT10 ......32 C1
Causeway Cl BH20 ......142 B3
Causeway La BH18 ......203 A6
Causeway The
 Hazelbury Bryan DT10 ......196 F4
 Milborne St Andrew DT11 ......79 C4
Cavalier Cl BA21 ......27 C4
Cavalier Ct BA21 ......27 C4
Cavalier Way BA21 ......27 C4
Cavan Cres BH17 ......87 A1
Cavendish Hall BA21 ......122 A3
Cavendish Pl BH1 ......122 A3
Cavendish Rd BH1 ......122 A3
Caversham Cl BH15 ......118 C2
Cawdor Rd BH3 ......121 B4
Caxton Cl BH23 ......125 A4
Cecil Ave
 Bournemouth BH8 ......122 B4
 Salisbury SP1 ......213 B1
Cecil Cl BH21 ......86 C3
Cecil Ct BH21 ......122 A4
Cecil Hill BH8 ......122 A4
Cecil Rd
 Bournemouth BH5 ......122 C2
 Poole BH12 ......120 B3
 Swanage BH19 ......179 A1
Cecil St BA20 ......27 B3
Cedar Ave
 Bournemouth BH10 ......89 B3
 Christchurch BH23 ......123 B4
 3 St.Leonards BH24 ......53 C2
Cedar Cl Upton BH16 ......118 A4
 1 Wool BH20 ......140 A1
Cedar Ct BH21 ......121 A4
Cedar Dr
 1 Easton/Weston BH16 ......186 C1
 Overcombe/Preston
  DT3 ......168 A4
 Sandford BH20 ......116 A1
 Wimborne Minster BH21 ......60 A3
Cedar Fields 1 BA22 ......193 A8
Cedar Gdns BH25 ......94 C1
Cedar Gr BA21 ......27 A3
Cedar Manor BH1 ......121 B2
Cedar Rd DT1 ......107 C1
Cedar Trad Pk 60 C3
Cedar Way BH22 ......61 B4
Cedars The BA21 ......121 B2
Celandine Cl BH23 ......92 A3
Celandine Rd 3 BA22 ......26 B3
Cellars Farm Rd BH6 ......124 A2
Celtic Cres BH11 ......134 C4
Cemetery Ave BH15 ......119 C3
Cemetery Rd
 10 Gillingham SP8 ......5 C1
 Portesham DT3 ......150 A4
 Wimborne Minster BH21 ......59 A3
Centenary Gdns BA8 ......19 A2
Centenary House 6
 BH21 ......124 A4
Centenary Way BH1 ......122 C3
Central Acre 13 BA20 ......27 B2
Central Ave
 Corfe Mullen BH21 ......86 B4
 Poole BH12 ......120 C3
Central Dr BH24 ......121 C3
Central Rd BA20 ......27 C2
Centre Pl BH24 ......55 A4
Centurion Rd BH17 ......199 E2
Cerleton Pk DT11 ......211 C6
Cerne Abbas BH21 ......122 A3
Cerne Abbas CE Fst Sch
 DT2 ......207 D4
Cerne Abbas Giant*
 DT2 ......207 D4
Cerne Abbey* DT2 ......207 D4
Cerne Cl BH9 ......90 A2
Chaddesley Glen
 BH13 ......147 C3
Chaddesley Pines
 BH13 ......147 C3
Chaddesley Wood Rd
 BH13 ......147 C3
Chafeys Ave BH14 ......167 A3
Chaffey Cl BH24 ......55 C4
Chaffeymoor Hill SP8 ......1 A1
Chaffinch Cl
 Bincombe DT3 ......152 B2
 Broadstone BH7 ......86 C1
 New Milton BH25 ......94 C1
Chafyn Gr Sch SP1 ......213 C3
Chalbury (Hill Fort)*
 DT3 ......153 A2
Chalbury Cl
 Overcombe/Preston
  DT3 ......168 A4
 Poole BH17 ......88 A1
Chalbury Ct
 7 Christchurch BH23 ......124 C3
 11 Poole BH14 ......120 A2
Chalbury Lodge BH13 ......168 A4
Chaldecott Gdns BH10 ......89 B2
Chaldon Rd BH17 ......87 C1
Chalfont Ave BH23 ......91 B2
Chalice Cl BH14 ......120 A2
Chalk Cl BH24 ......81 A1
Chalk Pit La
 Litton Cheney DT2 ......103 A1
 Wool BH20 ......139 C1
Chalk The 2 DT11 ......37 C1
Chalky Rd DT2 ......135 C1
Chalwell 2 DT11 ......199 F6
Chalwyn Ind Est BH12 ......120 A4
Chamberlaine Rd DT4 ......167 B2
Champerhayes La
 DT6 ......64 C3
Champions 1 DT8 ......204 C4
Chancery Cl 1 SP2 ......213 A3

Chancery La DT6 ......100 B3
Chandos La 61 C2
Chandlers DT9 ......30 B4
Chandlers Cl BH7 ......123 A4
Chandos Ave BH12 ......121 A4
Channel Ct
 Barton on Sea BH25 ......126 C4
 Bournemouth BH6 ......123 B2
Channel View Rd DT5 ......186 C2
Chant Cl BH31 ......124 B4
Chantmarle La DT2 ......206 B5
Chantry Cl BH21 ......93 C3
Chantry La DT8 ......204 C5
Chantry St DT6 ......204 C2
Chantry The BH1 ......122 A2
Chantry View BA22 ......193 D8
Chapel Cl
 Corfe Mullen BH21 ......86 B3
 Langton Herring DT3 ......150 B1
Chapel Gate BH23 ......90 B4
Chapel Gdns DT11 ......212 C2
Chapel Hill SP8 ......9 B1
Chapel La
 Bransgore BH23 ......93 A4
 Corfe Mullen BH21 ......86 B3
 Dinnington TA17 ......191 B8
 Henstridge BA8 ......19 B4
 Hurn BH23 ......90 B4
 Maiden Newton DT2 ......72 C4
 7 Milborne Port DT9 ......17 B1
 Osmington DT3 ......154 A2
 Pen Selwood BA9 ......1 B2
 2 Pimperne DT11 ......199 D3
 Poole BH15 ......119 B1
 Radipole DT3 ......152 B3
 Wimborne Minster BH21 ......59 A3
 Woodlands BH21 ......59 A3
 3 Yetminster DT9 ......194 C5
 Zennor BA12 ......1 C3
Chapel Mdw 6 DT9 ......194 C5
Chapel Pl 5 SP2 ......213 B3
Chapel Rd Poole BH14 ......120 A2
 Sturminster Newton
  DT10 ......197 A8
Chapel Rise DT6 ......54 C1
Chapel St
 Milborne St Andrew DT11 ......79 C4
 Shipton Gorge DT6 ......101 B2
Chapel View 1 DT2 ......78 A1
Chapelhay St DT4 ......167 B1
Chapelhay Steps DT4 ......167 B1
Charberry Rise DT6 ......96 C4
Charborough Rd BH16 ......84 B2
Charborough Park*
 BH20 ......83 C4
Charborough Pk*
 BH20 ......211 F1
Charborough Rd 1 BH17 ......87 A2
Charborough Way 1
 BH21 ......56 B2
Chard La
 Broadwindsor DT8 ......203 C2
 Wayford TA18 ......191 B2
Chard Rd
 Broadwindsor DT8 ......203 C2
 Crewkerne TA18 ......191 D4
Chard St TA20 ......202 D8
Chards Mead Rd DT6 ......100 B4
Charing Cl 2 BH7 ......55 B3
Charing Cross SP5 ......42 A3
Charles Cres BH25 ......95 A1
Charles Garrett Cl 7
 SP7 ......12 C2
Charles Gdns BH10 ......89 B1
Charles Keightley Ct
 BH21 ......59 B2
Charles Rd
 Burton Bradstock DT6 ......128 A4
 Christchurch BH23 ......124 C4
 Poole BH15 ......119 B2
 Yeovil BA21 ......27 C3
Charles St
 Blandford Forum DT11 ......212 B2
 Dorchester DT1 ......108 A1
 Radipole DT4 ......167 B2
 2 Salisbury SP2 ......213 A3
Charles's La 1 BH24 ......55 C1
Charlotte Cl
 Charminster DT2 ......107 C3
 Christchurch BH23 ......125 A3
 8 New Milton BH25 ......95 A1
 Poole BH12 ......121 B4
Charlton Beeches
 DT11 ......211 C2
Charlton Cl
 Bournemouth BH9 ......90 B2
 18 Crewkerne TA18 ......191 F4
 Hordle SO41 ......95 C2
Charlton La SP7 ......13 C1
Charlton Manor 1
 BH9 ......90 B2
Charlton Mead 4 DT11 ......211 D6
Charltons The DT2 ......121 C3
Charminster Ave BH9 ......90 A1
Charminster Cl BH8 ......90 A1
Charminster Pl BH8 ......90 B1
Charminster Rd BH8 ......90 A1
Charminster St Marys Fst Sch
 DT2 ......107 B3
Charmouth Cl DT7 ......96 B3
Charmouth Gr DT4 ......167 A1
Charmouth Heritage Coast
 Ctr* DT6 ......97 A4
Charmouth Rd DT7 ......96 B3
Charnock Rd SO41 ......95 C2
Charnwood Ave 8 BH9 ......90 A2

Charnwood Cl BH22 ......53 A1
Charnwood Rd SP2 ......213 A3
Charcombe BH11 ......88 B3
Charter Rd BH11 ......88 B3
Chartwell DT4 ......167 A3
Chase Cres SP5 ......188 C4
Chase The
 St.Leonards BH24 ......54 C3
 Verwood BH31 ......45 C3
Chaseborough Sq 4
 DT1 ......107 B1
Chaseside BH7 ......123 A4
Chaston La BA21 ......27 C4
Chatham Cl SP1 ......213 A4
Chatsworth Rd
 Bournemouth BH8 ......122 B3
 Poole BH14 ......120 A3
 Yeovil BA21 ......27 C4
Chatsworth Way BH25 ......94 C2
Chaucer Cl BH21 ......59 B3
Chaucer Rd BH13 ......147 C4
Chaucombe Pl BH25 ......94 C1
Cheam Rd BH18 ......96 C2
Cheap St DT9 ......30 A3
Checkridge La EX13 ......202 A2
Cheddington Rd BH9 ......90 A2
Cheddington Cl BH17 ......
Cheddington La DT8 ......204 D8
Cheese La DT1 ......150 C3
Cheese Mkt 10 SP1 ......213 B3
Chelmsford Rd BH16 ......118 A4
Chelmsford St DT4 ......167 B2
Chelston Ave BA21 ......27 B4
Cheltenham Rd BH12 ......120 B3
Chelwood Gate DT4 ......166 C2
Chene Rd BH21 ......59 A2
Chene The BH21 ......89 A1
Cherita Ave BH15 ......119 C3
Cheriton Ave BH23 ......123 B4
Cheriton Way BH21 ......59 B3
Cherrett Cl BH11 ......88 C2
Cherries Dr BH9 ......89 C1
Cherry Cl Poole BH14 ......120 A2
 Sandford BH20 ......143 A4
Cherry Ct BH14 ......120 A3
Cherry Gr BA22 ......61 B3
Cherry Hill Gdns
 BH16 ......118 A3
Cherry Hill Gr BH16 ......118 A3
Cherry Orch La
 Cann SP7 ......11 C1
 Gillingham SP8 ......5 B1
Cherry Tree DT6 ......100 A4
Cherry Tree Cl BA22 ......53 C2
Cherry Tree Ct
 9 Crewkerne TA18 ......191 F5
 8 New Milton BH25 ......95 A1
Cherry Tree Dr BA20 ......26 C1
Cherryfields SP8 ......5 C2
Chescombe Cl DT2 ......207 D3
Chescombe La DT11 ......210 B3
Cheselbourne Cty Fst Sch
 DT2 ......209 A2
Cheshire Dr BH8 ......91 A1
Chesil Beach Visitor Ctr*
 DT4 ......180 B2
Chesil View DT4 ......180 B4
Chesildene Ave BH8 ......90 B2
Chesildene Dr BH8 ......90 B2
Chessel Ave BH5 ......122 C2
Chessels 13 BA22 ......193 B8
Chester Cl DT1 ......107 A1
Chester Rd BH13 ......121 A1
Chesterfield Cl BH13 ......147 C4
Chesterfield Ct BH13 ......122 B2
Chestnut Ave
 Barton on Sea BH25 ......127 A4
 Bournemouth BH6 ......123 B2
 Ellingham Harbridge & Ibsley
  BH24 ......46 B3
 Wareham St Martin
  BH20 ......116 A2
Chestnut Cl BH20 ......143 A4
Chestnut Dr BH20 ......27 A2
Chestnut Gr
 Blandford Forum DT11 ......212 B2
 Ferndown BH21 ......60 C3
Chestnut Pl DT3 ......167 B4
Chestnut Rd DT6 ......100 B2
Chestnut Way
 Burton DT3 ......92 B2
 Dorchester DT1 ......107 B1
 Gillingham SP8 ......5 A3
Chetcombe Rd BA12 ......3 A1
Chetnole Cl BH17 ......88 A1
Chetnole Sta DT9 ......194 C2
Chettell Way DT11 ......212 B1
Chetwode Way DT4 ......107 B4
Cheverell Ave SP1 ......213 C4
Cheviot Cl BH31 ......45 A3
Cheviot Way BH31 ......45 A3
Cheviots The BH14 ......120 B2
Chewton Comm Rd
 BH23 ......126 A4
Chewton Farm Rd
 BH23 ......94 B1
Chewton Lodge BH23 ......126 A4
Chewton Way BH23 ......94 B1
Cheyne Cl DT5 ......186 C1
Cheyne Gdns BH4 ......121 B1
Chichester Cl SP2 ......213 B1
Chichester Rd 1 BH24 ......55 A4
Chichester Way BH23 ......125 A3
Chichester Wlk BH21 ......59 C1
Chick's Copse La
 Cattistock DT2 ......206 A5

Chick's Copse La continued
 Rampisham DT2 ......205 F5
Chickerell Cl BH9 ......90 A2
Chickerell CP Sch
 DT3 ......166 B3
Chickerell Hill DT3 ......166 A3
Chickerell Rd DT3 ......166 B2
Chideock Cl BH12 ......120 C3
Chideock Ct BH12 ......120 C3
Chideock Hill DT6 ......98 C4
Chigwell Rd BH8 ......90 A1
Chilbury Gdns DT2 ......155 B4
Chilcombe Hill (Fort)*
 DT2 ......102 C2
Chilcombe La
 Chilcombe DT6 ......102 B2
 Shipton Gorge DT6 ......102 B3
Chilcombe Rd BH6 ......123 A3
Childhay La DT8 ......203 C6
Chilfrome Cl DT4 ......87 B1
Chilfrome La
 Chilfrome DT2 ......206 B1
 Maiden Newton DT2 ......72 C4
Chiltern Cl
 Barton on Sea BH25 ......94 C1
 Poole BH12 ......121 B3
Chiltern Ct 5 BH23 ......124 C4
Chiltern Dr
 Barton on Sea BH25 ......126 C4
 Verwood BH31 ......45 A3
Chilton Gr BA21 ......27 B4
Chimes The BH4 ......121 A2
China La 1 DT11 ......199 F7
Chine Cres BH2 ......121 B1
Chine Cres Rd BH2 ......121 B1
Chine Wlk BH22 ......61 C1
Chinnock Hollow
 BA22 ......192 E8
Chippel La DT10 ......20 C1
Chipper La SP1 ......213 B3
Chiselbury Gr SP2 ......213 B1
Chisels La BH23 ......93 A3
Chiswell DT5 ......186 C4
Chiswell Rd BH17 ......87 B1
Chitten Hill BH20 ......115 B4
Choristers Sq SP1 ......213 B2
Chorley Cl BH15 ......119 B3
Chowins Rd 18 TA18 ......191 F4
Chris Cres BH16 ......118 B4
Christ the King RC Prim Sch
 BH1 ......89 A3
Christchurch Bay Rd
 BH25 ......126 C4
Christchurch By-pass
 BH23 ......124 B4
Christchurch Castle*
 BH23 ......124 B3
Christchurch Cty Jun Sch
 BH23 ......124 A4
Christchurch Cty Prim Sch
 BH23 ......124 A4
Christchurch Hospl
 BH23 ......123 C4
Christchurch Priory*
 BH23 ......124 B3
Christchurch Rd
 Barton on Sea BH25 ......126 B4
 Bournemouth BH1 ......122 B2
 Ferndown BH21 ......61 B1
 Hurn BH23 ......91 B3
 Ringwood BH24 ......55 A4
Christchurch Ski Ctr*
 BH23 ......63 A2
Christchurch Sta
 BH23 ......124 A4
Christie Miller Rd
 SP2 ......213 A3
Christopher Cl
 3 Salisbury SP2 ......213 A1
 Yeovil BA20 ......27 A1
Christopher Cres
 BH15 ......119 B3
Christophers BH21 ......59 B1
Christy's La SP7 ......12 C2
Chur La BA22 ......193 A8
Church Acre 22 DT1 ......108 A1
Church Cl
 Bear Hackett DT7 ......194 D6
 Bourton SP9 ......1 B1
 Bridport DT6 ......69 A1
 Chetnole DT9 ......194 D3
 5 Dorchester DT1 ......108 A1
 Fontmell Magna SP7 ......179 C2
 Longburton DT9 ......195 B7
 Stour Provost SP7 ......22 B4
 9 Swanage BH19 ......179 A1
 Todber DT10 ......21 B2
Church Farm SP6 ......43 A4
Church Hill
 Buckhorn Weston SP8 ......9 A3
 Dinnington TA17 ......191 B7
 Iwerne Minster DT11 ......37 C1
 Kington Magna SP8 ......21 A2
 Langton Herring DT3 ......150 B1
 Marnhull DT10 ......21 A2
 Milborne St Andrew DT11 ......79 C4
 Piddlehinton DT2 ......76 C4
 Shaftesbury SP7 ......12 B2
 Stalbridge DT10 ......19 B1
 13 Swanage BH19 ......179 A1
 West Stour SP8 ......10 A2

Church Hill continued
Woodlands BH21 ....44 A4
Church Hill La DT2 ...104 B4
Church Hill View DT2 ...207 A2
Church Knap DT4 ....180 B4
**Church Knowle Animal
Sanctuary & Rehoming Ctr★**
BH20 ....176 A4
Church La
Barwick BA22 ....193 E8
Bere Regis BH20 ....81 A1
❸ Blandford Forum DT11 .212 B2
Charlton Marshall DT11 ...211 C6
Chickerell DT3 ....151 B1
Christchurch BH23 ....124 A3
Coombe Keynes BH20 .....158 A3
Crewkerne TA18 ....192 A3
Damerham SP6 ....190 F2
East Orchard SP7 ....36 C4
Easton/Weston DT5 ....186 C1
Ferndown BH22 ....89 C4
Frampton DT2 ....73 C2
Godmanstone DT2 ....75 A4
Haselbury Plucknett
TA18 ....192 C5
Leigh DT9 ....209 D4
Margaret Marsh SP7 ....22 B1
New Milton BH25 ....94 C1
Osmington DT3 ....154 A2
Owermoigne DT2 ....155 B4
Piddletrenthide DT2 ....208 B3
Portesham DT3 ....150 A4
Rimpton BA22 ....15 A4
Shaftesbury SP7 ....12 C1
Stinsford DT2 ....108 C2
Stour Provost SP8 ....21 B4
❷ Sturminster Newton
DT10 ....197 D8
Sutton Waldron DT11 ......37 C2
Sydling St Nicholas DT2 ...207 A2
Wareham BH20 ....142 C2
Wool BH20 ....140 A1
Church Mead DT2 ......205 F1
Church Ope DT5 ....187 A2
Church Path
❷ Crewkerne TA18 ....191 E4
Litton Cheney DT2 ....103 B1
Yeovil BA21 ....27 B3
Church Rd
Bournemouth BH6 ....123 C2
Bradford Abbas DT9 ....28 B1
Durweston DT11 ....198 E3
Ferndown BH22 ....61 B3
Iwerne Minster DT11 ......37 C1
Maiden Newton DT2 ....72 C4
Overcombe/Preston
DT3 ....168 B4
Pimperne DT11 ....199 D4
Poole BH14 ....120 A2
❺ Shillingstone DT11 .....198 B6
Silton DT8 ....2 A1
Studland BH19 ....164 B1
Thornford DT9 ....194 D8
Three Legged Cross BH21 ..45 A1
West Lulworth BH20 ....172 B3
Church Row DT11 ......209 C6
Church St
Beaminster DT8 ....204 C4
Bridport DT6 ....100 B3
Burton Bradstock DT6 .....128 A4
Christchurch BH23 ....124 A3
Cranborne BH21 ....40 A4
Dewlish DT2 ....209 C1
❸ Dorchester DT1 ....108 A1
Fontmell Magna SP7 ....37 C4
Fordingbridge SP6 ....43 A4
Halstock BA22 ....193 C3
Henstridge BA8 ....19 A2
Hinton St George TA17 ...191 C7
Kington Magna SP8 ....9 B2
Lyme Regis DT7 ....96 B3
Mere BA12 ....3 A3
Merriott TA16 ....191 F7
Milborne Port DT9 ....17 B1
Poole BH15 ....119 A1
Puncknowle DT2 ....129 C3
Radipole DT3 ....152 A4
Shapwick DT11 ....56 A4
Sturminster Newton DT10 ..35 A1
Wareham BH20 ....142 C2
❷ West Stour BA22 ....193 A8
West Stour SP8 ....10 A1
❿ Wimborne Minster BH21 ..59 A3
Winterborne Kingston
DT11 ....81 C4
Yeovil BA20 ....27 B3
Yetminster DT9 ....194 C5
Church Track SP8 ....1 B1
Church View SP5 ....5 C1
Church Wlk
Littlebredy DT2 ....131 B4
Motcombe SP7 ....12 A4
Okeford Fitzpaine DT11 ...197 E4
Churchfield BH31 ....45 A3
Churchfield Cres
BH15 ....119 C2
Churchfield Ct BH15 ....119 C2
Churchfield La BH24 ....43 A1
Churchfield Rd BH15 ....119 C2
Churchfields Ind Est
SP2 ....213 A3
Churchfields Rd SP2 ....213 A3
Churchfoot La DT10 ....196 F3
Churchill Cl
Alderholt SP6 ....42 A3

Churchill Cl continued
Sturminster Marshall
BH21 ....56 B2
❹ Weymouth DT4 ....180 B4
Churchill Cres BH12 ....120 B3
Churchill Dro DT1 ....40 C4
Churchill Gdns BH12 ...120 B3
Churchill Rd
Blandford Forum DT11 ....212 B2
Bournemouth BH1 ....122 B3
Bovington Camp BH20 ....139 B4
Poole BH12 ....120 B3
Wimborne Minster BH21 ..59 C2
Churchill Way E SP1 ...213 B3
Churchill Way N SP1 ...213 B3
Churchill Way S SP1 ....213 B2
Churchill Way W SP2 ...213 B3
Churchmoor Rd BH21 ...60 A3
Churchward Ave DT3 ...153 A2
Churchwell St DT9 ....28 B1
Churlands Cl BA22 ....193 A8
Chydok Rd DT2 ....156 B2
Circle The
❺ Bournemouth BH9 ....90 A2
Poole BH13 ....147 C4
Claire Ct BH23 ....126 A4
Clammer Hill La TA18 ..191 F4
Clanfield DT9 ....29 C2
Clap La SP5 ....188 B4
Clappentail La DT7 .....96 A3
Clappentail Pk DT7 ......96 A3
Clapton Ct Gdns★
TA18 ....191 D1
Clapton Rd TA18 ....191 D3
Clare Ave DT4 ....166 C1
Claremont Ave
Bournemouth BH9 ....90 A1
Gillingham SP8 ....5 C2
Claremont Gdns DT6 ...100 B4
Claremont Rd
Bournemouth BH9 ....90 A1
Bridport DT6 ....100 B4
Clarence Cl DT5 ....186 C2
Clarence Pk Rd BH7 ....123 A3
Clarence Rd
Dorchester DT1 ....134 C4
Easton/Weston DT5 ....186 C2
❸ Poole BH14 ....120 A2
Yeovil BA20 ....166 C1
Clarence St BA20 ....27 B2
Clarendon Ave DT11 ....152 B1
Clarendon Cl
Broadstone BH18 ....87 A2
Gillingham SP8 ....5 B1
Clarendon Ct BH2 ....121 B1
Clarendon Rd
Bournemouth BH4 ....121 B2
Broadstone BH18 ....86 C2
Christchurch BH23 ....124 A3
Salisbury SP1 ....213 C3
Clark's La BH24 ....55 B4
Clark's La TA18 ....192 A3
Clarks Cl BA22 ....193 E2
Clatcombe La DT9 ....15 C2
Claudius Cl DT1 ....134 C4
Clay Castle TA18 ....192 C5
Clay Castle La TA18 ....192 C5
Clay La Beaminster DT8 ..204 C4
Chard DT7 ....129 C2
Clayesmore Prep Sch
DT11 ....37 C1
Claysmore Sch DT11 ...37 C1
Clayford Ave BH22 ......61 A4
Clayford Cl BH17 ....87 B1
Clayland Dr BH31 ....45 B3
Claylands La DT4 ....204 A3
Claypits La
Beer Hackett DT9 ....194 D6
Winfrith Newburgh DT2 ..157 A3
Clayton Cl
Radipole DT3 ....152 B2
Yeovil BA21 ....26 B3
Clearmount Rd DT4 .....180 C4
Cleasby Grange ❸ BH6 ..123 C2
Cleeves Cl BH12 ....88 B1
Clematis Cl BH23 ....125 B4
Clement Mews BH4 ......121 A2
Clement's La BA12 ....3 A2
Clements La DT5 ....186 C4
Clenston Rd DT2 ....210 C7
Cleve The BA21 ....26 C3
Cleveland Ave DT4 ......167 B4
Cleveland Cl BH25 ....126 B4
Cleveland Ct BH2 ....121 B1
Cleveland Gdns BH21 ...61 B3
Cleveland Rd BH1 ....122 B3
Cleverlawns DT3 ....148 C4
Cleves Cl DT4 ....180 C4
Cliff Ave BH19 ....179 B2
Cliff Cres BH25 ....126 C4
Cliff Dr
Christchurch BH23 ....125 B3
Poole BH13 ....147 C3
Cliff House ❿ BH6 ....123 C2
Poole DT6 ....128 A4
Cliff La DT6 ....128 A4
Cliff St BH25 ....126 C3
Cliff Way DT5 ....186 B1
Cliffe Rd BH25 ....126 C4
Clifford Rd BH9 ....90 A1
Clift La DT2 ....205 D1
Clifton Cl
Canford Magna BH19 .....179 B2
Yeovil BA21 ....28 A3
Clifton Ct

Clifton Ct continued
❿ New Milton BH25 ....95 A1
Clifton Gdns 61 B2
Clifton Maybank BA22 ..193 F8
Clifton Pl ❻ DT4 ....167 B2
Clifton Rd
Bournemouth BH6 ....123 B2
Bournemouth BH5 ....123 A2
Ringwood BH24 ....55 B4
Swanage BH19 ....179 A2
Clifton View ❸ BA22 ...193 F8
Clingan Rd BH6 ....123 B4
Clinton Cl BH23 ....94 A1
Clive Ct ❸ BH4 ....121 B2
Clive Rd
Bournemouth BH9 ....89 C1
Christchurch BH23 ....93 C1
Cliveden Ct BH22 ....61 B4
Clivia Ct DT3 ....152 C1
Cloisters The
Christchurch BH23 ....124 A3
❷ Ringwood BH24 ....55 C3
Close Dr ❺ TA18 ....192 A3
Close The
Barton on Sea BH25 ....127 A4
Blandford Forum DT11 ....212 B2
Broadstone BH18 ....86 C2
Charlton Marshall DT11 ...211 D6
❿ Merriott TA16 ....191 F7
❿ Pimperne DT11 ....199 D4
Ringwood BH24 ....55 A4
St.Leonards BH24 ....54 B2
Clough's Rd BH24 ....55 B4
Clovens Rd DT5 ....186 C4
Clover Cl BH23 ....125 B4
Clover Ct BH25 ....95 B2
Clover Dr BH17 ....86 C1
Cloverfields SP8 ....5 C2
Clovermead DT9 ....194 B6
Clowers The BH12 ......121 A4
Clovers Wlk ❸ BA20 ....27 B2
Clowes Ave BH17 ....124 A2
Clump Hill BH21 ....44 B1
Cluny Cres BH19 ....179 B1
Clyde Rd BH17 ....87 A1
Clyffe View DT2 ....137 B3
Clyppetts ❷ DT11 ....81 C4
Coach House Pl BH1 .....122 A3
Coach La
❿ Stourpaine DT11 ....198 F4
Wimborne St Giles
BH21 ....201 C7
Coach Rd The DT7 ....64 A1
Coastguard Rd
Langton Herring DT3 ......150 A1
Coastguard Way BH23 ..124 C3
Cobb Rd DT7 ....96 A2
Cobb's Rd BH21 ....59 C3
Cobbs La BH15 ....119 C3
Cobham Dr DT4 ....166 C2
Cobham Rd
Bournemouth BH9 ....90 A2
Ferndown BH21 ....61 A4
Ferndown Town BH22 .....52 B1
Sturminster Newton
TA18 ....192 D5
Henstridge BA8 ....18 C4
Kington Magna SP8 ....9 B2
Sturminster Newton
BH21 ....194 B5
Cockerell Cl DT1 ....59 C1
Cocklands DT2 ....197 D8
Cockles La Fleet DT4 ....166 C1
Weymouth DT4 ....167 A1
Cockpit Hill DT6 ....203 C4
Codge La BA22 ....192 D7
Codge La DT2 ....205 E5
Codogan Ct ❿ BH1 ......122 A2
Codogan Rd BH9 ....90 A2
Codogan Way BH21 .....86 C4
Codogan Wlk BH21 ......86 C4
Codgeane Rd BH17 ......87 B1
Codgeane Pl 193 C7
Coker Hill BA22 ....192 E8
Coker Hill La BA22 ......193 A7
Coker Rd BH20 ....140 B1
Cokers Frome DT1 ....108 A4
Coker's Cross DT8 ....203 A5
Cole's La DT7 ....12 A1
Colehill Cres BH9 ....90 A2
Colehill Fst Sch BH21 ...60 A4
Colehill La Holt BH21 ...55 B1
Wimborne Minster BH21 ..59 C4
Colehill Rd BH20 ....83 C3
Coleman Rd BH11 ....89 A2
Colemore Rd BH7 ....123 B4
Coleridge Gn BH23 ......124 C4
Coles Ave BH15 ....118 C1
Coles Cl DT11 ....35 B1
Coles Gdns BH15 ....118 C1
Coles La
Milborne St Andrew
DT11 ....209 F1
Yetminster DT9 ....194 B6
Colin Cl BH21 ....86 B3
Coll of Air Traffic Control
BH23 ....90 C4

Collaway La BA22 ....192 F8
College BA22 ....192 E8
College Arms Cl SP7 ....22 A4
College Gn BA21 ....27 B3
College Rd
Blandford Camp DT11 ....199 E3
Bournemouth BH5 ....123 A2
Ringwood BH24 ....55 B4
College St SP1 ....213 B3
Collett Cl DT3 ....153 A2
Colletts La BH20 ....177 A4
Collier's La BH20 ....139 C1
Collingbourne Ave
BH6 ....123 B4
Collingwood Cl ❼ DT11 ..199 D4
Collingwood Rd BH21 ...53 A3
Collins La
Ringwood BH24 ....55 A4
Weymouth DT4 ....180 B4
Colliton St DT1 ....108 A1
Collwood Cl BH15 ....119 B4
Collyer's Rise SP7 ....37 C2
Colman Ct BH1 ....122 B2
Colmer Rd BA21 ....27 B3
Cologne Rd
Bovington Camp BH20 ...140 A3
Wool BH20 ....139 C3
Colombine Cl BH23 ......93 A1
Colonnade Rd BH5 ....123 A3
Colonnade Rd W ❹
BH5 ....123 A3
Colt Cl BH21 ....60 A3
Columbia Rd BH10 ......89 B1
Columbia Trees La
BH10 ....89 B1
Columbian Way BH10 ...89 B1
Colville Cl BH5 ....123 A3
Colville Rd ❻ BH5 ....123 A3
Colway Cl DT7 ....96 A4
Colway La DT7 ....96 A4
Colwell Cl DT1 ....108 A3
Colway Ct ❼ DT7 ....96 A4
Combe Ave DT7 ....96 A4
Combe Cl SP8 ....5 C2
Combe La DT2 ....137 B3
Combe Pk BA21 ....27 A4
Combe Way DT2 ....137 B3
Comber Rd ❺ BH9 ......90 A2
Comet Cl DT4 ....166 C1
Comet Way BH23 ....125 A3
Comley Rd BH9 ....89 C1
Commercial Rd
Bournemouth BH2 ....121 C2
Poole BH14 ....120 A2
Radipole DT4 ....167 B1
❿ Swanage BH19 ....179 B1
Common Dro
❻ Child Okeford DT11 ...198 F8
Farnham DT11 ....188 B3
Common Hill DT8 ....203 E5
Common La
❿ Blandford Forum DT11 ..212 B2
Burton Bradstock DT6 ....128 B4
East Stour SP8 ....11 A2
Halstock BA22 ....193 C2
Haselbury Plucknett
TA18 ....192 D5
Henstridge BA8 ....18 C4
Kington Magna SP8 ....9 B2
Sturminster Newton
BH21 ....194 B5
Common Mead Ave SP8 ..5 C1
Common Mead La SP8 ...5 B1
Common Rd SP5 ....188 F4
Common The
Evershot DT2 ....206 A7
Hazelbury Bryan DT10 ...196 E5
Moreton DT2 ....138 B4
Common Wr La DT8 .....203 F5
Compton Abbas Airfield
SP5 ....24 C1
Compton Acres Gdns★
BH13 ....147 C4
Compton Ave BH14 ......120 B1
Compton Beeches
BH24 ....54 B3
Compton Cl
Verwood BH31 ....45 A4
Yeovil BA21 ....28 A4
Compton Cres BH22 .....53 B1
Compton Ct BH14 ....120 B1
Compton Gdns BH14 ....120 B1
Compton Rd
New Milton BH25 ....95 A1
Over Compton DT9 ....28 B3
Concorde Cl DT4 ....166 C1
Condor Cl BH21 ....60 A3
Coney's Castle (Fort)★
DT6 ....202 B4
Coneygar Cl DT6 ....100 B4
Coneygar La DT6 ....100 B4
Coneygar Rd DT6 ....100 B4
Conifer Ave BH14 ....120 A1
Conifer Cl
Christchurch BH23 ....91 B2
Ferndown BH22 ....61 C1
St.Leonards BH24 ....54 B2
Coniston Dr BH11 ....43 A1
Coniston Cl BH31 ....45 A3
Coniston Cres DT3 ....167 B4
Coniston Gdns BA21 ....27 A4
Coniston Rd BH20 ....140 B1
Connaught Cl BH25 ......94 C1
Connaught Cres BH12 ..120 C3
Connaught Gdns BH25 ..94 C1

Connaught Rd
Bournemouth BH5 ....123...
❷ Weymouth DT4 ....180...
Connell Rd BH15 ....119...
Conniger La BH20 ....142...
Consort Cl BH12 ....120...
Constable Cl BA21 ......28...
Constable Way SP2 .....213...
Constitution Hill Gdns
BH14 ....120...
Constitution Hill Rd
BH14 ....120...
Conway Cl BH25 ....95...
Conway Ct ❷❺ BH25 ...95...
Conway Dr DT2 ....126...
Conways Dr BH14 ....120...
Cook Cl BH24 ....55...
Cook Row BH21 ....59...
Cook's La DT10 ....33...
Cooke Gdns BH12 ....120...
Cooke Rd BH12 ....120...
Cooks La DT9 ....10...
Cookswell ❶ DT11 ....198...
Coolhurst BH14 ....147...
Coombe DT9 ....307...
Coombe Ave
Bournemouth BH10 ....89...
Radipole DT4 ....167...
Coombe Cl BA21 ....27...
Coombe Gdns BH10 ....89...
Coombe Hill BH19 ....178...
Coombe La
Castleton DT9 ....15...
Stoke Abbott DT8 ....203...
Coombe Rd
Dinnington TA17 ....191...
Poole BH14 ....78...
Salisbury SP2 ....213...
❺ Shillingstone DT11 .....198...
Winterbourne Steepleton
DT2 ....105...
Coombe St
Lyme Regis DT7 ....96...
Pen Selwood BA9 ....3...
Coombe St La BA21 .....27...
Coombe Valley Rd
Bincombe DT3 ....153...
Overcombe/Preston
DT3 ....168...
Coombe Wr La DT8 .....203...
Coombes Cl DT2 ....103...
Cooper Dean Dr BH8 ...90...
Cooper Gdns DT11 ......198...
Cooper's Cl ❷ BH20 ....142...
Coopers Dr DT6 ....100...
Coopers La BH31 ....45...
Copeland Dr BH14 ....120...
Copper Beech Cl
BH12 ....121...
Copper Beech Gdns
BH10 ....89...
Coppercourt Leaze ❺
BH21 ....59...
Copperm Way DT10 .....33...
Coppers Cl SP6 ....42...
Coppice Ave BH22 ......61...
Coppice Cl
New Milton BH25 ....95...
St.Leonards BH24 ....54...
Coppice St SP7 ....12...
Coppice The
Chickerell DT3 ....166...
Christchurch BH23 ....125...
Coppice View BH10 .....89...
Copse Ave BH25 ....95...
Copse Cl BH14 ....119...
Copse Hill DT10 ....197...
Copse Rd
Brympton BA22 ....26...
New Milton BH25 ....95...
Verwood BH31 ....45...
Copse Way BH23 ....125...
Copythorne Cl BH8 ......90...
Coral Ct ❷ BH12 ....121...
Coram Av DT7 ....96...
Corbar Rd BH23 ....123...
Corbiere Ave BH12 ......88...
Corbin La BH21 ....60...
Corbin Way DT6 ....68...
Cordery Gdns SP8 ....5...
Cordova Gdns DT6 ......100...
Corfe Castle★ DT6 .....161...
Corfe Castle Model Village★
BH20 ....177...
Corfe Castle Mus★ .....162...
Corfe Castle VC Prim Sch
BH20 ....177...
Corfe Halt Cl BH21 ......58...
Corfe Hills Sch BH18 ...86...
Corfe Lodge Rd BH18 ..86...
Corfe Mews BH15 ....119...
Corfe Rd Arne BH20 ....160...
Radipole DT3 ....167...
Corfe View Rd
Corfe Mullen BH21 ....86...
Poole BH14 ....120...
Corfe Way BH18 ....86...
Corfu BH13 ....147...
Corhampton Rd BH6 ....123...
Cornelia Cres BH12 .....121...
Corner Cl DT11 ....21...
Corner La SP7 ....12...
Corner The DT11 ....198...
Cornerways ❷ ❼ BH25 ..95...
Cornflower Dr BH23 .....125...
Cornford Hill DT9 ....196...

ornford Way BH23 ....125 B4
ornhill Way DT3 ....153 B2
ornish Gdns BH10 ....89 B1
ornpits La SP6 ....190 E2
ornwall Cl DT4 ....167 A2
ornwall Rd
 10 Dorchester DT1 ....107 C1
 Salisbury SP1 ....213 B4
 2 Swanage BH19 ....179 B1
oronation Ave
 Bournemouth BH9 ....89 C1
 Upton BH16 ....118 A4
 Yeovil BA21 ....27 A4
oronation Cl BH31 ....45 A4
oronation Rd
 Bridport DT6 ....100 B3
 1 Fortuneswell DT5 ....186 C4
 Gillingham SP8 ....5 C1
 Radipole DT3 ....167 B4
 Verwood BH31 ....45 A4
orporation Rd
 Bournemouth BH1 ....122 B3
 Weymouth DT4 ....167 A2
orpus Christi RC Prim Sch
 BH5 ....123 A3
orscombe Cl BH17 ....87 C1
orscombe Ct* DT2 ....205 B8
orton Cl DT2 ....128 A4
ortry Cl BH12 ....121 A4
ossins La 1 TA18 ....191 F4
otes Ave BH14 ....120 A2
otes Ct BH14 ....120 C4
othayes Dro DT2 ....209 A6
otlands Rd BH1 ....122 A2
otswold Cl BH23 ....124 C4
ottage Cl 2 BH20 ....140 B3
ottage Gdns BH12 ....120 B1
ottage Mews BH24 ....55 A4
otton Cl BH18 ....86 C3
ounter Cl DT11 ....212 C3
ountess Cl BH7 ....123 A4
ountess Gdns BH7 ....122 C4
ounty Mus* DT1 ....108 A1
ourt Ash BA21 ....27 A4
ourt Barton
 8 Crewkerne TA18 ....191 E4
 Easton/Weston DT5 ....186 C4
ourt Cl Bridport DT6 ....68 C1
 12 Christchurch BH23 ....124 C4
 ourt Gdns BA21 ....27 A4
ourt Hill
 Corscombe DT2 ....205 B8
 Damerham SP6 ....190 F2
 Swanage BH19 ....179 A1
ourt La
 Corscombe DT2 ....205 B8
 Milborne Port DT9 ....17 B2
 5 Stofold BA22 ....193 F8
ourt Orch Rd DT6 ....100 B4
ourt Rd
 Bournemouth BH9 ....90 A1
 Radipole DT3 ....152 A1
 Swanage BH19 ....179 A1
ourtauld Dr DT4 ....180 B4
ourtenay Cl BH20 ....142 C3
ourtenay Dr BH22 ....59 B3
ourtenay Rd BH14 ....120 A2
ourthill Fst Sch
 BH14 ....120 B2
ourthill Rd BH14 ....120 B2
ourtlands Rd DT5 ....186 C2
ourtleigh Manor 6
 BH5 ....122 B2
ourtney Cl DT11 ....198 E8
ourtney Pl BH23 ....86 B3
ourtney Rd SP1 ....213 C2
ourtyard Craft Ctr*
 BH16 ....117 A4
ourtyard The
 Christchurch BH23 ....124 B3
 Poole BH12 ....88 B1
ove Rd BH10 ....89 B1
ove Row 5 DT4 ....167 C1
ove St DT4 ....167 C1
ovena Rd BH6 ....123 C3
oventry Cl BH17 ....86 B2
oventry Cres BH17 ....87 A1
ow Dro BH20 ....81 B1
ow La Laverstock SP1 ....213 C3
 Long Bredy DT2 ....103 B1
 Salisbury SP1 ....213 C3
 Swanage BH19 ....179 A1
 Wareham BH20 ....142 C2
owards La DT4 ....149 A4
owdrey Gdns BH8 ....90 C1
owdrys Field 2 BH21 ....59 A3
owell Dr BH7 ....123 A4
owen Cl TA18 ....191 F3
owgrove Rd BH21 ....58 C3
owleaze 10 BH19 ....179 A1
owleaze DT2 ....133 B3
owleaze Rd DT2 ....136 A1
owley Cl DT4 ....167 C1
owley 7 BH17 ....119 B4
owleys Rd BH23 ....92 B1
owper Ave BH25 ....95 C1
owper Rd BH9 ....89 C1
owpitts La BH21 ....57 A1
owslip Rd BH18 ....86 C1
ox Ave BH9 ....90 A1
ox Hill DT2 ....134 B4
ox's La DT2 ....130 B4
oxstone La 2 BH19 ....179 A1
oy Pond Rd BH12 ....121 A3
crab La BA12 ....2 A4

Crab Orch Way BH21 ....45 A1
Crabbswood La SO41 ....95 C4
Crabton Cl Rd BH5 ....123 A3
Crabtree Cl BH23 ....92 B1
Crack La BH19 ....178 B2
Crackmore DT9 ....17 B1
Craigmoor Ave BH8 ....90 C1
Craigmoor Cl BH8 ....90 C1
Craigmoor Way BH8 ....90 C1
Craigside Rd BH24 ....53 C2
Craigwood Dr BH22 ....61 C2
Cranborne CE Fst Sch
 BH21 ....40 A4
Cranborne Cres BH12 ....120 C4
Cranborne Ct
 14 Bournemouth BH4 ....121 B2
 Bournemouth BH9 ....90 A1
Cranborne Cty Mid Sch
 BH21 ....40 A4
Cranborne Dr 8 SP7 ....12 C2
Cranborne Lodge*
 BH21 ....40 A4
Cranborne Pl BH25 ....94 C2
Cranborne Rd
 Alderholt SP6 ....41 B3
 Bournemouth BH2 ....121 C1
 Hinton Parva BH21 ....50 B3
 Swanage BH19 ....179 A2
 Wimborne Minster BH21 ....59 A3
 Wimborne Minster BH21 ....88 A1
Cranbrook Mews
 BH12 ....120 A3
Cranbrook Rd BH12 ....120 A3
Crane Cl BH31 ....45 A4
Crane Dr BH31 ....45 A4
Crane St BH31 ....40 A4
Crane Valley Golf Club
 ....44 B3
Crane Way BH21 ....122 C3
Cranebridge Rd SP2 ....213 B2
Cranemoor Ave BH23 ....93 C1
Cranemoor Cl BH23 ....93 C1
Cranemoor Gdns BH23 ....93 C1
Cranes Mdw DT2 ....208 A8
Cranes Mews BH15 ....119 B2
Cranesmoor Cl BH20 ....139 B3
Cranfield Ave BH21 ....59 B3
Cranford Ave DT1 ....167 C3
Cranleigh Cl BH6 ....123 C3
Cranleigh Gdns BH6 ....123 C3
Cranleigh Rd BH6 ....123 C3
Cranmer Rd BH9 ....121 C4
Cransley Ct BH4 ....121 B1
Crantock Gr BH8 ....90 C2
Cranwell Cl BH11 ....88 C2
Crate Hill BH20 ....197 C5
Crate La SP7 ....7 C3
Crawford Bridge*
 DT11 ....211 E5
Crawford Down Rd 4
 DT11 ....199 E2
Crawford Pk DT11 ....211 E4
Crawshaw Rd BH14 ....120 A1
Creasey Rd BH11 ....89 A3
Creech Grange*
 BH20 ....160 B1
Creech Rd BH12 ....120 B3
Creech Way DT4 ....167 A4
Creekmoor La BH17 ....119 A4
Crescent Ct BH25 ....126 C4
Crescent Dr BH25 ....126 C4
Crescent Rd
 Bournemouth BH2 ....121 C2
 Poole BH14 ....120 C2
 Verwood BH31 ....45 B3
 Wimborne Minster BH21 ....59 B2
Crescent St DT4 ....167 C2
Crescent The
 Barton on Sea BH25 ....126 B4
 3 Bournemouth BH7 ....122 C2
 14 Yeovil BA20 ....27 B2
Crescent Wlk BH22 ....61 C1
Crest Rd BH12 ....120 B4
Cresta Gdns BH25 ....61 C1
Crewkerne Sta TA18 ....192 A3
Cribb Cl BH17 ....119 C4
Crichel House* BH21 ....201 A3
Crichel La BH21 ....200 F1
Crichel Mount Rd
 BH14 ....147 B4
Crichel Rd BH9 ....122 A4
Cricket Cl BH23 ....124 C3
Cringle Ave BH6 ....124 A2
Crispen Cl BH23 ....125 C4
Criterion Arc 5 BH1 ....121 C2
Crock La DT6 ....100 C3
Crockford Cl BH23 ....95 A3
Croft Cl BH21 ....60 B3
Croft Rd
 Bournemouth BH9 ....89 C1
 Bransgore BH23 ....93 A3
 Christchurch BH23 ....124 C4
 Easton/Weston DT5 ....186 C2
 Ringwood BH24 ....47 C1
Croft The
 Wareham BH20 ....142 C2
 12 Yeovil BA20 ....27 B2
Crofton Ave BH12 ....120 C3
Crofton Cl BH23 ....93 A3
Crofton Pk BH21 ....27 B3
Crofton Rd BH21 ....27 B3
Cromer Gdns BH12 ....120 C3
Cromer Rd
 Bournemouth BH8 ....122 B4
 Poole BH12 ....120 C3

Cromwell Pl 9 BH5 ....123 A3
Cromwell Rd
 Bournemouth BH5 ....123 A3
 16 Dorchester DT1 ....108 A1
 Poole BH12 ....120 B3
 Weymouth DT4 ....167 A2
 16 Wimborne Minster BH21 ....59 B2
 Yeovil BA21 ....27 C3
Crook Hill (National Trust)*
 DT8 ....192 E1
Crook Hill DT6 ....204 C2
Crooked La BA9 ....4 B2
Crooked Oak Hill DT6 ....204 D1
Crookhays SP7 ....12 C2
Cropmead Ind Est
 TA18 ....191 F4
Crosby Rd BH4 ....121 B1
Cross La SP8 ....5 C4
Cross Rd
 Bradford Abbas DT9 ....28 B1
 1 Weymouth DT4 ....180 C4
Cross The
 2 Bradford Abbas DT9 ....28 B1
 3 Child Okeford DT11 ....198 C7
 3 Henstridge BA8 ....21 C2
 4 Okeford Fitzpaine DT11 ....197 F5
 Shillingstone DT11 ....198 B6
 Wool BH20 ....140 A1
Cross Way
 Bradford Abbas DT9 ....28 B1
 Christchurch BH23 ....91 B1
Crossfields DT9 ....28 C4
Crossmead Ave BH25 ....95 B3
Crosstree Cl DT2 ....136 A1
Crossway DT11 ....199 E3
Crossways 16 TA20 ....202 A8
Crossways The BH16 ....118 B4
Crouch La DT2 ....196 A6
Crow Arch La 8 BH24 ....55 B3
Crow La BH24 ....55 C3
Crow Hill Cl 2 BH25 ....119 C2
Crown Cl BH12 ....120 C3
Crown Ct
 St Andrew DT11 ....79 C4
 8 Wimborne Minster BH21 ....59 B3
Crown Farm Terr BH21 ....187 A3
Crown Mead BH21 ....59 B3
Crown Rd DT10 ....21 A1
Crown Wlk 8 BH7 ....122 C2
Crown Yd DT2 ....156 C3
Crowthorne La DT2 ....208 A7
Crumpets Dr BH16 ....84 A2
Crumplers Cl BH16 ....84 A2
Crusader Rd BH11 ....88 C2
Cruxton Farm Cotd
 BH21 ....59 B1
Cruxton La DT2 ....73 A3
Cucklington Gdns BH9 ....90 A2
Cuckoo Hill DT9 ....194 B4
Cuckoo La
 Broadwindsor TA20 ....202 F7
 Hilton DT11 ....209 C7
 Stinsford DT2 ....109 A3
Cuckoo Rd BH12 ....120 A4
Cudnell Ave BH11 ....88 C1
Cuffnells Cl BH24 ....47 B4
Cul-de-sac DT11 ....126 B4
Culford Cl BH8 ....90 C1
Culford Ct 1 BH8 ....122 A3
Cull Cl BH21 ....121 B4
Cull La BH25 ....95 B3
Cull Peppers Dish (Sink
 Hole)* DT2 ....112 A3
Culliford Cres BH17 ....87 C1
Culliford Rd DT1 ....135 A4
Culliford Rd N 18 DT1 ....108 A1
Culliford Way DT1 ....152 C2
Cullwood La BH25 ....95 B3
Culver Rd BH25 ....94 C1
Culver St 2 BH1 ....180 C4
Culverhays DT8 ....204 C4
Culverhayes Rd BH21 ....59 A3
Culverhayes Rd DT11 ....59 A3
Culverlake La EX13 ....202 D3
Culvers Cl DT9 ....194 C4
Cumber La SP8 ....5 B1
Cumberland Dr DT4 ....166 C2
Cumnor Rd BH1 ....122 A2
Cunnage La BA12 ....3 C1
Curlew Cl
 1 Chickerell DT3 ....166 B3
 Ferndown BH22 ....61 A4
Curlew Rd
 Bournemouth BH8 ....90 B1
 Christchurch BH23 ....125 A3
Curlews The BH21 ....45 B3
Curlieu Rd BH15 ....119 C3
Curriott Hill 9 TA18 ....191 E3
Curriott Hill Rd 9 TA18 ....191 E4
Curry Hole La DT2 ....193 D2
Curtis Ct DT9 ....196 A8
Curtis Rd DT9 ....189 A3
Curzon Ct 12 BH21 ....119 B4
Curzon Rd
 Bournemouth BH1 ....122 B3
 Poole BH14 ....120 A2
Curzon Way BH23 ....125 B4

Custard Hill BH21 ....201 B5
Custom House Quay
 DT4 ....167 B1
Cuthburga Rd BH21 ....59 B2
Cuthbury Cl BH21 ....59 A2
Cuthbury Gdns BH21 ....59 A3
Cutler Cl
 New Milton BH25 ....95 B2
 Poole BH17 ....87 B1
Cutlers Pl BH21 ....60 A3
Cutt Mill La DT10 ....34 C3
Cynthia Cl BH12 ....120 A4
Cynthia House BH12 ....120 A4
Cynthia Rd BH12 ....120 A4
Cypress Dr BH20 ....27 A1
Cypress Way 9 SP8 ....5 C1
Cyril Rd BH8 ....122 B3

D

Dacombe Cl BH16 ....118 B4
Dacombe Dr BH16 ....118 B4
Daggons Rd SP6 ....41 C3
Dagmar Rd DT1 ....107 C1
Dahlia Cl DT3 ....152 C1
Dairy Cl
 Christchurch BH23 ....124 B4
 Corfe Mullen BH23 ....86 A2
Dairy Field DT11 ....212 C3
Dairy Mdw La SP1 ....213 C2
Dakota Cl BH23 ....125 A4
Dale Ave DT4 ....194 C3
Dale Cl BH15 ....119 C3
Dale Rd BH15 ....119 C3
Dale Valley Rd BH15 ....119 C4
Daler Ct 18 BH20 ....142 C2
Dales Cl BH21 ....60 A3
Dales Dr BH21 ....60 A3
Dales La BH23 ....90 C4
Dalewood Ave BH8 ....88 C3
Dalkeith Rd
 Corfe Mullen BH21 ....86 B2
 Poole BH13 ....121 A1
Dalling Rd BH12 ....121 A3
Dalmeny Rd BH6 ....124 A2
Dalwoods DT9 ....30 A3
Damer's Rd DT1 ....107 B1
Damers Cty Fst Sch
 DT1 ....107 C1
Damory Ct 5 DT11 ....212 B2
Damory Ct St DT11 ....212 B2
Damory St DT11 ....212 B2
Dampier Pl 8 BA21 ....27 C3
Dampier St 3 BA21 ....27 C3
Dane Ct BH24 ....120 A2
Dane Dr BH22 ....61 C2
Danecourt Cl BH14 ....120 A4
Danecourt Rd BH14 ....120 A4
Danecrest Rd SO41 ....95 C2
Danehurst New Rd
 SO41 ....95 A4
Danes Cl BH21 ....121 C4
Danesbury Ave BH6 ....123 C2
Danesbury Mdws BH25 ....95 B2
Daneswood Rd BH25 ....95 B2
Daniel Dr BH20 ....142 B3
Daniel Gdns 18 BH15 ....119 B1
Danielsfield Rd BA20 ....27 A1
Dansie Cl BH14 ....120 A2
Darby La 6 DT6 ....128 A4
Darby's 6 DT6 ....119 B3
Darby's Cnr BH17 ....87 B1
Darby's La BH17 ....119 B4
Darby's La N BH17 ....119 B4
Darkie La Bransgore BH23 ....94 B4
 Fifehead Neville DT10 ....197 C6
 Mere BA12 ....3 A3
 Sandford Orcas DT9 ....15 B3
 Tincleton DT2 ....111 A3
 Witchampton BH21 ....200 F1
Darkie La BH19 ....179 A3
Darknoll La DT11 ....197 E6
Darley Rd BH21 ....60 A3
Darracott Rd BH5 ....123 A3
Darrian Ct BH16 ....118 A4
Darwin Ave BH23 ....91 C1
Darwin Cl DT3 ....152 B2
Darwin Ct 4 BH21 ....121 B4
D'Urberville Cl 4 DT1 ....134 C4
D'Urberville Dr BH19 ....179 A2
Davenant Cl 5 SP8 ....5 C1
Davenport Cl BH16 ....118 B4
David Way DT4 ....180 B4
David's La BH24 ....54 C3
David's Wlk DT1 ....134 C4
Davis Ct BH12 ....120 A3
Davis Field BH25 ....94 C1
Davis Gdns 4 DT10 ....35 B1
Dawkins Bsns Ctr
 BH15 ....118 B2
Dawkins Rd BH15 ....118 B2
Dawn Chorus BH21 ....120 A2
Dawn Cl BH10 ....89 A1
Dawn Cres DT4 ....180 B4
Daws Ave BH11 ....89 A1
Daws Ct BH21 ....121 C4
Day's Rd BH21 ....178 C1
Day's Rd DT9 ....189 C4
Daylesford Cl BH14 ....120 A4
De Courtenai Cl BH11 ....59 C1
De Haviland Rd BH23 ....125 A3
De Haviland Way
 BH23 ....125 A3

De Lisle Rd BH3 ....121 C4
De Mauley Rd BH13 ....147 C4
De Montfort Rd BH21 ....59 C1
De Moulham Rd BH19 ....179 A2
De Redvers Rd BH14 ....120 B1
De Vaux Pl SP1 ....213 B2
Deacon Gdns BH11 ....89 A3
Deacon Rd BH11 ....89 A3
Dean Cl BH15 ....118 C2
Dean La SP5 ....188 F6
Dean La Dro SP5 ....188 F4
Dean Pk Cres BH1 ....121 C2
Dean Pk Rd BH1 ....121 C2
Dean Swift Cres BH14 ....147 B4
Dean's Rd 18 BH5 ....123 A3
Deane Ave SP8 ....5 C1
Deane Way 5 TA20 ....202 A8
Deans Dro BH16 ....84 B1
Deans Gr BH21 ....59 B2
Deans Tr BH1 ....121 C2
Deanscroft Rd BH10 ....89 C2
Deansleigh 5 DT3 ....168 A4
Deansleigh Rd BH7 ....91 A1
Dear Hay La BH15 ....119 B1
Decies Rd BH14 ....120 A3
Dee Way BH15 ....119 A1
Deep Ford La DT2 ....194 C3
Deep La DT9 ....194 C3
Deepdene La BH11 ....88 C3
Deer Pk Cl BH25 ....94 C2
Deerleap Way BH25 ....95 A3
Delamere Gdns BH10 ....89 C2
Delft Mews BH12 ....124 B3
Delhi Cl BH12 ....120 B2
Delhi La DT5 ....187 A2
Delhi Rd BH9 ....89 C1
Delilah Rd BH15 ....118 B1
Delkeith Ct DT2 ....61 B2
Dell Cl BH18 ....86 C2
Dell The BH25 ....126 B4
Delph Rd BH21 ....87 B4
Delph Woods Woodland
 Trail* BH21 ....87 B4
Delta Cl BH23 ....125 A4
Denby Rd BH15 ....119 B2
Dene Cl BH24 ....47 C1
Dene Wlk BH22 ....61 C1
Denecote Lodge
 BH13 ....147 C4
Denes Ave BH12 ....3 A3
Deneve Ave BH17 ....87 B1
Denewood Copse BH22 ....52 C2
Denewood Rd BH22 ....52 C2
Denhall Cl DT10 ....35 A1
Denham Cl BH17 ....87 C2
Denham Dr Cann SP7 ....23 A3
 Christchurch BH23 ....93 C1
Denhay La DT6 ....67 B3
Denholm Cl BH24 ....47 C1
Denison Rd BH17 ....87 B1
Denison Rise SP1 ....213 C4
Denmark La BH15 ....119 B2
Denmark Rd
 Bournemouth BH9 ....89 C1
 Poole BH15 ....119 B2
Denmark Terr BH1 ....122 C3
Denmead BH25 ....95 A3
Denmead Rd BH6 ....124 A3
Dennetts La 19 BH15 ....119 A1
Dennis Rd
 Corfe Mullen BH21 ....86 B3
 Weymouth DT4 ....167 A1
Dennistoun Ave BH23 ....124 B3
Denwood Rd BH24 ....121 A2
Denzil Cl 3 BA22 ....193 A8
Derby Rd BH1 ....122 B2
Derby St DT4 ....167 B2
Dereham Way BH12 ....120 C3
Derritt La BH23 ....92 B4
Derrybrian Gdns BH25 ....95 A1
Derwent Cl
 Bournemouth BH9 ....90 A1
 Wareham BH22 ....62 A3
Derwent Gdns BH21 ....27 C3
Derwent Rd
 New Milton BH25 ....95 A3
 3 Weymouth DT4 ....180 B3
Derwent Way 3 BA22 ....26 C3
Derwentwater Rd BH21 ....59 B3
Deverel Cl BH23 ....124 A4
Devizes Rd SP2 ....213 A3
Devon Rd
 Christchurch BH23 ....123 C4
 Poole BH15 ....119 C3
 Weymouth DT4 ....167 B2
Devonshire Rd SP1 ....213 B4
Dew's Rd SP2 ....213 A3
Dewey's Way SP2 ....5 C1
Dewlands Orch DT9 ....194 E3
Dewlands Rd BH31 ....45 A4
Dewlands Way BH31 ....45 A4
Dewlish Cl BH17 ....88 A1
Dewlish House* DT2 ....78 C4
Diamond Cl SP6 ....43 A4
Diana Cl DT1 ....134 C4
Diana Ct BH23 ....124 B3
Diana Way BH21 ....86 C4
Dibbles La BA22 ....193 A8
Dibden Cl BH8 ....90 B2
Dick o'Th' Banks Cl
 DT2 ....137 B3
Dick o'Th' Banks Rd
 DT2 ....137 B3
Dickens Rd BH6 ....123 B4

Didcot Rd BH17 ....119 B4
Digby Rd DT9 ....30 A3
Diggory Cres DT1 ....135 A4
Dillons Gdns BH16 .....93 A4
Dilly La BH25 ....127 A4
Diments Gdns **2** DT6 .100 B4
Dinah's Hollow SP7 ....24 B3
Dingle Rd BH5 ....123 A2
Dingley Rd BH15 ....119 B3
Dinham Ct BH25 ....95 B2
Dinham Rd BH25 ....95 B2
Dinhay DT10 ....20 C2
Dinosaur Experience The*
..........................177 C1
Dinosaur Mus* DT1 ...108 A1
Diprose Rd BH21 ....86 C4
Discover Salisbury (Medieval
Hall)* SP1 ....213 B2
Disraeli Rd BH23 ......124 B3
Dock Rd DT5 ....101 B1
Dodhams Farm Cl DT6 ..68 C1
Doe Copse Way BH25 ...94 C2
Dogbury Gate DT2 ....207 C8
Dogdean BH21 ....59 B4
Dogwood Rd BH18 ......86 C1
Dolbery Rd N BH12 .....88 B1
Dolbery Rd S BH12 .....88 B1
Dollin's La **3** BH20 ...142 C2
Dollings The BH20 ....177 A4
Dolmans Hill BH16 .....84 A2
Dolphin Ave BH10 ......89 C3
Dolphin Cl **2** DT7 .....96 B3
Dolphin Ctr BH15 .....119 B1
Dolphin Ind Est SP1 ..213 C2
Dolphin La SP8 ....5 C2
Dolphin Pl BH25 ......127 A4
Dolphin St SP1 ....213 B2
Dominion Ctr* BH11 ....88 C2
Dominion Rd BH11 ......88 C2
Donaldson Rd SP1 ....213 B3
Doncaster Rd DT4 ....180 B1
Donhead Hollow SP7 ...25 B4
Donkey La
Bere Regis BH20 .....113 A3
Bridport DT6 ....100 B4
Burton Bradstock DT6 .128 A4
Donnelly Rd BH6 ....123 C3
Donnington Dr BH23 ..125 A4
Donoughmore Rd **1**
BH1 ....122 C2
Dorchester Cty Mid Sch
DT1 ....134 C4
Dorchester Gdns
BH15 ....119 C3
Dorchester Hill
Blandford St Mary DT11 .212 B1
Milborne St Andrew DT11 .79 C4
Winterborne Whitechurch
DT11 ....110 C2
Dorchester Mans DT1 .122 B2
Dorchester Mus*
DT1 ....108 A1
Dorchester Prep Sch
DT1 ....108 A1
Dorchester Rd
Affpuddle DT2 ....79 C1
Askerswell DT2 ....103 A2
Bincombe DT3 ....134 B1
Cerne Abbas DT2 ....207 D4
Closworth BA22 ....193 F6
Frampton DT2 ....74 A1
Loders DT6 ....101 B3
Lytchett Minster & Upton
BH16 ....119 A4
Maiden Newton DT2 ...73 A4
Melbury Osmond BA22 .194 A4
Poole BH15 ....119 C3
Radipole DT3 ....152 A1
Stratton DT2 ....106 B4
Sydling St Nicholas DT2 .207 A2
Tolpuddle DT2 ....79 A1
Upton BH16 ....118 A4
Wool BH20 ....139 C1
Yeovil BA20 ....27 B1
Dorchester S Sta DT1 ..108 A1
Dorchester W Sta
DT1 ....107 C1
Dormers The BH25 ......94 C1
Dornie Rd BH13 ....147 C4
Dorset Av BH22 ....61 B3
Dorset Cl DT4 ....167 A2
Dorset Cty Hospl DT1 .107 C1
Dorset Gall* BH20 ....142 C2
Dorset Grange BH23 ..123 A4
Dorset House BH13 ...121 A1
Dorset Lake Ave BH14 .147 A4
Dorset Lake Manor
BH14 ....120 A1
Dorset Leisure Ctr DT4 .97 A4
Dorset Rare Breeds Ctr*
SP8 ....11 B4
Dorset Rd
Bournemouth BH4 ....121 B3
Christchurch BH23 ...124 C4
Salisbury SP1 ....213 B4
Dorset St DT11 ....212 B2
Dorset Terr **8** DT4 ..167 B1
Dottery Rd DT6 ....68 A1
Double Comm DT6 .....97 A4
Douglas Ave BH23 ....124 A3
Douglas Cl BH16 ......118 B4
Douglas Gdns DT12 ..120 C3
Douglas Haig Rd SP1 .213 B3
Douglas Mews
Bournemouth BH6 .....123 C1

Douglas Mews continued
Upton BH16 ....118 B4
Douglas Rd
Bournemouth BH6 ....123 C2
Poole BH12 ....120 C3
Weymouth DT4 ....180 B3
Doulton Gdns BH14 ..120 A1
Doussie Cl BH16 .....118 B4
Dover Cl BH13 ....121 A2
Dover Rd Poole BH13 .121 A2
Weymouth DT4 ....180 B3
Dover St SP7 ....21 C1
Doves The DT3 ....152 B2
Doveshill Cres BH10 ..89 B2
Doveshill Gdns BH10 ..89 B2
Doveshill Mobile Home Pk
BH10 ....89 B2
Dowlands Cl BH10 .....89 B2
Dowlands Rd BH10 ....89 B2
Dowman Pl DT4 ....180 B3
Down End DT2 ....107 C3
Down House La DT6 ...99 C2
Down La Folke DT9 ...195 D8
Trent DT9 ....14 C1
Down Lodge Cl SP6 ...42 B3
Down Rd
3 Pimperne DT11 ..199 D4
Weymouth DT4 ....167 B1
Down Wood Rd **2** DT11 .199 E2
Down's La DT9 ....4 A4
Downash La EX13 ....202 B3
Downclose **17** DT4 ...180 B4
Downclose La TA18 ..192 C4
Downes St DT6 ....100 B3
Downey Cl BH21 ....88 C1
Downlands CP Sch
DT11 ....199 E3
Downlands Pl BH17 ..119 C4
Downleaze **1** BA20 ..26 C1
Downs La DT9 ....194 C5
Downside Cl
Blandford Forum DT11 .212 C2
Charmouth DT6 ....97 A4
Mere BA12 ....33 A3
Downsview Dr SP8 ......5 C2
Downsway SP1 ....213 B4
Downton Cl BH8 ....90 B2
Downton La SO41 ....127 C4
Downton Rd SP2 .....213 B1
Downview Rd SP6 ....160 B6
Doyne Rd BH14 ....120 C2
Dozens Cnr TA17 .....191 A7
Dragons Hill DT7 ......96 B4
Dragoon Way BH23 ..123 C4
Drake Ave DT3 ....166 B3
Drake Cl
Christchurch BH23 ...124 C3
New Milton BH25 ......94 C2
Ringwood BH24 ....47 C1
Drake Ct **2** BH15 ..119 B1
Drake Rd BH15 ....119 B1
Drake's La DT10 ......37 A3
Drake's Rd DT2 ....208 F3
Drakes Cres **6** TA20 .202 A8
Drakes Mdw BA22 ...193 C7
Drakes Rd BH22 ....61 C2
Draper Rd
Bournemouth BH11 ...89 A2
Christchurch BH23 ...124 C4
Drax Ave BH20 ....142 C3
Draycott Rd BH10 .....89 B1
Dreswick Cl BH23 ....123 B3
Drew Cl Bridport DT6 ..68 C1
Poole BH12 ....121 B4
Drew's La DT10 ....91 B3
Drewitt Ind Est BH11 ..88 C2
Drift End DT2 ....72 C4
Drift The TA20 ....202 B8
Drive The BH12 ......120 B3
Drones La SP7 ....23 B1
Drove La SP7 ....36 C3
Drove Rd DT10 ....32 C2
Drove The Arne BH20 .160 C4
Shapwick DT11 ....56 C4
Thornford DT9 ....194 D8
Winfrith Newburgh DT2 .156 C4
Droveway La BA21 ...14 A3
Droxford Rd BH6 .....123 A3
Druce La DT2 ....77 C2
Druids Cl BH22 ....61 B1
Druitt Rd BH23 ....124 C4
Drum La DT10 ....196 F3
Drummond Rd
Bournemouth BH1 ...122 B2
Swanage BH19 ....179 B1
Drury La DT6 ....204 C2
Drury Rd BH4 ....121 A1
Dry La SP8 ....5 B1
Dryden Cl
Salisbury SP2 ....213 B1
St.Leonards BH24 .....54 A3
Duart Ct BH25 ....95 B2
Duchy Cl DT1 ....135 B4
Duchy Manor Mid Sch
BA12 ....A3
Duck Island La BH24 ..55 A3
Duck La
Bournemouth BH11 ...88 C2
Salisbury SP1 ....213 C3
Stalbridge DT10 ....19 B1
Duck St Bridport DT6 .100 C2
Cattistock DT2 ....206 C2
Cerne Abbas DT2 ....207 D4
Chideock DT6 ....194 B3
Child Okeford DT11 ..198 C7
Hilton DT11 ....209 D5
Symondsbury DT6 .....99 C4
Winterborne Kingston
DT11 ....91 C4

Duck St continued
Wool BH20 ....140 A1
Duck's Nest (Long Barrow)*
SP6 ....190 F7
Ducking Stool La
BH23 ....124 A3
Duckpool La TA18 ....192 B8
Dudley Ave SO41 ......95 C2
Dudley Gdns BH10 .....89 B3
Dudley Pl **2** BH25 ...95 A1
Dudley Rd BH10 ....89 B3
Dudmoor Farm Rd
BH23 ....91 C2
Dudmoor La BH23 .....91 C2
Dudsbury Ave BH22 ...61 B2
Dudsbury Cres BH22 ..61 C2
Dudsbury Ct **9** BH21 .123 A4
Dudsbury Gdns BH22 ..89 C4
Dudsbury Rd BH22 ....61 B1
Dudsway Ct BH22 .....61 B2
Dugberry Hill DT6 .....70 A3
Dugdell Cl BH22 ......61 C3
Duke's Ave DT1 ......108 A1
Dukes Dr BH11 ....88 C3
Dukesfield BH23 ....91 B1
Dullar La BH21 ....56 B1
Dulsie Rd BH3 ....121 A4
Dumbarton Rd DT4 ..180 B3
Dumpton Gdns BH21 ..59 B4
Dunbar Cres BH23 .....93 C1
Dunbar Rd BH3 ....121 C3
Dunbury Fst Sch
Winterborne Kingston
DT11 ....81 C4
Winterborne Stickland
DT11 ....210 C7
Winterborne Whitechurch
DT11 ....210 C3
Dunbury La DT11 ....209 F6
Duncan Cres BH20 ..139 C3
Duncan Rd BH25 ......95 B2
Dunch La DT9 ....194 D3
Duncliff Rd BH6 ......124 A2
Duncliffe Cl DT10 ....33 C4
Duncombe Dr BH24 ...46 C2
Dundas Rd BH17 .....119 C4
Dundee Rd DT4 ......180 B3
Dune Crest BH13 ....147 B2
Dunedin Cl BH22 ......61 A2
Dunedin Dr BH22 .....61 A2
Dunedin Gdns BH22 ..61 A2
Dunedin Rd BH23 ....125 B4
Dunford Cl
Barton on Sea BH25 .126 C4
New Milton BH25 ......94 C1
Dunford Pl **6** BH19 ..179 A1
Dunford Rd BH12 ....120 B3
Dungeon Hill (Fort)*
DT9 ....195 F2
Dunkeld Rd BH3 .....121 C3
Dunlin Cl BH23 ....125 A3
Dunn's La
Iwerne Minster DT11 ..37 C1
Silton SP8 ....2 A1
Dunnock Cl BH22 .....61 A4
Dunsham La TA18 ....191 C2
Dunshay Manor*
BH19 ....177 B2
Dunspit La DT11 .....188 B1
Dunstans La BH15 ...120 A3
Dunyeats Rd BH18 ....87 A2
Durdells Ave BH11 ...89 A3
Durdells Gdns BH11 ..89 A3
Durland Cl BH25 ....95 A1
Durley Chine Ct BH2 .121 B1
Durley Chine Rd
BH2 ....121 B1
Durley Chine Rd S
BH2 ....121 B1
Durley Gdns BH2 ....121 C1
Durley Rd BH2 ....121 C1
Durley Rd S BH2 .....121 C1
Durlston Cres BH23 ..91 B2
Durlston Ct Sch BH23 .91 B2
Durlston Ctry Pk* ....
BH19 ....185 A4
Durlston Farm BH19 .179 A3
Durlston Rd
Poole BH14 ....120 B1
Swanage BH19 ....179 B1
Durnford Dro BH19 ..178 A1
Durngate St DT1 .....108 A1
Durnover Ct DT1 ....108 B1
Durrant DT10 ....197 D8
Durrant Cl DT9 ....30 A3
Durrant Rd
7 Bournemouth BH2 .121 C2
Poole BH14 ....120 B2
Durrington Pl BH7 ...123 A3
Durrington Rd BH7 ..123 A3
Durweston CE Fst Sch
DT11 ....198 E3
Durweston Cl BH9 ....90 A2
Dyke Head DT9 ......195 B6
Dymewood Rd BH21 ..53 A4

E

Eadon Cl DT3 ....168 A4
Eagle House Gdns
DT11 ....212 B2
Eagle House Sch
BH24 ....120 A2
Eagle Rd BH12 ....121 A2
Eaglehurst **5** BH12 .121 A2
Earl Cl **14** DT1 ......108 A1
Earle Rd BH4 ....121 B1
Earle St BA20 ....27 C2

Earlham Dr BH14 ....120 B2
Earls Cl DT9 ....30 B4
Earlsdon Way BH23 ..125 C4
Earlswood Dr SP6 .....42 A3
Earlswood Pk BH25 ...95 B2
Earthpits La SP5 .....189 E4
East Ave
Barton on Sea BH25 .126 B4
Bournemouth BH3 ....121 B3
East Borough BH21 ...59 A3
East Burton Rd BH20 .139 C1
East Cl BH25 ....126 B4
East Cliff DT7 ....96 B3
East Cliff Way BH23 .125 B4
East Coker Prim Sch
BA22 ....193 C7
East Coker Rd BA20 ..27 A1
East Dro BH19 ....178 A1
East Farm La DT2 ....155 B4
East Hill
Charminster DT2 .....107 B3
Evershot DT2 ....206 A7
East Howe La BH10 ...89 B2
East Knighton La DT2 .157 A4
East La TA18 ....192 B8
East Mill La DT9 ......30 B3
East Morden Dro BH20 .83 B3
East Overcliff Dr BH1 .122 B2
East Quay BH15 .....119 B1
East Quay Rd BH15 ..119 B1
East Rd DT6 ....100 C3
East St Beaminster DT8 .204 D4
Blandford Forum DT11 .212 B2
Bourton SP8 ....1 C1
Bridport DT6 ....100 B3
Chickerell DT3 ....166 B3
Corfe Castle BH20 ..162 A1
Crewkerne TA18 .....191 F4
Fortuneswell DT5 ...186 C4
Milborne Port DT9 ...17 B1
North Perrott TA18 ..192 C4
Poole BH15 ....119 B1
Radipole DT4 ....167 C1
Salisbury SP2 ....213 A3
Sydling St Nicholas DT2 .207 A2
Wareham BH20 ......142 C2
West Coker BA22 ....193 A8
9 Winterborne Kingston
DT11 ....81 C4
East View Rd BH24 ..155 B4
East Walls BH20 .....142 C2
East Way
Bournemouth BH8 ....90 B1
Corfe Mullen BH21 ...86 B3
East Weare Rd DT5 ..181 A1
East Wyld Rd DT4 ...167 A2
Eastbrook Row BH21 ..59 B2
Eastbury La BH21 ....123 A4
Eastcott Cl DT2 ......123 A4
Eastdown Ave DT3 ..167 C4
Eastdown Gdns DT3 .168 A3
Easter Rd BH9 ....90 A1
Eastfield **4** DT9 ...194 D8
Eastfield Ct BH24 .....55 C4
Eastfield La
North Perrott TA18 ..192 C4
Ringwood BH24 ....55 C4
West Chinnock BA22 .192 D8
Easthams Rd TA18 ..191 F4
Eastlake Ave BH12 ..120 B3
Eastland Rd BA21 ....27 C3
Eastlands
New Milton BH25 .....95 A1
10 Vetminster DT9 ...194 C5
Eastleaze Rd DT11 ..212 B3
Easton Hollow SP5 ..188 B7
Easton La DT5 ....187 A3
Easton Sq **4** DT5 .187 A2
Easton St DT5 ....187 A2
Eastop La DT10 ....33 A3
Eastville BA21 ....27 C3
Eastwell La DT10 ......35 A4
Eastwood Ave BH31 ..45 A4
Eaton Rd BH13 ....147 C3
Ebor Cl BH22 ....61 C1
Ebor Rd Poole BH12 .120 B3
Weymouth DT4 ......180 B4
Eccles Rd BH15 .....119 A1
Eddison Ave DT1 ....108 B1
Eddy Green Rd BH16 .84 C1
Eden Cl **2** BH1 .....122 A2
Eden Gr BH21 ....59 B2
Edgarton Rd BH17 ....87 B2
Edgehill Rd
Bournemouth BH9 ....89 C1
Bridport DT6 ....100 A3
Edgemoor Rd BH22 ...53 B1
Edifred Rd BH9 ....90 A2
Edison Rd SP2 ....213 A2
Edith Ct **2** SP8 ....5 C1
Edmondsham House*
BH21 ....40 B2
Edmondsham Rd
BH21 ....121 C2
Edmundsham House **26**
BH21 ....121 C2
Edmunds Cl BH25 .....95 A1
Edward Cl BA22 ....26 B3
Edward Cres BH20 ..142 C2
Edward Rd
Bournemouth BH11 ...89 A2
Christchurch BH23 ...124 C4
Dorchester DT1 ......107 C1
Poole BH14 ....120 B3
Edward St
Blandford Forum DT11 .212 B2

Edward St continued
4 Radipole DT4 .....167 C1
Edward Way Ct BH11 ..89 A3
Edwina Cl BH24 ......47 C1
Edwina Dr BH17 ......87 A2
Egdon Cl
Bere Regis BH20 ......81 A4
Ferndown BH22 ....61 A3
Egdon Ct BH16 ......118 A4
Egdon Dr BH21 ....87 C1
Egdon Glen DT2 .....137 C4
Egdon Rd
Dorchester DT1 ......135 A4
Northport BH20 .....142 A4
Egerton Gdns BH8 ..122 B4
Egerton Rd BH8 .....122 B4
Eggardon Cl **5** DT8 .204 C4
Eggardon Hill (Fort)*
DT6 ....71 A4
Egmont Cl BH24 ......54 C1
Egmont Dr BH24 .....54 C1
Egmont Gdns BH24 ..54 C1
Egmont Rd BH16 ....118 A4
Elbury View SP7 ......37 C1
Elder Rd BH20 ....81 A4
Elderberry La BH23 ..124 C3
Eldon Ave BH25 .....126 C4
Eldon Cl BH21 ....126 C4
Eldon Ct **9** BH14 ..120 A1
Eldon Pl BH4 ....121 B1
Eldon Rd BH9 ....89 C1
Eldon Terr **11** BH19 .179 A1
Eldons Dro BH16 .....84 B1
Eldridge Cl **3** DT1 ..134 C4
Eleanor Dr BH11 ......88 B1
Eleanor Gdns BH23 ..123 C1
Elfin Dr BH22 ....61 B3
Elgar Rd BH10 ....89 B1
Elgin Rd
Bournemouth BH3 ....121 B3
Poole BH14 ....120 A3
Elijah Cl BH15 ....118 C1
Eliot House **14** BH25 ..95 A3
Eliotts Dr BA21 ....27 A4
Elise Cl BH7 ....123 A4
Elizabeth Ave
Bridport DT6 ....100 B3
Christchurch BH23 ..123 C4
Elizabeth Cl **1** DT7 ..96 B3
Elizabeth Ct
12 Bournemouth BH1 ..122 A4
11 New Milton BH25 ..95 A3
Elizabeth Gdns BH23 ..125 B4
Elizabeth Pl DT1 ....107 B1
Elizabeth Rd
Blandford Forum DT11 .212 C2
Poole BH15 ....119 B1
Upton BH16 ....118 B4
Wimborne Minster BH21 ..59 B3
Elizabeth Way DT3 ..166 C1
Ellerslie Cl DT2 ......107 C1
Elles Rd BH20 ....139 B1
Ellesdon DT6 ....97 A4
Ellesfield Dr BH22 ....61 B1
Ellingham Dr BH24 ...46 C1
Ellingham Dro BH24 ..47 C1
Ellingham Rd BH25 ..126 B4
Elliot Rd BH11 ....88 C1
Elliott's Hill BA22 ....192 D4
Elm Ave
Christchurch BH23 ....91 C1
Holton Heath BH20 ..116 A4
New Milton BH25 ......95 A4
Elm Cl Matcombe SP7 ..7 A4
Overcombe/Preston
DT3 ....168 A4
Salisbury SP1 ....213 B2
Sturminster Newton DT10 ..35 B4
Elm Ct **1** BH25 ......95 A3
Elm Gdns BH4 ....121 B3
Elm Gr SP1 ....213 C2
Elm Gr Rd SP1 ......213 B3
Elm Tree Wlk BH22 ..89 C4
Elmes Rd BH9 ....89 C1
Elmgate Dr BH7 .....123 A4
Elmhurst Ave BA21 ...27 B3
Elmhurst Rd
Bournemouth BH11 ...89 A3
Ferndown BH22 ....53 A4
Elmhurst Way BH22 ..53 A4
Elmore Dr BH24 ....54 A1
Elmrise Prim Sch BH11 ..89 A3
Elms Ave BH14 ......120 A2
Elms Cl BH14 ....120 A2
Elms Way BH6 ....123 C2
Elmstead Rd BH13 ..147 C4
Elmwood Way BH23 .126 A4
Elphinstone Rd BH23 ..94 A3
Elsdon's La DT6 ....64 A3
Elston Medieval Village of*
DT2 ....207 A3
Eltham Cl BH7 ....123 A4
Elvin Cl SO41 ....95 C3
Elwell Cl DT6 ....100 C3
Elwell Manor Gdns
DT4 ....167 B3
Elwell St DT3 ....152 A3
Elwood Cl BH20 ....142 C4
Elwyn Rd BH1 ....122 B2
Elysium Ct BH22 ......61 C2
Elziver Cl DT3 ....166 B3
Embankment Way
BH24 ....55 A4
Emberley Cl BH22 ....54 A2
Emerald Cl BH24 .....54 A1
Emerson Cl BH15 ...119 B1
Emerson Rd
Poole BH15 ....119 B1

merson Rd continued
Weymouth DT4 .....167 A4
mily Cl BH23 .....92 A1
mily La BH14 .....120 C3
mley La ■ BH21 .....201 C1
mmadale Rd DT4 .....167 A2
mmanuel CE Mid Sch BH11 .....45 A3
mmdale Cl DT4 .....167 A2
mmdale Ct DT3 .....168 A4
mpool Cl DT2 .....137 B3
ncombe Cl BH12 .....120 C4
ncombe Rd BH20 .....142 B2
ndfield Cl BH23 .....91 C1
nfield Rd
Bournemouth BH9 .....90 A1
Christchurch BH23 .....91 C1
ndless St SP1 .....213 B3
nfield Cres BH15 .....119 C3
nfield Cl BH15 .....119 C3
nglands Way BH11 .....88 B2
nkworth Rd DT3 .....168 A4
nsbury Ave BH10 .....89 B1
nsbury La BH10 .....89 B1
nsbury Ct BH10 .....89 C1
nsbury Pk Rd BH9 .....89 C1
nterprise Way BH23 .....90 B4
piphany CE Prim Sch BH9 .....90 A2
rica Dr BH21 .....86 B3
rickson Rd BH12 .....89 B2
rin Rd BH20 .....139 C4
rinbank Mans BH1 .....122 B3
rpingham Rd BH17 .....121 A3
smonde Way BH17 .....119 C3
splanade
Bridport DT6 .....100 A1
Poole BH13 .....147 C4
Portland BH5 .....186 C4
Radipole DT4 .....167 C2
ssex Ave BH23 .....91 C1
ssex Rd DT4 .....167 B2
ssex Sq SP2 .....213 A1
stcourt Rd SP1 .....213 B3
thelbert Rd BH21 .....59 B2
ton Gdns BH4 .....121 B2
trick Rd BH13 .....121 A1
ucalyptus Ave BH24 .....54 B1
uston Gr BH24 .....55 B3
vans Cl
Bournemouth BH11 .....88 C1
St.Leonards BH24 .....54 A3
velyn Mews ■ BH9 .....89 C1
velyn Rd BH9 .....90 A1
vening Glade BH22 .....61 C2
ventide Homes BH8 .....90 C1
verdene Cl BH21 .....60 B1
verdene Dr DT4 .....166 C2
verdene Rd ■ DT1 .....135 A4
verest Rd
Christchurch BH23 .....124 C4
Weymouth DT4 .....167 B1
verets La ■ DT11 .....198 B5
verglades Cl BH22 .....61 B4
vergreen Cl BH21 .....53 A4
vergreens BH24 .....54 A4
vering Ave BH21 .....88 B1
vering Gdns BH12 .....88 B1
versleigh Rd BH12 .....121 B1
verton Ho ■ BA20 .....27 B2
vesham Ave BA21 .....26 C3
vesham Cl BH7 .....123 A4
vesham Cl BH13 .....121 A1
kbourne Manor BH1 .....122 B2
xbury Dr BH11 .....88 C3
xcelsior Rd BH14 .....120 B2
xeter Cres BH2 .....121 C2
xeter Ct BH23 .....126 A4
xeter House Specl Sch SP1 .....213 B4
xeter La BH1 .....121 C1
xeter Pk Mans BH2 .....121 C1
xeter Rd BH2 .....121 C1
■ Swanage BH19 .....179 B1
xeter St SP1 .....213 B2
xton Rd BH6 .....123 C2
ynon Mews BH4 .....55 A3
ype Down Rd DT6 .....99 C3
yres Way SP1 .....213 B2

F

actory Hill SP8 .....1 C2
actory La
■ Buckland Newton DT2 .....207 F8
Tatworth & Forton TA20 .....202 A8
actory Rd BH16 .....118 B3
air Lea BH21 .....212 C1
air Mile Road DT2 .....212 C1
airclose DT1 .....135 A4
aircourt ■ BH21 .....95 A4
aircross Ave DT4 .....167 B1
airey Cl SP1 .....213 A4
airfax Dr BH16 .....99 A3
airfield
Christchurch BH23 .....124 A4
Crewkerne TA18 .....191 E4
Sherborne DT9 .....30 A4
airfield Bglws BH23 .....124 A4
airfield Cl
Christchurch BH23 .....124 A4
■ Okeford Fitzpaine DT11 .....197 F6

Fairfield Cl continued
Wimborne Minster BH21 .....59 C3
Fairfield Pk DT7 .....96 B3
Fairfield Rd
Barton on Sea BH25 .....126 C4
Blandford Forum DT11 .....212 B2
■ Dorchester DT1 .....108 A1
Iwerne Courtney or Shroton DT11 .....198 E7
Salisbury SP1 .....213 B4
Wimborne Minster BH21 .....59 B2
Fairhavon Ct ■ BH5 .....122 C2
Fairhouse Rd BA22 .....193 F8
Fairies Dr BH22 .....61 C2
Fairles SP7 .....13 A1
Fairlie BH24 .....47 C1
Fairlie Pk BH24 .....47 B1
Fairlight La SO41 .....204 A4
Fairmead Rd BA21 .....27 C4
Fairmead Sch BA21 .....27 C4
Fairmile Par BH23 .....91 C1
Fairmile Rd BH23 .....91 C1
Fairoak Way ■ DT8 .....204 A7
Fairthorn Ct ■ BH21 .....121 C2
Fairview Dr BH18 .....87 A3
Fairview Pk BH14 .....120 B2
Fairview Rd
Broadstone BH18 .....87 A3
Salisbury SP1 .....213 C3
Weymouth DT4 .....180 B4
Fairway BH14 .....147 B4
Fairway Dr
Christchurch BH23 .....123 C3
Wareham Town BH20 .....142 B3
Fairway The BH25 .....127 A4
Fairway View BH22 .....27 C3
Fairwinds BH13 .....147 A2
Fairwood Rd BH31 .....45 C3
Fairy Bridge Wlk ■ SP8 .....5 C2
Fairy Cres SP6 .....5 C2
Falcon Dr BH23 .....125 A3
Falconer Dr BH15 .....118 C2
Falconsway SP2 .....213 B1
Falkland Sq ■ BH15 .....119 B1
Fallows The BH25 .....95 A3
Fancy Rd BH12 .....120 A4
Fancy's Row BH21 .....116 A2
Fantley La SP8 .....2 A3
Far Ends ■ BH21 .....120 A2
Faraday Rd SP2 .....213 A3
Farcroft Rd BH12 .....120 A3
Farfrae Cres DT1 .....135 A4
Farley Rd SP1 .....213 C2
Farm Cl Radipole DT4 .....167 A4
Ringwood BH24 .....55 B4
Farm La
Christchurch BH23 .....125 A3
Salisbury SP2 .....213 A3
West Lulworth BH20 .....172 B5
Farm La S BH21 .....127 A4
Farm Rd
Bradford Abbas DT9 .....28 B1
Ferndown DT2 .....52 C1
Farmdene Cl BH23 .....91 C1
Farmer Palmers Farm Pk* BH16 .....84 B4
Farmers Wlk ■ BH21 .....59 C3
Farnham Rd BH12 .....120 C4
Farr's Orch ■ TA16 .....191 F7
Farriers Cl BH21 .....60 A3
Farrington Cl ■ DT11 .....134 C4
Farrington BH21 .....121 B1
Farwell Cl BH22 .....53 C1
Farwell Rd BH12 .....88 B1
Faversham
Bournemouth BH2 .....121 C2
Radipole DT4 .....167 A3
Fawcett Rd BH25 .....94 C1
Fawley Gn BH8 .....90 C3
Fawn Gdns BH25 .....94 C2
Fellowsmead DT10 .....20 C2
Felton Cres BH23 .....125 C4
Felton Rd BH14 .....119 C3
Fenleigh Cl BH25 .....95 A1
Fennel Rd BA21 .....3 A1
Fennel Way BA22 .....26 B3
Fenton Rd BH6 .....123 B3
Fenway Ct DT1 .....108 B1
Fenwick Ct BH8 .....122 C3
Fern Bank
■ Bournemouth BH2 .....121 C2
Three Legged Cross BH21 .....53 A4
Fern Barrow BH12 .....42 B3
Fern Cl Alderholt SP6 .....42 B3
Burton BH23 .....92 B1
Fern Hill SP8 .....11 A1
Ferncroft Gdns BH10 .....89 B3
Ferndale Gdns BA21 .....27 A3
Ferndale Rd
New Milton BH25 .....95 A3
Radipole DT4 .....52 C1
Ferndown Forest Golf Club BH22 .....52 C1
Ferndown Fst Sch BH22 .....61 B3
Ferndown Ind Est BH21 .....60 C4
Ferndown Mid Sch BH22 .....61 B3
Ferndown Upper Sch BH22 .....61 B3
Ferne Hollow SP5 .....188 A8
Fernery Rd BA21 .....27 C3

Fernglade BH25 .....95 A2
Fernheath Cl BH11 .....89 A2
Fernheath Rd BH11 .....89 A2
Fernhill Ave DT4 .....167 B3
Fernhill Cl BH17 .....88 A1
Fernhill Flats ■ BH21 .....121 C2
Fernhill Gate BH25 .....95 A3
Fernhill La BH25 .....95 A3
Fernhill Rd BH25 .....95 A3
Fernhill Rise BA22 .....61 B2
Fernlea Cl
Ferndown BH22 .....61 B2
St.Leonards BH24 .....54 A2
Fernlea Gdns BH22 .....61 B2
Fernside Ave BH14 .....119 C2
Fernside Ct BH15 .....119 C2
Fernside Rd
Bournemouth BH9 .....121 C4
Ferndown BH22 .....53 A1
Poole BH15 .....119 C2
Fernway Cl BH21 .....60 A2
Fernwood Cl BH24 .....54 B3
Ferris Ave BH8 .....90 B1
Ferris Pl BH8 .....90 B1
Ferry Rd
Bournemouth BH6 .....123 C2
Hamworthy BH15 .....119 A1
Studland BH19 .....147 A1
Ferry Way BH13 .....147 A2
Ferrymans Way DT4 .....180 B4
Feversham Ave BH8 .....90 C1
Feversham Rd ■ BH13 .....213 B4
Fiddleford Manor* DT10 .....197 F8
Field Barn Dr DT4 .....167 A3
Field La Gillingham SP8 .....9 B1
Pen Selwood BA9 .....1 A4
Field Pl
Barton on Sea BH25 .....95 A4
Verwood BH31 .....45 A4
Field View Rd ■ DT11 .....212 B2
Field Way
Christchurch BH23 .....93 B1
■ Gillingham SP8 .....86 C4
Field's Cl ■ DT11 .....210 C3
Fieldfare Cl DT3 .....152 B2
Fielding Rd BA21 .....27 C3
Fieldings The SP8 .....9 B1
Fields Mead DT11 .....100 A4
Fields Oak BH21 .....212 B2
Fields The BA12 .....3 A3
Fieldway BH21 .....121 A3
Filehead Hill SP8 .....20 C4
Filbridge Rise DT10 .....35 B1
Filford La DT6 .....67 C4
Filleul Rd BH20 .....115 C1
Finches The DT3 .....152 B2
Finchfield Ave BH11 .....88 C2
Finchley Rd SP2 .....213 A3
Findlay Pl BH19 .....178 C2
Fineshade ■ BH23 .....147 C4
Fippenny Hollow ■ 197 F5
Fir Ave
Holton Heath BH20 .....116 A2
New Milton BH25 .....95 A1
Fir Cl BH22 .....53 A2
Fir Dr DT3 .....153 B2
Fir Tree Cl
Dorchester DT1 .....107 B1
Netherbury BH20 .....68 A3
St.Leonards BH24 .....53 C1
Fir Tree Hill SP6 .....42 B3
Fir Tree La BH23 .....91 B3
Fir Vale Rd BH1 .....121 C2
Firbank Rd BH9 .....122 A4
Firch La DT6 .....101 A3
Firecrest Cl DT3 .....152 B2
Firfield BH21 .....60 A3
Firs Glen Rd
Bournemouth BH9 .....121 C4
Ferndown BH22 .....53 A1
Verwood BH31 .....45 A4
Firs La BH14 .....147 A4
Firs The BH1 .....122 A2
Firshill BH23 .....125 C4
Firside Rd BH21 .....60 A2
First Cliff Wlk ■ DT6 .....100 A1
First Marine Ave BH25 .....127 A4
Firsway BH16 .....118 B4
Firtree Cres SO41 .....95 C2
Fisher's Cl DT11 .....212 B2
Fisher's La TA17 .....191 A7
Fisherbridge Rd DT3 .....168 B4
Fisherman's Ave BH5 .....123 A2
Fisherman's Wlk BH5 .....123 A2
Fishermans Cl DT3 .....166 B3
Fishermans Rd BH15 .....119 B1
Fishers Cl DT9 .....14 C1
Fishers Pl DT3 .....170 A4
Fisherton Island SP2 .....213 A2
Fisherton Manor Mid Sch SP2 .....213 A3
Fisherton St SP2 .....213 A2
Fisherway La TA19 .....191 A5
Fishey La SP7 .....24 C4
Fishpond Bottom Rd DT6 .....202 D1
Fishweir Fields ■ DT6 .....68 C1
Fishweir La DT6 .....68 C1
Fitzharris Ave BH9 .....121 C4
Fitzmaurice Rd BH23 .....123 C4
Fitzpain Cl BH22 .....61 B1

Fitzpain Rd BH22 .....61 B1
Fitzwilliam Cl BH11 .....89 A2
Fitzworth Ave BH16 .....118 B2
Five Acres DT6 .....97 A4
Five Marys (Tumuli)* DT2 .....156 B3
Fiveways Specl Sch BA21 .....27 C3
Flaghead BH13 .....147 C3
Flaghead Chine Rd BH13 .....147 C3
Flaghead Rd BH13 .....147 C3
Flambard Ave BH23 .....92 A1
Flambard Rd BH14 .....120 B2
Flanders Cl DT10 .....21 A1
Flax La DT9 .....17 A4
Flax Way BA21 .....180 A4
Flaxfield Dr ■ TA18 .....191 F4
Flaxfield Rd DT8 .....204 B7
Flazen Cl BH11 .....88 B2
Fleet Ct DT3 .....166 C2
Fleet La DT3 .....166 A3
Fleet Rd DT3 .....165 C3
Fleet St DT8 .....204 D4
Fleet View DT4 .....166 C2
Fleet's Cnr BH17 .....119 A4
Fleetpoint Bsns Ctr BH15 .....119 A3
Fleets Est BH15 .....119 B3
Fleets La BH15 .....119 B3
Fleetsbridge Bsns Ctr BH17 .....119 A4
Fleetwood Ct BH15 .....119 B4
Fletcher Cl BH10 .....89 B2
Fletcher Rd BH10 .....89 B2
Flood La DT6 .....100 B2
Floral Farm BH21 .....60 A1
Florence Rd
Bournemouth BH5 .....122 C2
Dorchester DT1 .....134 C4
Poole BH14 .....120 B2
Florin Mall ■ BH7 .....123 A4
Floriston Gdns BH25 .....95 B2
Flower Ct ■ BH21 .....59 C3
Flowers Dro BH16 .....84 B2
Flushing Mdw BA21 .....28 A3
Folke La DT9 .....31 A4
Folkstone Rd SP2 .....213 A1
Folly Cl SP2 .....213 A1
Folly Farm La BH24 .....54 C3
Folly Fields BA21 .....27 A4
Folly La
Blandford St Mary DT11 .....212 B1
Gillingham SP8 .....9 A1
Kington Magna SP8 .....9 C2
Nether Compton DT9 .....28 C4
Wool BH20 .....140 A1
Folly Mill Gdns DT6 .....100 B3
Folly Mill La DT6 .....100 B3
Font La DT8 .....204 B2
Font Villas BA22 .....193 B7
Fontmell Magna St Andrews CE Sch SP7 .....37 C3
Fontmell Rd BH18 .....87 B2
Foot's Hill SP7 .....24 A4
Footners La BH23 .....91 C2
Ford Cl BH22 .....53 A2
Ford Down La DT2 .....208 A7
Ford La Corscombe DT2 .....205 B7
Ferndown BH22 .....62 A4
Forde Abbey* TA20 .....202 D8
Forde Pk BH23 .....26 C4
Fordhay BA22 .....192 E7
Fordingbridge Rd SP6 .....42 B4
Fordington Gdns ■ DT1 .....108 A1
Fore St Evershot DT2 .....206 F4
Thorncombe TA20 .....202 E6
Forehill Cl DT3 .....168 A4
Foreland Cl BH23 .....91 B2
Foreland Rd BH16 .....118 B2
Forest Cl
Christchurch BH23 .....93 B1
Verwood BH31 .....45 C2
Forest Ct BH25 .....55 C3
Forest Ct Hills ■ BH24 .....55 C3
Forest Edge Rd BH24 .....53 A3
Forest Edge Rd BH20 .....142 C4
Forest Hill BH20 .....27 A1
Forest La
Corfe Castle BH20 .....162 C1
Verwood BH31 .....45 A4
Forest Links Rd BH21 .....59 B3
Forest Oak Dr BH25 .....95 A3
Forest Pines BH25 .....95 A2
Forest Rd
Bournemouth BH22 .....53 A2
Poole BH13 .....121 A1
Forest Rise BH23 .....93 B1
Forest View
Crossways DT2 .....137 B3
New Milton BH25 .....94 B1
Forest View Cl BH9 .....90 A1
Forest View Dr BH9 .....90 A1
Forest View Rd BH9 .....90 A1
Forest Way
Christchurch BH23 .....93 B1
Ferndown BH22 .....53 A2
Forestlake Ave BH24 .....55 C3
Forestside Gdns BH24 .....47 C1
Forestside The BH31 .....45 C3
Forge End DT8 .....10 B1
Forge La
East Chinnock BA22 .....192 E8
Zennor BA12 .....1 C1
Forsters La DT6 .....69 A1

Forsyth Gdns BH10 .....89 B1
Fort Cumberland Pl BH15 .....118 B1
Fortescue Rd
Bournemouth BH3 .....122 A3
Poole BH12 .....120 B3
Fortuneswell DT6 .....186 C4
Forty Foot Way DT6 .....100 A1
Forum Sch The DT11 .....198 B6
Foss Way TA17 .....191 C8
Fosse Cl BA21 .....26 C4
Fosse Way BA21 .....26 C4
Fossett Way DT4 .....180 A4
Fosters DT9 .....30 B3
Fosters Hill DT9 .....196 B5
Fosters Mdws ■ DT11 .....198 B6
Fosters Spring BH16 .....84 B1
Fotherby Cres SP1 .....213 C4
Foundry Cl DT6 .....100 A4
Foundry Knapp DT6 .....100 A4
Foundry La DT6 .....100 B3
Foundry Sq ■ TA18 .....191 F4
Fountain Mead ■ SP7 .....12 C2
Fountain Way BH23 .....124 A3
Four Acres DT5 .....186 C2
Four Wells Rd BH21 .....60 A1
Fouracre Cl DT6 .....100 B4
Fourgates Rd BH21 .....107 C1
Fourth Cliff Wlk DT6 .....100 A1
Fowler's Hill SP1 .....213 C2
Fowler's Rd SP1 .....213 B2
Fox Cl DT6 .....69 A1
Fox La DT11 .....60 B3
Fox La Terr DT10 .....35 B1
Fox Mdws ■ TA18 .....191 F5
Foxbury BH20 .....139 B4
Foxbury Rd
St.Leonards BH24 .....62 C4
St.Leonards BH24 .....54 A1
Foxcote ■ BA20 .....26 C1
Foxcote Gdns BH25 .....94 C2
Foxcroft Dr BH21 .....60 A3
Foxes Cl BH31 .....45 C3
Foxglove Cl
Christchurch BH23 .....125 B4
Gillingham SP8 .....5 C1
Foxglove Pl BH25 .....95 B2
Foxglove Way
Radipole DT3 .....152 C1
Yeovil BA22 .....26 B3
Foxhill Cl BH15 .....118 A4
Foxhill ■ BH19 .....179 A1
Foxhills BH31 .....45 B3
Foxhills Cres BH16 .....84 B2
Foxhills Dr BH16 .....84 B2
Foxhills Rd BH16 .....84 B2
Foxholes ■ BH6 .....123 C2
Foxholes Rd
Bournemouth BH6 .....123 C2
Poole BH15 .....119 C3
Foxs Cl DT9 .....196 B5
Foxwell La TA18 .....192 C7
Foxwood Ave BH23 .....124 C3
Foyle Hill SP7 .....12 B3
Framerville Rd BH20 .....139 C4
Frampton Cl BH25 .....95 B3
Frampton Pl BH24 .....55 B3
Frampton Rd
Bournemouth BH9 .....122 A4
■ Pimperne DT11 .....199 D4
Frances Ct ■ BH23 .....126 A4
Frances Rd BH1 .....122 A3
Francesca Ct ■ BH23 .....124 C4
Francesca Grange ■ BH23 .....124 C3
Francesca Lodge ■ BH23 .....124 C3
Franchise St DT4 .....167 B1
Francis Ave BH11 .....88 B2
Francis Ave Ind Est BH11 .....88 B2
Francis Rd Poole BH12 .....120 C3
Weymouth DT4 .....167 A1
Francis Way SP2 .....213 B1
Frank Wareham Cottage Homes The BH9 .....90 A2
Frankland Cres BH14 .....120 C2
Franklin Cl DT4 .....167 A1
Franklin Rd
Bournemouth BH9 .....90 A2
New Milton BH25 .....95 A1
Weymouth DT4 .....167 A2
Franklyn Cl BH16 .....118 A4
Frankston Rd BH6 .....123 C2
Frankston Rd BH6 .....123 B2
Fraser Ave BH14 .....120 C4
Fraser Ct BH25 .....94 C2
Fraser Rd BH21 .....120 C4
Freame Way SP8 .....5 B1
Freda Rd BH23 .....123 C3
Frederica Rd BH9 .....121 C4
Freedom Ave BA21 .....27 A3
Freemans Cl BH21 .....60 A1
Freemans Rd BH21 .....60 A1
Freemantle Rd DT4 .....166 C1
Freesia Cl DT3 .....152 C1
Fremington Ct ■ BH25 .....95 A2
French Mill La
Cann SP7 .....23 C4
Shaftesbury SP7 .....12 C1
French Mill Rise SP7 .....12 C1
French Rd BH17 .....87 A1
French's Farm Rd BH16 .....117 A4

Frensham Cl BH10 ....89 C2
Freshwater Cl **8** DT5 ....186 C1
Freshwater Dr BH15 .....118 B2
Freshwater Rd BH23 ....125 B3
Friar Waddon Rd
 Chickerell DT3 ....151 C4
 Radipole DT3 ....152 A4
Friar's Orch **8** SP1 ....213 B2
Friars Ave BA21 ....26 C3
Friars Cl **2** DT1 ....135 B4
Friars Gate BH23 ....125 B3
Friars Moor DT10 ....35 B1
Friars Rd BH23 ....125 A3
Friars Wlk BH25 ....127 A4
Friary Hill BH25 ....108 A1
Friary La
 Dorchester DT1 ....108 A1
 Salisbury SP1 ....213 B2
Friary The SP1 ....213 B2
Friday's Heron BH21 ......44 A4
Frinton Cl **6** BH14 ....120 A2
Fritham Gdns BH8 ....90 B2
Frizzel's Hill DT10 ......196 F4
Frobisher Ave BH12 ......88 C1
Frobisher Cl
 Christchurch BH23 .....124 C3
 8 Ringwood BH24 ......47 C1
Frog La
 Dinnington TA17 ....191 B8
 Fordingbridge SP6 ....43 A4
 Iwerne Courtney or Shroton
 DT11 ....198 F2
 Motcombe SP7 ....30 A1
Frogham Hill SP6 ....43 C3
Frogmore La DT2 ....71 C4
Frome Ave BH20 ....139 C1
Frome Bridge* DT2 ...110 B1
Frome La DT2 ....72 C4
Frome Rd BH20 ....142 B2
Frome Terr DT1 ....108 A1
Frome Valley Rd DT2 ....37 C3
Frome View
 Bradford Peverell DT2 ...107 A3
 Maiden Newton DT2 ......73 A4
Front La BH21 ....56 B3
Front St East Stour SP8 ..10 C2
 Portesham DT3 ....132 A1
Froom's La BH20 ....81 B1
Frost Rd BH11 ....88 C2
Froud Way BH21 ....86 B2
Froxfield Rd DT11 ......212 B3
Fry's Cl DT3 ....150 A4
Fry's La DT2 ....75 A4
Fryer Cl BH11 ....89 B3
Fryers Copse BH21 ......60 B3
Fryers Rd BH21 ....52 C4
Frys Cl BH16 ....89 A3
Fudge Hill DT2 ....205 A8
Fulbrooks Cl DT6 ....100 B4
Fulbrooks La DT6 ....100 B4
Fulmar Rd BH23 ....125 A3
Fulwood Ave BH11 ....88 C3
Furge Gr BA8 ....19 A2
Furge La BA8 ....19 A2
Furland Rd **8** TA18 ...191 F4
Furlands DT5 ....186 C2
Furlong La DT9 ....17 C2
Furlong The BH24 ....55 A4
Furlongs The DT9 ....30 A4
Furnell Rd BH15 ....119 B1
Furze Croft BH25 ....95 A1
Furze Hill Dr BH14 ......120 B1
Furze The **9** BA20 ....26 C1
Furzebrook Cl BH17 .....87 C2
Furzebrook Rd BH20 ....161 A2
Furzehill BH21 ....50 C1
Furzelands Rd
 Verwood BH21 ....45 A1
 Verwood BH21 ....53 A4
Furzey Rd BH16 ....118 A3
Furzy Cl DT3 ....168 A4

G

Gabriel Gn **1** DT1 .....135 A4
Gainsborough DT9 ....17 B1
Gainsborough Ave
 BH25 ....95 A3
Gainsborough Ct **11**
 BH5 ....123 A3
Gainsborough Dr DT9 ...29 C3
Gainsborough Hill DT9 ...30 B2
Gainsborough Rd
 Bournemouth BH7 .....122 C4
 St.Leonards BH24 ....54 A3
Gainsborough Way
 BA21 ....28 A4
Gale Cres DT6 ....100 B3
Gales Hill DT2 ....207 E7
Gallop Way BH12 ....121 B4
Gallop's La BH20 ....83 B1
Galloway Rd BH15 ....118 B2
Gallows Cnr
 Iwerne Courtney or Shroton
 DT11 ....44 A4
 Milton Abbas DT11 ....209 D3
Gallows Dr BH22 ....61 C1
Gallows Hill Arne BH20 .161 B2
 Owermoigne DT2 ......155 B3
Gallwey Rd DT4 ....180 B4
Galton Ave BH23 ....123 C3
Gannetts Pk BH19 .....179 A2
Garden Cl Bridport DT6 .100 B4
 Litton Cheney DT2 .....103 A1

Garden Cl continued
 New Milton BH25 ....95 A1
Garden Ct BH1 ....122 B3
Garden House **17** BH1 ...122 A2
Garden Wlk BH22 ....61 C4
Garden-Lane BH24 ......54 A2
Gardens Cres BH14 ....147 A4
Gardens Ct **7** BH15 ....119 C2
Gardens Rd BH14 ......147 A4
Gardenside **1** DT6 ....97 A4
Gardner Ct BH23 ....123 C4
Gardner Rd
 Christchurch BH23 ....123 C4
 Ringwood BH24 ....55 B3
Garfield Ave
 Bournemouth BH9 .....122 B3
 Dorchester DT1 ....134 C4
Garland Cres DT1 ......135 A4
Garland Rd BH15 ......119 B2
Garlands La DT11 ......197 D4
Garrett Rd BA20 ....26 C2
Garsdale Cl BH11 ......89 A3
Garston Hill DT3 ......166 B3
Gartells **1** DT10 .....197 A4
Garth Cl BH24 ....53 C2
Garth Rd BH9 ....90 A1
Gas La
 Hinton St George TA17 .191 C7
 Salisbury SP2 ....213 A3
Gascoigne's La SP7 ....12 C1
Gascoyne La DT2 ......107 A3
Gashay La EX13 ....202 E3
Gasper St BA12 ....1 B3
Gassons La DT6 ....66 A2
Gate Cl EX13 ....202 A3
Gatemore Rd DT1 ......138 C1
Gateway The BH13 ....120 C2
Gawthorne Dr SP2 .....213 A1
Gaydon Rise BH11 .....88 C2
Gaza Rd BH20 ....139 B4
Gazelle Rd BA20 ......26 C2
Geelong Cl DT3 ....152 C1
Geneva Ave BH6 ......123 B3
Gent Cl DT11 ....212 C3
George St (South) **9**
 ....213 A3
George St Bridport DT6 .100 B1
 Salisbury SP2 ....213 A3
 Sherborne DT9 ....30 A3
Georges Cl DT6 ....97 A4
Georges Mews BH21 ...86 B4
Georgian Cl BH24 .....55 B4
Georgian Way BH22 ...89 C2
Georgina Cl BH12 .....121 B4
Georgina Talbot House
 BH12 ....121 A4
Gerald Rd BH3 ....122 A3
Germaine Cl BH23 ....125 C4
Gerrards Gn DT8 ......204 D4
Gervis Cres BH14 .....120 A2
Gervis Pl BH2 ....121 C2
Gervis Rd BH1 ....122 A2
Giant's Grave* DT2 ...209 A4
Gibbs Gn BH16 ....84 B1
Gibbs La DT6 ....64 B2
Gibbs Marsh Trading Est
 DT10 ....20 A2
Gibson Rd BH17 ......119 C4
Giddy Gn La BH20 ....139 C1
Giddy Gn Rd BH20 ....139 C1
Giddylake BH21 ....59 B3
Gifle View **2** DT9 ...194 D8
Gigant St SP1 ....213 B2
Gigg La SP6 ....8 C2
Gilbert Cl SP6 ....42 B3
Gilbert Ct **5** BH20 ...139 C1
Gilbert Rd
 Bournemouth BH1 ....122 B3
 Swanage BH19 ....179 A1
Gilbert Way SP1 ......213 C4
Giles Cl DT2 ....107 A3
Giles's La
 Bishop's Caundle DT9 .196 A7
 Morden BH21 ....83 B2
Gillam Rd BH10 ....89 B3
Gillett Rd BH12 ....121 A4
Gillingham DT11 ......90 B2
Gillingham CP Sch SP8 ..5 C1
Gillingham Milton Prim Sch
 SP8 ....5 C3
Gillingham Mus* SP8 ...5 C1
Gillingham Sch SP8 ....6 A1
Gillion Ct **13** BH23 ...128 C3
Gipsy La DT6 ....68 C1
Gipsy's Dro DT10 .....197 C7
Girt La DT2 ....205 F7
Glacis DT5 ....187 A4
Gladdis Rd BH11 .....60 A4
Glade The BH24 ......54 A3
Gladelands Cl BH18 ...86 C2
Gladelands Mobile Home Pk
 BH22 ....61 C4
Gladelands Way BH18 .86 C2
Gladstone Cl
 Bridport DT6 ....100 C4
 Christchurch BH23 ....124 B3
 2 Radipole DT3 .....152 C1
Gladstone Rd
 Bournemouth BH7 ....122 C3
 Poole BH12 ....120 B3
Gladstone Rd E BH7 ...122 C3
Gladstone Rd W BH1 ...122 C3
Glamis Ave BH10 .....89 C3
Glastonbury Ct BA21 ..26 C3
Gleadowe Ave BH23 ...123 C3
Glebe Cl
 Abbotsbury DT3 ......149 B4

Glebe Cl continued
 Bridport DT6 ....100 B3
 Maiden Newton DT2 ....72 C4
 Osmington DT3 ....169 A4
 8 Thornford DT9 ....194 D8
Weymouth DT4 ....167 B1
Glebe Cottage* DT2 ...169 C3
Glebe Ct **4** DT11 .....37 C1
Glebe Gdns SP7 ....12 A4
Glebe Rd BH16 ....84 B2
Glebe The
 8 Durweston DT11 ...198 E3
 8 Iwerne Minster DT11 ..37 C1
Glebefields DT2 ....106 C4
Glebeford Cl DT2 ......155 C4
Glebeland Cl DT3 ......136 A4
Glebeland La DT6 ......65 C4
Glebelands **6** TA16 ...191 F7
Glen Ave DT4 ....167 B1
Glen Cl BH25 ....126 B4
Glen Fern Rd BH1 .....122 A2
Glen Rd
 Bournemouth BH5 .....122 C2
 Poole BH14 ....120 A2
 6 Swanage BH19 .....179 A1
Glen Spey BH25 ....95 B1
Glen The BH12 ....120 B3
Glenair Ave BH14 .....120 A2
Glenair Cres BH14 ....120 A2
Glenair Rd BH14 ......120 A2
Glenavon BH25 ....95 B1
Glencairn Rd BH23 ....93 C1
Glencoe Rd
 Bournemouth BH7 .....122 C4
 Poole BH12 ....120 B3
Glendale Cl
 Christchurch BH23 ....91 B2
 Wimborne Minster BH21 ..59 B1
Glendale Cres SP1 ....213 C2
Glendale Ct BH23 .....91 B2
Glendale Rd BH6 ......124 A2
Glendinning Ave DT4 ..167 B3
Glendon Ave BH10 ....89 B3
 SP2 ....213 A3
Glendrive BH23 ....126 B4
Gleneagles BH23 ......123 C3
Gleneagles Ave BH14 .120 B1
Gleneagles Cl BH22 ...61 C3
Glenferness Ave BH4 ..121 B3
Glengariff Rd BH14 ....120 B2
Glengarry BH25 ....95 B1
Glengarry Way BH23 ..125 B3
Glenives Cl BH24 ......54 A2
Glenmeadows Dr BH10 ..89 A3
Glenmoor (Girls) Sch
 BH10 ....89 B1
Glenmoor Cl BH10 ....89 B1
Glenmoor Rd
 Bournemouth BH9 ....89 B1
 Ferndown BH22 ....61 B2
Glenmore Rd
 Salisbury SP1 ....213 C4
 Weymouth DT4 ....167 A2
Glenmount Dr BH14 ...120 A2
Glennie Way DT3 ......166 B2
Glenroyd Gdns BH6 ...123 C2
Glenside BH25 ....126 A4
Glenthorne Ave BA21 ..27 B4
Glenville Cl BH23 .....94 A1
Glenville Gdns BH10 ..89 B1
Glenville Rd
 Bournemouth BH10 ....89 B1
 Christchurch BH23 ....94 A1
 Yeovil BA21 ....27 B4
Glenwood Cl DT2 .....53 A1
Glenwood La BH22 ....53 A1
Glenwood Rd
 Ferndown BH22 ....53 A1
 Verwood BH31 ....45 A3
Glenwood Way BH22 ..53 A1
Glissons BH22 ....61 A1
Globe Cl **8** BH19 ....178 C1
Globe La BH15 ....119 B1
Globe Orch TA18 .....192 C6
Gloucester Cl DT3 ....166 C2
Gloucester Mews DT4 .167 B2
Gloucester Rd
 Bournemouth BH7 ....122 C3
 8 Dorchester DT1 ...107 C1
Poole BH12 ....120 B3
Gloucester St DT4 ....167 B2
Glovers Cl **2** BH21 ...17 B1
Glue Hill DT10 ....197 C8
Glyde Path Rd DT1 ...108 A1
Glyn Pl SP7 ....24 B3
Glynville Cl BH21 ....60 A4
Glynville La BH21 ....60 A4
Glynville Rd BH21 ....60 A4
Goathill Rd DT9 ......194 E6
Goathorn Cl BH16 ....118 B2
God's Blessing La BH21 ..51 A2
Godley Rd SP2 ....213 B1
Godmanstone Cl DT2 .88 A1
Godolphin Sch SP2 ...213 C2
Godolphin Sch Douglas
 House SP1 ....213 C3
Godshill Cl BH8 ....90 B2
Gold Hill
 Child Okeford DT11 ...198 B8
 Shaftesbury SP7 ......12 C1
Gold St DT10 ....33 B4
Goldcrest Cl DT3 .....152 B2
Goldcroft BA21 ....27 B3
Goldcroft Ave DT4 ...167 A2
Goldcroft Rd DT4 ....167 B2
Golden Gates BH13 ...147 A2

Golden Hill DT10 .....32 C1
Golden Sands BH13 ...147 A2
Goldenleas Ct BH11 ...88 B2
Goldenleas Dr BH11 ...88 B2
Goldensands Pool & Leisure
 Ctr BA20 ....27 B2
Goldfinch Cl BH25 ....94 C1
Goldfinch Rd BH17 ....118 C4
Golding's La DT9 .....17 B1
Golf Links Rd
 Broadstone BH18 .....87 A3
 Ferndown BH22 ....61 C2
Goliath Rd BH15 .....118 B1
Good Rd BH12 ....120 B4
Goodwin's La BH20 ...83 C2
Goose Hill DT3 ....124 C4
Goosacre La BA22 ...26 B1
Gordon Cres **11** DT4 ..166 C1
Gordon Ct BH4 ....121 B2
Gordon Mount BH23 ..126 A4
Gordon Rd
 Bournemouth BH11 ...122 B2
 Christchurch BH23 ...126 A4
 Poole BH12 ....121 A3
 6 Swanage BH19 ...179 A1
 Wimborne Minster BH21 ..59 C2
 Yeovil BA21 ....27 C3
Gordon Rd S BH12 ...121 A3
Gordon Way BH23 ....92 B1
Gordon's La DT9 .....195 A8
Gore Cross DT6 ....68 C1
Gore Cross Way **8** DT6 ..68 C1
Gore Grange BH25 ...94 C1
Gore Hill BH20 ......142 C4
Gore La DT6 ....68 C1
Gore Rd BH25 ....94 C1
Gore Rd Ind Est BH25 ..94 C1
Gorey Ave BH22 .....88 B1
Gorleston Rd BH12 ...120 C3
Gorley Lynch SP6 ....43 C2
Gorley Rd BH24 .....47 C4
Gorse Cl
 New Milton BH25 ....95 B2
 St.Leonards BH24 ...53 C2
Gorse Hill Cl BH15 ...119 C3
Gorse Hill Cres BH15 .119 C3
Gorse Hill Rd BH15 ..119 C3
Gorse La BH16 ....118 B4
Gorse Rd BH21 ....86 B3
Gorsecliff Ct **7** BH5 ..122 B2
Gorsecliff Rd BH10 ...89 B1
Gorsefield Rd BH25 ..95 A2
Gorseland Ct BH22 ..61 C2
Gort Rd
 Bournemouth BH11 ..89 A2
 Poole BH17 ....87 A1
Gosling Cl BH17 .....119 C4
Gough Cl **11** TA16 ...191 F7
Gough Cres BH17 ....87 A1
Goughs Cl DT10 .....35 A1
Gould's Hill
 Radipole DT3 ....152 A4
 Winterborne St Martin
 DT2 ....52 B2
Goulds Hill Cl DT3 ...152 A4
Gover Cl BH20 ......143 A1
Gover Rd SP7 ....13 A1
Grafton Ave DT4 ....167 A3
Grafton Cl
 Bournemouth BH3 ...122 A4
 Christchurch BH23 ...124 B3
Grafton Rd BH3 .....122 A3
Grammar Sch La BH21 ..59 A2
Granby Cl DT4 ......166 C2
Granby Ind Est DT4 ..166 C2
Granby Rd BH9 .....90 A1
Granby Way DT4 ....167 A3
Grand Ave BH6 .....123 B2
Grand Par **22** BH15 ..119 A1
Grange BH21 ....50 C1
Grange Arch* BH20 ..175 B4
Grange Ct **16** BH1 ...122 A2
Grange Gdns
 Poole BH12 ....120 C4
 Salisbury SP1 ....213 C3
Grange Hill BH20 ...160 B1
Grange La DT8 .....203 D5
Grange Pk **1** DT9 ...194 D8
Grange Rd
 Bournemouth BH6 ...123 B2
 Broadstone BH18 ....87 A2
 Christchurch BH23 ..125 A4
 Church Knowle BH20 ..160 B2
 Radipole DT3 ....167 C3
 St.Leonards BH24 ..54 C3
Grange Rd Bsns Ctr
 BH23 ....125 A4
Grange Sch The BH23 ..124 C4
Grangecroft Rd **6** DT5 ..186 C2
Grangewood Hall DT2 ..59 B3
Grans Barrow (Long
 Barrow)* SP6 ....190 C6
Grant's Ave BH1 ....122 B3
Grantham Rd BH1 ...122 C3
Grantley Rd **8** BH5 ...122 C2
Grants Cl BH1 ....122 C4
Granville Gdns **6** SP7 ..12 C2
Granville Pl **22** BH1 ...121 C2
Granville Rd
 Bournemouth BH5 ...122 C2
 Poole BH12 ....120 B3
 Weymouth DT4 ......167 B1
Granville Way DT9 ...30 B4
Grasmere Cl
 Christchurch BH23 ...91 B2
 1 Salisbury SP2 ...213 A1
Grasmere Gdns BH25 ..95 A3

Grasmere Rd
 Bournemouth BH5 123
 Poole BH13 147
 Radipole DT3 167
Grass Royal BA21 27
Grass Royal Jun Sch
 BA21 27
Gravel Hill BH18 88
Gravel La
 Charlton Marshall DT11 ..211
 Ringwood BH24 55
Gray Cl BH17 119
Gray's Yd **2** BH15 ..119
Graycot Cl BH10 89
Grays DT4 167
Grays Cl SP7 12
Grayson Ct BH22 61
Great Cnr BA21 26
Great Down La DT10 ..21
Great George St DT4 ..167
Great Head La DT2 ...266
Great Hill BA9 1
Great La SP7 12
Great Ovens Dr BH20 ..142
Great Pit La BA22 ...15
Great Western Rd **11**
107
Great Western Terr
 Radipole DT4 167
 Yeovil BA21 27
Greaves Cl BH10 ...89
Grebe Cl
 Broadstone BH17 ...118
 2 Chickerell DT3 ..166
 Christchurch BH23 ..125
Green Acres BH23 ..124
Green Acres Cl BH24 ..54
Green Bottom BH21 ..60
Green Cl
 Bere Regis BH20 81
 Bradpole DT6 100
 Charlton Marshall DT11 ..211
 Poole BH15 119
 Sturminster Newton DT10 ..35
Green Dr SP6 42
Green Gdns BH15 ...119
Green La Ashmore SP5 ..39
 Barton on Sea BH25 ..127
 Bournemouth BH10 ..89
 Bridport DT6 100
 Chickerell DT3 166
 Crossways DT2 137
 East Chinnock BA22 ..192
 Ferndown BH22 61
 Hooke DT8 205
 Kington Magna SP8 ..9
 New Milton BH25 94
 Ringwood BH24 55
 Stour Provost SP7 ..22
 Sturminster Marshall
 DT11 56
 Tatworth & Forton
 TA20 202
 West Coker BA22 ...193
 Weymouth DT4 180
Green Loaning **5** BH23 ..124
Green Mead BA21 ...26
Green Pit Knapp DT6 ..65
Green Pk BH1 122
Green Rd
 Bournemouth BH9 ...122
 Poole BH15 119
Green St **11** SP7 191
Green The
 8 Hazelbury Bryan DT10 ..197
 Mappowder DT10 ...196
 Puddletown DT2 78
 Salisbury SP1 213
 Sherborne DT9 30
Greenacre
 Barton on Sea BH25 ..127
 Charminster DT2 107
Greenacre Cl BH16 ..118
Greenacres BH13 ...121
Greenacres Cl BH10 ..89
Green's **17** SP1 213
Greenclose La BH21 ..59
Greencroft St SP1 ...213
Greenfield Gdns BH25 ..127
Greenfield Rd
 8 Charlton Marshall
 DT11 211
 Poole BH15 119
Greenfields BH12 ...120
Greenfinch Cl BH21 ..86
Greenfinch Wlk BH24 ..55
Greenford CE Prim Sch
 DT2 72
Greenford La
 Compton Valence DT2 ..104
 Frome Vauchurch DT2 ..72
Greenham La TA18 ..203
Greenhayes
 Broadstone BH18 ...87
 Chard DT6 96
 2 Okeford Fitzpaine DT11 ..197
Greenhays Rise BH21 ..59
Greenhill
 Blandford Forum DT11 ..212
 Radipole DT4 167
 Sherborne DT9 30
Greenhill Cl BH21 ...59
Greenhill La BH21 ...59
Greenhill Rd
 Wimborne Minster BH21 ..59
 Yeovil BA21 27
Greenhill Terr **4** DT5 ..186
Greenings Ct DT11 ..212

eens Cross Dr 4 DT8 ....204 C4
eenside ST25 ....127 A3
eensleeves Ave
?18 ....87 A3
eesome Dr BH22 ....61 C3
?ne
2 Child Okeford DT11 ....198 C7
me Regis DT7 ....96 A3
eenway CI DT3 ....59 B1
eenway Cres BH16 ....118 A4
eenway La DT11 ....198 B7
eenway Rd DT3 ....152 B1
eenways
?rndown BH22 ....125 C4
aston/Weston DT5 ....186 C2
?enways Ave BH8 ....90 B2
?enways Ct BH22 ....61 C2
eenwood Ave
?rndown BH22 ....61 C3
?ole BH14 ....147 B4
?isbury SP1 ....213 C3
eenwood Copse
?24 ....54 A2
eenwood Rd
?ournemouth BH9 ....121 C4
?2 BH21 ....26 C4
eenwood Way 8 BH24 ....54 A2
eenwoods 32 BH24 ....95 A1
?nfield Rd BH9 ....89 C2
?nville Ct BH24 ....47 C1
?nville Ct
?Bournemouth BH4 ....121 B2
?Poole BH15 ....119 B1
?nville Rd BH12 ....59 B2
?esham Rd BH9 ....90 A1
?exy Cross DT2 ....205 E7
?exy Mare & Her Colts (Long ?arrow) The P 131 B2
?eyfriars CI SP1 ....213 B2
?eys Bridge* DT1 ....108 B1
?eys Rd 8 TA16 ....191 F7
?eystoke Ave BH11 ....88 C3
?eystones CI DT7 ....137 B3
?ibb View TA20 ....202 E6
?iffin Ct BH21 ....59 B2
?iffins Ct 7 SP7 ....213 B3
?iffiths Gdns BH10 ....89 A3
?imsey La SP8 ....4 C4
?osvenor 15 BH1 ....122 A2
?osvenor CI DT1 ....53 C3
?osvenor Cres DT1 ....135 A4
?osvenor Ct
?Bournemouth BH1 ....122 B2
?hristchurch BH23 ....124 A3
?osvenor Gdns BH1 ....122 C2
?osvenor Rd
?ournemouth BH4 ....121 B2
?orchester DT1 ....135 A4
?aston/Weston DT5 ....186 C2
?adipole DT4 ....167 B3
?ove Ave
?haftesbury SP7 ....12 C2
?albridge DT10 ....33 B4
?rquage BH19 ....179 B1
?ove End
?adipole DT4 ....167 B3
?oole BH13 ....27 A3
?ove Cty Inf Sch DT5 ....187 A3
?ove La
?hobsbury DT3 ....149 A3
?othenhampton DT6 ....101 A3
?ortesham DT3 ....150 C3
?albridge DT10 ....33 B4
?ove Orch DT10 ....33 B4
?ove Orch 3 BH24 ....128 A4
?ove The
?ournemouth BH1 ....89 C2
?hristchurch BH23 ....107 C1
?orchester DT1 ....135 A4
?rndown BH22 ....61 B2
?erwood BH31 ....45 B3
?oveley Bsns Ctr
?123 ....124 C3
?oveley Rd
?hristchurch BH4 ....121 A1
?hristchurch BH23 ....124 C3
?owery Ave BH5 ....122 C2
?ower Gdns BH12 ....89 A2
?ugs La BH12 ....94 C1
?yphon Leisure Ctr
?9 ....30 A4
?yphon Sch The DT9 ....30 B4
?ard Ave BH2 ....26 B3
?ernsey La BH12 ....88 B1
?ernsey St BH12 ....121 A3
?est Rd BH21 ....122 A3
?est Rd BH16 ....118 A4
?uilder La SP1 ....213 C1
?uildford DT4 ....167 B3
?uildhall Ct 33 BH15 ....119 A1
?uildhall Mus* BH15 ....119 A1
?uildhill Rd BH6 ....123 C2
?ainevere CI BH21 ....26 C4
?ulliver CI BH14 ....147 B4
?ulliver CI BH21 ....59 B3
?ullivers Orch DT6 ....101 B2
?ulway Mead 7 TA20 ....202 A8
?undry La DT6 ....100 B3

Gundry Rd DT6 ....100 C4
Gunn La 3 DT11 ....198 B5
Gunners La BA22 ....26 B3
Gunville Cres BH19 ....90 A2
Gunville Down Rd
DT11 ....199 F4
Gunville La
East Coker BA22 ....193 D8
Hermitage DT2 ....195 C2
Gunville Rd DT11 ....199 F4
Gurjun CI BH16 ....118 A4
Gurney Rd BH21 ....86 C3
Gussage Rd BH12 ....120 C4
Gwenlyn Rd BH16 ....118 B3
Gwynne Rd BH12 ....120 C4
Gyllas Way SP8 ....5 C2
Gypshayes BH19 ....178 A1
Gypsy La
Easton/Weston DT5 ....186 C2
Ringwood BH24 ....55 B4
2 Weymouth DT4 ....167 B1

H

Haarlem Mews BH23 ....124 B4
Hackney DT2 ....205 A7
Hadden La BH8 ....122 B4
Haddon La DT10 ....19 C1
Haddons Dr BH21 ....52 C3
Hadley Way BH18 ....86 C2
Hadow Rd BH10 ....89 B2
Hadrian CI BH22 ....61 B1
Hadrian Way BH21 ....86 C4
Hahnemann Rd BH2 ....121 C1
Haig Ave BH13 ....147 A2
Haimes La SP7 ....12 C2
Hainault Dr BH31 ....45 B3
Haines La DT8 ....203 A5
Hains La DT10 ....20 C3
Haking Rd BH23 ....124 B4
Halcyon Ct BH15 ....119 B3
Hale Ave BH25 ....95 A1
Hales Gdns BH25 ....95 A1
Hales Mdw BH21 ....123 C4
Half Acre La DT8 ....204 C4
Half Acres DT9 ....30 A3
Half Hide Down SP5 ....188 B3
Half Moon St DT9 ....30 A3
Halfpenny La SP5 ....39 B4
Halfway Way BH25 ....125 A4
Hall Rd DT1 ....88 C2
Hallet Ct DT7 ....96 A3
Hallet Gdns BA20 ....27 B2
Halls Rd BH16 ....60 B3
Hallum CI SP1 ....213 C4
Halsey Gn DT2 ....196 B3
Halstock CI DT3 ....168 B4
Halstock Cres BH17 ....87 B1
Halter Path BH15 ....118 C2
Halter Rise BH21 ....60 B3
Halton CI BH23 ....93 A4
Halves Cotts BH21 ....177 A4
Halves La BA22 ....193 B8
Ham La Ferndown BH21 ....60 C2
5 Gillingham SP8 ....9 A3
Marnhull DT10 ....20 B2
Trent DT9 ....15 A1
Ham Mdw DT10 ....20 B2
Hamble Rd BH15 ....94 C1
Hambledon CI
Blandford Forum DT11 ....212 C2
Todber DT10 ....21 B2
Hambledon Gdns
Blandford Forum DT11 ....212 C2
Bournemouth BH6 ....123 B3
Hambledon Hill (Hill Fort)*
DT11 ....198 B7
Hambledon View DT10 ....35 B1
Hambleton Rd BH7 ....123 A4
Hambro CI BH21 ....186 C4
Hamcroft DT5 ....186 C2
Hamilton CI
10 Bournemouth BH4 ....122 A3
5 Wimborne Minster SP1 ....59 A3
Hamilton Rd
Bournemouth BH1 ....122 B3
Christchurch BH23 ....124 C2
Hamworthy BH15 ....118 C1
Radipole DT3 ....152 C1
Salisbury SP1 ....213 B3
Hamilton Way DT1 ....94 A4
Hamlands DT1 ....105 C1
Hamlon CI BH11 ....89 A2
Hammett CI DT2 ....79 B1
Hammond Ave BH14 ....167 A3
Hammond St DT10 ....88 B1
Hammonds Mead DT6 ....97 A4
Hampden La BH6 ....123 A3
Hampreston CE Fst Sch
BH21 ....60 C2
Hampshire CI BH23 ....91 C1
Hampshire CI 6 BH21 ....121 C2
Hampshire CI The
BH8 ....90 C1
Hampshire Hatches La
BH24 ....55 A2
Hampshire House
BH2 ....121 C2
Hampshire Rd DT4 ....166 C2
Hampton Dr DT3 ....132 A1
Hampton CI 8 BA22 ....193 F8

Hampton Dr BH24 ....47 B1
Hampton Stone Circle*
DT3 ....131 C1
Hamworthy Fst Sch
BH15 ....118 C1
Hamworthy Mid Sch
BH15 ....118 C1
Hamworthy Park*
BH15 ....118 C1
Hamworthy Sta BH16 ....118 B2
Hanbury Rd 7 BH19 ....179 A1
Handley St BH24 ....55 A4
Handley Lodge BH12 ....120 C4
Hands La DT3 ....149 A4
Hanford Cl
DT11 ....198 D6
Hanford House Sch
DT11 ....198 D6
Hanham Rd DT12 ....121 A4
Hanham Rd
Corfe Mullen BH21 ....86 B3
Wimborne Minster BH21 ....59 B3
Hankinson Rd BH9 ....122 A4
Hannam's CH BH16 ....84 B2
Hannington PI BH7 ....123 A3
Hannington Rd BH7 ....123 A3
Hanover CI DT10 ....35 A1
Hanover Ct DT11 ....212 B2
Hanover Gn BH17 ....119 C4
Hanover House BH15 ....119 B2
Hanover La SP8 ....5 B1
Hanover Rd DT4 ....167 B3
Happy Island Way
DT6 ....100 C4
Harbeck Rd BH9 ....122 A4
Harbin's Pk* DT11 ....199 D8
Harbour BA21 ....26 C3
Harbour CI BH13 ....147 B3
Harbour Cres BH23 ....124 C3
Harbour Ct
Barton on Sea BH25 ....126 C4
Christchurch BH23 ....124 C3
Poole BH13 ....147 C3
Harbour Hill CI
BH15 ....119 C3
Harbour Hill Cres
BH15 ....119 C3
Harbour Hill Rd BH15 ....119 C3
Harbour Hospl The
BH15 ....119 B2
Harbour Lights BH15 ....119 C2
Harbour Prospect
BH14 ....147 B4
Harbour Rd
Bournemouth BH6 ....124 A2
Sherborne DT9 ....30 B4
Harbour View CI
BH14 ....120 A3
Harbour View Ct
BH23 ....124 A3
Harbour View Rd
Fortuneswell DT5 ....186 C4
Poole BH14 ....120 A2
Harbour Watch BH14 ....147 B4
Harbour Way DT9 ....30 A4
Harbridge Dro BH24 ....42 C2
Harbridge Sch BH24 ....46 C4
Harcombe CI BH17 ....87 C2
Harcombe Rd DT7 ....64 A2
Harcourt Mews 7 BH5 ....123 A3
Harcourt CI BH23 ....123 A4
Harcourt Terr SP2 ....213 A2
Harding's La SP8 ....6 A1
Hardwick St 3 DT1 ....167 C2
Hardy Ave DT4 ....167 A1
Hardy Cl
2 Beaminster DT8 ....204 D4
Ferndown BH22 ....21 A2
Marnhull DT10 ....21 A2
Martinstown DT2 ....133 B3
New Milton BH25 ....94 C2
Hardy Cres
Stalbridge DT10 ....33 B4
Wimborne Minster DT11 ....59 B2
Hardy Ct 26 TA18 ....191 F4
Hardy Mon (National Trust)*
DT2 ....132 B2
Hardy Rd Bridport DT6 ....100 C4
Ferndown BH22 ....61 A4
Poole BH14 ....120 B2
Wareham BH20 ....142 B1
Hardy's Birthplace (National
Trust)* DT2 ....132 B2
Hardy's La DT8 ....203 D6
Hare La Cranborne BH21 ....40 C3
Hordle SO41 ....95 C2
Hare La Pottery*
DT11 ....41 A3
Hares Gn BH11 ....123 A4
Harewood Ave BH7 ....123 A4
Harewood Cres BH7 ....122 C4
Harewood Gdns BH7 ....122 C4
Harewood Pl BH7 ....122 C4
Harford Rd BH12 ....120 B4
Hargrove La DT10 ....33 C2
Harkwood Dr BH15 ....118 C2
Harland Rd BH6 ....124 A2
Harleston Villas 17 BH21 ....59 B2
Harley Gap BH21 ....201 B8
Harley La BH21 ....201 A5
Harman's Cross Sta
BH19 ....177 C3
Harness CI BH21 ....60 A3
Harnham CE Jun & Inf Sch
SP2 ....213 A1
Harnham Rd SP2 ....213 A2
Harnwood Rd SP2 ....213 A1
Harp Stone* BH20 ....175 C3

Harper Rd
21 Crewkerne TA18 ....191 F4
Salisbury SP2 ....213 A4
Harpitts La
Kington Magna SP8 ....9 C2
West Stour SP8 ....10 A2
Harpway La BH23 ....92 B3
Harrier Dr BH21 ....125 B4
Harrington CI BH23 ....125 C4
Harrington Ct BH23 ....125 C4
Harris Way BH25 ....95 A3
Harrison Ave BH1 ....122 B3
Harrison CI BH23 ....122 B3
Harrison Way BH22 ....53 A2
Harrow CI BH23 ....93 A4
Harrow Rd BH23 ....93 A3
Harry Barrow CI 1 BH21 ....59 B3
Harry Lodge's La SP8 ....5 A1
Hart's CI BH25 ....94 C2
Hart's La Holt BH21 ....51 B2
Nether Compton DT9 ....29 A3
Harting Rd BH6 ....124 A2
Hartland CI DT2 ....209 B5
Hartfoot La DT2 ....209 B5
Hartfoot La DT2 ....209 B5
Hartington CI SP2 ....213 A3
Hartley St SP1 ....195 B1
Hartmoor Hill SP8 ....9 B3
Hartnell CI BH21 ....86 B3
Hartsbourne Dr BH7 ....123 A4
Harvard CI 4 SP2 ....213 A1
Harvey Rd
Bournemouth BH5 ....123 A3
Oakley BH21 ....87 C4
Harveys CI DT7 ....64 A2
Harwell Rd BH17 ....119 B4
Harwood Ct BH25 ....94 C2
Haselbury Plucknett VC Fst
Sch TA18 ....192 C5
Haskells Rd BH12 ....120 A4
Haslemere Ave BH23 ....126 A4
Haslemere PI BH23 ....126 A4
Hasler Rd BH17 ....119 B4
Haslop Rd BH23 ....93 B1
Hastings Rd
Bournemouth BH8 ....90 C1
Poole BH17 ....87 A1
Hatch Pond Rd BH17 ....119 B4
Hatches La SP1 ....213 C2
Hatfield Ct BH25 ....94 C2
Hatfield Gdns BH7 ....123 A4
Hathaway CI SP1 ....213 A4
Hathaway Rd BH6 ....123 B2
Hatherden Ave BH19 ....119 C4
Hathermead Gdns
BH21 ....27 C4
Havelins CI DT11 ....198 E4
Havelock Rd BH12 ....121 A3
Havelock Way BH23 ....93 B1
Haven Ct BH13 ....147 A2
Haven Gdns BH25 ....95 A1
Haven Rd
Corfe Mullen BH21 ....86 B3
Poole BH13 ....147 C4
Havenhurst BH13 ....147 C3
Haverstock BH9 ....90 A2
Haviland Mews BH7 ....122 C3
Haviland Rd
Bournemouth BH1 ....122 C3
Ferndown BH22 ....61 A4
Haviland Rd E 8 BH7 ....122 C3
Haviland Rd W 9 BH7 ....122 C3
Hawden Rd BH11 ....89 A1
Hawk CI BH24 ....60 A4
Hawkchurch Gdns
BH17 ....87 C1
Hawkchurch Prim Sch
EX13 ....202 B3
Hawkcombe Way EX13 ....202 B3
Hawkcombe St SP2 ....23 C1
Hawker CI BH21 ....59 C1
Hawker's La SP7 ....22 C4
Hawkesdene La SP7 ....12 C1
Hawkeswood CI SP7 ....12 A4
Hawkesworth CI 13 SP3 ....153 A2
Hawkins CI 2 BH24 ....47 C1
Hawkins Rd BH12 ....88 C1
Hawkins Way BA21 ....26 C2
Hawkridge SP2 ....213 B1
Hawkwood Rd BH5 ....122 C2
Haworth CI BH23 ....92 A1
Hawthorn Ave SP8 ....5 C1
Hawthorn CI
5 Dorchester DT1 ....107 C1
New Milton BH25 ....95 A3
Radipole DT4 ....167 A3
5 Shaftesbury SP7 ....213 A3
Hawthorn Dr BH17 ....86 C1
Hawthorn Rd
Bournemouth BH9 ....121 C4
Burton BH23 ....92 C4
Yeovil BA21 ....27 C4
Hawthorne CI 15 TA18 ....191 F5
Hawthorne Rd DT1 ....107 C1
Hawthorns The
Christchurch BH23 ....124 C3
Stalbridge DT10 ....33 C4
Haxen La TA17 ....191 A8
Haycock Way 2 BH21 ....56 B2
Haycombe DT11 ....198 E3
Haycrafts La BH19 ....177 C2
Haydon Hollow DT9 ....31 B3
Haydon La
Frome St Quintin DT2 ....206 D7
Lydlinch DT10 ....197 A6
Haydon Rd DT11 ....121 A1
Haye CI DT7 ....96 A3

Haye La DT7 ....96 A3
Hayes Ave BH7 ....122 C3
Hayes CI BH21 ....60 A2
Hayes La BH21 ....60 A3
Hayes The DT8 ....203 E5
Hayeswood Fst Sch
BH21 ....60 A3
Hayeswood Rd BH21 ....60 A3
Haylands DT5 ....186 C2
Haymoor Ave DT3 ....167 C4
Haymoor Mid Sch
BH17 ....87 C1
Haymoor Rd BH15 ....120 A4
Haynes Ave BH15 ....119 B2
Haysoms CI BH25 ....95 A1
Hayters Way SP6 ....42 B3
Hayward Cres BH31 ....45 A3
Hayward La DT11 ....198 B7
Hayward Way DT11 ....44 C3
Haywards Ave DT3 ....167 B4
Haywards Farm CI
BH31 ....45 A3
Haywards La
Child Okeford DT11 ....198 C7
Corfe Mullen BH21 ....86 B4
Hazel CI Alderholt SP6 ....42 B3
Christchurch BH23 ....93 B1
Hazel Ct DT2 ....129 C4
Hazel La DT2 ....129 C4
Hazel View 11 TA18 ....191 F5
Hazeldene BH18 ....87 A2
Hazeldown Ave DT3 ....167 C4
Hazell Ave BH10 ....89 A1
Hazelton CI BH7 ....123 A4
Hazelwood Ave BH23 ....94 C2
Hazelwood Dr BH31 ....45 B2
Hazlebury Rd BH17 ....119 A4
Hazlemere Dr BH24 ....54 A2
Hazzard's Hill BA12 ....3 A3
Head La SP8 ....10 B2
Head's La BH10 ....89 C3
Headland CI BH7 ....186 C1
Headlands Bsns Pk
BH24 ....47 B1
Headless Cross BH10 ....89 B3
Heads Farm CI BH10 ....89 C3
Headstock Rd TA20 ....202 B7
Headswell Ave BH10 ....89 C2
Headswell Cres BH10 ....89 C2
Headswell Gdns BH10 ....89 C2
Heanor CI BH10 ....89 B1
Heath Ave BH15 ....119 B3
Heath CI
Bovington Camp BH20 ....139 B4
Wimborne Minster BH21 ....60 A4
Heath Farm CI BH22 ....61 B2
Heath Farm Rd BH22 ....61 B2
Heath Farm Way BH22 ....61 B2
Heath Gn Rd BH19 ....164 A1
Heath Rd
Christchurch BH23 ....94 A1
Hordle SO41 ....95 C2
St Leonards BH24 ....54 C2
Heathcote Rd BH5 ....122 C2
Heather Cl
Bournemouth BH8 ....90 B2
Christchurch BH23 ....94 A1
Corfe Mullen BH21 ....86 C3
St Leonards BH24 ....54 A2
Heather Dell BH16 ....118 A4
Heather Dr BH22 ....61 B4
Heather Fields 18 SP8 ....5 C2
Heather Lodge 2 BH25 ....95 A1
Heather Rd
Bournemouth BH10 ....89 B2
Yeovil BA21 ....27 C4
Heather View Rd
BH12 ....120 C4
Heather Way
Ferndown BH22 ....61 B4
Yeovil BA21 ....27 C4
Heatherbank Rd BH4 ....121 B2
Heatherbrae La BH16 ....118 A3
Heatherdown Rd BH22 ....53 B1
Heatherdown Way
BH22 ....53 B1
Heatherlands Fst Sch
BH12 ....120 B3
Heatherlands Rise
BH12 ....120 B3
Heatherlea Rd BH6 ....123 B2
Heathfield Ave BH12 ....121 A4
Heathfield Rd BH22 ....53 B1
Heathfield Way BH22 ....53 A1
Heathlands CI DT2 ....137 B3
Heathlands Ave BH22 ....53 B1
Heathland CI BH23 ....92 B2
Verwood BH31 ....45 B3
Heathlands Prim Sch
BH11 ....89 A3
Heathwood Ave BH25 ....126 C4
Heathwood Rd
Bournemouth BH9 ....121 C4
Weymouth DT4 ....167 A2
Heathy CI BH25 ....126 C4
Heaton Rd BH10 ....89 A1
Heavy Horse Ctr*
BH21 ....40 C1

Heavytree Rd BH14 .....120 A2
Heber's La TA17 ....191 A5
Heckford La BH15 ......119 B2
Heckford Rd
  Corfe Mullen BH21 ....86 B3
  Poole BH15 ....119 B2
Heddington Dr DT11 ...212 B3
Hedgerley BH25 ....127 A4
Heights App BH16 ......118 B4
Heights Rd BH16 ....118 B4
Helen La ❹ DT4 ....167 C1
Helena Rd BA20 ....26 C1
Helena Terr SP1 ....213 B3
Helic Ho ❷ BH21 ....59 B3
Hell Cnr DT21 ....194 D1
Hell La DT6 ....99 A4
Helston Cl DT3 ....132 A1
Helyar Rd BH8 ....90 C1
Hembury Rd DT2 ....102 B4
Hemlet's Cl DT6 ....68 C1
Hemsbach Ct ❻ BH20 ..142 C2
Henbury Cl
  Corfe Mullen BH21 ....86 B3
  Poole BH17 ....88 A1
Henbury Hall (English
  Heritage)* BH21 ....56 C1
Henbury Rise BH21 ......86 B3
Henbury View Fst Sch
  BH21 ....86 B3
Henbury View Rd BH21 ..86 B3
Henchard Cl BH22 ....61 B1
Hendford ❻ BA20 ....27 B2
Hendford Hill BA20 .....89 B1
Hendford Gr BA20 ....27 B2
Hendford Hill BA20 .....27 A2
Hendford Rd BH10 ......89 B1
Hendre Cl BH19 ....178 C1
Hengist Rd BH1 ....122 B2
Hengistbury Head Nature
  Reserve* BH6 ....124 C1
Hengistbury Head Nature
  Trail* BH6 ....124 B2
Hengistbury Rd
  Barton on Sea BH25 ....126 C4
  Bournemouth BH6 ......124 A2
Henhayes La ❶ TA18 ...191 F4
Henley Gdns BH7 ....123 A4
Henley View ❼ TA18 ...191 F3
Henning Way DT9 ....17 B2
Henning's Pk Rd BH15 .119 C3
Henry Cl DT4 ....180 C4
Henry's Way DT7 ....96 B3
Henstridge CE VC Prim Sch
  BA8 ....19 A3
Henstridge Trad Est
  BA8 ....20 A3
Henville Rd ❹ BH8 ....122 B3
Herbert Ave BH12 ......120 B4
Herbert Ct BH12 ....120 B4
Herbert Hospl BH4 .....121 A1
Herbert Rd
  Bournemouth BH4 ......121 A1
  New Milton BH25 ....95 A2
  Poole BH13 ....121 A1
Herberton Rd BH6 .....123 B3
Herblay Cl BA21 ....28 A3
Herbury La DT9 ....21 C4
Hercules Rd BH15 .....118 B2
Hereford Cres DT4 ....167 A2
Hereford Rd DT14 .....167 A2
Heritage Ct BH13 .....147 C4
Herm Rd BH12 ....88 B1
Hermitage La DT17 ....195 B1
Hermitage Rd BH14 ...120 A3
Hermitage The BH14 ..120 A3
Hern La SP6 ....43 B3
Heron Cl
  ❸ Dickerell DT3 .....166 B3
  Overcombe/Preston
    DT3 ....168 A3
Heron Cl Rd BH13 .....122 A4
Heron Dr BH21 ....60 A4
Heronswood SP2 ......213 B1
Herrington Rd DT1 ....135 A4
Herrison Rd DT2 ....75 C1
Herston CE Sch BH19 .178 C1
Herston Halt Sta
  BH19 ....178 C2
Herstone Cl DT7 ....87 C1
Hertford Ct ❶❷ BH23 ..126 A4
Hertford Rd BA21 ....28 A4
Hesketh Cl BH24 ......145 B3
Hestan Cl BH23 ....91 B2
Heston Way BH22 ....52 C2
Hetherly Rd DT11 .....167 B4
Hewish La TA18 ....191 E4
Hewitt Rd BH15 ....118 C2
Hewlett's Dro DT10 ...197 C7
Heysham Rd BH10 ......87 A2
Heytesbury Rd BH6 ...123 B3
Hibberd Way BH10 ......89 B1
Hibberds Field DT11 ...40 A4
Hibbs Cl
  Northport BH20 ....142 C3
  Upton BH16 ....118 B4
Hickes Cl BH11 ....88 C2
Hickory Cl BH16 ....118 A4
High Brow BH22 ....61 B3
High Cl BH21 ....56 B2
High E St DT1 ....108 A1
High Howe Cl BH11 ......88 C2
High Howe Gdns BH11 ...88 C2
High Howe La BH11 ......88 C2

High Lea BA21 ....27 B4
High Lea Sch BH21 ......50 B4
High Marryats BH25 ...127 A4
High Mead BH22 ....61 A1
High Mead La BH22 ......61 A1
High Oaks Gdns BH11 ...88 C2
High Pines BH23 ....125 B4
High Pk Rd BH23 ....86 C2
High Ridge Cres BH25 ..95 B3
High St Ashmore SP5 ....39 B4
  Broadwindsor DT8 .....203 E5
  Burton Bradstock DT6 ..128 A4
  Child Okeford DT11 ....198 C7
  Christchurch BH23 ....124 A3
  Corscombe DT2 ....205 A8
  Cranborne BH21 ....40 A4
  Damerham SP6 ....190 F3
  East Chinnock BA22 ...192 E8
  ❼ Easton/Weston DT5 .186 C1
  Fortuneswell DT5 .....186 C4
  Gillingham SP8 ....5 C1
  Hardington Mandeville
    BA22 ....193 A6
  Henstridge BA8 ....19 A2
  Hinton St George TA17 .191 C7
  Lytchett Matravers BH16 .84 A2
  Milborne Port DT9 ......17 B1
  Piddlehinton DT2 ....76 C4
  Poole BH15 ....119 B1
  Puddletown DT2 ....82 A2
  Rimpton BA22 ....15 A4
  Ringwood BH24 ....55 A4
  Salisbury SP1 ....213 B2
  Shaftesbury SP7 ....12 C1
  Shapwick DT11 ....68 B1
  Saxpenny Hundley SP5 .189 A4
  Spetisbury DT11 ....211 E5
  St.Leonards BH24 ....54 A3
  Stalbridge DT10 ....33 B4
  Sturminster Marshall
    BA22 ....56 B2
  Swanage BH19 ....178 A1
  Sydling St Nicholas DT2 .207 A2
  Tarrant Monkton DT11 .200 B3
  Thorncombe TA20 ......202 E5
  Toller Porcorum DT2 ....71 B4
  Weymouth DT4 ....180 B4
  Wimborne Minster BH21 .59 A2
  Winfrith Newburgh DT2 .156 C3
  Wool BH20 ....140 A1
  Yeovil BA20 ....27 B2
  Yetminster DT9 ....194 C5
  Zeale SP8 ....1 C2
High St Cl BH20 ....140 A1
High St Fordington
  DT1 ....108 A1
High St N BH15 ....119 B2
High Trees
  Broadmayne DT2 ......136 B1
  Poole BH13 ....147 D4
High Trees Wlk BH22 ...61 B4
High St W
  Dorchester DT1 ....107 C1
  Weymouth DT4 ....167 B1
High Way BH18 ....86 C2
Highacres DT6 ....69 B1
Highbridge Rd BH14 ...120 B2
Highbury Ave SP2 .....213 A3
Highbury Cl
  New Milton BH25 ....95 A1
  ❷ Salisbury SP2 .....213 A3
Highbury Fst Sch SP2 .213 A3
Highcliff Rd DT7 ....96 A3
Highcliffe Castle*
  BH23 ....125 C4
Highcliffe Castle*
  BH23 ....126 A4
Highcliffe Jun Sch
  BH23 ....93 C1
Highcliffe Rd
  Christchurch BH23 ....125 B4
  Swanage BH19 ....179 B2
Highcliffe Sch BH23 ...93 B1
Highdown DT9 ....167 C4
Higher Barn Cl SP7 .....24 B3
Higher Beadon TA16 ...191 E7
Higher Blandford Rd
  Corfe Mullen BH18 ......86 C3
  Shaftesbury SP7 ....13 A1
Higher Bullen BA22 ...193 F8
Higher Cheap St DT9 ...30 A3
Higher Coombses
  TA20 ....202 A8
Higher Day's Rd BH19 .178 C1
Higher Dro DT2 ....205 F2
Higher Easthams La
  TA18 ....192 A5
Higher End DT3 ....166 A3
Higher Eype Rd DT6 .....99 C3
Higher Filbank BH20 ..177 A4
Higher Gdns BH20 .....177 A4
Higher Gunville ❺ DT9 ..17 B1
Higher Kingsbury DT9 ..17 B2
Higher Kingsbury Cl
  DT9 ....17 B2
Higher Kingston BA21 ..27 B3
Higher Mere Pk* BA12 ...7 A4
Higher Merley La BH21 .86 C4
Higher Ream BA21 ......26 C3
Higher Sea La DT6 ......97 A4
Higher Shaftesbury Rd
  DT11 ....212 B4
Higher St Bridport DT6 ..69 A1
  Iwerne Minster DT11 ....37 C1
  Lillington DT9 ....194 F7
  Merriott TA16 ....191 F8
  Morden BH20 ....83 B2
  Okeford Fitzpaine DT11 .197 F5
  West Chinnock TA18 ...192 B8

Higher St La DT8 ......205 C3
Higher Westbury DT9 ...28 B1
Highfield TA18 ....192 B8
Highfield Ave BH24 .....55 B4
Highfield Cl
  Charminster DT2 ......107 B4
  Corfe Mullen BH21 ......86 C3
Highfield Dr BH24 ......47 B1
Highfield Gdns DT6 ...204 C2
Highfield House ❶❷
  BH14 ....120 A2
Highfield Rd
  Bournemouth BH9 ....89 C1
  Corfe Mullen BH21 ......86 C3
  Ferndown BH22 ....62 A2
  Ringwood BH24 ....55 B4
  Salisbury SP2 ....213 A3
  Yeovil BA21 ....27 C3
Highfields DT11 ....212 C2
Highgate La DT7 ....136 B3
Highgrove SP8 ....5 C2
Highgrove Cl ❺ DT1 ...135 A4
Highland Ave BH23 .....94 A1
Highland Rd
  Poole BH14 ....120 A3
  Weymouth DT4 ....167 B2
  Wimborne Minster BH21 .59 B3
Highland View Cl BH21 ..59 B3
Highlands Cres BH10 ...89 B2
Highmoor
  Barton on Sea BH25 ...127 A4
  Salisbury SP2 ....213 B1
Highmoor Cl
  Corfe Mullen BH21 ......86 B3
  Poole BH14 ....120 A2
Highmoor Rd
  Bournemouth BH11 ......89 A1
  Corfe Mullen BH21 ......86 B3
  Poole BH14 ....120 B2
Hightown Gdns BH24 ...55 B3
Hightown La BH24 ......55 B3
Hightrees Ave BH8 .....90 C1
Highview Cl BH21 ....91 C2
Highview Gdns BH12 ..120 B4
Highwood Cl SP6 ....41 C3
Highwood La BH24 .....47 C1
Highwood Rd BH24 .....47 C1
Hilary Rd BH17 ....87 B1
Hilcot Way DT11 ......212 B3
Hilda Rd BH12 ....120 C4
Hill Rd BH15 ....119 B3
Hilfield La DT2 ....194 F1
Hill Brow DT9 ....29 C2
Hill Cl Bransgore BH23 ..93 A4
  ❶ Bridport DT6 ......100 A1
Hill Crest Rd BH12 ...120 C4
Hill House Cl DT9 ......30 B4
Hill La Bransgore BH23 ..93 A4
  Burton BH23 ....92 C1
Hill Rd Lyme Regis DT7 ..96 A3
  Swanage BH19 ....179 A3
Hill Rise DT6 ....100 A1
Hill Rise Rd BH7 ....96 A3
Hill St BH15 ....119 B1
Hill View
  Bishop's Caundle DT9 ...196 A7
  Charminster DT2 ......107 B3
  ❸ Hazelbury Bryan DT10 .197 A4
  Maiden Newton DT2 .....73 A4
  Osmington DT2 ....169 A4
  Swanage BH20 ....27 C3
Hill View Cl TA18 .....192 B7
Hill View Prim Sch
  BH10 ....89 C2
Hill View Rd
  Ferndown BH22 ....61 B4
  ❸ Salisbury SP1 .....213 B2
Hillary Rd BH24 ....54 A3
Hillard Ct ❼❷ BH20 ...142 C2
Hillary Rd BH23 ....124 C4
Hillborne Gdns ❹ BA21 .26 C3
Hillbourne Fst & Mid Schs
  BH17 ....87 A1
Hillbourne Rd
  ❶❷ Weymouth DT4 .....180 B4
  Corfe Mullen BH18 ......86 C3
Hillbury Rd SP6 ....42 B3
Hillcrest Ave BH22 .....61 B4
Hillcrest Cl
  Bournemouth BH9 ....90 A2
  Sturminster Newton
    DT10 ....197 C8
Hillcrest Hospl BH10 ...89 B1
Hillcrest Rd
  Bournemouth BH9 ....90 A2
  Corfe Mullen BH18 ......86 B3
  Weymouth DT4 ....180 C4
Millfort Cl DT1 ....134 C4
Hillgrove Ave BA20 .....27 A1
Hilling La DT2 ....207 F8
Hillingdon DT6 ....100 C4
Hillingdon Ct BA21 ...206 D1
Hillman Rd BH14 ......120 B3
Hillmeadow BH31 ....45 B2
Hillside La BH31 ....179 A1
Hillside CI BA12 ....2 C3
Hillside Cty Fst Sch
  BH31 ....45 A4
Hillside Dr BH23 ....91 B2
Hillside Gdns BH21 .....86 B2
Hillside Mews BH21 .....86 B2
Hillside Rd
  Blandford Camp DT11 ..199 E3
  Corfe Mullen BH21 ......86 B3
  Poole BH12 ....120 C4
  Verwood BH31 ....45 B3
  Woodlands BH21 ....44 B3

Hillside Rd continued
  Swanage BH19 ....179 B2
Hillside Terr ❹ BA20 ...27 C3
Hillside West ❺ BA22 .193 F8
Hilltop Cl BH22 ....61 A1
Hilltop Rd
  Corfe Mullen BH21 ......86 C3
  Ferndown BH22 ....61 A1
Hillview DT6 ....68 C1
Hillview Est ❶❷ DT6 ...100 B4
Hillwer Rd
  Bournemouth BH10 ......89 B2
Hilmar Dr SP8 ....5 C1
Hiltom Rd BH24 ....55 B4
Hilton Cl BH15 ....120 A3
Hilton Rd BH25 ....95 A2
Hilton Rd Cl DT11 ......79 C4
Hinchcliffe Cl BH15 ...118 C1
Hinchcliffe Rd BH15 ..118 C1
Hine Town La DT11 ....198 B6
Hine's Mead La DT12 ..103 B1
Hingsdon La DT6 ......204 B2
Hintock St DT1 ....107 B1
Hinton Admiral Mews
  BH23 ....93 C1
Hinton Admiral Sta
  BH23 ....93 C1
Hinton Cl
  Blandford Forum DT11 .212 B3
  Hinton St George TA17 .191 D7
Hinton Cross BA22 .....14 A3
Hinton La DT10 ....135 B4
Hinton Rd
  Bournemouth BH1 ......121 C2
  West Crewkerne TA18 ..191 E5
Hinton St George Prim Sch
  TA17 ....191 C7
Hinton St Mary Roman Villa
  (site of)* DT10 ....35 A2
Hinton Wood DT11 ......35 A1
Hinton Wood BH1 ......122 A1
Hinton Wood Ave BH23 ..93 C1
Hintonwood La BH23 ...93 C1
Hitchen ❸ TA16 ....191 F7
Hive Cl DT6 ....128 B4
Hive Gdns BH13 ....147 B3
Hoadley Gn SP1 ....213 C4
Hobart Rd BH25 ....94 C1
Hobbs Pk BH24 ....54 A2
Hobbs Rd BH12 ....120 B4
Hobgoblin DT11 ....37 C1
Hoburne Ct BH23 ......93 B1
Hoburne Gdns BH23 ....93 B1
Hoburne La BH23 .....125 B4
Hoburne Rd BH19 .....179 A1
Hod Dr DT11 ....198 E5
Hod Hill (Roman Fort)*
  DT11 ....198 E5
Hod View ❷ DT11 .....198 F4
Hodder's La DT7 ....64 A1
Hodges Cl BH12 ....117 C4
Hodway La DT11 ....198 D5
Hogarth Way BH8 ....91 A1
Hogshill St DT8 ....204 C4
Hogue Ave BH10 ....89 B3
Holbaek Cl DT11 ......133 A4
Holbury Cl BH8 ....90 C2
Holcombe Cl DT3 ......168 B4
Holcombe Mead DT2 ...208 A6
Holcombe Rd BH16 ....118 A3
Holdenhurst Ave BH7 ..123 B4
Holdenhurst Rd BH8 ...91 A2
Holditch Ct* TA20 ....202 B5
Holditch La TA20 .....202 A5
Holditch La DT6 ....202 A5
Holdcroft La DT6 .....202 E1
Hole House La DT10 ...197 D8
Holebrook La DT10 ....196 F7
Holes Bay Rd BH15 ...119 A2
Holeshle Rd BH23 .....94 C2
Holland Rd DT4 ....167 B2
Holland Way
  Blandford Forum DT11 .212 B3
  Corfe Mullen BH18 ......86 C3
Hollands Cl BH20 .....176 C4
Hollands Mead Ave
  DT2 ....155 B4
Hollands Wood Dr
  BH25 ....95 A3
Holles Cl ❶❷ TA20 ...202 A8
Hollies The
  ❸ Crewkerne TA18 ...191 E3
  Yeovil BA21 ....27 C3
Hollis Way BA22 ....193 D3
Hollow Hill DT2 ....198 C2
Hollow La TA17 ....191 B7
Hollow Oak Rd BH20 ..113 A4
Hollow Oak Rd DT2 ...142 C1
Hollow The
  Affpuddle DT2 ....112 A3
  Child Okeford DT11 ...198 C8
  Sixpenny Hundley SP5 .189 A4
Hollow Way DT6 ....100 B2
Holloway Ave BH11 ....88 C3
Holloway La DT11 .....198 C8
Holloway Rd DT11 .....108 A1
Hollowell Cl SP2 .....213 A1
Holly Cl
  ❸ Dorchester DT1 ...107 C1
  ❷ Sandford BH20 ....116 A1
  ❶ St.Leonards BH24 ...53 C2
Holly Gdns BH23 ....92 B1
Holly Gn Rise BH11 ....88 C2
Holly Gr Merriott TA18 .191 F5
  Verwood BH31 ....45 A3

Holly Hedge La BH17 ...11
Holly La
  Broadwindsor DT8 203
  Christchurch BH23 9
  New Milton BH25 9
Holly Lodge ❺ BH12 ...12
Holly Rd DT6 116
Hollymoor Cl BH23 204
Hollymoor Comm La
  DT8 204
Hollymoor Gdns ❶❷ BH23 .204
Hollymoor La DT8 204
Holm Cl BH24 42
Holm Hill La BH23 94
Holm Oak Cl BH31 45
Holm St DT3 162
Holme La
  East Holme BH20 160
  Stoke BH20 141
Holme Rd BH23 124
Holmead Wlk DT1 107
Holmes Rd BH19 178
Holmfield Ave BH7 123
Holmhurst Ave BH23 ...92
Holmlea ❶❷ DT11 212
Holmwood Garth ❹
  BH24 ....
Holnest Pk* DT9 195
Holnest Rd BH17 87
Holt Heath National Nature
  Reserve* BH21 51
Holt Hill DT9 31
Holt La
  Bishop's Caundle DT9 ...196
  Holt BH21 51
  Melbury Osmond DT2 ...194
  South Perrott DT8 192
  Stourton Caundle DT10 ..32
Holt Rd Holt BH21 51
  Horton BH21 52
  Poole BH12 120
  Wool BH20 139
Holten's La BA22 192
Holton Heath Sta
  BH16 116
Holton Heath Trading Pk
  BH16 116
Holton Rd BH16 116
Holway TA20 202
Holway La
  Cattistock DT2 206
  Evershot DT7 206
Holwell Dro DT9 195
Holwell Prim Sch DT9 .196
Holwell Rd DT10 196
Holworth Cl BH11 88
Holy Trinity Jun & Inf Sch
  DT4 167
Holy Trintiy CE VA Prim Sch
  BA20 27
Holyrood Cl BH17 119
Holywell Cl BH17 87
Home Dr BA21 27
Home Farm Cl DT6 10
Home Farm La BA22 ...15
Home Farm Way BH31 ..45
Home Farm La BA22 ...44
Home Rd BH11 89
Homedale House BH2 ..121
Homedene House
  BH15 119
Homefield
  ❻ Child Okeford DT11 .198
  Mere BA12 ....
  Milborne St Andrew DT11 .79
  Shaftesbury SP7 12
Homefield House ❶❸
  BH25 95
Homefield Ind Prep Sch
  BH15 123
Homefield Ind Senior Sch
  BH23 92
Homelake House
  BH14 120
Homelands Est BH23 ..123
Homelands House
  DT2 62
Homeleigh House ❺
  BH5 95
Homemill House ❺
  BH25 95
Homeoaks House
  BH2 121
Homeside Rd BH9 90
Homestour House ❶
  BH23 ....
Homeview House
  BH15 ....
Homewood Cl BH25 95
Honey Bun Mdw DT10 ..196
Honeybourne Cres
  BH6 124
Honeycombe Rise DT9 ..29
Honeyfields ❶❺ SP8 5
Honeymead La DT10 35
Honeysuckle Cl DT13 ..152
Honeysuckle Gdns ❷
  DT11 198
Honeysuckle La BH17 ..86
Honeysuckle Way
  BH23 125
Honeywood House
  BH14 147
Hood Cl BH10 89
Hood Cres BH10 89
Hooke Cl BH17 87
Hooke (School)*
  DT8 205

Hooper's La BA22 ...193 F7
Puncknowle DT2 ...129 C3
Hop Cl BH16 ...117 A4
Hope Bottom DT6 ...204 C2
Hope Cl DT2 ...137 B3
Hope Cross SP8 ...9 A3
Hopkins Cl BH8 ...91 A1
Hopmans Cl BH16 ...84 A2
Hopsfield DT11 ...79 C4
Horace Rd 10 BH5 ...122 C2
Hordle House Sch SO41 ...127 C3
Horn Hill View DT8 ...204 C4
Horn Pk* DT8 ...204 B5
Hornbeam Cl DT4 ...167 A3
Hornbeam Way BH21 ...59 C3
Horncastles La 1 DT9 ...30 A1
Horning Rd BH12 ...120 C3
Horsa Cl BH6 ...123 C2
Horsa Ct BH6 ...123 C2
Horsa Rd BH6 ...123 C2
Horsecastles DT9 ...30 A3
Horsecastles La DT9 ...29 C3
Horsfields SP8 ...5 C2
Horsehill La DT8 ...204 A3
Horseponds SP7 ...12 B2
Horseshoe Cl BH21 ...60 A3
Horseshoe Ct 1 BH11 ...121 C2
Horseshoe Rd TA20 ...202 D7
Horseshoe The BH13 ...147 B2
Horsey Knap DT2 ...205 E7
Horsey La
East Chelborough DT2 ...205 E7
Yeovil BA20 ...27 B2
Horsford St DT4 ...167 C1
Horsham Ave BH10 ...89 B3
Horton Cl
Bournemouth BH9 ...90 B2
Bridport DT6 ...100 C3
St.Leonards BH24 ...53 C3
Wimborne St Giles BH21 ...40 A1
Woodlands BH21 ...201 F3
Horton Twr* BH21 ...201 E1
Horton Way BH31 ...44 C3
Horyford Cl DT3 ...168 B4
Hosier's La 22 BH15 ...119 A1
Hosker Rd BH5 ...123 A2
Hospital La
Allington DT6 ...100 A4
Sherborne DT9 ...30 A3
Horton Heath Nature Reserve* BH24 ...116 C2
Houlton Rd BH15 ...119 C2
Hound St DT9 ...30 A3
Hounds Way BH21 ...60 A3
Houndstone Cl BA21 ...26 A2
Houndstone Ct 2 BA22 ...26 B3
Hounslow Cl BH15 ...118 C1
Howard Cl
Bothenhampton DT6 ...101 A4
Christchurch BH23 ...124 C3
Weymouth DT4 ...180 C4
Howard Rd
Bournemouth BH8 ...122 B4
Bridport DT6 ...100 C3
9 Swanage BH19 ...179 A5
Verwood BH31 ...45 A3
Yeovil BA21 ...28 A3
Howard's La BH20 ...142 C2
Howard Cl 1 DT6 ...100 B4
Howe Cl
Christchurch BH23 ...124 C3
New Milton BH25 ...94 C2
Howe La BH31 ...45 A2
Howe's Eype La DT6 ...99 C3
Howell House BH11 ...59 C4
Howeth Cl BH10 ...89 B2
Howeth Rd BH10 ...89 B2
Howton Cl BH10 ...89 B3
Howton Rd BH10 ...89 B3
Hoxley Rd BH10 ...89 B2
Hoyal Rd BH15 ...118 A2
Hudson Cl Poole BH12 ...88 B1
Ringwood BH24 ...55 C4
Hudson Rd SP1 ...213 A4
Hughes Bsns Ctr BH23 ...125 A4
Hugh Rd BH11 ...88 C2
Huish Cp Sch BA20 ...27 B3
Hull Cl BH11 ...88 C2
Hull Rd BH11 ...88 C2
Hull Way BH11 ...88 C2
Hulse Rd SP1 ...213 B3
Humber Chase BH20 ...142 B3
Humber Rd BH22 ...62 A3
Humpy La DT9 ...31 A1
Hundred Stone* BA21 ...27 B4
Hundredstone Cl BA21 ...27 B4
Hunger Hill BH15 ...119 B1
Hungerford Hill SP6 ...43 C3
Hungerford Rd BH8 ...90 B2
Hunt Rd
Blandford Forum DT11 ...212 C3
Christchurch BH23 ...124 C4
Poole BH15 ...119 C2
Hunt's Hill DT11 ...21 C3
Hunter Cl
Christchurch BH23 ...125 A4
Wimborne Minster BH21 ...60 B3
Hunters Cl BH31 ...45 C3
Hunters Mead SP7 ...7 A1
Huntfield Rd BH9 ...90 A1
Huntick Rd
Lytchett Matravers BH16 ...84 C2

Huntick Rd continued
Lytchett Minster & Upton BH16 ...85 A1
Huntingdon Dr BH21 ...59 C1
Huntingdon Gdns BH23 ...92 A1
Huntley Down DT11 ...209 F1
Huntly Rd BH3 ...121 B4
Hunts Mead DT9 ...29 C2
Huntvale Rd BH9 ...90 A2
Hurdles The BH23 ...123 C4
Hurn Cl BH24 ...54 C3
Hurn Ct BH8 ...91 A2
Hurn Ct La BH23 ...54 C3
Hurn La BH24 ...54 C3
Hurn Rd
Christchurch BH23 ...91 B2
St Leonards & St Ives BH24 ...54 C2
Hurn Way BH23 ...91 B1
Hurricane Cl DT2 ...137 B3
Hursley Cl BH7 ...123 B4
Hurst Bridges* DT2 ...111 B1
Hurst Cl
Barton on Sea BH25 ...126 B4
Christchurch BH23 ...94 B1
Hurst Ct 6 BH23 ...126 A4
Hurst Hill BH14 ...147 B4
Hurst Rd Moreton DT2 ...127 B1
Ringwood BH24 ...47 B1
Hurstbourne Ave BH23 ...93 C1
Hurstdene Rd BH8 ...90 B1
Hussar Cl BH23 ...123 C4
Hussey's DT10 ...20 C1
Hutchins Cl DT1 ...134 C4
Hyacinth Cl BH17 ...86 C1
Hyde CE Prim Sch SP6 ...43 C3
Hyde Cl BH21 ...26 C3
Hyde Gdns 6 DT11 ...199 D4
Hyde La SP6 ...43 C3
Hyde Rd
Bournemouth BH9 ...89 B3
Wool BH20 ...140 A3
Hyde The
New Milton BH25 ...94 C2
Swanage BH19 ...178 B1
Hydes La DT10 ...196 D7
Hynesbury Rd BH23 ...125 A4
Hythe Rd BH15 ...118 C2
Hythe The DT3 ...166 B3

Ibbertson Cl BH8 ...90 C1
Ibbertson Rd BH8 ...90 C1
Ibbertson Way BH8 ...90 C1
Ibbett Rd BH10 ...89 B2
Ibsley Cl BH8 ...122 B3
Ibsley Dro BH24 ...44 C4
Icen La Bincombe DT3 ...152 B2
Shipton Gorge DT6 ...101 C2
Icen Rd DT3 ...167 B4
Icen Way DT1 ...108 A1
Iddesleigh Rd BH3 ...122 A3
Ilford Bridge Home Pk BH23 ...123 B4
Ilford Cl BH23 ...123 C3
Ilford Gdns BH23 ...123 B4
Ilford La BH23 ...123 C3
Ilchester Rd
Weymouth DT4 ...167 B2
Yeovil BA21 ...27 A4
Ilminster Rd BH19 ...179 A1
Ilsington House* DT2 ...78 B1
Ilsington Rd DT2 ...109 C4
Imber Dr BH23 ...125 C4
Imber Rd SP7 ...13 A2
Imbre Ct BH13 ...147 C4
Imperial Cl 4 BH13 ...147 C4
Incline Rd
Fortuneswell DT5 ...181 B1
Portland DT5 ...187 A3
India Ave SP2 ...213 A3
Ingarth 8 BH6 ...123 C2
Inglegreen Cl BH10 ...89 B1
Inglesham Way BH15 ...118 C2
Inglewood Ave BH8 ...90 C1
Inglewood Dr BH25 ...95 A1
Ingram Wlk 10 BH21 ...59 B2
Ingworth Rd BH12 ...121 A3
Innsworth Rd BH23 ...125 A4
Innesmay SP5 ...187 A3
Inner Breakwater Rd DT5 ...181 B1
Insley Cres BH18 ...86 C3
Institute Rd BH19 ...179 B1
Inveraron BH23 ...124 C2
Invercylde House BH14 ...120 A2
Inverclyde Rd BH14 ...120 B2
Inverleigh Rd BH6 ...123 B3
Inverness Rd BH13 ...147 C4
Ipswich Rd BH4 ...121 A2
Iris Gdns 6 SP8 ...5 C1
Iris Rd BH9 ...89 C1
Irvine Way BH23 ...124 C4
Isaacs Cl BH21 ...121 A4
Island View Ave BH23 ...125 A3
Island View Rd BH25 ...126 B4
Isle of Purbeck Golf Club BH20 ...178 C4
Isle Rd DT5 ...186 C2
Ivamy Pl BH11 ...88 C1
Ivel Ct BA20 ...27 C2
Ivelway 14 TA18 ...191 F4
Ivers Coll DT10 ...20 C2

Ivor Rd
Corfe Mullen BH21 ...86 B2
Poole BH15 ...119 A1
Ivy Cl 4 Gillingham SP8 ...5 B1
St.Leonards BH24 ...53 C2
Ivy La BH24 ...54 A3
Ivy Mead BA22 ...3 A3
Ivy Rd BH21 ...87 B4
Ivy St SP1 ...213 B2
Iwerne Cl BH9 ...90 A2

Jack Paul Cl BA12 ...3 A3
Jack the Treacle Eater (Folly)* BA22 ...27 C1
Jack's Hedge Cnr BH21 ...189 F2
Jacklin Ct BH18 ...87 A3
Jackson Gdns BH12 ...120 B3
Jackson Rd BH12 ...120 B3
Jacmar Ct 8 BH25 ...95 A1
Jacobean Cl BH23 ...94 A1
Jacobs Ladder 2 DT11 ...198 C7
Jacobs Rd BH15 ...118 C1
Jacqueline Rd BH12 ...120 B4
James Cl DT11 ...212 C3
James Day Mead BH19 ...179 A3
James Rd
Dorchester DT1 ...134 C4
Poole BH12 ...121 A3
James St Salisbury SP2 ...213 A3
Weymouth DT4 ...167 B1
Jameson Rd BH9 ...89 C1
Janred Ct BH25 ...126 C4
Jarvis Cl DT11 ...33 B4
Jarvis Way DT10 ...33 B4
Jasmine Cl
Crewkerne TA18 ...191 F5
Yeovil BA22 ...26 B3
Jasmine Way 2 DT4 ...180 A4
Jaundrells Cl BH25 ...95 B2
Jay's Ct BH23 ...126 A4
Jeanneau Cl 7 SP7 ...12 C2
Jefferson Ave BH1 ...122 B3
Jellicoe Cl BH14 ...119 C3
Jellicoe Dr BH23 ...124 C3
Jenner Way DT3 ...152 B2
Jennings Rd DT1 ...120 B1
Jennys La BH16 ...84 A2
Jephcote Rd BH11 ...88 B2
Jeremy Cl BH20 ...140 A1
Jersey Cl BH12 ...88 B1
Jersey Rd BH12 ...88 B1
Jesmond Ave BH23 ...125 C4
Jesop Cl 1 SP8 ...5 C2
Jessica Ave BH31 ...44 C4
Jessop Cl BH20 ...89 C2
Jessop Rd BH20 ...60 A3
Jessopp Ave BH21 ...100 C4
Jessopp House 6 BH21 ...59 B3
Jessy's Ave DT1 ...152 B2
Jewell Cl SP1 ...213 C4
Jewell Rd BH8 ...91 A1
Jimmy Brown Ave BH23 ...53 A3
Johns Rd BH20 ...142 B3
Johnson Rd BH21 ...61 A4
Johnston Rd BH15 ...119 B4
Johnstone Rd BH23 ...124 C3
Jolliffe Ave BH15 ...119 B2
Jolliffe Rd BH15 ...119 B2
Jopps Cnr BH23 ...92 B2
Jordan Hill Roman Temple* DT3 ...168 A4
Jordan Way 5 DT3 ...152 B2
Joshua Cl BH15 ...118 C1
Journeys End DT6 ...100 A3
Jowitt Dr BH25 ...94 C1
Joyce Dickson Cl 8 BH24 ...55 B3
Joys Rd BH21 ...89 B3
Juan's La SP8 ...9 B1
Jubilee Cl
Corfe Mullen BH21 ...86 A2
Radipole DT4 ...167 B2
Ringwood BH24 ...55 B2
Jubilee Cres BH12 ...120 B3
Jubilee Cross BH16 ...85 A2
Jubilee Ct 5 SP2 ...213 A3
Jubilee Gdns BH10 ...89 B1
Jubilee La
Corfe Castle BH20 ...177 A4
Jubilee Rd
Bournemouth BH6 ...123 B3
Poole BH12 ...120 B4
Swanage BH19 ...178 C1
Julia Cl BH23 ...125 C4
Julian's Rd BH21 ...59 A2
Julyan Ave BH12 ...121 A4
Jumpers Ave BH23 ...123 C4
Jumpers Rd BH23 ...123 C4
Junction Rd
Bournemouth BH9 ...121 C4
Hamworthy BH16 ...118 B2
Juniper Cl
Ferndown BH22 ...61 B4
Three Legged Cross BH21 ...53 A4
Yeovil BA20 ...27 A2
Juniper Flats BH23 ...123 C4
Juniper Gdns 7 SP8 ...5 C1
Juniper Way BH23 ...123 C4
Jupiter Way DT3 ...152 B2
Justin Gdns BH10 ...89 C2

K

Kamptee Copse BH25 ...95 A3
Kangaw Pl BH15 ...119 A1
Katherine Chance Cl BH23 ...92 B2
Katterns Cl BH23 ...91 C1
Kay Cl BH23 ...124 C3
Kayes Cl BH14 ...119 C3
Keats House 17 BH25 ...95 A1
Keeble Cl BH10 ...89 B3
Keeble Cres BH10 ...89 B3
Keeble Rd BH10 ...89 B3
Keepers La BH21 ...60 C2
Keighley Ave BH18 ...86 C3
Keith Rd BH3 ...121 B4
Kellaway Rd DT4 ...167 B2
Kellaway Terr DT4 ...167 B2
Kelly Cl BH17 ...119 C4
Kelsall Gdns BH25 ...95 A2
Kelsey Rd SP1 ...213 B3
Kemp Rd BH9 ...121 C4
Kemp Welch Ct BH12 ...121 A4
Kempston Rd DT4 ...167 A3
Ken Rd BH6 ...123 C2
Kendalls La SP8 ...5 C2
Kenilworth DT4 ...167 A3
Kenilworth Cl BH25 ...94 C2
Kenilworth Ct
Christchurch BH23 ...124 A4
11 Poole BH15 ...119 B4
Kenmoor Cl DT11 ...199 E3
Kenmore Dr BA21 ...27 B3
Kennard Ct BH25 ...94 C2
Kennard Rd BH25 ...94 C2
Kennart Rd BH17 ...119 A4
Kennel La DT2 ...206 C2
Kennels La DT9 ...195 C2
Kennett Ct 10 BH23 ...126 A4
Kennington Rd BH17 ...119 B3
Kennington Sq 5 BH20 ...142 C2
Kensington Dr BH2 ...121 B3
Kensington Rd 8 SP2 ...213 A3
Kent Cl DT4 ...166 C2
Kent House 20 BH21 ...121 B2
Kent La BH24 ...43 A1
Kent Rd Poole BH12 ...121 A3
12 Tatworth TA20 ...202 A8
Kentisworth Rd DT10 ...20 C1
Kents La 8 TA20 ...202 A8
Kenwyn Cl BH10 ...100 C4
Kenwyn Cl BH24 ...55 B4
Kenyon Rd BH15 ...119 C4
Keppel Cl BH24 ...55 B4
Kerley Rd BH2 ...121 C1
Kestrel Cl
Bournemouth BH22 ...61 A4
Upton BH16 ...118 A4
Kestrel Ct BH24 ...55 B4
Kestrel View DT3 ...152 B2
Kestrel Way BH23 ...42 B3
Keswick Ct BH25 ...95 A3
Keswick Rd
Bournemouth BH5 ...122 C3
New Milton BH25 ...95 A3
Keverstone Ct BH11 ...122 B2
Key La BH15 ...119 A1
Keyes Cl
Christchurch BH23 ...124 C3
Poole BH12 ...88 B1
Keynston Down Rd 7 DT11 ...199 E2
Keysworth Ave BH16 ...126 C4
Keysworth Dr BH20 ...143 A4
Keysworth Rd BH16 ...118 B2
Khartoum Rd DT4 ...167 B1
Khyber Rd BH12 ...120 B3
Kiddles BA21 ...27 C3
Kidmore Cl 2 DT6 ...100 C4
Kilbride BH12 ...121 A2
Kilkicks Hill DT5 ...186 C4
Killock BH23 ...147 C4
Kilmarnock Rd BH9 ...90 A1
Kilmington Way BH23 ...125 C4
Kiln Cl BH21 ...86 B2
Kimber Rd BH11 ...88 B2
Kimberley Cl
Christchurch BH23 ...123 C4
1 Radipole DT3 ...152 C1
Kimberley Rd
Bournemouth BH6 ...123 B3
Poole BH14 ...120 B3
Kimmeridge Ave BH12 ...120 B3
Kimmeridge Cl DT1 ...167 A4
Kine Bush La SP8 ...10 A4
King Alfred's Mid Sch SP7 ...13 A2
King Arthur Dr BA21 ...26 C4
King Barrow (Tumulus)*
Alderholt SP6 ...41 B3
Studland BH19 ...145 C2
King Charles Way DT6 ...100 C4
King Cl BH24 ...54 B2
King Down Dro BH21 ...49 B2
King Down Rd DT11 ...199 D4
King Edmund Ct SP8 ...5 C1
King Edward Ave BH9 ...90 A1
King Edward Ct BH9 ...90 A1
King Edward's Dr DT1 ...209 F5
King Fisher Way BH23 ...125 A3
King George Ave BH9 ...89 C1

King George Mobile Home Pk BH25 ...94 C1
King George St 7 BA20 ...27 B2
King George V Rd BH20 ...139 C4
King John Ave BH11 ...88 B3
King John Dr BH11 ...88 B3
King John's House* BH21 ...188 B4
King Richard Dr BH11 ...88 B3
King St Bridport DT6 ...100 B3
Fortuneswell DT5 ...186 C4
Radipole DT4 ...167 B2
Wimborne Minster BH21 ...59 B2
King's Ave BH23 ...123 C3
King's Barrow* BH20 ...160 C4
King's Ct Pal* SP8 ...6 A1
King's Cres SP2 ...213 A2
King's La DT6 ...70 B3
King's Mill Rd DT10 ...34 A3
King's Pk Athletic Ctr BH7 ...122 C3
King's Pk Dr BH7 ...122 C3
King's Pk Rd BH7 ...122 C3
King's Pk Sch BH1 ...122 C3
King's Rd
Blandford Forum DT11 ...212 B3
Bournemouth BH3 ...122 A4
Salisbury SP1 ...213 B3
Thornford DT9 ...194 D7
King's St BH21 ...56 B3
Kingcombe Cross Roads DT2 ...205 E3
Kingcombe La DT2 ...205 E3
Kingcombe Rd DT8 ...205 C3
Kingcombe Nature Reserve* DT2 ...205 D3
Kingcup Cl BH18 ...86 C1
Kingfisher Cl
Bournemouth BH22 ...123 C3
Ferndown BH22 ...53 A1
Salisbury SP2 ...
Weymouth DT4 ...180 B3
Kingfisher Pk Homes 3 BH21 ...89 C2
Kingfisher Way BH23 ...47 B1
Kingfishers 2 BH23 ...124 A3
Kingfishers The BH31 ...45 B3
Kinghton Heath Ind Est BH11 ...88 C2
Kingland Cres BH15 ...119 B4
Kingland Rd BH15 ...119 B4
Kings Arms La BH24 ...55 A4
Kings Arms Row BH24 ...55 A4
Kings Ave BH14 ...120 B1
Kings Cl Ferndown BH22 ...53 A1
Longburton DT9 ...195 B8
Kings Cres DT9 ...30 A4
Kings Hill 8 SP7 ...12 C2
Kings La La DT9 ...201 F4
Kings Mead DT2 ...78 A1
Kings Pk Com Hospl BH7 ...122 C3
Kings Rd
Dorchester DT1 ...108 A1
New Milton BH25 ...95 B2
Radipole DT3 ...167 B4
Sherborne DT9 ...30 A4
Kings Rd E BH19 ...179 A1
Kings Rd W BH19 ...179 A1
Kingsbere Ave BH10 ...89 A1
Kingsbere Cres DT11 ...135 A4
Kingsbere Gdns BH23 ...126 A4
Kingsbere La SP7 ...13 A2
Kingsbere Rd
Overcombe/Preston DT3 ...119 C3
Poole BH15 ...119 C3
Kingsbridge Rd BH14 ...120 B2
Kingsbury's La BH24 ...55 A4
Kingscourt Cl 4 SP8 ...6 A1
Kingscourt Rd SP8 ...6 A1
Kingsland Ct BH11 ...55 B4
Kingsland Rd SP2 ...213 A3
Kingsleigh Fst Sch BH10 ...89 B2
Kingsleigh Jun Sch BH10 ...89 B2
Kingsleigh Sec Sch BH10 ...89 B2
Kingsley Ave BH6 ...124 A2
Kingsley Cl BH6 ...124 A2
Kingsmead Ct 9 BH21 ...59 B2
Kingsmill Rd BH17 ...119 C4
Kingston BA20 ...27 B3
Kingston DT11 ...212 B3
Kingston Cl DT10 ...100 C4
Kingston Hill DT10 ...176 C2
Kingston La DT10 ...196 F4
Kingston Lacy House (NT)* BH21 ...58 A4
Kingston Maurward Agricultural Coll DT2 ...108 C3
Kingston Maurward Gdns & Animal Pk* DT2 ...108 C2
Kingston Rd BH15 ...119 B2
Kingston Russell House* DT2 ...131 A4
Kingston Russell Stone Circle* DT2 ...131 A4

Kingston View BA21 ....27 B3
Kingsway
Ferndown BH22 ....61 A4
Lyme Regis DT7 ....96 B3
Kingsway Cl BH23 ....91 C1
Kingswell Cl BH10 ....89 A1
Kingswell Gdns BH10 .....89 A1
Kingswell Gr BH10 ....89 A1
Kingswell Rd BH10 ....89 A1
Kingswood BH4 ....121 B1
Kingswood Cl 6 BH19 ....178 C1
Kingswood Rd 6 TA18 ...191 F3
Kinross Rd BH3 ....121 C3
Kinsbourne Ave BH10 ....89 A1
Kinson Ave BH15 ....120 A4
Kinson Gr BH11 ....120 A4
Kinson Pk Rd BH10 ....89 B3
Kinson Pottery Ind Est
BH14 ....120 A3
Kinson Prim Sch BH11 ....89 A3
Kinson Rd BH10 ....89 B1
Kiosks The 20 BH15 .....119 B1
Kipling Rd BH14 ....120 A3
Kirby Cl BH15 ....119 C3
Kirby Way BH6 ....123 B2
Kirkham Ave BH23 ....92 B2
Kirkleton Ave DT4 ......167 B3
Kirkway BH18 ....87 A2
Kit La DT2 ....155 B4
Kitchener Cres BH17 ......87 A1
Kitchener Rd DT4 ....167 A2
Kite's Nest La SP8 ....1 C1
Kitford La DT11 ....197 C3
Kithill TA18 ....191 F3
Kitscroft Rd BH10 ....89 B3
Kitt Hill DT9 ....30 A3
Kittiwake Cl BH6 ....123 C3
Kivel Ct SP2 ....213 B3
Kiwi Cl BH15 ....119 C2
Knacker's Hole La
TA20 ....202 F4
Knap Barrow (Long
Barrow)* SP6 ....190 D6
Knapp Cl BH23 ....124 A4
Knapp Mill Ave BH23 ....124 A4
Knapp The
Chickerell DT3 ....166 B3
Fontmell Magna DT11 ....37 C3
Hilton DT11 ....209 D6
Shaftesbury SP7 ....12 B2
Knapps DT11 ....198 B6
Knighton Heath Cl
BH11 ....88 C2
Knighton Heath Rd
BH11 ....88 C2
Knighton House Sch
DT11 ....198 E3
Knighton La
Broadmayne DT2 ....136 B1
Oakley BH21 ....88 B4
Knighton Pk BH25 ......126 C4
Knights Cl BH21 ....212 B1
Knights Rd BH11 ....88 B3
Knightsbridge Ct BH12 .121 C1
Knightsdale Dr DT4 ....167 A1
Knightsdale Rd Swimming
Pool DT4 ....167 A1
Knightstone Cswy TA14 .142 C2
Knightstone Rise DT6 ....68 C1
Knightwood Cl BH23 ....125 B4
Knobcrook Rd 3 BH21 ....59 A3
Knole Cl BH22 ....122 B2
Knole Gdns BH1 ....122 B2
Knole Rd BH1 ....122 B2
Knoll Gdns*
Ferndown BH31 ....60 C2
St.Leonards BH24 ....54 A2
Knoll La BH21 ....86 A4
Knoll Manor BH21 ......121 C3
Knoll Pl SP8 ....5 C2
Knoll Rise DT3 ....152 C1
Knollsea Cl 8 BH19 .....179 B1
Knotts Cl BH12 ....198 C2
Knotts Paddock DT9 ....30 B3
Knowl La DT6 ....101 B4
Knowle Cross DT8 ......203 D6
Knowle Hill BH20 ......140 A1
Knowle La BH24 ....119 F1
Knowle Wood Knap 4
BH20 ....140 A1
Knowles 1 BH23 ....124 C4
Knowlton Church (remains
of)* BH21 ....201 D5
Knowlton Circles*
BH21 ....201 D5
Knowlton Gdns BH9 ......90 A2
Knowlton Rd BH17 ....87 C2
Knyveton Rd BH1 ....122 A2
Knyveton Rd BH1 ....122 A2
Kyrchil La BH21 ....59 C3
Kyrchil Way BH21 ....59 C4

L

La Retraite Sch SP1 ....213 B3
Labrador Dr BH15 ......119 B1
Laburnam Way SP8 ....5 B1
Laburnum Cl
Ferndown BH22 ....61 A3
Radipole DT3 ....167 A3
1 Sandford BH20 ......116 A1
Verwood BH31 ....45 A4
Laburnum Cres 18 TA18 .191 F5

Laburnum House 6
BH10 ....89 C2
Laburnum Way BA20 ....26 C1
Lacey Cres BH15 ....120 A3
Lackington Dro DT2 ....208 B1
Lacy Cl BH21 ....59 B3
Lacy Dr BH21 ....59 B3
Lady Baden Powell Way
DT11 ....212 C3
Lady Caroline's Dr
DT11 ....210 D7
Lady Mead Cl 3 DT5 ...187 A2
Lady's Well* DT2 ....195 C1
Lagado Cl BH14 ....147 B4
Lagland Ct 12 BH15 ....119 B1
Lagland St BH15 ....119 B1
Lagoon Cl BH14 ....147 A4
Lagoon Rd BH14 ....147 A4
Laidlaw Cl DT2 ....121 A4
Lake Ave BH15 ....118 B1
Lake Cres BH15 ....118 C2
Lake Dr BH15 ....118 B1
Lake Gr BH25 ....95 A2
Lake La DT6 ....100 B2
Lake Rd
Bournemouth BH9 ....89 A3
Hamworthy BH15 ....118 C1
Verwood BH31 ....45 B3
Lake View Manor BH25 ..95 A2
Lakefields BA22 ....193 B7
Lakegate La DT1 ....194 A5
Lakeside BH24 ....55 C3
Lakeside Gdns DT5 .....167 A4
Lakeside Pines BH25 ....95 A2
Lakeside Rd BH13 ......121 A1
Lakeview Dr BH24 ....55 C3
Lakewood Rd BH23 ......93 C1
Lamb Plot DT9 ....194 D2
Lambert Cl 8 DT9 ......17 B1
Lambert's Castle (Fort)*
DT6 ....202 E2
Lambourne Ct TA18 ....191 F5
Lambs Cl BH17 ....87 B1
Lambs La BH21 ....56 B2
Lambsfield DT9 ....30 B4
Lambsgreen La BH21 ....58 C1
Lammas St SP8 ....5 C2
Lampton Cl BH20 ......139 C1
Lampton Gdns BH9 .....89 C1
Lancaster Cl
Christchurch BH23 .....125 B4
Corfe Mullen BH18 ......86 C3
Lancaster Dr
Bournemouth BH8 ....90 B2
Corfe Mullen BH18 ......86 C3
Verwood BH31 ....45 A3
Lancaster Rd
Dorchester DT1 ....108 A1
Ferndown BH22 ....61 A4
Radipole DT3 ....152 A1
Lancer Cl BH23 ....124 C4
Lanchards 4 DT11 .....198 B6
Lanchards La DT11 ....198 B5
Lander Cl BH15 ....119 B2
Landers Reach BH16 ....84 B1
Landford Gdns BH8 .....90 B1
Landford Way BH8 ......90 B1
Landscombe Vale
DT2 ....208 A8
Landseer Rd 18 BH4 ...121 B2
Landshire La
Fifehead Magdalen SP8 ..20 B3
Henstridge BT10 ....18 C1
Stalbridge BA8 ....19 B2
Lane Cl DT11 ....212 C3
Lane End BH31 ....79 C4
Lane The
4 Bournemouth BH8 ...122 B3
Corfe Castle BH20 .....176 C2
Lanehouse Rocks Rd 1
DT4 ....180 B4
Lanes The BH25 ....95 A3
Lane-side SP7 ....12 C2
Lang Rd TA18 ....191 E3
Langdon Ct BH14 ......120 B2
Langdon La
Beaminster DT8 ....204 E4
Chideock DT6 ....98 C4
Langdon Rd BH14 ......120 B2
Langdons DT9 ....30 B4
Langdons Way 11 TA20 .202 A8
Langfords La SP7 ....12 B1
Langham Ct BH23 ....93 C1
Langham La SP8 ....4 C1
Langley Chase BH23 ....54 A3
Langley Rd
Christchurch BH23 ......93 C1
Poole BH14 ....120 C2
Langmead Pl 3 TA18 ..191 F5
Langmead Rd TA18 ....191 F5
Langmead Sq 7 TA18 ..191 F5
Langmoor La EX13 ....202 A2
Langside Ave BH12 ....121 A4
Langside Sch BH12 ....121 A4
Langton Ave DT4 ......180 B3
Langton Cl BH25 ....127 A4
Langton Cres DT11 ....212 C2
Langton Cross* DT3 ...152 A4
Langton Dene 27 BH4 ..121 B2
Langton Matravers Mus*
BH19 ....178 A2
Langton Matravers Prim Sch
BH19 ....178 A1
Langton Rd
Blandford Forum DT11 .212 C2
Bournemouth BH7 .....122 C3
Lansdell Ct 6 BH15 ....119 C2
Lansdowne Cres BH1 ..122 A2

Lansdowne Gdns BH1 ..122 A2
Lansdowne House 13
BH1 ....122 A2
Lansdowne Rd
Bournemouth BH1 .....122 A3
Bridport DT6 ....100 B2
Lansdowne Sq DT4 ....167 B1
Lansdowne The BH1 ...122 A2
Lapwing Rd BH21 ....60 A4
Lara Cl BH8 ....90 B2
Larch Cl
Broadstone BH17 ....86 C1
Hordle SO41 ....95 C2
Wimborne Minster BH21 .59 C3
Sandford BH20 ....143 A4
St.Leonards BH24 ....54 B2
Larch Way BH22 ....61 B4
Larcombe La DT6 ....69 B3
Lark Rd BH23 ....125 A3
Larkhill Rd Yeovil BA21 .27 A3
Yeovil Without BA21 ....26 C4
Larks Cl BH22 ....61 A4
Larks Rise BH22 ....61 A4
Larksfield Ave BH9 ......90 B2
Larkshill Cl BH25 ....95 A2
Larksmead DT11 ....212 C3
Larkspur Cl DT4 ....167 C3
Larkspur Cres BA21 ....26 C4
Larmer Tree Victorian
Pleasure Gdn* SP5 ....188 B3
Lascelles Cl 18 BH7 ....123 A3
Lascelles Rd BH7 ......123 A3
Latch Farm Ave BH23 ..124 A4
Latimer Rd BH9 ....121 C4
Latimers Cl BH23 ....93 C1
Launches The BH20 ....172 B3
Laundry La SP7 ....12 B2
Laurel Ave BH20 ....116 A1
Laurel Cl 1 Bridport DT6 .100 A4
Christchurch BH23 ......93 B1
Hordle SO41 ....95 C2
St.Leonards BH24 ....54 A2
West Coker BA22 ......193 B8
Laurel Dr BH18 ....87 B2
Laurel Gdns BH18 ......87 B2
Laurel La DT4 ....54 A2
Laurels The
7 Crewkerne TA18 ....191 F5
Ferndown BH22 ....61 B4
8 Gillingham SP8 ......5 C1
Iwerne Courtney or Shroton
DT11 ....198 E7
Lavender Cl
Ferndown BH22 ....61 B3
Poole BH12 ....120 C3
Lavender Rd BH31 ....45 C3
Lavender Rd
Bournemouth BH8 ......90 B2
Hordle SO41 ....95 C2
Lavender Villas 1
BH23 ....126 A4
Lavender Way BH18 .....86 B2
Laver's La TA20 ....202 C6
Laverstock BH25 ....126 C4
Laverstock Pk SP1 ....213 C3
Laverstock Pk W SP1 ..213 C3
Laverstock Rd SP1 ....213 C3
Lavinia Rd BH12 ....120 B4
Lawford Rd BH9 ....90 A2
Lawn View BH25 ....94 B3
Lawns Cl BH21 ....60 B3
Lawns Rd BH21 ....60 A3
Lawns The
Charmouth DT6 ....97 A4
Christchurch BH23 ....126 A4
Lawrence Cl BH8 ......122 B3
Lawrence Dr
Crossways DT2 ....137 B3
Poole BH13 ....147 C4
Lawrence La Hyde SP5 ...43 B2
Wimchampton BH21 ....86 C1
Lawrence of Arabia's
Cottage* BH20 ....112 B1
Lawrence of Arabia's Grave*
DT2 ....138 C4
Lawrence Rd BH4 ....47 C1
Lawson Rd BH12 ....120 A3
Layard Dr BH21 ....59 B1
Laymoor La BH21 ....60 B3
Layton Cl DT4 ....167 C1
Layton La SP7 ....12 C1
Layton Rd DT4 ....167 C1
Le Neubourg Way SP8 ...5 C1
Le Patourel Cl BH23 ...124 B4
Lea Cl BA21 ....27 B4
Lea Rd BH8 ....180 A4
Lea The BH31 ....45 B3
Lea Way BH11 ....88 C3
Leaden Hall Sch SP2 ..213 B2
Leamington
Bournemouth BH9 .....122 A4
Weymouth DT4 ....166 C1
Leaphill Rd BH7 ....123 A3
Learoyd Rd BH17 ......119 C4
Leaze La BA21 ....28 A2
Lechlade La BA21 ......192 C1
Lechlade Gdns BH7 ....123 A4
Ledbury Rd BH23 ......124 C3
Ledgard Cl BH14 ......120 C2
Lee Ct BH22 ....61 B2
Lee La DT6 ....45 A4
Leedam Rd BH10 ....89 B2
Leeds Cres DT4 ....166 C1
Lees Cl BH23 ....91 B3
Leeson Cl 2 BH19 .....178 C1
Leeson Dr BH22 ....61 A3
Leeson House Field Studies
Ctr* BH19 ....178 B1
Leeson Rd BH7 ....122 C4
Leet Cl 1 DT5 ....181 A1
Leet Ct DT9 ....29 C2

Legg La BH21 ....59 B2
Legion Cl
Dorchester DT1 ....134 C4
Hamworthy BH15 ......118 C1
Legion Rd
Hamworthy BH15 ......118 C1
Yeovil BA21 ....27 A3
Leicester Rd BH13 ....120 C2
Leigh Comm BH21 .....59 C3
Leigh Gdns BH21 ......59 C3
Leigh La Halstock BA22 .193 C3
Ibberton DT11 ....197 D3
Wimborne Minster BH21 .59 C3
Leigham Vale Rd BH6 ..123 B2
Leigh Rd
New Milton BH25 ....95 A2
Wimborne Minster BH21 .59 C3
Leigham Vale Rd BH6 ..123 B2
Lennox Cl DT4 ....167 B2
Lentham Cl BH17 ......87 B1
Lenthay Cl DT9 ....29 C2
Lenthay Rd DT9 ....29 C2
Lerrett Cl DT3 ....166 B3
Leslie Rd
Bournemouth BH9 .....121 C4
Poole BH14 ....120 A2
Lessingham Ave DT4 ..180 B3
Letton Cl DT11 ....212 C4
Letton Pk* DT11 ......212 C3
Leven Ave BH4 ....121 B3
Leven Cl BH4 ....121 B2
Levet's La 5 BH15 ....119 A1
Lewell Way DT2 ....136 B2
Lewens Cl BH21 ....59 B2
Lewens La BH21 ....59 B2
Lewesdon Cl 8 DT8 ...204 C4
Lewesdon Dr BH18 ....86 C2
Lewesdon Hill (National
Trust)* DT8 ....203 E4
Leybourne Ave BH10 ...89 B2
Leybourne Cl BH10 .....89 B3
Leydene Ave BH8 ....90 C1
Leydene Cl BH8 ....90 C1
Leyland Rd BH12 ......88 C1
Leyside BH23 ....124 C3
Leyton Conyers 16
BH13 ....147 C4
Liberty Cl BH23 ......53 B3
Liberty Ct BH23 ......123 C4
Library Mews BH12 ...120 B3
Library Rd
Bournemouth BH9 .....89 C1
Ferndown BH22 ....61 B3
Poole BH12 ....120 C3
Lichfield Rd DT4 ......167 A1
Liddington Cres 11 DT1 .212 B3
Liddon Mill TA18 ......191 C5
Lighthouse Rd BH19 ..185 B4
Lilac Cl BH24 ....55 B4
Lilliput CE Fst Sch
BH14 ....147 B4
Lilliput Cl BH14 ....120 A2
Lilliput Rd BH14 ......147 B4
Limber Rd BA22 ....26 B3
Lime Cl Dorchester DT1 .134 C4
Poole BH15 ....119 C3
Lime Hill DT6 ....64 A3
Lime Kiln BA21 ....26 C3
Lime Kiln La BA8 ....19 A2
Lime Kiln Rd BH16 .....84 B2
Lime Kiln Way SP2 ....213 B1
Lime Tree Ave BH22 ...61 B3
Lime Tree Rd BH24 ....27 A1
Lime Tree Cl SP6 ....42 B2
Limekiln Cl 2 DT5 ....186 C1
Limerick Cl 3 DT9 ....17 B1
Limes The SP7 ....12 A4
Limited Rd BH9 ....90 A1
Lin Brook Dr BH24 ....55 A4
Linclieth Rd 3 BH20 ..140 A1
Lincoln Ave
Bournemouth BH1 .....122 B3
Christchurch BH23 .....91 C1
Lincoln Rd Poole BH12 .120 B4
2 Weymouth DT4 ....166 C1
Lindberg Rd BH21 ......61 A4
Linden Ave DT1 ....108 A1
Linden Cl
Ferndown BH22 ....61 B1
Salisbury SP1 ....213 C3
Linden Gdns 1 BH24 ..55 A4
Linden Pk SP7 ....13 A1
Linden Rd
Bournemouth BH9 ......90 A2
Ferndown BH22 ....61 B1
Poole BH12 ....120 B3
Swanage BH19 ....179 A1
Yeovil BA20 ....27 A3
Lindens The BH23 .....179 A2
Lindford Rd DT4 ......166 C1
Lindinar Rd BH24 ......47 C1
Lindisay Manor 16 BH12 .121 A2
Lindsay Pk 8 BH13 ....121 A2
Lindsay Rd BH13 ......121 A2
Lindum Cl 3 BH12 ....121 A2
Lineside BH23 ....124 B4
Linford Cl BH25 ....95 A2
Linford Rd BH24 ....47 C1
Ling Rd BH12 ....88 C1
Lingdale Rd BH6 ......123 B3
Lingfield Ave BA21 ...27 C4
Lingfield Grange BH14 .121 A1
Lington Cl DT3 ....137 B3
Lingwood Ave BH23 ..124 C3
Linhorns La BH25 ......94 B3
Link Rd BH24 ....47 C1
Link Rise BH21 ....86 C3
Link Way SP1 ....213 C4
Linkhay 12 TA20 ......202 A8

Linkhay Cl 11 TA20 ...202 A8
Links Dr BH23 ....91 B3
Links Rd Poole BH14 ..120 B3
Weymouth DT4 ....167 A1
Links View Ave BH14 ..120 C3
Linkside Ave BH8 .....122 C4
Linmead Dr BH11 ......89 A4
Linnet Cl Radipole DT3 .152 B3
Ringwood BH24 ....55 C4
Linnet Ct BH25 ....94 C2
Linnet La DT2 ....205 D6
Linnet Rd BH17 ....118 C4
Linnetsdene 7 SP2 ...213 B4
Linsay Rd BH20 ....139 C1
Lintern La SP8 ....1 A1
Linthorpe Rd BH15 ....119 C1
Linwood Mix Sch BH9 .122 A4
Linwood Rd BH9 ......122 A4
Lionheart Cl BH11 .....88 B1
Lions Hill Way BH24 ...53 C1
Lions La BH24 ....53 C1
Lions Wood BH24 ......54 A1
Liscombe Cl DT4 ......107 B
Litchford Rd BH25 .....95 B
Little Barrs Dr BH25 ..94 B
Little Britain DT1 ......108 B
Little Content La SP7 ..12 C2
Little Croft Rd BH12 ..120 A
Little Cl BH14 ....147 B
Little Dewlands BH31 ..44 C
Little England DT11 ....79 C
Little Forest Mans 10
BH1 ....122 A
Little Forest Rd BH4 ..121 C
Little Fosters BH14 ...147 C
Little La DT11 ....198 A
Little Lonnen BH21 ....59 C
Littlecroft Ave BH9 ....90 A
Littledown SP7 ....12 C
Littledown Ave BH7 ...122 C
Littledown Dr BH7 ....122 C
Littlefield DT9 ....29 C
Littlefield La SP5 .....189 A
Littlemead
Broadmayne DT2 ......136 A
Radipole DT3 ....152 C
Littlemead Cl BH17 ...119 A
Littlemill La SP6 ......190 F
Littlemoor Ave BH11 ..88 B
Littlemoor CP Sch
DT3 ....152 C
Littlemoor Rd
Overcombe/Preston
DT3 ....168 A
Radipole DT3 ....152 B
Littleton Dro DT11 ....211 B
Littletowns DT11 ......212 B
Littleview Rd DT4 ....166 C
Litton Hill DT2 ....103 A
Litton La
Askerswell DT2 ....102 C
Litton Cheney DT2 ....103 A
Puncknowle DT2 ......129 C
Liverpool Rd 3 DT1 ..166 C
Livingston Rd DT2 ....120 B
Livingstone Rd
Bournemouth BH5 ....123 A
Christchurch BH23 .....124 B
Wimborne Minster BH21 .59 C
Llewellin Cl BH16 .....118 B
Llewellin Ct BH16 ....118 B
Load La DT2 ....194 C
Loaders Cl BH9 ....122 A
Locarno Rd BH19 ......179 A
Loch Rd BH14 ....120 C
Lockeridge Cl DT11 ...212 B
Lockett's La DT11 ....207 F
Locks La
Glanvilles Wootton DT9 .195 E
Loders DT6 ....101 C
Stratton DT2 ....106 C
Locksley Dr BH22 ......61 B
Lockwood Terr SP8 ....11 A
Lockyer's Mid Sch
BH21 ....86 B
Lockyer's Rd BH21 ....86 C
Lockyer's Way BH16 ..84 B
Lockyers Dr BH22 .....61 C
Lodbourne Gdns 6 SP8 ..5 C
Lodbourne Gn 7 SP8 ...5 C
Lodbourne Terr 5 SP8 ..5 C
Lodden View SP8 ......11 A
Loders CE Prim Sch
DT6 ....69 B
Loders Cl BH17 ....87 B
Loders La DT6 ....101 C
Lodge Cl BH14 ....120 C
Lodge Ct BH14 ....120 C
Lodge Rd
Christchurch BH23 ....123 C
Holt BH21 ....51 A
Lodge The BH4 ....121 B
Lodmoor Ave DT3 ....180 B
Lodmoor Ctry Pk*
DT3 ....167 C
Loewy Cres BH12 ......88 B
Lombard Ave BH6 .....123 B
Lombardy Cl BH31 ....45 B
Lomer La SP5 ....42 C
Lomond Dr DT4 ......167 B
London Cl
20 Dorchester DT1 ....108 A
Piddlehinton DT2 ......76 C
London La BH23 ......63 C
London Rd
Dorchester DT1 ....108 A
Milborne Port DT9 ....17 C

London Rd continued
Salisbury SP1 ....213 C4
London Row DT2 ....76 C4
Lone Pine Dr BH22 ....61 C1
Lone Pine Way BH22 ......61 C1
Long Acre DT5 ....187 A2
Long Ash La
Cattistock DT2 ....206 E2
Frampton DT2 ....74 A2
Frome St Quintin DT2 ...206 D6
Maiden Newton DT2 ....73 C3
Long Barrow La DT8 .....204 B3
Long Bredy Hut La
DT2 ....103 C1
Long CI BA21 ....26 C3
Long Cross SP7 ....12 C2
Long Entry DT7 ....96 B3
Long Furlong La BA22 ..193 C8
Long Hill BA12 ....2 C3
Long La
Bothenhampton DT6 .....100 C2
Bourton SP8 ....1 A1
Cann SP7 ....24 A4
Colehill BH21 ....51 A1
Cucklington BA9 ....4 A1
Puddletown DT2 ....78 A1
Ringwood BH24 ....55 B2
Whitechurch Canonicorum
DT6 ....65 B4
Wimborne Minster BH21 ..59 C4
Long Mdw DT2 ....195 A2
Long Mead BA21 ....26 C3
Long Rd BH10 ....89 B3
Long St
Cerne Abbas DT2 ....207 D4
Sherborne DT9 ....30 B3
Longacre Dr BH22 ....61 A2
Long's La DT6 ....100 C4
Longbarrow CI BH8 ......91 A1
Longbury Hill La SP8 ....5 A2
Longcroft Rd
Weymouth DT4 ....167 A2
Yeovil BA21 ....27 B3
Longdown Rd DT9 ....194 D7
Longespee Rd BH21 .....47 B4
Longfield Dr
Bournemouth BH11 ....89 A3
Ferndown BH22 ....89 C4
Longfield Rd DT4 ....167 B1
Longfleet CE Comb Sch
BH15 ....119 B2
Longfleet Rd BH15 ......119 C4
Longford St DT1 ....194 C7
Longforward Hill
TA17 ....191 B8
Longforward La TA17 ..191 B8
Longhayes Ave DT6 ....100 A4
Longhill SP2 ....213 B1
Longland SP7 ....223 A3
Longland's La
Littlebredy DT2 ....131 C4
Winterbourne Abbas
DT2 ....105 A3
Longlands La BA22 .....193 C8
Longlat Gdns BH25 ......94 C2
Longman's Rd BA21 ....201 A3
Longmead SP7 ....12 C2
Longmeadow La BH17 ..118 C4
Longspee Sch SH17 ...119 B4
Longstone CI DT6 ....186 C1
Longstone CI DT6 ....186 C1
Longmen Rd BH21 ....51 B1
Lonnen Wood CI BH21 ..60 A4
Lonsdale Rd BH3 ....121 C3
Looke La DT2 ....129 C3
Lopen Rd DT1 ....194 C7
Lordsmead Rd BA12 ....3 A2
Lorne Pk Rd BH1 ....122 C3
Lorne CI DT1 ....107 C1
Lorton La DT3 ....152 A2
Loscombe's Well Rd
DT6 ....66 B1
Lotmoor Hill SP8 ....10 B3
Louise Rd DT1 ....107 C1
Louse La DT11 ....211 E4
Louviers Rd DT3 ....152 C1
Love La Marshall DT10 ..21 A2
Salisbury SP1 ....213 B2
Shaftesbury SP7 ....12 B1
Love La DT6 ....66 B1
Lovelands DT2 ....193 A1
Lovells Mead DT10 ......193 A1
Loveridge La 16 TA20 ..202 A8
Loverley La BH31 ....201 B3
Low's Hill La DT9 ....225 C4
Lower Acreman St DT9 ..30 A3
Lower Ashley Rd BH25 ..95 B1
Lower Beadon TA16 ...191 F7
Lower Blandford Rd
Broadstone BH18 ....87 A2
Cann SP7 ....24 A4
4 Shaftesbury SP7 ....12 C1
3 Shaftesbury SP7 ....13 A1
Lower Boyston La DT6 ..16 C2
Lower Catherston Rd
DT6 ....65 A1
Lower Comm La BH21 ..53 B4
Lower Comm Rd DT11 ..36 B3
Lower Coombes
DT20 ....202 A8
Lower E Coker Rd
BA20 ....27 A1
Lower Fairmead Rd
BA21 ....27 C4
Lower Golf Links Rd
BH18 ....87 A3

Lower Gunville 4 DT9 ..17 B1
Lower Hillside Rd
BH20 ....140 A1
Lower Kingsbury DT9 ..17 B2
Lower N Rd SP5 ....188 C5
Lower Odcombe BA22 ..26 A2
Lower Putton La DT3 ..166 B3
Lower Ream BA22 ....26 C3
Lower Ream DT12 ......26 C3
Lower Sch La 2 DT11 ..212 B1
Lower Sch La DT6 ....97 A4
Lower St Lillington DT9 ..194 F7
Merriott TA16 ....191 F7
Morden BH20 ....43 A4
Okeford Fitzpaine DT11 ..197 F6
Salisbury SP2 ....213 B2
West Chinnock TA18 ....192 B8
Witchampton BH21 ......200 F1
Lower St Alban St 4
DT4 ....167 B1
Lower St Edmund St 5
DT4 ....167 B1
Lower Steppes DT6 ....167 B1
Lower Townsend DT6 ..128 A4
Lower Walditch La
DT6 ....100 C3
Lower Way DT3 ....166 B3
Lower Wraxhill Rd
BA20 ....27 A1
Lowesmore CI BH14 ..120 B2
Lowther Gdns 8 BH2 ..122 B3
Lowther Rd
Bournemouth BH8 ......122 A3
Poole BH14 ....120 B3
Lox La SP7 ....24 A4
Lubbecke Way DT1 .....108 B3
Lucas Rd BH15 ....119 A1
Lucerne Ave BH6 ....123 B3
Lucetta La DT1 ....135 A4
Luckham CI BH9 ....90 B1
Luckham Gdns BH9 ....90 B1
Luckham PI BH9 ....90 A1
Luckham Rd BH9 ....90 A1
Luckham Rd E BH9 .....90 A1
Ludbourne Rd DT9 ......30 B3
Ludlow Rd DT4 ....166 C1
Ludney La SA17 ....191 A7
Lufton Manor Coll
BA22 ....26 A4
Lufton Trad Est BA22 ..26 B4
Lufton Way BA22 ....26 B4
Lulworth Ave BH15 ....118 C1
Lulworth Castle*
BH20 ....158 B1
Lulworth CI BH15 ....118 C1
Lulworth Cove Heritage Ctr*
BH20 ....172 B3
Lulworth Cres DT4 .....167 B4
Lulworth Rd BH20 ......140 A1
Lumber La BH21 ....201 C5
Lumby Dr BH24 ....55 B4
Lumby Dr Pk BH24 ......55 B4
Lurmer St SP7 ....37 C3
Luscombe Rd BH14 ...120 B2
Luther Rd BH1 ....121 C4
Luton Down Rd 4 DT11 ..199 F7
Luton Down Rd BH21 ..200 A2
Lyatts Hill BA22 ....193 A6
Lych Gate Ct BH24 .....55 C3
Lyde La BA21 ....26 A3
Lyde Rd BA21 ....27 A4
Lydford Gdns BH11 ....89 A1
Lydford Rd BH11 ....89 A1
Lydfords La SP8 ....5 B1
Lydwell CI
Bournemouth BH11 ......88 C3
Weymouth DT4 ....180 C4
Lyell Rd DT4 ....120 B3
Lyewater TA18 ....191 E4
Lyme Cres DT6 ....125 C4
Lyme CI
Crewkerne TA18 ....191 E3
Lyme Regis DT7 ....96 A4
Lyme Rd
Crewkerne TA18 ....191 E3
Lyme Regis DT7 ....96 B4
Lyme Regis Golf Club
DT7 ....96 B4
Lyme Regis Leisure Ctr*
DT7 ....96 A4
Lyme Regis Marine
Aquarium* DT7 ....96 B3
Lyme Regis Philpot Mus*
DT7 ....96 B3
Lymes CI 3 DT4 ....180 B4
Lymington Rd
Christchurch BH23 ......95 B1
Highcliffe BH23 ....125 A3
Lynch CI Mere BA12 ....3 A3
Milborne St Andrew DT11 ..79 B4
Lynch La
Hardington Mandeville
BA22 ....193 A6
Weymouth DT4 ....166 C1
Lynch Rd DT4 ....166 C1
Lyndale Rd DT4 ....180 B3
Lyndhurst Rd BH23 ....93 B3
Lyndon Ct BH21 ....91 C1
Lynes La BH24 ....55 A4
Lynnoor Rd DT4 ....167 C3
Lynn Rd BH17 ....87 C1
Lynric CI BH25 ....127 A4
Lynton Cres DT4 ....91 B2
Lynwood CI BH22 ....61 B4

Lynwood Dr BH21 ....87 C4
Lynx Trad Est BA20 ....26 C2
Lynx W Trading Est
BA20 ....26 C2
Lyon Ave BH25 ....95 A2
Lyon Rd BH12 ....88 C3
Lysander CI BH23 ......125 B4
Lysander Rd BA20 .....26 C2
Lystra Rd BH9 ....90 A2
Lytchett Dr BH18 ....87 A2
Lytchett La BH20 ....140 A2
Lytchett Matravers CP Sch
BH16 ....84 B1
Lytchett Minst Upper Sch
BH16 ....84 A4
Lytham Rd BH18 ....87 A4
Lytton Rd BH1 ....122 B3

M

Mabey Ave BH10 ....89 B1
Macandrew Rd BH13 ..147 C4
Macaulay Rd BH18 .....87 A2
Macklin Rd SP2 ....213 A3
Macmillan Way DT2 ....131 A3
Maclean Rd BH11 ......88 C2
Macville Ave BH10 .....140 A1
Madeira Rd
Bournemouth BH1 ......122 A2
Poole BH14 ....120 B3
Madeline CI BH12 .....120 A4
Madeline Cres BH12 ..120 A4
Madison Ave BH1 ....122 B3
Mag's Barrow DT6 .....61 C1
Magna CI
Bournemouth BH11 .....88 C3
Yeovil BA21 ....27 C4
Magna Gdns BH11 .....88 B4
Magna Rd BH11 ....88 B4
Magnolia CI
Bournemouth BH6 ......123 A4
3 Radipole DT3 ....152 C1
Magnolia House 6 BH9 ..89 C2
Magpie CI BH6 ....123 A4
Magpie Gr BH25 ....94 C1
Maiden Beech Mid Sch
TA18 ....191 E3
Maiden Castle* DT1 ..134 A3
Maiden Castle Rd 4
DT2 ....73 A4
Maiden CI DT4 ....167 C1
Maidment CI BH11 ....88 C2
Main Rd
Fortuneswell DT5 ....181 B1
Tolpuddle DT2 ....79 B1
West Lulworth BH20 ....172 B3
Main St Bridport DT6 ..100 C2
Chideock DT6 ....196 A3
Iwerne Courtney or Shroton
DT11 ....198 F7
Maincombe CI 2 TA18 ..191 E3
Maitlands The BH2 .....121 B1
Major's Comm DT2 ....208 A7
Majorca Mans 11 BH2 ..121 A1
Malan CI BH11 ....119 C4
Malcomb CI BH6 ....124 A2
Mallams DT5 ....186 C4
Mallard Bldgs 8 BH25 ..95 A2
Mallard CI
Bournemouth BH8 ......90 B1
Christchurch BH23 ......125 A3
Salisbury SP2 ....213 A3
Mallard Rd
Bournemouth BH8 ....90 B1
Wimborne Minster BH21 ..60 A4
Mallory CI BH23 ....124 C4
Mallow CI
Broadstone BH18 ....88 C3
Christchurch BH23 ......125 B4
Mallows The BH25 .....95 B2
Malmesbury Pk BH8 ..122 B3
Malmesbury Pk PI 7
BH8 ....122 A3
Malmesbury Pk Prim Sch
BH8 ....122 A3
Malmesbury Pk Rd
BH8 ....122 A3
Malmesbury Rd BH24 ..54 A2
Malmesbury Way BA21 ..26 C3
Maloren Way BH22 .....61 B4
Malta CI 2 DT1 ....107 C1
Malthouse BH1 ....119 B1
Malthouse La
8 Salisbury SP2 ....213 B3
Trent DT9 ....194 F8
Malthouse Mdw 4 DT3 ..150 A4
Maltings The
Bournemouth BH11 .....88 C3
Cerne Abbas DT2 ....207 D4
Poole BH15 ....119 C2
Salisbury SP1 ....213 B3
Weymouth DT4 ....180 C4
Malvern CI BH9 ....90 A2
Malvern CI
3 Bournemouth BH9 ..90 A1
2 Christchurch BH23 ..124 C4
7 Yeovil BA21 ....26 C3
Malvern Rd BH9 ....90 A1
Malvern Terr DT4 ....167 A1

Mampitts La SP7 ....13 A1
Mampitts Rd SP7 ....13 A1
Mandalay CI BH11 ......45 A3
Mandale CI BH11 ....89 A2
Mandale Rd BH11 ......88 C2
Mandeville CI DT4 .....180 A4
Mandeville Rd DT4 ....180 A4
Mandeville Stoke La
DT6 ....66 A4
Mangerton La DT6 ......69 A2
Mangerton Water Mill*
DT6 ....69 B2
Mangle Cave Hill
BH12 ....191 C5
Manning Ave BH23 .....93 B1
Manning's Heath Rd
BH12 ....88 C4
Manningford Rd DT11 ..212 B3
Mannings Heath Works
BH12 ....88 C4
Mannington PI 10 BH2 ..121 C2
Mannington Way BH22 ..52 C1
Manor Ave
Lyme Regis DT7 ....96 A3
Poole BH14 ....88 B1
Manor CI
Bradford Abbas DT9 ....28 B1
Dewlish DT2 ....209 C1
Ferndown BH22 ....61 C3
1 Portesham DT3 ....150 A4
South Perrott DT8 ....192 C1
Stratton DT2 ....46 C4
Templecombe BA8 ......18 B4
Manor Ct
Ringwood BH24 ....55 B4
Verwood BH31 ....45 A3
Manor Dr
9 Merriott TA16 ....191 F7
West Coker BA22 ....193 B8
Manor Farm CI
Litton Cheney DT2 ......103 B1
New Milton BH25 ....94 C1
Manor Farm La DT2 ...133 C3
Manor Farm Rd
Bere Regis DT2 ....81 A1
Bournemouth BH10 .....89 C2
Salisbury SP1 ....213 C3
Manor Farmyard BH8 ..91 A2
Manor Fields BH16 ....100 C3
Manor Gdns
12 Beaminster DT8 ....204 D4
2 Ringwood BH24 ....55 B4
Verwood BH31 ....45 A3
Manor Gr DT7 ....96 A3
Manor La
Manor Deverell DT2 ....106 C3
Verwood BH31 ....45 A3
Manor Pk BH15 ....119 A3
Manor PK CE Fst Sch
DT1 ....135 A2
Manor Rd
Bournemouth BH1 ....122 B2
Christchurch BH23 ......124 A3
Dorchester DT1 ....135 A4
Gussage St Michael
BH21 ....200 F6
Mere BA12 ....2 C2
Milborne Port DT9 ....17 C2
New Milton BH25 ....95 A2
Radipole DT3 ....167 A4
Ringwood BH24 ....55 B4
Poole BH14 ....120 B3
Salisbury SP1 ....213 C3
Stourpaine DT11 ....198 F4
Studland BH19 ....164 B1
Swanage BH19 ....179 A1
Verwood BH31 ....45 A3
Yeovil BA20 ....27 B2
Manor St BA22 ....193 B8
Manor Vale 18 DT8 ....204 D4
Manor View BH31 ......191 F3
Manor Way BH31 ....45 A4
Mansard Ct BH13 ......147 A2
Manscombe Abbey*
DT6 ....90 B1
Mansel CI BH12 ....121 B4
Mansfield Ave BH14 ...88 B1
Mansfield CI
Ferndown BH22 ....61 B1
Poole BH14 ....88 B1
Mansfield Rd
Bournemouth BH9 ....89 C1
Poole BH14 ....120 B2
Ringwood BH24 ....55 A4
Manshay La DT6 ....203 A1
Manston Rd DT10 ....35 B1
Manston CI BH15 ......118 C2
Manton Rd BH15 ......118 C2
Manwell CI BH19 ......179 A1
Manwell Rd BH19 ......179 A1
Manwell's La 16 BH19 ..179 A1
Maple CI
Barton on Sea BH25 ..127 A4
Christchurch BH23 ......125 C4
4 Overcombe/Preston
DT3 ....168 A4
Sandford BH20 ....143 A4
Shaftesbury SP7 ....12 C2
Maple Ct
15 Crewkerne TA18 ...191 F5
Ferndown BH22 ....61 B4
Yeovil BA20 ....27 A2
Maple Gdns DT6 ....100 B3
Maple Lodge BH4 .....121 A3
Maple Rd
Bournemouth BH9 ......121 C4
Poole BH15 ....119 C4
Maple Way SP8 ....5 B1
Maplecroft 4 SP2 .....213 B1

Mapperton CI BH17 ....87 C1
Mapperton Hill DT6 .....2 C1
Mapperton House*
DT8 ....204 F2
Mapperton La DT6 ......69 A4
Mapperton La DT6 ......69 A4
Mapgowder Ct 9 DT10 ..208 F8
Marabout CI BH23 ....124 B4
Marchwood Rd BH10 ..89 B2
Margards La BH31 ....45 A3
Margaret PI DT1 ....107 C1
Marian CI BH21 ....86 B2
Marian Rd BH21 ....86 B2
Marianne Rd
Poole BH12 ....121 B4
Wimborne Minster BH21 ..60 A4
Marie CI DT4 ....120 B4
Marie Rd DT1 ....107 C1
Marina Ct
21 Bournemouth BH5 ..122 C2
Christchurch BH23 ......126 A4
Marina Dr BH14 ....120 A1
Marina Gdns DT4 ......167 A1
Marina Rd SP1 ....213 C2
Marina Twrs 24 BH5 ..122 C2
Marina View 6 BH23 ..124 A3
Marine CI DT5 ....186 C4
Marine Dr BH25 ....126 C4
Marine Dr E BH25 .....127 A4
Marine Dr W BH25 ....126 C4
Marine Par DT7 ....96 A2
Marine Par E BH23 ...123 B2
Mariners Ct BH23 ......125 A3
Mariners Dr BH19 .....179 A1
Mariners Way BH23 ...166 B3
Marion CI BH23 ....126 C4
Markers CI BH23 ....124 A4
Mark's La BH23 ....95 A3
Market CI BH15 ....119 C4
Market PI
Blandford Forum DT11 ..212 B2
Ringwood BH24 ....55 A4
Sturminster Newton DT10 ..35 A1
Market St
Abbotsbury DT3 ....149 A4
Poole BH15 ....119 C4
Radipole DT4 ....167 B1
Yeovil BA20 ....27 B3
Market Way BH21 ......59 B2
Markets La DT6 ....101 C2
Markham Ave
Bournemouth BH10 .....89 B4
Weymouth DT4 ....167 A1
Markham Rd BH10 .....89 B3
Markham Rd BH9 ......122 A4
Marks Rd BH9 ....89 C2
Marl CI BA21 ....27 A4
Marl La DT9 ....28 B3
Marlborough Ave DT4 ..180 B4
Marlborough Ct
21 Bournemouth BH4 ..121 B2
7 Poole BH12 ....121 A2
3 Wimborne Minster DT1 ..59 B3
Marlborough Mans 2
BH7 ....123 A3
Marlborough Rd 7
Marlborough Rd
Bournemouth BH4 ......121 B2
Poole BH12 ....120 B2
Salisbury SP1 ....213 B3
Yeovil BA21 ....28 C3
Marler House BH4 .....121 A2
Marley Ave BH25 ....94 C2
Marley CI
New Milton BH25 ....94 C2
Overcombe/Preston
DT3 ....153 B2
Marline Rd BH12 ....120 B3
Marlott Rd Gillingham SP8 ..5 C2
Poole BH15 ....119 B3
Marlow Dr BH23 ....91 C2
Marlow Rd DT4 ....167 B1
Marlpit Dr BH23 ....94 A1
Marlpit La BH25 ....95 A4
Marmion Gn BH23 ....124 C4
Marnhull Rd
Hinton St Mary DT10 ..35 A3
Poole BH15 ....119 B3
Marpet CI BH11 ....88 C3
Marquis CI DT4 ....166 C1
Marquis Way BH11 .....88 B3
Marriage La DT10 ....35 A3
Marrowbone La DT6 ..100 C3
Marryat Ct
Christchurch BH23 ......91 C1
New Milton BH25 ....94 C2
Marryat Rd BH25 ....94 C2
Marsh Gate DT6 ....100 B2
Marsh La
Christchurch BH23 ......91 C1
Hazelbury Bryan DT10 ..196 F2
Henstridge BA8 ....18 B3
Ibberton DT11 ....197 D3
Pen Selwood BA9 ....4 A1
Salisbury SP1 ....213 A3
Upton BA16 ....118 A4
Wincanton BA9 ....8 C4
Winterborne Kingston
DT11 ....81 C4
Yeovil BA21 ....27 A4
Marsh Rd DT4 ....167 B1
Marsh The DT9 ....194 F3 B8
Marsh Way
18 Pimperne DT11 .....199 D4
Swanage BH19 ....178 C1
Marshal Rd BH17 ....87 A1

Marshall Row 5 BH19 ....179 B1
Marshallsay Rd DT3 ...166 B3
Marshfield BH21 ....59 C4
Marshlands Cl BH23 ...124 B3
Marshwood Ave BH17 ..87 C2
Marshwood CE Prim Sch
DT6 ....202 F2
Marston Cl
Blandford Forum DT11 ..212 B3
New Milton BH25 ....95 A3
Marston Gn BH23 ....93 C1
Marston Rd
Castleton DT9 ....29 C4
New Milton BH25 ....95 A3
2 Poole BH15 ....119 A1
Sherborne DT9 ....30 A4
Martel Cl DT2 ....136 A1
Martello House 10
BH13 ....147 C4
Martello Pk BH13 ......147 C4
Martello Rd BH13 ......147 C4
Martello Rd S BH13 ...147 C4
Martello Twrs BH13 ....147 C4
Martells The BH25 .....127 A4
Martin Cl BH17 ....118 C4
Martin Dro End SP6 ...190 A7
Martin Kemp-Welch Sch The
BH12 ....120 B4
Martin's La SP8 ....5 B4
Martin's St SP7 ....12 C1
Martindale Ave BH11 ...60 A3
Martingale Cl BH16 ....118 B4
Martins Cl
Ferndown BH22 ....61 C4
3 Salisbury SP2 ....213 B1
Martins Dr BH22 ....61 C4
Martins Hill Cl BH23 ...92 B1
Martins Hill La BH23 ...92 B1
Martins Way BH22 ....61 C4
Martinscroft Rd 4 DT5 .186 C2
Martleaves Cl 6 DT4 ..180 B4
Martyr Cl DT1 ....134 C4
Marvell Cl BH17 ....123 A4
Mary Cossins Cl DT11 .212 B3
Mary Gdns 4 DT11 ....197 F6
Mary La BH22 ....52 C1
Mary St BA21 ....27 B3
Maryland Rd BH16 .....118 B2
Maskew Cl DT3 ....166 B3
Mason's La DT8 ....204 A4
Masters Ct BH4 ....121 C2
Masterson Cl BH23 ...124 B4
Matchams Cl BH24 ......63 A4
Matchams La BH23 ......63 A1
Matlock Rd BH22 ....61 B2
Matthews Rd BA21 ......27 C3
Maud Rd DT1 ....107 C1
Maudlin Cross TA20 ...202 E8
Maudlin La TA20 ....202 F8
Maumbury Rd DT1 .....107 C1
Maumbury Rings *
DT1 ....135 A4
Maundeville Cres
BH23 ....124 A3
Maundville Rd BH23 ...123 C4
Maunsell Ave DT3 .....153 A2
Maureen Cl BH12 ......120 A4
Maurice Rd BH8 ....122 B4
Max Gate (NT)* DT1 ....90 A1
Maxwell Rd
Bournemouth BH9 ......122 A4
Broadstone BH18 ....86 C2
Poole BH13 ....147 C4
May Gdns
Bournemouth BH11 ......88 C2
Christchurch BH23 ....94 A1
May Gr DT11 ....211 D6
May La DT11 ....199 D7
May Terr Gdns DT3 ...166 B3
Maycroft Rd DT4 ....167 B1
Mayfair BH21 ....121 B1
Mayfair Gdns BH11 .....89 A2
Mayfair Rd SP1 ....213 C3
Mayfield Ave BH14 ....120 C2
Mayfield Cl
Ferndown BH22 ....61 B3
Radipole DT4 ....167 A3
Mayfield Dr BH22 ....61 B3
Mayfield Rd
Bournemouth BH9 ....90 A1
Yeovil BA21 ....27 C3
Mayfield Way BH22 .....61 B3
Mayford Rd BH12 ......121 A3
Mayhill Rd BH4 ....85 A1
Mc Creery Rd DT9 ......17 A3
Mcintyre Rd BH23 ......91 A4
Mckay Way DT4 ....166 C1
Mckinley Rd BH4 ......121 B1
Mcwilliam Cl BH12 ......90 A1
Mcwilliam Rd 2 BH9 ...90 A1
Mead Ave BA21 ....26 B3
Mead Bower DT5 ......186 C1
Mead Cl BH18 ....87 A1
Mead La Allington DT6 .100 A4
Gussage All Saints BH21 .201 A5
Mead Rd
Corfe Castle BH20 .....177 A4
Radipole DT4 ....167 A3
Meadow Cl
Bransgore BH23 ....93 A4
Cattistock DT2 ....206 C2
Chickerell DT3 ....166 B3
Ferndown BH22 ....61 B1
Henstridge BA8 ....19 A3

Meadow Cl continued
Ringwood BH24 ....55 B4
Sopley BH23 ....92 A4
Stalbridge DT10 ....33 B4
Meadow Ct
5 Bournemouth BH9 ....90 A2
16 Wimborne Minster BH21 .59 B2
Meadow Ct La BH20 ....90 A2
Meadow Farm La BH21 ..86 A4
Meadow Gr BH31 ....45 B3
Meadow La Burton BH23 ..92 B1
Wool BH20 ....140 A1
Meadow Rd (South) 10
SP2 ....213 A3
Meadow Rd
7 Charlton Marshall
DT11 ....211 D6
New Milton BH25 ....95 A2
Ringwood BH24 ....55 B4
4 Salisbury SP2 ....213 A3
Yeovil BA21 ....27 C4
Meadow Rise BH18 .....86 C3
Meadow View
7 Blandford Forum DT11 .212 C1
Bradford Peverell DT2 ..107 A3
Cattistock DT2 ....206 B2
Charminster DT2 ....107 B3
7 Stofold BA22 ....193 F8
Meadow View Cl
BH20 ....142 C2
Meadow View Rd
Bournemouth BH11 ......88 C2
Radipole DT4 ....152 B2
Meadow Way
Barton on Sea BH25 ....97 A4
Charmouth DT6 ....97 A4
Ringwood BH24 ....55 B4
Verwood BH31 ....45 B2
Meadowbank BH16 ....118 B4
Meadowcroft SP8 ....11 A4
Meadowland BH23 .....126 C1
Meadows Cl BH16 .....108 B1
Meadows Cl BH16 .....118 B4
Meadows Dr BH16 ....118 B4
Meadows The
Gillingham SP8 ....11 A4
Pimperne DT11 ....199 C3
Meadowside 4 DT8 ...204 A7
Meadowsweet Rd
BH17 ....118 C4
Meads Cl DT2 ....194 A2
Meads The DT9 ....17 B1
Meadu's La BH20 ......162 B2
Meadway DT6 ....100 A1
Meadway The BH23 .....93 B1
Melbourne Cl DT11 ...212 B3
Median Way BH15 .....118 C2
Mediar Cl BH21 ....92 B1
Medway Dr DT3 ....168 A4
Medway Rd BH22 ....62 A3
Meech Cl DT10 ....100 B2
Meech Way DT2 ....75 C1
Meerhay La DT6 ....204 D5
Meerhay Manor*
DT8 ....204 D5
Meeting House La
BH24 ....55 A4
Melancholy La BH20 ..142 C1
Melbourne Rd BH23 ...91 C1
Melbourne St DT4 .....167 B2
Melbourne St DT4 .....167 B2
Melbury Abbas Mill*
SP7 ....24 A3
Melbury Ave BH12 ....120 C4
Melbury Down * SP5 ...24 C2
Melbury House* DT2 ..194 A1
Melbury Pk* DT2 ....194 A1
Melbury Rd
Weymouth DT4 ....167 B2
Yetminster DT9 ....194 C5
Melbury Way SP7 ....13 A2
Melchester Cl 11 SP8 ..5 A2
Melcombe Ave DT4 ...167 C3
Melcombe Pl 1 DT4 ...167 C2
Melford Cl BH21 ....122 A2
Mellstock Ave DT1 ....107 C1
Mellstock Cres BH20 .142 B3
Mellstock Rd BH15 ...119 B3
Melplash Ct* DT6 .....202 F5
Melrose Cl SP40 ....95 B2
Melrose Rd BA21 ....27 A3
Melstock Ave DT3 .....168 A4
Melton Ct BH13 ....120 C2
Melverley Gdns BH21 ..59 B3
Melville Rd BH9 ....121 C4
Melvin Cl SP1 ....213 C2
Melway Gdns 11 DT11 .198 C2
Melway La DT11 ....198 C2
Memorial Ave 19 TA18 .191 F4
Memorial Rd BA22 ......26 B3
Mendip Cl
New Milton BH25 ....95 B1
Verwood BH31 ....45 A3
Mendip Ct 4 BH23 .....45 A3
Mendip Rd BH31 ....45 A3
Menin Rd BH20 ....162 B2
Mentone Rd 2 BH14 ..120 A2
Meon Rd BH7 ....123 A4
Mercery Rd DT1 ....107 B4
Mere Castle* BA12 .....2 C3
Mere Fst Sch BA12 .....3 A3
Meredith Cl
Christchurch BH23 ....124 B4
Halstock BA22 ....193 C3
Meriden Cl BH13 ......147 C4
Meridians The BH23 ..123 C3

Merino Way BH22 ....53 A1
Merlewood Cl BH22 ....90 C2
Merlewood Ct 19 BH25 ..95 A2
Merley Dr BH23 ....126 A4
Merley Fst Sch BH21 ...59 B1
Merley Gdns BH21 ......59 C1
Merley House BH21 .....59 B1
Merley House La BH21 ..59 B1
Merley House Mus*
BH21 ....59 C1
Merley Pk Rd
Corfe Mullen BH21 ......86 C4
Wimborne Minster BH21 .59 B1
Merley Rd DT4 ....180 B3
Merley Ways BH21 .....59 C1
Merlin Ave N DT3 .....152 A2
Merlin Ave S DT3 .....152 A2
Merlin Cl BH24 ....55 C3
Merlin Way BH23 ......125 A3
Mermaid Ct DT3 ....180 B3
Mermond Pl BH19 .....179 B1
Merredin Cl DT3 ....152 B2
Merrefield Ave BH18 ...87 A3
Merrefield Ct BH18 .....87 A3
Merrefield Dr BH18 .....87 A3
Merrifield BH21 ....40 B3
Merriott Fst Sch TA16 .191 F7
Merriott Rd
Hinton St George TA17 ..191 F7
Merriott TA18 ....191 F6
Merritown La BH23 .....90 B4
Merrivale Ave BH10 ...123 C3
Merrow Ave DT2 ....138 C2
Merrow Chase 1 BH13 .147 C4
Merryfield Cl
8 Christchurch BH23 ...126 A4
3 Poole BH15 ....119 C2
Merville Gdns BH9 ....121 C4
Methuen Cl 2 BH8 .....122 B3
Methuen Dr 1 SP1 ....213 C2
Methuen Rd
Bournemouth BH8 .....122 A3
Poole BH17 ....87 A1
Mews The 1 BH2 ......121 B2
Meyrick Ave SP2 ......213 B1
Meyrick Cl BH23 ....93 A4
Meyrick Pk Cres BH3 .121 C3
Meyrick Pk Mans 5
BH2 ....121 C2
Meyrick Rd BH1 ....121 C2
Michelgrove Rd BH5 ..122 C2
Michelmersh Gn BH8 ..90 A1
Mickleham Cl BH12 ...121 A4
Middle Brook BH11 .....89 A3
Middle Field La DT9 ...15 B3
Middle Gn 1 DT8 ....204 A4
Middle La Martin SP6 ..190 A7
Ringwood BH24 ....55 B4
Middle Path TA18 .....191 E4
Middle Rd
Bournemouth BH10 .....89 B3
Lytchett Matravers BH16 .84 A1
New Milton SO41 ....95 C4
Poole BH15 ....119 C3
Sturminster Marshall
BH21 ....56 C2
Sway SO41 ....95 C4
Middle St Bridport DT6 ..99 A4
Burton Bradstock DT6 .128 A4
Crewkerne TA18 ....192 A3
Dewlish DT2 ....95 A4
Rimpton BA22 ....15 A4
Salisbury SP2 ....213 A2
3 Yeovil BA20 ....27 C2
Middlebere Cres
BH16 ....118 B2
Middlebere Dr BH20 ..142 B3
Middlefield BH20 ....142 C2
Middlefield La TA13 ...191 F8
Middlehill Dr BH21 .....60 A3
Middlehill Rd BH21 .....60 A3
Middlemarsh St DT1 ..107 B1
Middleton Rd
Bournemouth BH9 ......89 C1
Ringwood BH24 ....55 B4
Salisbury SP2 ....213 A3
Midland Rd BH9 ....89 C1
Mideleaze DT9 ....29 C3
Midney La SP8 ....4 A4
Midway Path BH13 ....147 B2
Midwood Ave BH8 ......90 C1
Milborne Cres BH12 ..120 C4
Milborne Port CP Sch
DT9 ....17 B1
Milborne St Andrew CE Fst
Sch DT11 ....79 C4
Milbourne Rd DT2 ......61 B3
Milburn Cl 3 BH4 ......121 B1
Milburn La DT9 ....196 A7
Milburn Rd BH4 ....121 A2
Miles Ave BH20 ....142 C4
Miles Gdns DT3 ....93 C3
Milestone Rd BH15 ...119 B3
Milestone Way DT7 ...28 C1
Milford Cl BH22 ....53 A1
Milford Ct SP8 ....4 A2

Milford Manor Gdns
SP1 ....213 C2
Milford Mill Rd SP1 ...213 C2
Milford Rd SP1 ....213 C2
Milford Rd
Barton on Sea BH25 ...127 A4
Dorchester DT1 ....107 C1
Yeovil BA21 ....27 B3
Milford St SP1 ....213 B2
Military La DT10 ....197 A4
Mill Cl BA22 ....193 C8
Mill End SP6 ....190 F2
Mill Gn DT7 ....96 B3
Mill Hill Cl BH14 ....120 B3
Mill Hollow La SP7 .....24 A3
Mill House Cider Mus*
DT2 ....137 C2
Mill La Bourton DT9 .....59 B4
Bradford Abbas DT9 ...28 B1
Cann SP7 ....29 C3
Cattistock DT2 ....206 B2
Cerne Abbas DT2 ......207 D4
Charminster DT2 ....107 B4
Chetnole DT9 ....194 D2
Chideock DT6 ....99 A2
Christchurch BH23 .....126 A4
Cranborne BH21 ....40 B3
Crewkerne TA18 ....191 F3
Durweston DT11 ......198 E3
East Coker BA22 ....193 C7
Edmondsham BH21 ....40 A2
Halstock BA22 ....193 C3
Hawkchurch EX13 .....202 C3
Hurn BH23 ....91 A3
Ibberton DT11 ....197 D3
Kingstone TA17 ....191 B8
Lyme Regis DT7 ....96 B3
Lyme Regis DT7 ....96 B3
Manhull DT10 ....20 C2
Mere BA12 ....3 A3
Misterton TA18 ....192 B3
Poole BH14 ....120 B2
Shapwick DT11 ....56 C3
Stour Provost SP8 ......21 B4
Stratton DT2 ....106 C4
Symondsbury DT6 ......99 C4
Trent DT9 ....14 C2
Wareham BH20 ....142 C2
West Coker BA22 ......193 B8
Wimborne Minster BH21 .59 A3
Winterbourne Abbas
DT2 ....105 C4
Wootton Fitzpaine DT6 ..64 B2
Yeovil BA20 ....27 B2
Yetminster DT9 ....194 C5
Zeale SP8 ....11 A4
Mill Rd
Christchurch BH23 ....124 A4
Salisbury SP2 ....213 A2
Mill Rd N BH8 ....90 B2
Mill Rd S BH8 ....90 B1
Mill Rise SP6 ....1 C1
Mill St
Blandford Forum DT11 .212 B2
Broadstone BH21 ....58 A1
Burton Bradstock DT6 .128 A4
Corfe Mullen BH21 ......57 A3
Dorchester DT1 ....108 A1
Fontmell Magna SP7 ...37 C3
Puddletown DT2 ....78 A1
Radipole DT3 ....152 A2
Rimpton BA22 ....15 A4
Mill Stream App SP2 .213 B3
Milbank House 5 BH21 .59 B3
Millbrook
Salisbury SP1 ....213 C3
17 Yeovil BA20 ....27 B2
Millbrook Cl 2 DT11 ..198 C8
Millbrook Ct 3 DT11 ..198 C8
Milldown CE Fst Sch
DT11 ....212 B3
Milldown CE Mid Sch
DT11 ....212 A3
Milldown Rd DT11 ....212 A3
Millennium Way SP2 ..213 B1
Miller Cl BH25 ....95 B2
Miller Rd BH23 ....124 B4
Miller's Cl DT1 ....107 C2
Miller's Hill DT7 ....17 A3
Miller's La
Farnham DT11 ....200 D8
Sixpenny Handley DT11 .188 C1
Millers Cl DT3 ....153 B2
Millfield
Beaminster DT8 ....204 D5
Broadstone BH17 ......119 A4
New Milton BH25 ....94 C2
Millhams Cl BH10 ....89 A3
Millhams Dr BH10 ......89 A3
Millhams Rd BH10 .....89 A3
Millhams St BH23 .....124 A3
Millhams St N BH23 ..124 A3
Mills Rd DT3 ....169 B4
Mills The BH12 ....120 C4
Millstream Ct
Broadstone BH17 ......119 A4
Wimborne Minster BH21 .59 B2
Millyford Cl BH25 .....126 B4
Milne Rd BH17 ....87 A1
Milner Rd BH4 ....121 B1
Milom La
Athelhampton DT2 ....110 B4
Puddletown DT2 ....78 B1
Milton Abbas CE Prim Sch
DT11 ....209 F5
Milton Abbey Sch
DT11 ....209 E5
Milton Cl Poole BH14 ..120 B2

Milton Cl continued
Radipole DT4 ....167 B1
Yeovil BA21 ....26 C1
Milton Cres DT3 ....167 B1
Milton Ct BH25 ....95 B1
Milton Gr BH25 ....95 A2
Milton La DT11 ....198 D1
Milton Mead BH25 .....94 C2
Milton Rd
Bournemouth BH8 .....122 A4
Milborne St Andrew DT11 .79 C
Poole BH14 ....120 B2
Salisbury SP2 ....213 B3
Weymouth DT4 ....167 B1
Wimborne Minster BH21 .59 B
Milton Terr DT4 ....167 B1
Milton Villas BH8 ......122 A4
Milvers La DT6 ....101 A3
Milverton Cl BH23 ......93 C
Mimosa Ave BH21 .....87 C
Minerva Cl DT1 ....134 C
Minstead Rd BH10 .....89 B
Minster St 11 SP1 ....213 B
Minster View BH21 .....59 B
Minster Way BH16 ...118 A
Minterne Gdns* DT2 ..207 C
Minterne Grange
BH14 ....147 B
Minterne Rd
3 Bournemouth BH9 ...90 A
Christchurch BH23 ....124 A
Poole BH14 ....147 B
Minton Mews DT1 ....121 C
Mission Hall La DT3 ..153 B
Mission Rd BH18 ....87 A
Misterton Sch TA18 ..192 A
Mistover Cl DT1 ....135 A
Mistover Rd BH20 ....142 B
Mitchell Cl BH25 ......127 A
Mitchell Rd
Ferndown BH21 ....61 A
Poole BH17 ....119 C
Mitchell St 1 DT4 ......167 C
Mitchelmore Rd BA21 ..27 B
Mithras Cl DT1 ....134 C
Miz Maze* DT9 ....194 F
Moat Cl BH4 ....121 B
Moat La BH25 ....126 C
Moats Cotts DT2 ......209 C
Moberly Rd SP1 ....213 B
Mockbeggar La BH24 ..47 B
Modbury Village*
DT2 ....129 A
Moffat Rd BH23 ....124 B
Mohun Castle* DT8 ..192 C
Mohune Way DT3 .....166 B
Mohuns Pk* BA8 ....19 A
Moigne Ct* DT2 ....135 C
Molyneux Rd BH25 .....95 B
Mompesson House*
SP1 ....213 B
Monaco Ct BH4 ....122 A
Moneyfly Rd BH31 .....45 B
Monkey World*
BH20 ....140 A
Monks Cl BH22 ....62 A
Monks Dale BH22 ......26 C
Monks Way BH11 ......88 B
Monkshood Cl BH23 ...93 A
Monkswell Gn BH23 ..124 B
Monkton Cl BH22 ....61 B
Monkton Cres BH12 ..120 C
Monkton Down Rd 5
DT11 ....199 E
Monkton Dro BH21 ...189 C
Monkton Hill DT12 ...153 C
Monkton Wyld Cross
DT6 ....64 A
Monkton Wyld La DT6 ..64 A
Monkwood La DT6 ....203 E
Monkworthy Dr BH24 ..54 A
Monmouth Ave DT3 ..167 B
Monmouth Cl BH31 ....45 B
Monmouth Dr BH31 ....45 A
Monmouth Gdns DT8 ..204 C
Monmouth Rd
Dorchester DT1 ....108 A
Wareham BH20 ....142 B
Yeovil BA21 ....27 C
Monmouth St 5 DT7 ...96 B
Monsal Ave DT1 ....61 B
Montacute Sch BH17 ..87 C
Montacute Way BH21 ..87 C
Montagu Pk BH23 .....126 A
Montagu Rd BH23 ....126 A
Montague Rd BH5 ....123 A
Monterey Dr SO41 .....95 C
Montgomery Ave BH11 ..89 A
Montgomery Gdns
SP2 ....213 A
Montrose Cl
1 Easton/Weston DT5 .186 C
Verwood BH31 ....45 A
Montrose Dr BH10 ......89 A
Montrose Rd BA21 ....28 A
Moonrakers BH13 .....147 C
Moonrakers Way BH23 ..93 C
Moor La
Broadwindsor DT8 ....203 B
Buckhorn Weston SP8 ...4 B
East Coker BA22 ......193 D
Gillingham SP8 ....9 B
Hardington Mandeville
BA22 ....193 A
Sturminster Marshall
BH21 ....56 B
Moor Rd
Broadstone BH18 ....87 A

oor Rd *continued*
wanage BH19 ....179 A3
oor The DT2 ....78 A1
oor View Rd BH15 ....119 C4
oorcombe Dr DT3 ....153 A2
oorcroft Ave BH23 ....92 B1
oordown Ave DT3 .....167 C4
oordown Cl BH9 ......90 A2
oordown St John's CE Prim
Sch BH9 ....89 C1
oore Ave BH11 ....89 A2
oore Cl BH25 ....94 C1
oorfield Gr BH9 ....89 C1
oorfield Rd DT5 ....187 A2
oorfields Rd BH13 ....147 C4
oorhaven BH22 ....61 B3
oorhills 14 BH21 ....59 B2
oorings Cl BH15 ....118 C1
oorings The 7 BH23 ....124 A3
oorland Ave BH25 ....126 C4
oorland Cres BH16 ....118 A4
oorland Gate BH24 ....55 B3
oorland Par BH16 .....118 A4
oorland Rd BH1 ....122 B2
oorland Way BH16 ....118 A4
oorlands Coll BH23 ....92 A3
oorlands Rd
erndown BH22 ....53 A2
Merriott TA18 ....191 E6
erwood BH31 ....45 A4
oorlands Rise BH22 ....53 A2
oorlea 11 BH8 ....122 A3
oors Cl BH23 ....91 A4
oors Valley Ctry Pk*
BH24 ....46 A1
oorside Ave DT4 .....167 C4
oorside Cl BH11 ....89 A2
oorside Rd
ournemouth BH11 ....89 A2
Corfe Mullen BH21 ....86 B3
erndown BH22 ....53 A1
oortown Dr BH21 ......88 A4
oortown House BH24 ..55 B3
oortown La BH24 ....55 B2
oorvale Rd BH9 ....90 A1
orway La DT9 ....15 C2
orant Ct 14 BH25 ....95 A2
orant Rd BH24 ....47 B1
oray Ct 14 BH21 ....59 A3
orden Ave BH22 ....61 B2
orden La BH20 ....82 B2
orden Rd
ournemouth BH9 ....89 C1
andford BH20 ....142 C4
Wareham St Martin
BH20 ....115 C2
oreton Dr
Moreton DT2 ....138 C4
urners Puddle DT2 ......112 A1
oreton House* DT2 ....138 C4
oreton Pk* DT2 ......138 C3
oreton Rd
ournemouth BH9 ....90 A2
rossways DT2 ....137 C3
oreton Sta DT2 ....137 C4
oreton's La BH20 .....142 C2
organ's La SP5 ....189 E5
oriconium Quay
H15 ....118 B1
orington Ct 8 BH8 ....122 A3
orley Cl
ournemouth BH5 ....123 A3
urton BH23 ....92 B2
orley Rd BH5 ....123 A3
orley Way BH22 ....61 C2
ornish Rd BH13 ....120 C1
orris Rd Poole BH17 ..119 B4
Wool BH20 ....139 C3
orrison Ave BH12 ....120 C3
orrison Rd BH19 ......179 A1
orston DT9 ....194 D8
ortain Cl DT11 ....212 B3
ortimer Cl BH23 ......125 A3
ortimer Rd BH8 ....90 A1
ossley Ave BH12 ....89 A1
osterton Down La
Misterton TA18 ....191 F1
Mosterton DT8 ....192 A1
otcombe CE Sch SP7 ..12 A4
otcombe Grange Prep Sch
P7 ....7 A1
otcombe Rd
Poole BH13 ....121 A1
haftesbury SP7 ....12 C2
ount Ave BH25 ....95 A1
ount Cl BH25 ....95 A1
ount Grace Dr BH14 ..147 B4
ount Heatherbank 30
H1 ....121 C2
ount Joy DT6 ....100 B2
ount La DT6 ....99 C2
ount Pleasant
ridport DT6 ....100 B4
hristchurch BH23 ....125 A3
ast Lulworth BH20 ......158 C1
ingwood BH24 ....55 B4
Wareham Town BH20 ....142 C2
eovil BA21 ....27 C3
ount Pleasant Ave N
T3 ....167 A4
ount Pleasant Ave S
T3 ....167 B4
ount Pleasant Dr
H8 ....90 C1
ount Pleasant La 3
H19 ....179 B1
ount Pleasant Rd
H15 ....119 B2

Mount Rd
Bournemouth BH11 ....89 A2
Poole BH14 ....120 A3
Mount Scar BH19 ......179 A1
Mount Skippet Way
DT2 ....137 B3
Mount The
8 Blandford Forum DT11 .212 B2
Ringwood BH24 ....55 C4
Mountain Ash Rd 4
DT1 ....107 C1
Mountbatten Cl
Christchurch BH23 ....125 A3
Weymouth DT4 ....180 A4
Mountbatten Ct BH25 ....94 C2
Mountbatten Dr BH22 ....61 B3
Mountbatten Gdns BH8 ..90 C1
Mountbatten Rd BH13 ..121 A1
Mounters Cl DT10 ....20 C1
Mountjoy Cl BH21 ....59 C1
Mountjoy Sch DT6 ....100 B2
Mower La DT11 ....37 A3
Mowes La DT10 ....34 C4
Mowleaze 1 BA22 ....193 F8
Moyles Ct Sch BH24 .....47 C3
Moynton Cl DT2 ....137 B3
Muchelney Way BA21 ....26 C4
Muddox Barrow La
BH20 ....81 A3
Muddyford La DT6 ....98 B4
Mude Gdns BH23 ....125 A3
Mudeford BH23 ....125 A3
Mudeford Cty Inf Sch
BH23 ....124 C3
Mudeford Cty Jun Sch
BH23 ....124 C3
Mudeford Gn Cl BH23 ..124 C3
Mudeford La BH23 .....124 C3
Mudford Rd BA21 ....27 B4
Mudros Rd DT11 ....199 E3
Mulberry Ct
4 Christchurch BH23 ....124 A4
Sixpenny Handley SP5 ..189 B4
Mulberry Gdns
16 Crewkerne TA18 ......191 F4
Fordingbridge SP6 ....43 A4
Mullins Cl BH12 ....121 B4
Munden's La DT9 ....31 A1
Munks Cl 3 SP2 ....213 A2
Munster Rd BH14 ....120 B2
Murley Rd BH9 ....122 A4
Murray-Smith Dr BA22 ..26 B3
Musbury Cl DT10 ....20 C2
Musbury La DT10 ....20 C2
Muscliff Prim Sch BH9 ..90 B2
Muscliffe La BH9 ....90 A3
Muscliffe Rd BH9 ....89 C1
Museum of Childhood*
BH8 ....122 C3
Museum of Electricity*
BH23 ....124 A4
Museum of S Somerset*
BA20 ....27 B2
Musgrave Pl 4 DT4 .....167 C2
Muston La DT11 ....82 A4
Mustons La 4 SP7 ....12 C2
Mutton St DT6 ....203 A1
Myrtle Cl
10 Beaminster DT8 ....204 C4
Hordle SO41 ....95 C2
Myrtle Rd BH8 ....122 B3

N

Nada Rd BH23 ....93 B1
Nag's La TA18 ....191 B1
Nairn Ct BH3 ....121 C4
Nairn Rd
Bournemouth BH3 ....121 C3
Poole BH13 ....147 C4
Naish Holiday Village*
BH25 ....126 B4
Naish Rd BH25 ....126 C4
Nallers La DT2 ....102 C3
Namu Rd BH9 ....89 C1
Nansen Ave BH15 ....119 B3
Napier Cres SP1 ....213 C3
Napier Rd BH15 ....118 B2
Napiers Way DT11 ....37 C2
Narrow La BH24 ....47 C1
Naseby Rd BH9 ....90 A1
Nash Ct* DT10 ....21 A2
Nash La
Chillington TA17 ....191 A6
East Coker BA20 ....193 C8
Marnhull DT10 ....21 A2
Marshwood DT6 ....202 E2
Yeovil BA20 ....26 C1
Nathan Cl BA20 ....26 C1
Nathen Gdns BH15 ......118 B2
Nations Rd SP8 ....10 A3
Navarac Ct BH14 ....120 B2
Nea Cl BH23 ....125 B4
Nea Dr BH24 ....46 C2
Nea Rd BH23 ....125 C4
Neacroft Cl BH25 ....126 B4
Neal's La DT9 ....194 D2
Neathem Rd BA21 ....27 C4
Neighbourhood Ctr
BH17 ....87 C1
Nelson Cl BH25 ....94 C2
Nelson Ct 10 BH15 ......119 B1
Nelson Dr BH23 ....124 C3
Nelson Rd
Bournemouth BH4 ....121 A2
Salisbury SP2 ....213 B3
Tarrant Monkton DT11 ...199 F3

Nether Abber Village (site
of)* BA22 ....14 B4
Nether Mead 1 DT11 ...197 F6
Netheravon Rd SP1 .....213 B3
Netherby La DT8 ....204 A3
Nethercoombe La DT9 ...30 A4
Netherhall Gdns BH4 ...121 B2
Netherhay La DT8 ......203 C8
Netherstoke La BA22 ...193 C3
Netherton La BA22 .....193 F6
Netherton Rd
Weymouth DT4 ....167 B1
Yeovil BA21 ....27 C4
Netherwood Pl BH21 .....59 A3
Netley 8 BA21 ....26 C3
Netley Cl BH15 ....120 A4
Netmead La DT11 ......198 B8
Nettlebed Nursery SP7 ..12 C2
Nettlecombe SP7 ....13 A2
Nettleton Cl BH17 ......119 C4
Neville Cl SP1 ....213 C4
New Barn Rd DT3 ......149 A4
New Bond St DT4 ....167 B2
New Borough Rd BH21 ...59 B2
New Bridge Rd SP1 ....213 B2
New Canal SP1 ....213 B2
New Cl Bourton SP8 ....1 C1
Haselbury Plucknett
TA18 ....192 B5
New Cl Gdns DT4 ....167 B1
New Cotts BH21 ....60 C1
New Cross Gate DT11 ..198 A7
New Cut BA12 ....3 A3
New Field La DT11 .....198 D8
New Fields Bsns Pk
BH17 ....119 B4
New Gd DT5 ....187 A4
New Harbour Rd
BH15 ....119 A1
New Harbour Rd S
BH15 ....146 A4
New Harbour Rd W
BH15 ....119 A1
New Harnham Rd SP2 ..213 B1
New Inn St DT6 ....204 C2
New La Cann SP7 ....13 A1
Caundle Marsh DT9 ......195 E8
Haselbury Plucknett
TA18 ....192 C6
Morden BH20 ....83 B2
Motcombe SP7 ....12 A4
New Milton BH25 ....94 C3
Stour Provost SP8 ....11 A1
New Line BH20 ....161 B2
New Merrifield BH21 .....59 C4
New Milton Inf Sch
BH25 ....95 A1
New Milton Jun Sch
BH25 ....95 A1
New Milton Sta BH25 ....95 A2
New Orch BH15 ....119 A1
New Par BH10 ....89 C2
New Pk Rd BH6 ....123 B2
New Quay Rd BH15 .....119 A1
New Rd Arne BH20 ......143 A1
Bournemouth BH10 ....89 C3
Bovington Camp BH20 ...139 B4
Bryanston DT11 ....212 A2
Brympton BA22 ....26 B3
Castleton DT9 ....30 A2
Corfe Castle BH20 ....162 C1
Ellingham Harbridge & Ibsley
BH24 ....47 B4
Ferndown BH22 ....61 C2
Gillingham SP8 ....6 A1
Haselbury Plucknett
TA18 ....192 D5
Hinton St George TA17 ..191 C7
Loders DT6 ....101 C4
Lytchett Minster & Upton
BH16 ....116 C4
Odcombe BA22 ....26 A3
Poole BH12 ....120 B3
Portesham DT3 ....150 A4
Portland DT5 ....186 C3
Radipole DT4 ....167 B2
Shaftesbury SP7 ....12 B2
Shapwick DT11 ....48 B1
Stalbridge DT10 ....33 B4
Stoborough Green BH20 .160 C4
Stofold BA22 ....193 F8
Sturminster Newton
DT10 ....197 D7
West Crewkerne TA18 ....191 B4
Weymouth DT4 ....167 B1
Winsham TA20 ....202 C8
Winterborne Stickland
DT11 ....198 B1
Woodlands BH21 ....44 B4
Wool BH20 ....139 C1
Zeale SP8 ....2 A2
New St
9 Dorchester DT1 ....108 A1
Easton/Weston DT5 ......187 A2
Marnhull DT10 ....20 C1
North Perrott TA18 ....192 C4
9 Poole BH15 ....119 A1
Puddletown DT2 ....78 A1
Radipole DT4 ....167 C1
Ringwood BH24 ....55 B3
Salisbury SP1 ....213 B2
Wareham BH20 ....142 C2
New St La Loders DT6 ....69 B1
Symondsbury DT6 ....99 C3
Newberry Gdns 8 DT4 ..167 C1
Newberry Rd DT4 ....167 B1
Newbery La TA18 ....192 A3
Newbury SP8 ....6 A1

Newbury Dr BH10 ....89 B1
Newchester Cross
TA16 ....191 E7
Newcombe La DT2 ......108 C2
Newcombe Rd
Bournemouth BH6 ....123 C3
Ferndown BH22 ....53 A2
Newcroft Gdns BH23 ...124 A4
Newcross DT9 ....195 B8
Newell DT9 ....30 A3
Newell House Sch DT9 ..30 A3
Newfield Rd DT11 ......199 D5
Newfoundland Cl
BH19 ....183 B4
Newfoundland Dr
BH15 ....119 B1
Newhaven DT2 ....105 C1
Newland DT9 ....30 B3
Newland La DT9 ....195 F3
Newlands Rd
Bournemouth BH7 ....123 A3
Christchurch BH23 ....124 C4
New Milton BH25 ....95 A1
Newlands Way BH18 .....86 B2
Newlyn Way BH12 ......120 C4
Newman Cl 3 DT11 ....212 C3
Newman's La BH22 ....52 C3
Newmans Cl BH22 ....53 A3
Newmorton Rd BH9 ......90 A2
Newport La BH20 ....82 B1
Newstead Rd
Bournemouth BH6 ....123 B2
Weymouth DT4 ....167 B2
Newton Cl Gillingham SP8 ..5 C1
Sturminster Newton
DT10 ....197 D8
Newton Hill DT10 ....197 D8
Newton Manor Cl 2
BH19 ....179 A1
Newton Morrell BH14 ..120 B2
Newton Rd
Barton on Sea BH25 .....127 A4
Barwick BA20 ....27 C2
Maiden Newton DT2 ......73 A4
Poole BH13 ....147 C4
Stofold BA22 ....193 F8
Sturminster Marshall
BH21 ....56 B2
Swanage BH19 ....179 B1
1 Yeovil BA20 ....27 C2
Newton Rise 4 BH19 ...179 A1
Newton Surmaville*
BA20 ....27 C2
Newton's Rd DT4 ....167 C1
Newtown DT8 ....204 C4
Newtown Bsns Ctr
BH12 ....120 A4
Newtown Hill BH20 .....157 C2
Newtown La
Corfe Mullen BH21 ....86 B4
Ellingham Harbridge & Ibsley
BH24 ....43 C1
Verwood BH31 ....45 B3
Newtown Rd BH31 ....45 B2
Nicholas Cl BH23 ....94 A1
Nicholas Gdns BH10 .....89 B1
Nichole Ct BH12 ....120 A4
Nicholson Cl BH17 .....119 C4
Nightingale Cl BH31 .....45 B3
Nightingale Dr DT3 ....152 B2
Nightingale La 4 BH15 .119 B1
Nightjar Cl BH17 ....118 C4
Nimrod Way BH21 ....60 C3
Nine Stones (Stone Circle)*
DT2 ....105 B1
Noade St SP5 ....25 B1
Noah Henville Cnr 4
DT11 ....81 C4
Noake Rd DT9 ....29 C3
Noble Cl BH11 ....88 C1
Noel Rd BH10 ....89 A1
Noel The BH25 ....95 B2
Nonesuch Cl 3 DT1 ....135 A4
Noon Gdns BH31 ....45 B3
Noon Hill Dr BH31 ....45 B3
Noon Hill Rd BH31 ....45 B3
Norburton DT6 ....128 A4
Norcliffe Cl BH10 ....89 A2
Norden Dr BH20 ....142 B3
Norden La DT2 ....72 C4
Norden Sta BH20 ....161 C1
Nordon Rd DT11 ....212 B3
Nordons DT6 ....100 C3
Norfolk Ave BH23 ....91 C1
Norfolk Rd
Salisbury SP2 ....213 A2
Weymouth DT4 ....167 A2
Norleywood BH23 ....125 C4
Norman Ave BH12 ......121 A3
Norman Cl DT6 ....100 C4
Norman Gdns BH12 ....121 A3
Normandy Dr BH23 .....124 B4
Normandy Way
Dorchester DT1 ....107 C1
Hamworthy BH15 ....118 B1
Normanhurst Ave BH8 ...90 C1
Normanton Cl BH23 ......91 C1
Norris Cl BH24 ....54 A2
Norris Gdns BH25 ....95 A1
Norrish Rd BH12 ....120 B3
North Allington DT6 ....100 B4
North Ave
Bournemouth BH10 ....89 B3
Lyme Regis DT7 ....96 A3
North Bestwall Rd
BH20 ....142 C2
North Bowood La DT6 ..203 F2
North Bridge* BH20 ....142 B2

North Cres DT9 ....17 B2
North Cswy BH20 ....142 C3
North Dorset Leisure Ctr
SP8 ....6 A1
North End DT9 ....194 F3
North End La SP6 ....42 C2
North Gr DT11 ....199 E3
North Hill Cl DT6 ....128 A4
North Hill Way DT6 .....100 B2
North La
Hardington Mandeville
BA22 ....193 A7
Yeovil BA20 ....27 B3
North Lodge Rd BH14 ..120 C2
North Mills Rd DT6 .....100 B4
North Perrott Rd
TA18 ....192 C5
North Pk DT2 ....73 C2
North Pl DT11 ....212 B2
North Poulner Rd BH24 ..47 B1
North Quay DT4 ....167 B1
North Rd Ashmore SP5 ....25 B1
Bournemouth BH7 ....122 C3
Chideock DT6 ....99 A4
Mere BA12 ....3 A3
Poole BH14 ....120 A2
Sherborne DT9 ....30 B4
Weymouth DT4 ....180 A4
North Rew La DT2 ......106 A1
North Sq Chickerell DT3 ..166 B3
2 Dorchester DT1 ....108 A1
North St
Beaminster DT8 ....204 D4
Bere Regis BH20 ....81 A1
Bradford Abbas DT9 ....28 B1
Bridport DT6 ....100 B4
Charminster DT2 ....75 B1
Crewkerne TA18 ....191 F5
Fontmell Magna SP7 ....37 C4
Haselbury Plucknett
TA18 ....192 C6
Langton Matravers
BH19 ....178 A1
Mere BA12 ....3 A3
Milborne Port DT9 ....17 B1
Poole BH15 ....119 B1
Salisbury SP2 ....213 A3
Wareham BH20 ....142 C2
Winterborne Kingston
DT11 ....81 C4
Winterborne Stickland
DT11 ....210 C7
North Terr BA21 ....27 C3
North Walls BH20 ....142 C2
North Wlk SP1 ....213 B2
Northay La EX13 ....202 C3
Northbourne Ave BH10 ..89 B3
Northbourne Gdns
BH10 ....89 C3
Northbourne Pl 3 BH10 ..89 B3
Northbrook Rd
Broadstone BH18 ....87 A1
Swanage BH19 ....179 A1
Yeovil BA21 ....27 C4
Northcote Rd BH1 ......122 A2
Northernhay 1 DT1 ....108 A1
Northey Rd BH6 ....123 C3
Northfield La TA17 .....191 B8
Northfield Rd BH24 ......47 B1
Northleigh La BH21 ......59 C3
Northmead Dr BH17 ....118 C4
Northmere Dr BH12 ....120 C4
Northmere Rd BH12 ....120 C4
Northmoor Way BH20 ..142 B3
Northover BH3 ....121 C3
Northover Cl
Burton Bradstock DT6 ....128 B4
Piddletrenthide DT2 ......208 B2
Northover La SO41 ......95 C4
Northport Dr BH20 .....142 C3
Nortoft Rd BH8 ....122 A3
Norton Cl BH23 ....124 B4
Norton La
Durweston DT11 ....198 D3
Netherbury DT6 ....204 C2
Norton Rd BH9 ....121 C4
Norway Cl 3 BH9 ....89 C1
Norway La DT8 ....203 F4
Norwich Ave BH2 ....121 B2
Norwich Ave W BH2 ....121 B2
Norwich Ct 12 BH2 .....121 C2
Norwich Mans 4 BH2 ...121 B2
Norwich Rd
Bournemouth BH2 ....121 C2
Weymouth DT4 ....167 B1
Norwood Pl BH5 ....123 A3
Nothe Fort* DT4 ....167 C1
Nothe Par DT4 ....167 C1
Nottington La
Chickerell DT3 ....151 B1
Radipole DT3 ....152 A1
Nouale La BH24 ....55 C4
Noyce Gdns BH8 ....91 A1
Nuffield Hospl BH5 .....122 C2
Nuffield Ind Est BH17 ..119 B4
Nuffield Rd BH17 ....119 B4
Nugent Rd BH6 ....124 A2
Nundico BH20 ....142 C2
Nursery Gdns
Bridport DT6 ....100 C4
Mere BA12 ....3 A3
Nursery Rd
Blandford Forum DT11 ...212 B2
Bournemouth BH9 ....90 A2
Ringwood BH24 ....55 B3

Nursery Rd continued
Salisbury SP2 ...213 A3
Yeovil BA20 ...27 B2
Nursling Gn BH8 ...90 B1
Nutcombe Cl DT6 ...97 A4
Nutcrack La BA20 ...142 C1
Nutgrove Ave DT4 ...166 C1
Nuthatch Cl
Broadstone BH17 ...118 C4
Ferndown BH22 ...61 A4
Radipole DT3 ...152 B2
Nutley Cl BH11 ...88 C2
Nutley Way BH11 ...88 C2
Nutmead Cl ■ DT11 ...198 C8
Nyland La SP8 ...8 B1

O

Oak Ave
Christchurch BH23 ...123 B4
Holton Heath BH20 ...116 A2
Oak Cl Corfe Mullen BH21 ...86 B3
Ferndown BH22 ...61 C1
Oak La Corscombe DT2 ...205 C6
Ringwood BH24 ...55 B4
Oak Mews BH12 ...120 B3
Oak Rd Alderholt SP6 ...42 A3
Bournemouth BH8 ...122 B3
New Milton BH25 ...95 B2
Upton BH16 ...118 B3
Oak Vale La BA8 ...19 A2
Oakbury Dr DT3 ...168 A4
Oakdale Rd BH15 ...119 C3
Oakdale S Rd Mid Sch
BH15 ...119 B3
Oakdene Cl BH21 ...59 B3
Oakdene Rd BH20 ...139 C1
Oakfield Rd BH15 ...119 B3
Oakfield St DT11 ...212 B2
Oakford Cl BH8 ...90 B2
Oakham Grange BH22 ...61 C2
Oakhurst Cl BH22 ...53 A1
Oakhurst La BH22 ...53 A1
Oakhurst Rd BH22 ...53 A1
Oakland Wlk BH22 ...61 C1
Oaklands Cl BH31 ...45 A3
Oaklands Rd BA21 ...27 C4
Oakleigh ■ BA20 ...26 C1
Oakleigh Way BH23 ...125 C4
Oakley Gdns BH16 ...118 A4
Oakley Hill BH11 ...59 B1
Oakley La
Farnham DT11 ...188 D2
Oakley BH21 ...59 C1
Oakley Pl DT4 ...167 B1
Oakley Rd BH21 ...59 B1
Oakley Straight BH21 ...59 C1
Oakmead Coll of Tech
BH11 ...88 C2
Oakmead Gdns BH11 ...88 C2
Oakmead Rd BH17 ...118 C4
Oaks Dr BH24 ...53 C2
Oaks Mead BH11 ...45 A4
Oaks The Gillingham SP8 ...5 C1
Verwood BH31 ...45 A4
Oaktree Cl BH20 ...142 C1
Oakwood
Bournemouth BH3 ...121 C4
West Knighton DT2 ...136 B2
Oakwood Ave BH25 ...95 B2
Oakwood Cl BH9 ...90 A1
Oakwood Ct BH25 ...95 A2
Oakwood Dr ■ DT11 ...37 C1
Oakwood Rd
Bournemouth BH9 ...90 A1
Christchurch BH23 ...93 C1
Oasis Mews BH16 ...118 A4
Oasis The ■ DT11 ...121 A2
Oates Rd BH9 ...89 C1
Oathill La
Broadwindsor TA18 ...203 A7
West Crewkerne TA18 ...191 B1
Oban Rd BH3 ...121 C4
Oborne Rd DT9 ...30 B4
Ocean Hts ■ BH5 ...122 C2
Octagon Theatre*
BA20 ...27 B2
Odcombe Hollow
BA22 ...192 E8
Odstock Rd DT2 ...213 B1
OK Mobile Home Pk
BH23 ...125 A4
**Okeford Fitzpaine CE Prim
Sch** DT11 ...197 F5
Okeford Rd BH18 ...87 B2
Old Bakery Cl ■ DT11 ...199 D3
Old Bakery The DT8 ...203 E5
Old Barn Cl
Christchurch BH23 ...91 B1
Ringwood BH24 ...55 B4
Old Barn Farm Rd
BH21 ...53 B3
Old Barn Rd
Bere Regis BH20 ...81 A1
Christchurch BH23 ...91 B1
Old Barn Way DT2 ...27 A1
Old Bincombe La DT3 ...151 B2
Old Blandford Rd SP2 ...213 A2
Old Bound Rd BH16 ...118 B3
Old Boundary Rd SP7 ...12 C1
Old Bowden Way DT9 ...17 B2
Old Brickfields DT2 ...138 A1
Old Bridge Rd BH6 ...123 B4
Old Cann Rd SP7 ...13 A1

Old Castle Rd DT4 ...180 C4
Old Chalk Pit BH20 ...81 A1
Old Chapel Dr BH21 ...84 B2
Old Christchurch La ■
BH1 ...121 C2
Old Christchurch Rd
BH1 ...121 C2
Old Church Rd DT6 ...100 C2
Old Church Sch DT8 ...204 D4
Old Coastguard Rd
BH13 ...147 A2
Old Ct Mews BH14 ...120 A2
Old Depot Rd DT5 ...181 B1
Old Farm Cl BH24 ...47 C1
Old Farm Gdns BH21 ...212 B3
Old Farm Rd BH15 ...119 C3
Old Farm Way DT2 ...137 B3
Old Forge Cl BH16 ...116 C3
Old Forge Rd BH21 ...60 C3
Old Furzebrook Rd
BH20 ...160 C4
Old Generator House The
BH12 ...121 A2
Old Granary Cl DT3 ...153 B2
Old Ham La BH21 ...60 B2
Old Highway Mews
BH21 ...59 B2
Old Hitchen ■ TA16 ...191 F7
Old Hollow BA12 ...3 A3
Old Kiln Rd
Ridge BH20 ...143 A1
Upton BH16 ...118 A3
Old Lifeboat House (Mus)*
BH15 ...119 B1
Old Lyme Hill DT6 ...96 C4
Old Lyme Rd DT6 ...96 C4
Old Manor Cl BH21 ...59 B3
Old Manor Hospl SP2 ...213 A3
Old Mdws Wlk SP2 ...213 A2
Old Mill La DT10 ...21 A2
Old Mills DT2 ...71 C4
Old Milton Gn BH25 ...94 C1
Old Milton Rd BH25 ...95 A1
Old Mkt Rd BH21 ...59 C3
Old Mulberry Cl BH10 ...89 A1
Old Oak Way DT11 ...210 C3
Old Orch BH15 ...119 B1
Old Orch Cl DT10 ...196 F8
Old Pines Cl BH22 ...61 C2
Old Pound Cl BH16 ...84 B2
Old Pound Ct SP8 ...1 B1
Old Priory Rd BH6 ...123 C2
Old Rd Odcombe BA22 ...26 A2
Wimborne Minster BH21 ...59 A3
Old Rd The DT9 ...18 A1
Old Rectory Cl
■ Charmouth DT6 ...97 A4
Corfe Mullen BH21 ...86 B4
Old Rectory La DT9 ...195 E3
Old Rope Wlk The
BH15 ...118 C1
Old Ropewalk BH15 ...119 A1
Old Sandpit La BH16 ...84 B2
Old Sawmill Cl BH31 ...45 A4
Old Sch Cl
Ferndown BH22 ...61 B3
Folke DT9 ...31 A1
Poole BH14 ...120 A2
Old Sch La
Hinton St Mary DT10 ...35 A3
Iwerne Minster DT11 ...37 C1
Old Sch The DT2 ...72 C4
Old St Salisbury SP2 ...213 B1
Sturminster Marshall
BH21 ...56 C2
Old St John's Mews
BH9 ...89 C2
Old Sta Gdns BA8 ...19 A3
Old Sta Rd
Radipole DT3 ...152 A2
■ Yeovil BA20 ...27 B2
Old Stacks Gdns ■ BH24 ...55 C3
Old Town Mews ■
BH15 ...119 B1
Old Vicarage Cl BH10 ...89 C3
Old Vicarage Gdn DT7 ...96 A3
Old Wareham Rd
Corfe Mullen BH21 ...86 A2
Poole BH12 ...120 A4
Olga Rd DT1 ...107 C1
Olivers Mead ■ DT11 ...198 C8
Olivers Rd BH21 ...60 A3
Olivers Way BH21 ...60 A3
Onslow Gdns BH21 ...59 B3
Onslow House BH21 ...59 B3
Ophir Gdns ■ BH8 ...122 B3
Ophir Rd BH8 ...122 A3
Oratory Gdns BH13 ...147 C4
Orchard Ave
Bridport DT6 ...100 B4
Poole BH14 ...119 C1
Orchard Chase ■ DT1 ...199 F7
Orchard Cl
■ Charmouth DT6 ...97 A4
Cheselbourne DT2 ...209 A3
Christchurch BH23 ...124 A3
Corfe Mullen BH21 ...86 B4
Ferndown BH22 ...61 C3
Fontmell Magna SP7 ...37 C3
Lytchett Minster & Upton
BH16 ...118 A3
■ Okeford Fitzpaine DT11 ...197 F6
Ringwood BH24 ...55 B4
■ Stourpaine DT11 ...198 F4
Sturminster Newton
DT10 ...35 B1
Sydling St Nicholas DT2 ...207 A3

Orchard Cl continued
■ West Coker BA22 ...193 A8
Orchard Cres DT6 ...100 B4
Orchard Ct
■ New Milton BH25 ...95 A2
Verwood BH31 ...45 B3
Orchard Dr DT3 ...168 A4
Orchard Gr BH25 ...95 A1
Orchard La
Corfe Mullen BH21 ...86 B4
■ Crewkerne TA18 ...191 F4
Thorncombe TA20 ...202 E6
■ Winterborne Kingston
DT11 ...81 C4
Orchard Leigh ■ BH25 ...95 A1
Orchard Mead DT8 ...203 E5
Orchard Mews
Christchurch BH23 ...124 A3
■ Gillingham SP8 ...5 C1
Orchard Rd
Gillingham SP8 ...5 C1
Milborne Port DT9 ...17 B1
Orchard Rise
■ Crewkerne TA18 ...191 F4
Milborne St Andrew DT11 ...79 C4
Orchard St
Blandford Forum DT11 ...212 B2
Bournemouth BH2 ...121 C2
Dorchester DT1 ...108 A1
■ Yeovil BA20 ...27 A2
Orchard The
Blandford Forum DT11 ...212 B3
Bournemouth BH11 ...88 B3
Bransgore BH23 ...93 B4
Hazelbury Bryan DT10 ...196 F3
Radipole DT3 ...152 A2
Sixpenny Handley SP5 ...189 A4
Winfrith Newburgh DT2 ...156 C3
Orchard Way
■ Misterton TA18 ...192 A2
■ Mosterton DT8 ...204 A8
Orchard Wlk
■ Bournemouth BH1 ...121 C2
Osborne Rd
New Milton BH25 ...95 A2
Poole BH14 ...120 A2
Swanage BH19 ...179 A1
Osborne House ■
BH25 ...95 A2
Osbourne Rd DT6 ...100 B4
Osmay Rd DT9 ...17 B1
Osmington Dro DT2 ...136 A1
Osmington White Horse*
DT3 ...153 C2
Osprey Cl BH23 ...125 A3
Osprey Rd BH14 ...120 B4
Ossemsley Manor House
BH23 ...94 B3
Ossemsley S Dr BH25 ...94 A4
Oswald Cl BH9 ...89 C1
Oswald Rd BH9 ...89 C1
Otter Cl Upton BH16 ...118 A3
■ Verwood BH31 ...45 B3
Otter Rd BH15 ...119 C3
Otters Wlk BH25 ...95 B3
Ottery La DT9 ...30 A3
Oval Gdns BH20 ...142 C1
Oval The BH20 ...172 C4
Over Links Dr BH14 ...120 B1
Overbury Cl DT4 ...166 C1
Overbury Rd BH14 ...120 A2
Overcliffe Mans BH1 ...122 B2
Overcombe Cl DT3 ...168 A4
Overcombe Cl BH17 ...87 C1
Overcombe Dr DT3 ...168 A4
Overlands Rd DT4 ...180 A4
Overton Cl DT7 ...96 B4
Ovington Ave BH7 ...123 A4
Ovington Gdns BH7 ...123 B4
Owermoigne CE Prim Sch
DT2 ...155 B7
Owl Sanctuary* BH24 ...55 C3
Owls Rd
Bournemouth BH5 ...122 C2
Verwood BH31 ...45 B3
Owlshotts BH13 ...147 C4
Owlswood ■ SP2 ...213 B1
Ox Dro
Berwick St John SP5 ...188 B7
Bower Chalke SP5 ...189 A8
Oxen Rd ■ TA18 ...191 F4
Oxencroft ■ SP7 ...12 C2
Oxey Cl BH25 ...95 A1
Oxford Ave BH6 ...123 A3
Oxford La BH11 ...88 A1
Oxford Rd
Bournemouth BH1 ...122 A2
■ Yeovil BA21 ...28 A4
Oxhayes DT8 ...203 C8
Ozone Terr DT7 ...96 A2

P

Paceycombe Way DT1 ...107 B1

Packers' Way ■ TA18 ...192 B3
Paddington Cl BH11 ...88 B2
Paddington Gr BH11 ...88 B2
Paddock Cl
Ferndown BH21 ...61 A3
Lytchett Matravers BH16 ...84 B2
Shaftesbury SP7 ...13 A1
Sixpenny Handley SP5 ...189 A3
St Leonards BH24 ...54 A2
Paddock Gr BH31 ...45 B3
Paddock The DT2 ...136 A4
Paddock Wlk DT9 ...17 B1
Paddock's Cross DT6 ...67 A4
Paddock's La DT6 ...67 A4
Paddocks Cl BH12 ...120 A2
Paddocks The
Bournemouth BH10 ...89 A2
■ Iwerne Minster DT11 ...37 C1
■ Mosterton DT8 ...204 A8
Thornford DT9 ...194 D8
Padfield Cl BH6 ...123 C3
Padget Rd BH24 ...47 C1
Padstow Pl SP6 ...43 A4
Page Dr ■ DT5 ...186 C1
Pageant Dr DT9 ...30 A3
Pageants Cl DT6 ...68 C1
Paget Cl BH21 ...60 A4
Paget Rd BH11 ...89 A2
Paisley Rd BH6 ...123 C3
Palfrey Rd BH10 ...89 B3
Palma Ct BH23 ...126 A4
Palmer Pl BH25 ...95 A2
Palmer Rd Poole BH15 ...119 B3
Salisbury SP2 ...213 A3
Palmers La DT11 ...211 D7
Palmerston Ave BH23 ...124 B3
Palmerston Cl BH16 ...118 B4
Palmerston Rd
Bournemouth BH1 ...122 C3
Poole BH14 ...120 B2
Upton BH16 ...118 A4
Pamphill CE Fst Sch
BH21 ...58 C3
Panorama Rd
Poole BH13 ...147 A2
Swanage BH19 ...179 A1
Pans Cnr BH22 ...61 C2
Parade The
Barton on Sea BH25 ...94 C1
■ Bournemouth BH6 ...123 C2
New Milton BH25 ...95 B2
Poole BH17 ...87 A1
Paradise La BH20 ...83 B2
Paradise Rd BH21 ...59 A3
Paradise St ■ BH15 ...119 A1
Parcroft Gdns DT9 ...27 A3
Parcroft Jun Sch BA20 ...27 A3
Pardys Hill BH21 ...86 B4
Parfields BA20 ...27 A3
Parham Cl BH25 ...94 C2
Parham Rd BH10 ...89 B1
Parish Rd BH15 ...119 C2
Park Ave BH10 ...89 B3
Park Cl Burton BH23 ...92 B2
New Milton BH25 ...95 B3
■ Stourpaine DT11 ...198 F4
Park Cnr DT10 ...115 B4
Park Dr
Holton Heath BH20 ...116 A2
Verwood BH31 ...45 A4
Park Est Rd BH15 ...186 C2
Park Gate Mews ■
BH1 ...121 C2
Park Gdns
Christchurch BH23 ...124 C4
Yeovil BA20 ...27 B3
Park Gr DT10 ...106 C2
Park Hill DT11 ...211 C6
Park Homer Dr BH21 ...60 A3
Park Homer Rd BH21 ...59 C3
Park La Alderholt SP6 ...42 C3
Bournemouth BH10 ...89 C2
Evershot DT2 ...206 A7
Henstridge BA8 ...18 B4
Henstridge BA8 ...19 A4
Melbury Sampford DT2 ...194 A1
Radipole DT3 ...167 B3
Salisbury SP1 ...213 B4
Shapwick DT11 ...128 B1
Thorncombe TA20 ...202 D7
Wayford TA18 ...191 B1
Wimborne Minster BH21 ...59 B2
Wimborne St Giles BH21 ...201 E7
Woodlands BH21 ...44 A3
Park La Rd BH15 ...119 C1
Park Lands DT11 ...212 B2
Park Mead Rd DT4 ...180 B4
Park Pl BH14 ...119 C2
Park Rd
Barton on Sea BH25 ...94 C1
Blandford Forum DT11 ...212 B2
Bournemouth BH8 ...122 A3
Bridport DT6 ...100 B4
Easton/Weston DT5 ...187 A2
Henstridge BA8 ...19 A2
New Milton BH25 ...95 B3
Poole BH14 ...120 A2
Stalbridge DT10 ...33 B4
Swanage BH19 ...179 B1
Yeovil BA20 ...27 B3
Park St Radipole DT4 ...167 B2
Salisbury SP1 ...213 B3
Yeovil BA20 ...27 B2
Park The
Barton on Sea BH25 ...126 B4
Yeovil BA20 ...27 B3

Park View
Crewkerne TA18 ...191 F4
New Milton BH25 ...95 B3
■ Poole BH15 ...119 C2
Park View Mews BH25 ...95 A2
Park Way BH22 ...53 A2
Park Wr La DT8 ...203 C3
Park's La DT2 ...130 C1
Parkelea ■ BH21 ...56 B2
Parker Rd BH9 ...121 C4
Parkers Cl BH24 ...47 C1
Parkland Cl BH24 ...45 C1
Parkland Dr BH25 ...126 C2
Parkland Pl BH25 ...95 A1
Parkside
Christchurch BH23 ...93 B1
Ringwood BH24 ...55 A3
Parkside Gdns BH10 ...89 C1
Parkside Rd BH14 ...120 B1
Parkstone Ave BH14 ...120 B1
Parkstone Gram Sch
BH17 ...120 A4
Parkstone Hts BH14 ...119 C1
Parkstone Rd BH15 ...119 C2
Parkstone Sta BH14 ...120 A2
Parkview DT2 ...121 C1
Parkway DT6 ...97 A4
Parkway Dr BH8 ...122 C2
Parkwood La ■ BH5 ...123 A2
Parkwood Rd
Bournemouth BH5 ...123 A2
Wimborne Minster BH21 ...59 B2
Parley Cl BH22 ...61 C1
Parley Cross BH22 ...61 C1
Parley Fst Sch BH22 ...61 B1
Parley La BH23 ...90 B4
Parley Rd BH9 ...90 A1
Parmiter Dr BH21 ...59 C3
Parmiter Rd BH21 ...59 C3
Parmiter Way BH21 ...59 C3
Parnham House*
DT8 ...204 C1
Parr Gr ■ DT11 ...199 C7
Parr House ■ BH14 ...120 A1
Parr St BH14 ...120 A1
Parrett & Axe CE Prim Sch
DT8 ...204 A7
Parrett Mead DT8 ...192 C1
Parricks La EX13 ...202 A2
Parsonage Barn La
BH24 ...55 B4
Parsonage Ct ■ BH8 ...122 B3
Parsonage Gn DT9 ...213 A2
Parsonage Hill BH21 ...200 C6
Parsonage La ■ BH21 ...201 E7
Parsonage Rd
Bournemouth BH1 ...122 A2
Bridport DT6 ...100 B4
Parsonage St SP7 ...37 C1
Parsonage The SP5 ...179 A2
Parsons Cl BH17 ...179 A1
Parsons La DT2 ...102 C2
Parsons Pool ■ SP7 ...12 C2
Partridge Cl BH23 ...125 A3
Partridge Dr BH14 ...120 A4
Partridge Gr BH25 ...95 A4
Partridge Wlk BH14 ...120 A4
Partway DT10 ...196 F7
Partway La
Hardington Mandeville
BA22 ...192 F2
Hazelbury Bryan DT10 ...196 F3
Thorncombe TA20 ...202 E8
Pascoe Cl BH14 ...120 A4
Pasture Way DT6 ...100 C4
Patchins Rd BH16 ...118 A3
Patchins The BH14 ...147 A4
Patson Hill La DT9 ...15 E4
Pattinson Cl BA21 ...27 C4
Paul's Mead DT5 ...186 C2
Pauls Way DT2 ...137 B3
Pauncefote Rd BH5 ...123 A3
Pauntley Rd DT4 ...124 C4
Pavan Gdns BH10 ...89 B1
Pavilion Theatre*
DT4 ...167 C1
Pavyotts La BA22 ...193 A7
Payne Cl BH21 ...53 A1
Payne's Hill ■ SP1 ...213 B3
Paynes Ct DT2 ...76 C2
Peace Cl BH23 ...93 A3
Peaceful La DT10 ...196 E8
Peacemarsh Farm Ct ■
SP8 ...5 C2
Pear Ash La BA9 ...1 B4
Pear Cl BH22 ...121 A4
Pear Tree Cl
Alderholt SP6 ...42 A4
Bransgore BH23 ...93 A4
Pearce Ave BH14 ...120 A4
Pearce Rd BH14 ...120 A4
Pearce Rd BH16 ...118 A4
Pearce-Smith Ct
BH25 ...126 C4
Pearl Gdns BH10 ...89 B3
Pearl Rd BH10 ...89 B3
Pearson Ave BH14 ...120 B4
Pearson Gdns BH10 ...89 B3
Peatons La BH16 ...84 A2
Peckham Ave BH25 ...95 A4
Peeks Mews BH6 ...123 C2
Peel Cl
Blandford Forum DT11 ...212 B2
Poole BH12 ...120 A4
Pegasus Ct
Bournemouth BH1 ...122 A2
■ New Milton BH25 ...95 A2
Pegasus Lodge BH22 ...61 B3

eggy's La TA18 .....192 C5
elham Cl BH23 .....124 B3
elican Mead BH24 .....55 C3
emberton Cl DT3 .....152 B2
embroke Cl BA21 .....28 A4
embroke Ct 11 BH23 .....126 A4
embroke Rd
Bournemouth BH4 .....121 A1
Poole BH12 .....120 B4
en Mill Cty Inf Sch
BA21 .....27 C3
en Mill Hill BA9 .....1 C2
en Mill Trading Est
BA21 .....28 A3
encraig BH13 .....121 A2
endomer Rd BA22 .....193 B5
enelope Ct 18 BH23 .....126 A4
engelly Ave BH10 .....89 C3
enmore Rd DT9 .....15 B3
enn Cl BH25 .....94 C1
enn Cross DT6 .....64 B1
enn Hill BA20 .....27 B2
enn Hill Ave BH14 .....120 B2
enn Hill Pk BA20 .....27 B2
enn House Day Hospl
BA20 .....27 B2
enn La BA22 .....193 A6
ennant Way BH23 .....124 C4
enney's Hill DT8 .....204 D8
ennine Ct 8 BH23 .....124 C4
ennine Way BH31 .....45 A3
ennington Cl BH22 .....52 C1
ennington Cres BH22 .....52 C1
ennington Rd BH22 .....52 C1
ennsylvania Rd DT5 .....187 A2
enny Hedge BH25 .....127 A4
enny La 6 BH7 .....122 C2
enny Plot DT7 .....96 A3
enny St Radipole DT4 .....167 B2
1 Sturminster Newton
DT10 .....197 D8
enny Way BH23 .....125 B3
enny's Cnr SO41 .....95 C2
enny's Ct BH22 .....61 B3
enny's La BH21 .....40 A4
enny's Mead BH21 .....40 A4
enny's Wlk BH22 .....61 B3
ennyfarthing St SP1 .....213 B3
ennywell Gdns BH25 .....95 B2
enrith Cl BH31 .....45 A3
enrith Rd BH5 .....123 A2
enrose Cl BH16 .....84 B1
enrose Rd BH22 .....61 B3
entons Hill SP6 .....43 C3
entridge La DT10 .....34 B2
epper Hill DT11 .....198 B5
ercy Gdns DT11 .....212 B2
ercy Rd
Bournemouth BH5 .....122 C2
Yeovil BA21 .....27 C3
eregrine Rd BH23 .....125 A3
ergin Cres BH17 .....119 A4
ergin Way BH17 .....119 A4
errott Hill Sch TA18 .....192 B4
erry Gdns BH15 .....119 B1
erry St TA20 .....202 A7
erryfield Gdns BH7 .....123 A4
ersley Rd BH10 .....89 C2
erth Cl BH23 .....91 C1
erth St DT4 .....167 A2
eter Grant Way BH22 .....61 B3
eter St 3 BA20 .....27 B2
eters Cl BH16 .....118 B3
eters Rd BH22 .....61 C2
etersfield Pl BH7 .....123 A4
etersfield Rd BH7 .....123 A4
etersham La BH21 .....51 A2
etersham Rd BH17 .....119 A4
etit Rd BH9 .....90 A2
etter's Way BA20 .....27 B2
etitts Cl DT9 .....28 B1
ettridge La BA12 .....3 A3
ettycrate La DT6 .....98 C3
etwyn Cl BH22 .....62 A3
everell Ave E DT1 .....107 B1
everell Rd BH16 .....118 A2
everil Cl BH24 .....54 A3
everil Point Rd BH19 .....179 B1
everil Rd BH19 .....179 B1
helipps Rd BH21 .....86 C3
hilip Rd DT11 .....212 C3
hillips Rd DT10 .....21 A1
hyldon Cl BH12 .....120 A3
hyldon Rd BH12 .....120 A3
iccadilly La DT11 .....56 B4
ickard Rd BH22 .....61 C4
ickering Cl BH18 .....87 A1
icket La DT8 .....192 C1
ickett La BA21 .....27 B4
icketts Cross DT2 .....74 A2
ickford Rd BH9 .....89 C1
iddle La DT2 .....207 D3
iddle Valley Fst Sch
DT2 .....208 B2
idney Hill DT10 .....196 F3
iece Rd DT9 .....17 B2
iece The 2 TA16 .....191 F7
ierston Fields SP8 .....5 B3
ig Hill BA22 .....193 A7
ig Shoot La BH23 .....90 C3
igeon Cl
Blandford Forum DT11 .....212 B1
Winfrith Newburgh DT2 .....156 C3
ikes La BH19 .....183 B4
ile La DT10 .....32 C3
ilford Heath Rd BH21 .....60 A4
ilford La BH21 .....51 B1
ilgrim Pk BH24 .....55 C4

Pilgrim's Cl BH25 .....95 B2
Pilgrims Way
Broadstone BH17 .....119 A4
4 Radipole DT4 .....167 C1
Pill Mdw SP8 .....9 B2
Pilot Hight Rd BH11 .....89 A2
Pilsdon Cl 7 DT8 .....204 C4
Pilsdon Dr BH17 .....87 C2
Pilsdon La DT6 .....203 C3
Pilsdon Manor* DT6 .....203 C2
Pilsdon Pen (Hill Fort)*
DT6 .....203 C4
Pilwell DT10 .....21 A2
Pimperleaze Rd BA12 .....3 C1
Pimpern Cl BH17 .....87 C1
Pimperne CE VC Fst Sch
DT11 .....199 D4
Pimpernel Ct 6 SP8 .....5 B1
Pine Ave
Bournemouth BH6 .....123 B2
Poole BH12 .....120 C3
Pine Cl
Barton on Sea BH25 .....126 C4
Corscombe DT2 .....205 B8
Ferndown BH22 .....61 B4
Pine Cres
Christchurch BH23 .....125 C4
Holton Heath BH20 .....116 A2
Pine Dr Poole BH13 .....120 C2
St.Leonards BH24 .....54 A2
Pine Glen Ave BH22 .....61 B4
Pine Grange 4 BH1 .....122 A2
Pine House BH25 .....95 A2
Pine Lodge 15 BH13 .....147 C4
Pine Manor Rd BH24 .....53 C3
Pine Mans 3 BH1 .....122 B2
Pine Pk Mans 16 BH13 .....121 A2
Pine Rd Alderholt SP6 .....42 A3
Bournemouth BH9 .....122 A4
Broadstone BH21 .....58 C1
Pine Ridge DT7 .....96 B4
Pine Tree Ave BA20 .....27 A2
Pine Tree Cl BH21 .....59 B3
Pine Tree Glen BH4 .....121 B2
Pine Vale Cres BH10 .....89 C2
Pine View DT6 .....100 A3
Pine View Cl
Upton BH16 .....118 B3
Verwood BH31 .....44 C4
Pine View Rd BH31 .....44 C4
Pine Wlk
Lyme Regis DT7 .....96 A2
Verwood BH31 .....45 B3
Pineapple La DT6 .....68 B3
Pinebeach Ct BH13 .....147 D4
Pinecliffe Ave BH6 .....123 B2
Pinecliffe Rd BH25 .....126 B4
Pineholt Cl BH24 .....54 B3
Pinehurst Ave BH23 .....124 C3
Pinehurst Rd BH22 .....53 A1
Pinemoor Cl DT3 .....167 C4
Pines Mews 11 DT8 .....204 D4
Pines The BH13 .....121 A1
Pineside BH9 .....122 A4
Pinesprings Dr BH18 .....86 C1
Pinetree Wlk BH17 .....118 C4
Pinewood Ave BH10 .....89 B3
Pinewood Cl
Bournemouth BH10 .....89 B3
Christchurch BH23 .....94 A1
Upton BH16 .....118 A4
Pinewood Gdns BH22 .....61 B4
Pinewood Rd
Christchurch BH23 .....93 C1
Ferndown BH22 .....61 B4
Hordle SO41 .....95 C2
Poole BH13 .....121 A1
St.Leonards BH24 .....54 A2
Upton BH16 .....118 A4
Pinford La DT9 .....30 C3
Pink End BH22 .....61 C2
Pink Knoll Hollow DT9 .....15 C4
Pipers Ash 2 BH24 .....55 C4
Pipers Dr BH23 .....125 A4
Pipit Cl DT3 .....152 B2
Pippin Cl BH23 .....91 C1
Pirates La DT4 .....180 A4
Pit Hill TA17 .....191 B7
Pit Rd TA17 .....191 B7
Pitcher Cl 3 DT11 .....81 C4
Pitchers DT6 .....68 A3
Pitfield Cnr BA22 .....15 A3
Pitman's La DT6 .....66 A1
Pitt Cl DT11 .....212 B1
Pitt La DT6 .....65 C2
Pitt's Dro BH21 .....49 C1
Pittmore Rd BH23 .....92 B1
Pitts La
Melbury Abbas SP7 .....23 C3
Sedgehill And Semley SP7 .....7 B3
Pitts Orch DT10 .....35 A1
Pitts Pl BH25 .....95 B1
Pitwines Cl BH15 .....119 B1
Pix Mead Gdns SP7 .....13 A1
Place Mill* BH23 .....124 A3
Placket La BA20 .....27 A1
Plain The DT2 .....109 A3
Plaisters La DT3 .....153 B2
Plant Pk Rd BH24 .....54 C1
Plantaganet Chase
BA20 .....27 A1
Plantaganet Cres BH11 .....88 B3
Plantagenet Pk BA20 .....27 A2
Plantagenet Way 8 SP8 .....5 B1
Plantation Ct BH17 .....87 B1
Plantation Dr BH23 .....94 A1
Plantation Rd BH17 .....87 B1
Plassey Cl DT1 .....107 C1

Plassey Cres BH10 .....89 B3
Playfield Cl 2 BA8 .....19 A2
Playfields Dr BH12 .....120 C3
Pleasance Way BH25 .....94 C2
Pleck Hill DT10 .....196 E3
Pleck La DT2 .....209 B7
Plecy Cl BH22 .....61 B1
Plemont Cl BH12 .....88 C1
Plocks The DT11 .....212 B2
Plot La DT9 .....14 C1
Plott La BA8 .....19 B3
Plough Est DT11 .....212 B3
Plover Cl 11 DT9 .....17 B1
Plover Ct BA21 .....26 C3
Plover Dr DT3 .....166 B3
Plover Rd DT9 .....17 B1
Plowman Cl DT10 .....21 A2
Plum Orch DT9 .....28 C4
Plumbley Mdws 6 DT11 .....81 C4
Plumer Rd BH17 .....87 A1
Podington Mdws DT3 .....166 B3
Pokesdown Com Prim Sch
BH5 .....123 A3
Pokesdown Sta BH7 .....123 A3
Polans DT9 .....194 D2
Polden Rd 7 SP1 .....213 C2
Policemans La BH16 .....117 A4
Pollards La DT2 .....155 B4
Pomona Cl BH22 .....61 B3
Pompey's Cnr BH21 .....61 A2
Pompey's La BH22 .....61 A1
Pond Cl Henstridge BA8 .....19 A2
New Milton BH25 .....95 A2
Pond Head BH21 .....51 B3
Pond Wlk DT10 .....33 B4
Ponsonby Rd BH14 .....120 B2
Pony Dr BH16 .....118 B4
Poole Aquarium &
Serpentarium*
BH15 .....119 B1
Poole Commerce Ctr
BH12 .....120 C3
Poole Gram Sch BH17 .....87 B1
Poole High Sch BH15 .....119 B2
Poole Hill BH2 .....121 C2
Poole Hospl BH15 .....119 B2
Poole La BH11 .....89 A3
Poole Rd
Bournemouth BH2 .....121 B2
Lytchett Matravers BH16 .....84 C3
Poole BH12 .....121 A2
Sturminster Marshall
BH21 .....56 B1
Upton BH16 .....118 B4
Wimborne Minster BH21 .....59 B2
Poole Sta BH15 .....119 B2
Poole's Ct 4 DT7 .....96 B3
Poop Hill TA18 .....192 C8
Poop Hill La TA18 .....192 C8
Poorhouse La DT6 .....66 B4
Pope's Hill DT2 .....205 F1
Pope's La DT9 .....17 B1
Popes Rd BH15 .....119 B3
Poplar Cl
Bransgore BH23 .....93 B4
Christchurch BH23 .....126 A4
6 Poole BH15 .....119 A1
Wimborne Minster BH21 .....59 B3
Poplar Cres BH24 .....55 B4
Poplar Hill 3 DT11 .....198 B6
Poplar La BH23 .....93 B4
Poplar Rd BH25 .....95 B2
Poplar Way BH24 .....55 B4
Pople's Well TA18 .....191 E4
Poppy Cl
Christchurch BH23 .....125 B4
Upton BH16 .....117 A4
Yeovil BA22 .....26 B3
Poppyfields SP8 .....5 C2
Porchester Ct 12 BH1 .....122 A3
Porchester Pl BH8 .....122 A3
Porchester Rd BH8 .....122 A3
Port La DT6 .....101 B2
Port Regis Sch SP7 .....12 A3
Portarlington Cl BH2 .....121 B1
Portarlington Rd BH4 .....121 B1
Portchester Boys Sch
BH7 .....123 A4
Portelet Cl BH12 .....88 B1
Porter Rd BH17 .....119 A4
Porters La BH21 .....60 B3
Portesham CE Prim Sch
DT3 .....150 A4
Portesham Gdns BH9 .....90 A2
Portesham Hill DT3 .....132 A1
Portesham Way BH17 .....87 C2
Portfield Cl BH23 .....124 A4
Portfield Rd BH23 .....124 A4
Portfield Sch BH23 .....124 A3
Portiere House BH11 .....89 A2
Portland Ave SP2 .....213 A1
Portland Beach Rd
DT4 .....180 C2
Portland Castle* DT5 .....181 A1
Portland Cres DT4 .....167 A1
Portland Ct DT7 .....96 A3
Portland Hospl DT5 .....181 A1
Portland Mus* DT5 .....187 A2
Portland Pl BH2 .....121 C2
Portland Port DT5 .....181 B1
Portland Rd
Bournemouth BH9 .....122 A4
Weymouth DT4 .....180 B4
Portland Tophill Jun Sch
DT5 .....187 A2
Portman Cres BH5 .....123 A2
Portman Ct BA22 .....192 E8
Portman Dr 5 DT11 .....198 C8

Portman Rd
Bournemouth BH7 .....122 C3
11 Pimperne DT11 .....199 D4
Portman Terr BH5 .....123 A2
Portmore Cl BH18 .....87 B3
Portmore Gdns DT4 .....167 B1
Portnell's La BA12 .....1 C2
Portreeve Dr BA21 .....27 B3
Portswood Dr 2 BH9 .....90 A2
Portway DT2 .....102 B3
Portwey Cl DT4 .....167 B1
Possessions Cnr SP5 .....25 A2
Post Gn Rd BH16 .....116 C4
Post Office Bldgs BH9 .....121 C4
Post Office La
6 Poole BH15 .....119 B1
St.Leonards BH24 .....54 B3
Post Office Rd
41 Bournemouth BH1 .....121 C2
Gillingham SP8 .....5 B3
Potterne Way BH21 .....45 B2
Potters Way
Poole BH14 .....120 B1
Salisbury SP1 .....213 C2
Pottery La DT4 .....167 B2
Pottery Lines BH20 .....142 C4
Pottery Rd BH14 .....120 A1
Poulner Hill BH24 .....55 C4
Poulner Jun & Inf Sch
BH24 .....47 C1
Poulner Pk BH24 .....47 C1
Pound Cl
Charminster DT2 .....107 B3
Poole BH15 .....119 C3
Ringwood BH24 .....55 B4
Stalbridge DT10 .....33 B4
Yeovil BA21 .....26 C3
Pound Cottage Visitor Ctr*
DT2 .....205 E2
Pound Hill
Corscombe DT2 .....205 B7
Witchampton BH21 .....200 F1
Pound La
Bishop's Caundle DT9 .....196 A7
Burstock DT8 .....203 D5
3 Christchurch BH23 .....124 A3
Damerham SP6 .....190 E3
Dewlish DT2 .....209 C1
21 Dorchester DT1 .....108 A1
Gillingham SP8 .....5 B1
5 Okeford Fitzpaine DT11 .....197 F5
Poole BH15 .....119 C3
Shaftesbury SP7 .....13 A2
Wareham BH20 .....142 C2
Wootton Fitzpaine DT6 .....64 A3
Pound Piece
Easton/Weston DT5 .....186 C2
Maiden Newton DT2 .....72 C4
Pound Rd
Hawkchurch EX13 .....202 C2
Lyme Regis DT7 .....96 A3
Thornford DT9 .....194 D8
Pound St DT7 .....96 A3
Poundbury Cres DT1 .....107 C1
Poundbury Rd DT1 .....107 C2
Poundbury W Ind Est
DT1 .....107 C1
Povington Barrow*
BH20 .....159 B1
Powell Rd BH14 .....120 A2
Powerscourt Rd BH25 .....126 C4
Powis Cl BH25 .....95 A2
Powys Cl DT1 .....134 C4
Poxwell Dro DT2 .....154 A3
Poxwell Manor* DT2 .....154 C2
Prankerds Rd 12 DT9 .....17 B1
Preetz Way DT11 .....212 C3
Preston Cl BH16 .....118 B4
Preston Cty Comp Sch
BA21 .....26 C3
Preston Gr BA20 .....27 A3
Preston La BH23 .....92 B2
Preston Rd
Overcombe/Preston
DT3 .....153 B2
Poole BH15 .....119 B3
Radipole DT3 .....167 C3
Yeovil BA22 .....26 B3
Preston VC Prim Sch
BA21 .....27 A3
Preston Way BH23 .....125 B4
Prestwood Cl BH25 .....94 C1
Pretoria Terr DT4 .....167 B1
Priest La BH23 .....92 A4
Priest's House Mus & Gdns*
BH21 .....59 A2
Priest's Rd BH19 .....179 A1
Priest's Way BH19 .....178 C1
Priestlands DT9 .....30 A4
Priestlands La DT9 .....30 A4
Priestley Rd BH10 .....89 A1
Prime La DT6 .....65 C4
Primrose Cl 3 SP8 .....5 B1
Primrose Gdns BH17 .....86 C1
Primrose Hill BA22 .....193 B7
Primrose La BA21 .....14 A1
Primrose Way
Christchurch BH23 .....125 B4
Corfe Mullen BH21 .....86 C4
Primula Cl DT3 .....152 C1
Prince of Wales Rd
Bournemouth BH4 .....121 B2
Dorchester DT1 .....108 A1
3 Weymouth DT4 .....167 B1
Prince of Wales Sch The
DT1 .....134 B4
Prince's Dr DT4 .....167 B3
Prince's Pl BH25 .....95 B2

Prince's St DT1 .....108 A1
Princes Cl BH22 .....61 B3
Princes Ct 6 BH12 .....121 A2
Princes St BA20 .....27 B2
Princess Ave BH23 .....124 A3
Princess Rd
Bournemouth BH4 .....121 A2
Bridport DT6 .....100 B3
Poole BH12 .....121 A2
Swanage BH19 .....179 A1
Pringles Cl BH22 .....61 C3
Pringles Dr BH22 .....61 C3
Priors Cl BH23 .....125 B4
Priors Cnr 2 BH21 .....201 D1
Priors Rd BH17 .....119 A4
Priors Wlk 7 BH21 .....59 A3
Priory CE Prim Sch The
BH23 .....124 A3
Priory Cl BA20 .....26 C1
Priory Gdns
3 Pimperne DT11 .....199 D3
3 Spetisbury DT11 .....211 E5
West Moors BH22 .....62 A4
Priory Glade BA21 .....26 C3
Priory House BH23 .....124 B3
Priory Ind Pk BH23 .....125 A4
Priory La DT6 .....100 B3
Priory Quay BH23 .....124 B3
Priory Rd
Bournemouth BH2 .....121 C1
Portland DT5 .....186 C3
West Moors BH22 .....62 A4
Priory Sq 9 SP2 .....213 B3
Priory View Ct 5 BH23 .....124 A3
Priory View Pl 7 BH9 .....90 A2
Priory View Rd
Bournemouth BH9 .....90 A2
Burton BH23 .....92 B1
Privet Rd BH9 .....121 C4
Promenade BH23 .....125 A3
Prospect Cl 2 SP8 .....6 A1
Prospect Cres BH19 .....179 A2
Prospect Pl Mere BA12 .....2 C3
9 Weymouth DT4 .....167 B1
Prospect Rd
Dorchester DT1 .....107 C1
Lytchett Matravers BH16 .....84 B2
Prosperous St 14 BH15 .....119 B1
Prout Hill 9 DT8 .....204 D4
Prunus Cl BH22 .....61 A4
Prunus Dr BH22 .....61 A4
Pryors Wlk BH16 .....84 B1
Pud Brook 9 DT9 .....17 B1
Puddledock La DT3 .....153 B2
Puddletown CE Fst Sch
DT2 .....78 A1
Puddletown Cres BH17 .....87 C1
Puddletown Rd
Arne BH20 .....142 A2
Bere Regis BH20 .....140 C4
East Stoke BH20 .....113 A1
Pugmill La DT3 .....166 B3
Pullman Ct BH22 .....52 C1
Pullman Way BH24 .....55 B3
Pulmans La 4 TA18 .....191 F4
Purbeck Ave BH15 .....118 C1
Purbeck Cl Loders DT6 .....101 C4
Lytchett Matravers BH16 .....84 B2
Upton BH16 .....118 A4
Weymouth DT4 .....167 A1
Purbeck Ct
Bournemouth BH5 .....123 A2
3 Christchurch BH23 .....124 C4
Purbeck Dr BH31 .....45 A3
Purbeck Gdns BH14 .....119 C3
Purbeck Hts BH14 .....120 A3
Purbeck Information &
Heritage Ctr* BH20 .....142 C2
Purbeck Rd
Barton on Sea BH25 .....126 B4
Bournemouth BH2 .....121 C1
Lytchett Matravers BH16 .....84 B2
Purbeck Sch The
BH20 .....142 B2
Purbeck Sports Ctr
BH20 .....142 B1
Purbeck Terr Rd
BH19 .....179 B1
Purbeck Toy Mus*
BH20 .....144 B2
Purbeck View 13 BH19 .....178 C1
Purbeck View Sch
BH19 .....179 A2
Purchase Rd BH12 .....121 B4
Purewell BH23 .....124 B3
Purewell Cl BH23 .....124 C3
Purewell Cross BH23 .....124 C3
Purewell Cross Rd
BH23 .....124 B4
Purewell Ct 11 BH23 .....124 C4
Purns Mill La SP8 .....5 C3
Pussex La BH23 .....91 A4
Putt's La DT9 .....16 A4
Putton La DT3 .....166 B3
Puxey La
Shillingstone DT11 .....198 B5
Sturminster Newton
DT10 .....197 B7
Pye Cl BH21 .....86 C4
Pye Cnr BH21 .....59 A2
Pye La Cranborne BH21 .....41 A3
Tatworth & Forton TA20 .....202 B8
Wimborne Minster BH21 .....59 A2
Pymore La DT6 .....68 B2

Pymore Rd
Bradpole DT6 ....68 C1
Bridport DT6 ....100 B4

Q

Quantock Ct **7** BH23 ....124 C4
Quar Cl DT10 ....196 E1
Quarr Dr DT9 ....30 A4
Quarr Hill Morden DT6 ...83 B1
Wool BH20 ....140 A1
Quarr La Sherborne DT9 ..30 A4
Symondsbury DT6 ....99 B3
Quarry Chase **7** BH4 ..121 B2
Quarry Cl
Shipton Gorge DT6 ....101 B2
Stour Provost SP8 ....21 B4
Sturminster Newton DT10 ..35 A1
12 Swanage BH19 ....178 C3
Wimborne Minster DT1 ....60 A4
Quarry Dr BH21 ....60 A4
Quarry Fields Ind Est
BA12 ....2 C3
Quarry La
Bothenhampton DT6 ....100 C2
Bradford Abbas DT9 ....28 B2
Longburton DT9 ....195 B8
Melbury Abbas SP7 ....24 A3
Quarry Rd BH21 ....60 A4
Quarterjack Mews 1
BH21 ....59 B2
Quay Point **1** BH15 ....119 B1
Quay Rd BH23 ....124 A3
Quay The Poole BH15 .....119 B1
8 Wareham Town BH20 ..142 C2
Quayle Dr BH11 ....88 C3
Quayside DT6 ....100 B1
Quebec Pl **8** DT4 ......167 B2
Queen Anne Dr BH21 ......87 C4
Queen Elizabeth Ct
BH21 ....59 A2
Queen Elizabeth's Sch
BH21 ....58 C3
Queen Manor Rd SP1 .....213 C2
Queen Mary Ave BH9 ......89 C1
Queen St Gillingham SP8 ...5 C1
Radipole DT4 ....167 C2
Salisbury SP1 ....213 B3
4 Wetminster DT9 ......194 C5
Queen's Ave
Christchurch BH23 ....124 A3
Dorchester DT1 ....134 C4
Queen's Copse La BH21 ...51 B4
Queen's Pk Ave BH8 ......122 B4
Queen's Pk Gdns BH8 .....122 B4
Queen's Pk Rd BH8 ....122 B4
Queen's Pk S Dr BH8 .....122 B4
Queen's Pk W Dr BH8 .....122 B4
Queen's Rd
Blandford Forum DT11 ....212 C2
Bournemouth BH4 ....121 B2
Christchurch BH23 ....124 C3
Corfe Mullen BH21 ....86 B3
Poole BH14 ....120 B2
Swanage BH19 ....179 A1
Queens Ct BH22 ....52 C1
Queens Ct
5 Bournemouth BH4 ....121 B2
New Milton BH25 ....95 B2
Queens Gdns BH21 ....121 B2
Queens Gr
New Milton BH25 ....95 B2
Pen Selwood BA9 ....95 B2
Queens Mead **11** BH19 .179 A1
Queens Rd
Bradford Abbas DT9 ....28 B1
Bridport DT6 ....100 B3
Ferndown BH22 ....61 B4
Fortuneswell DT5 ....186 C4
Mere BA12 ....3 A3
Radipole DT3 ....167 B4
Salisbury SP1 ....213 B3
Queens Wlk DT7 ....96 A3
Queensberry Rd SP1 .....213 B4
Queensbury Mans 7
BH1 ....122 A2
Queensland Rd
Bournemouth BH5 ....123 A3
Weymouth BH20 ....167 A2
Queensmead **4** BH21 ..59 B3
Queensway
New Milton BH25 ....94 C2
Ringwood BH24 ....55 B4
Yeovil BA20 ....27 B3
Queensway Pl BA22 ....27 B2
Queenswood Ave BH8 ....90 C1
Queenswood Dr BH22 .....61 B4
Queenwell DT6 ....68 C1
Quibo La DT4 ....167 A2
Quince La BH21 ....59 C3
Quinton Cl BH23 ....125 C4
Quomp The BH24 ....55 B4

R

R L Stevenson Ave
BH4 ....121 A2
Rabin Hill DT10 ....35 A1
Rabling La BH19 ....179 A2
Rabling Rd BH19 ....179 A2
Racedown Rd DT11 ....199 E3
Rachel Cl BH12 ....120 B4
Radcliffe Rd SP2 ....213 B1

Radipole La
Chickerell DT4 ....166 C2
Radipole DT4 ....167 A3
**Radipole Lake Nature
Reserve*** DT4 ....167 B2
Radipole Pk Dr DT4 ......167 B3
Radipole Prim Sch
DT3 ....167 A4
Radipole Rd BH17 ....88 A1
Radnor Rd SP1 ....213 B4
Raglan Gdns BH11 ....89 A1
Raglan Terr BA21 ....27 A4
Railway Dr BH21 ....59 A2
Railway Terr 4 SP8 ......6 A1
Raleigh Cl
Christchurch BH23 ....124 C3
New Milton BH25 ....94 C2
8 Ringwood BH24 ......55 C4
Raleigh Rd Poole BH15 ...88 C1
Stalbridge DT10 ....33 C4
Ralph Rd BH21 ....86 C4
Ram La DT11 ....48 B1
Ram's Hill DT10 ....21 C1
Rampant Wlk DT1 ....134 C4
Rampart Rd SP1 ....213 B3
Rampisham Hill DT8 .....205 C3
Ramsbury DT10 ....196 D5
Ramsbury Cl DT11 ....212 B3
Ramsbury Ct DT11 ....212 B3
Ramsey Ct BH25 ....94 C2
Randall Cl DT3 ....166 B3
Randalls Hill BH16 ....85 A1
Randolph Rd
2 Bournemouth BH1 ....122 C2
Poole BH14 ....120 B3
Ranelagh Ct BH23 ....125 C4
Ranelagh Rd
Christchurch BH23 ....125 C4
Radipole DT4 ....167 B2
Rashley Rd DT3 ....166 B3
Raspberry La SP7 ....12 B1
Ratcliff's Gdn SP7 ....12 B1
Ratleigh La DT9 ....196 A3
Ravana Cl **4** BH8 ......122 A3
Raven Way BH23 ....123 A3
Ravenscourt Rd BH6 .....123 B3
Ravenscroft **8** SP2 ....213 B1
Ravensdale Cl BH12 .....120 B3
Ravenshall BH2 ....121 B1
Ravine Cl BH13 ....147 C4
Ravine Gdns 5 BH13 ..147 C4
Ravine Rd
Bournemouth BH5 ....123 A2
Poole BH13 ....147 C4
Rawles Way DT6 ....100 B4
Rawlsbury Camp*
DT11 ....209 B8
Rawston Down Rd 6
DT11 ....199 E2
Rax La DT6 ....100 B4
Raymond Cl BH31 ....45 B3
Raymond Rd DT4 ....166 C1
Rayners Dr BH12 ....120 B3
Reap La DT5 ....186 C1
Rebbeck Rd BH7 ....123 A3
Reckleford BA20 ....27 B3
Reckleford Cty Inf Sch
BA21 ....27 B4
Recreation Rd BH12 .....120 C3
Rectory Ave BH21 ....58 B1
Rectory Cl DT2 ....136 A1
Rectory Gdns DT11 ......198 F7
Rectory La
Child Okeford DT11 ......198 C7
Hardington Mandeville
BA22 ....193 A7
Puncknowle DT2 ....129 C3
Studland BH19 ....164 B1
West Stafford DT2 ....136 A4
Rectory Rd
Broadmayne DT2 ....136 A1
Piddlehinton DT2 ....76 C4
Poole BH15 ....119 B3
Salisbury SP2 ....213 A2
Rectory Way DT4 ....167 A2
Red Horn Cl BH16 ....118 B2
Red House Mus & Gdns*
BH23 ....124 A3
Red La
Corfe Mullen BH21 ....86 A4
Seaborough DT8 ....191 E1
Sixpenny Handley SP5 ...189 A3
Todber DT10 ....21 B2
Red Lion Cl **3** BH10 ...197 D8
Red Oaks Cl BH22 ....61 A4
Red Post Blaxworth DT11 ..82 A4
Poyntington DT9 ....16 B2
Red Roofs BH22 ....61 C2
Red Wing Rd DT9 ....17 B1
Redan Cl BH23 ....125 C4
Redbreast Rd BH9 ....90 A2
Redbreast Rd N BH9 .....90 A2
Redbridge La DT2 ....137 C3
Redbridge Rd DT2 ....137 C3
Redcliff View DT4 ....167 C1
Redcliffe Cl BH23 ....92 B2
Redcliffe Rd **4** BH23 ..124 B3
Redcotts La BH21 ....59 A3
Redcotts Rd BH21 ....59 A3
Redford Cl SP1 ....213 C4
Redgate Pk TA18 ....191 E5
Redhill Ave BH9 ....89 C2
Redhill Cl BH10 ....89 C2
Redhill Cres BH9 ....89 C2
Redhill Dr BH10 ....89 C2
Redhill Dr BH10 ....89 C2
Redhill Pk Homes 1
BH10 ....89 C2

Redhoave Rd BH17 ....87 C1
Redhole La
Castleton DT9 ....16 A1
Sherborne DT9 ....30 A4
Redlands
Christchurch BH23 ....125 A4
Poole BH21 ....120 C3
Redlands La DT8 ....203 F5
Redman La SP7 ....24 A3
Redmans View BH11 .....45 A3
Redpoll Cl **1** DT3 .....152 B2
Redsails BH13 ....147 A2
Redshank Cl BH17 ....86 C1
Redvers Rd BH23 ....124 C4
Redwood Cl BH24 ....55 B4
Redwood Dr BH22 ....61 B4
Redwood Rd
Upton BH16 ....118 A4
Yeovil BA21 ....28 A4
Reed View Cl DT4 ....167 A3
Reedling Cl DT3 ....152 B2
Reeves Orch BH21 ....56 B3
Reforne DT5 ....186 C2
Reforne Cl **1** DT5 .....187 A2
Regency Cres BH23 .....123 C4
Regency Dr **7** BH23 ...152 B2
Regent Dr BH22 ....122 C4
Regent Way BH23 ....124 A4
Regents The **2** BA21 ...26 C3
Regimental Mus*
SP1 ....213 B2
Reid St BH23 ....124 A4
Remstone Rd
Oakley BH21 ....87 B4
Swanage BH19 ....179 A2
Remus Cl DT1 ....134 C4
Renault Dr BH18 ....87 A1
Renfrew Cl DT1 ....134 C4
Renscombe Rd BH19 ....183 A4
Restharrow BH1 ....122 A2
Retreat Rd BH21 ....59 B2
Revels Hill DT2 ....207 E7
Rew La DT2 ....208 A3
Rex La DT3 ....166 B3
Rex's La BA22 ....27 C1
Reynard Ct BH15 ....119 C2
Reynards Way DT3 ......153 B2
Rhine Rd BH20 ....139 C3
Rhode La DT7 ....64 A1
Rhosewood Dr DT11 ....153 A2
Rhydderch Way **9** TA18 ..191 F4
Ribble Cl BH18 ....87 A1
Ribbonwood Hts
BH14 ....120 A2
Ricardo Cres BH23 ......125 A3
Rice Gdns BH16 ....118 B2
Rice Terr BH16 ....118 B2
Richard Cl BH16 ....118 A4
Richards Way SP2 ....213 A2
Richmond Cl DT9 ....30 A3
Richmond Ct
15 Bournemouth BH5 ..122 C2
7 New Milton BH25 ....95 A2
Richmond Gdns BH1 ....122 C2
Richmond Gn DT9 ....30 A3
Richmond Hill DT1 ......121 C2
Richmond Hill Dr BH2 ..121 C2
Richmond Pk Ave
BH8 ....122 B4
Richmond Pk Cl BH8 ....122 B3
Richmond Pk Cres
BH8 ....122 B4
Richmond Pk Rd BH8 ...122 B4
Richmond Rd
1 Blandford Forum DT11 ..212 C2
Poole BH14 ....120 B2
4 Salisbury SP2 ....213 A3
Sherborne DT9 ....30 A3
Swanage BH19 ....179 A1
Wimborne Minster BH21 ..59 B2
Yeovil BA20 ....27 B2
Richmond Rise BH8 .....122 B3
Richmond Way BA21 .....26 C3
Richmond Wood Rd
BH8 ....122 B4
Ricketts La DT10 ....35 A1
Rickhay Rise TA18 ......192 B8
Ridge Dro DT10 ....196 F5
Ridge La
Hazelbury Bryan DT10 ...196 D5
West Coker BA22 ....193 A8
Ridge The DT9 ....16 C3
Ridge Way
Shaftesbury DT2 ....76 C1
Ridgeback La DT6 ....69 C4
Ridgefield Gdns BH23 ..125 A4
Ridgemead **6** BA20 ...26 C1
Ridgemount Gdns
BH15 ....118 C2
Ridgeway Bradpole DT6 ..68 C1
Broadstone BH18 ....87 A2
Corfe Mullen BH21 ....86 B4
Ferndown BH22 ....89 C4
3 Sherborne DT9 ....30 A3
Ridgeway La
Child Okeford DT11 .....198 C8
Hinton St Mary DT10 ....35 A2
Ridgeway Rd SP1 ....213 B3
Ridgway TA18 ....192 B8
Ridley Rd BH9 ....121 C4
Ridout Ct BH10 ....89 A1
Ridwood DT1 ....99 A3
Rigg La DT9 ....14 C1
Riggs Gdns BH11 ....88 C1
Rigler Rd BH15 ....119 A1
Rimbrow Cl DT3 ....153 B2
Rimbury Way BH23 .....124 A4

Ring St DT10 ....33 B4
**Ringmoor (Settlement &
Field System)***
DT11 ....197 F3
Rings The DT11 ....79 C4
Ringstead Cres DT3 .....168 A3
Ringwood CE Inf Sch
BH24 ....55 B4
Ringwood Cty Jun Sch
BH24 ....55 B3
Ringwood La BH21 ......201 E7
Ringwood Rd
Alderholt SP6 ....42 B3
Bournemouth BH11 ......88 C2
Bransgore BH23 ....93 B3
Christchurch BH23 ......94 A1
Ferndown BH22 ....61 B4
Fordingbridge SP6 ....43 B3
Hyde SP6 ....43 C2
Poole BH12 ....120 A4
Sopley BH23 ....92 A4
St.Leonards BH24 ....53 C1
Three Legged Cross BH21 ..52 C4
Verwood BH31 ....45 B3
Ringwood Recn Ctr
BH24 ....55 B4
Ringwood Rd Pk BH11 ...88 C2
Ringwood Sch BH24 .....55 B3
Rip Croft DT5 ....186 C1
Ripon Rd BH9 ....90 A1
Ripp's La DT2 ....207 F4
Rise The DT4 ....167 A3
Ritchie Pl BH22 ....52 C2
Ritchie Rd
Bournemouth BH11 ......89 A2
Yeovil BA22 ....26 B3
River Cl BH21 ....59 B3
River La **2** DT11 ......211 D6
River Pk BH6 ....123 B3
River View SP8 ....5 C1
River Way
Charmouth DT6 ....97 A4
Christchurch BH23 ......91 A1
Riverbourne Rd SP1 ....213 C2
Riverdale La BH23 ......124 A3
Riverlea Rd DT2 ....124 A3
Rivermead Gdns BH23 ..91 C1
Rivers Mead DT10 ....35 B1
Rivers Rd BA21 ....27 C4
Riverside **1** BH21 ......59 B2
Riverside Rd BH6 ....124 A2
Riversdene DT11 ....48 A3
Riverside
3 Beaminster DT8 .....204 D4
8 Bournemouth BH10 ..89 C2
Ringwood BH24 ....55 A3
Riverside Ave BH7 ....91 B1
Riverside Cl DT1 ....213 C3
Riverside La BH6 ....123 B3
Riverside Pk BH23 ......124 A3
Riverside Pk Ind Est
BH21 ....59 B2
Riverside Rd
Blandford Forum DT11 ..212 C2
Bournemouth BH6 ......123 C3
Ferndown BH22 ....52 C1
Salisbury SP1 ....213 C3
Rivers Mews BH23 ....59 B2
Riverstreet Ct BH23 ....124 A3
Rivervale DT6 ....100 B4
Riviera Ct
3 Bournemouth BH1 ...121 B2
8 Poole BH13 ....147 C4
Riviera **22** BH1 ....121 A2
Rixon Cl DT10 ....35 B1
Rixon Hill DT10 ....35 A1
Roberts La BH17 ....119 A4
Roberts Pl DT1 ....107 C1
Roberts Rd
Bournemouth BH7 ....123 A3
Poole BH17 ....87 A1
Robertson Rd BH20 .....139 B4
Robin Cl **2** DT3 ......152 B2
Robin Cres BH25 ....94 B3
Robin Gr BH25 ....94 C1
Robins Cl **7** BH21 ....59 B2
Robins Garth DT1 ....108 A1
Robins Gdn DT2 ....209 A2
Robins Way BH23 ....123 A3
Robinson Hts DT10 .....33 B4
Robinswood Dr BH22 ...61 B4
Robsall Cl BH12 ....120 C4
Robville Ct BH6 ....123 A3
Rochbank La BH11 ......89 A2
Rockbourne Gdns
BH25 ....126 B4
Rockbourne La SP6 .....190 F3
Rockford Cl DT3 ....123 C2
Rockhampton Cl DT3 ...152 B2
Rockley Rd BH15 ....118 C1
Rocks La DT2 ....209 A4
Rockway DT6 ....101 B2
Rocky Knap DT3 ....167 B4
Rod Hill La DT2 ....78 A1
Rodden Cl DT4 ....180 B4
Rodden House* DT3 ..152 B3
Rodden La DT3 ....150 B3
Rodden Row DT3 ....149 A4
Rodgett Cres BH20 .....142 C4
Rodney Cl DT1 ....121 A4
Rodney Ct
Christchurch BH23 ......125 A3
Poole BH15 ....119 B1
Rodney Dr BH23 ....124 C3
Rodway DT1 ....59 B2
Rodwell Ave DT4 ....167 B1
Rodwell Cl BH10 ....89 B2
Rodwell Rd DT4 ....167 B1

Rodwell St DT4 ....167 B1
Roe Ave BA22 ....26 B2
Roe La BA22 ....27 A3
Roebuck Cl BH25 ....95 A4
Roeshot Cres BH23 ......93 C4
Roeshot Hill BH23 ....93 B4
Roke Rd BH20 ....80 A2
Rolfe Cres DT3 ....166 B4
Rollestone St **13** SP1 ..213 B3
Rolls Bridge La SP8 ......5 C1
Rolls Bridge Way SP8 ....5 C1
Rolls Mill Bridge*
DT10 ....197 D1
Roman Cl DT3 ....167 B4
Roman Hts BH21 ....86 C1
Roman Rd
Corfe Mullen BH18 ......86 C1
Dorchester DT1 ....134 C4
Osmington DT3 ....154 A4
Radipole DT3 ....167 B4
Roman Way BH21 ....58 B2
Romer Rd SP2 ....213 B1
Romney Cl BH10 ....89 C2
Romney Rd BH10 ....89 C2
Romsey Rd BH21 ....28 A4
Romulus Cl DT1 ....134 C4
Rook Hill Rd BH23 ......125 C4
Rook La DT11 ....210 C4
Rook St DT3 ....3 A4
Rookery Cl
7 Gillingham SP8 ......6 A4
2 Gillingham SP8 ......11 A4
Rookery La
St.Leonards DT3 ....203 C4
Uplyme DT7 ....64 A4
Rookery The DT2 ....130 C2
Roosevelt Cres BH17 ...86 C2
Rope Walks DT6 ....100 B4
Roper's La BH20 ....142 C2
Ropers La BH16 ....118 B2
Roping Rd BA21 ....27 B
Ropley Rd BH7 ....123 A3
Rosamond Ave DT6 ....101 B
Rosamund Ave BH21 ....59 C
Roscrea Cl BH6 ....124 A
Roscrea Dr BH6 ....124 A
Rose Cres BH15 ....119 C
Rose Ct **3** Gillingham SP8 ..6 A
Poole BH15 ....119 C
Rose Gdn The BH23 .....91 B
Rose Gdns BH9 ....90 A
Rose La **1** TA18 ......191 E
Rose's La DT3 ....150 A
Rosebank La DT11 ......212 C
Rosebery Gdns **3** SP8 ..5 C
Rosebery Ave BA21 .....27 C
Rosebery Cl BH31 ....45 C
Rosebery Rd BH5 ....123 A
Rosebud Ave **8** BH9 ...90 A
Rosecrae Cl BH25 ......94 C
Rosecroft Rd DT4 ....166 C
Rosedale Cl **8** BH23 ..124 C
Rosefields **11** DT11 ...212 B
Roselyn Cres DT9 ....31 A
Rosemary Cl SP1 ....213 C
Rosemary Ct **14** BH23 ..124 A
Rosemary Gdns BH12 ..120 A
Rosemary La
Abbotsbury DT3 ....149 A
4 Salisbury SP1 ....213 B
Rosemary Rd BH12 .....120 B
Rosemary St DT3 ....17 B
Rosemount Rd BH4 ....121 A
Rosewood Gdns BH25 ..94 C
Roslin Gdns BH3 ....121 B
Roslin Rd BH3 ....121 C
Roslin Rd S BH3 ....121 C
Ross Cl BH20 ....139 C
Ross Gdns BH11 ....88 B
Ross Glades BH3 ....121 C
Ross Rd BH24 ....47 C
Rossiters Quay BH23 ...124 B
Rossley Cl BH23 ....93 C
Rossmore Par BH12 ....120 B
Rossmore Rd BH12 .....120 B
Rotary Cl BH21 ....59 C
Rothbury Pk BH25 ......95 A
Rotherfield Rd
Bournemouth BH5 ......123 A
Christchurch BH23 ....94 A
Rotherham Rd DT5 .....181 B
Rothesay Dr BH23 .....125 C
Rothesay Rd
Bournemouth BH5 ......121 B
Dorchester DT1 ....135 A
Rotterdam Dr BH23 ....124 B
Rougemont Cl SP1 .....213 B
Rough Down La DT6 ....65 A
Rough Height BH19 ....179 A
Roumelia La BH5 ....122 C
Roundham Gdns
Bridport DT6 ....100 B
Weymouth DT4 ....167 A
Roundhaye Rd BH11 ....88 C
Roundhayes Cl DT4 ....167 A
Roundways* BH11 .....88 C
Row The DT10 ....38 C
Rowan Cl
Christchurch BH23 .....125 B
Ringwood BH24 ....167 A
St Leonards & St Ives
BH24 ....53 C
Sandford BH20 ....143 A
Rowan Dr
Broadstone BH17 ....86 C
Christchurch BH23 .....125 B
Verwood BH31 ....45 B

owan Way BA20 ....27 A2
owbarrow Cl
  Poole BH17 ....87 C1
  Salisbury SP2 ....213 B1
owbarrow Dr TH9 .....14 C2
owbarrow La BH21 ....200 F2
owden Hill La DT10 ...32 C1
owena Rd BH6 ....123 C3
owland Ave BH15 .....119 C3
owlands Hill BH21 ....59 B3
owlands Rd **5** DT11 ..198 F4
owls La BA9 ....4 A2
ownhams Rd BH8 .....90 B2
oyal Arc **5** BH7 .....122 C2
oyal Armoured Corps Tank Mus* BH20 ......139 C3
oyal Bournemouth Gen Hospl The BH7 .....91 A1
oyal Manor Sch DT5 .186 C2
oyal Oak Rd BH21 ...123 A4
oyal Signals Mus* DT11 ......199 E3
oyal Victoria Hospl BH4 ......121 B2
oyster Cl BH17 .....87 B2
oyston Dr BH21 ....59 B3
oyston Pl BH25 ....127 A4
ozel Manor BH13 ...121 A1
ozelle Rd BH14 ....120 B2
uben Dr BH15 .....118 B1
uddock Cl BA22 ...95 A2
uddock Cl BA22 ...193 B8
uddock Way BA22 .193 A8
ue La DT9 ....31 C2
ufford Gdns BH6 ..123 C3
ufus Castle* DT5 .187 A2
ugby Rd BH17 ....87 A1
uins La DT6 ......99 A3
unnymede Ave BH11 .88 C3
unnymede Rd BA21 .27 C4
unton Rd BH12 ....120 B3
unway The BH23 ..125 A4
ural La DT2 ......73 C2
uscombe La DT6 ..69 C3
ushall La BH21 ...86 A3
ushcombe Fst Sch BH21 ....86 B3
ushcombe Way BH21 .86 C3
ushetts Cl **7** DT5 .186 C1
ushford Warren BH23 ....124 C2
ushmere Rd BH9 ..123 B4
ushmore Golf Club SP5 ....188 C5
ushmore Pk* SP5 .188 C5
ushton Cres BH3 ..121 C3
uskin Ave BH9 ....90 A2
uskin Rd BH9 .....89 B3
Russell Ave
  Swanage BH19 .....179 A1
  Weymouth DT4 .....167 A1
Russell Cotes Art Gall & Mus* BH1 ......122 A1
Russell Cotes Rd BH1 122 A1
Russell Ct **8** BH25 ..95 A2
Russell Dr
  Christchurch BH23 .124 B3
  Swanage BH19 .....179 A1
Russell Gdns
  Hamworthy BH16 ..118 B2
  St.Leonards BH24 ..54 B3
Russell Rd **7** DT4 ..167 A1
Russell Ct BH22 ....61 B3
Russet Way BH20 ..26 C1
Rutland Manor **9** BH21 121 A2
Rutland Rd
  Bournemouth BH9 .122 A4
  Poole BH14 ....91 C1
  Weymouth DT4 .....167 A2
Ryall Rd Poole BH17 .87 B1
  Whitechurch Canonicorum DT6 ....66 B1
Ryall's La DT9 ....196 A7
Ryan Cl Ferndown BH22 .61 B4
  Northport BH20 ...142 C3
Ryan Gdns
  Bournemouth BH11 .89 A3
  Christchurch BH23 .125 B4
  Langton Matravers BH19 .178 A1
Rydal Cl BH23 ....91 B2
Rydal Mews BH21 ..59 B3
Rye Gdns BA20 ....26 C1
Rye Hill BH20 .....81 A1
Rye Hill Cl BH20 ..81 A1
Rye Wr La TA18 ..193 A1
Ryecroft Ave BH11 .88 C3
Ryefields Cl BA22 ..193 B8
Ryemead La DT4 ..180 B3
Ryland's La DT4 ..180 A4
Rymbury SP7 ....153 B2
Ryme Rd DT9 ....194 B5

S

Sackmore Gn DT10 .20 C2
Sackmore La DT10 .20 C2
Sackville St DT11 ..81 C4
Sadborow La TA20 .202 E5
Saddle Cl BH21 ....60 B3
Saffron Ct BH11 ....88 B2
Saffron Dr BH23 ...125 A4
Saffron Way BH11 ..88 B2
St Adlem's CE Comb Sch BH21 ....121 A3
St Alban St DT4 ...167 B1
St Alban's Ave BH8 .122 A4
St Alban's Cres BH8 .122 A4

St Aldhelm's Rd BH8 ..122 A4
St Aldhelm's Cl BH14 ..120 C2
St Aldhelm's Chapel* BH19 ....183 A2
St Aldhelm's Cl BH13 ..120 C2
  Poole BH13 ....120 C2
  Sherborne DT9 ....29 C3
St Andrew's Cl DT9 .194 E3
St Andrew's Rd BH6 .68 C1
St Andrews BH23 ..124 A3
St Andrews Rd DT3 .167 B3
St Andrews CE Prim Sch
  Overcombe/Preston DT3 ......168 A4
  Yetminster DT9 ...194 C6
St Andrews CE **4** DT1 .135 A4
St Andrews Dr DT6 .97 A4
St Andrews Ind Est DT6 ....100 C4
St Andrews Mdw DT7 .96 A3
St Andrews Rd
  Broadstone BH18 ...87 A3
  Yeovil BA20 ....27 A3
St Andrews View SP7 .37 C4
St Ann Pl SP1 .....213 B2
St Ann's Cl DT11 ..213 B2
St Ann's Hospl BH13 147 C3
St Anne's Ave BH6 .123 A3
St Anne's Gdns BA21 .27 A3
St Anne's Rd
  Upton BH16 ....118 A4
  Weymouth DT4 ....180 C4
St Annes Cl SP7 ...23 B3
St Anthony's Rd BH2 121 C3
St Antonys Leweston Sch DT9 ....195 A7
St Aubyns Cl **3** BH15 .119 A1
St Augustin's Rd BH12 59 B3
St Augustines RC Prim Sch TA18 ....191 F4
St Bartholomews CE VC Fst Sch TA18 ....191 F4
St Brelades CE VC Fst Sch BH18 ....120 B1
St Brelades Ave BH12 88 B1
St Catharines Rd BH19 ....185 B4
St Catherine's Chapel* DT11 ....209 F5
St Catherine's Cres **2** BH23 ....91 C1
St Catherine's Par BH23 ....91 C1
St Catherine's RC Prim Sch BH21 ....60 A3
St Catherine's Way BH23 ....91 B2
St Catherines Chapel* DT3 ....149 A3
St Catherines RC Sch DT6 ....100 B4
St Clair Rd Poole BH13 147 C4
  Salisbury SP1 .....213 B1
St Cleeves Way BH22 .61 B2
St Clement & St John CE Inf Sch BH8 ....122 C3
St Clement's Gdns BH1 ....122 B3
St Clement's Rd BH8 .122 B3
St Clements La BH15 .119 A1
St Clements Rd BH15 120 A4
St David's Ave BA21 .27 B4
St David's Cl **3** BH11 .122 C3
St David's Rd
  Upton BH16 ....118 A4
  Weymouth DT4 ....180 B4
St Denys **2** BH25 ..95 A1
St Edmund St **6** DT4 .167 B1
St Edmund's Church St SP1 ....213 B3
St Edward's Sch BH15 .119 C4
St Edwards **5** SP7 .12 C1
St Edwards Cl BH20 .177 A4
St Francis Rd SP1 ..213 B4
St Gabriel's Cl DT6 .98 B4
St George's Almshos **3** BH15 ....119 A1
St George's Ave
  Bournemouth BH8 .122 B4
  Poole BH18 ....119 B2
  Radipole DT4 .....167 C3
  Yeovil BA21 ....27 B4
St George's Cl
  Bournemouth BH8 .122 B4
  Christchurch BH23 .125 B4
  Langton Matravers BH19 .178 A1
St George's Cl **2** BH1 122 C3
St George's Dr BH22 .61 B2
St Georges Hill DT7 .96 A3
St Georges Mans **10** BH5 ....122 C2
St Georges Rd DT11 .108 B1
St Gildas Sch BA21 ..27 B3
St Giles Cl DT11 ...99 A4

St Giles's House* BH21 ....201 E6
St Gregorys CE Prim Sch DT10 ....20 C1
St Helen's La DT2 ..206 B2
St Helen's Rd
  Dorchester DT1 ...107 C1
  Sandford BH20 ...143 A4
  Weymouth DT4 ...166 C2
St Helier Ave DT3 ..152 A2
St Helier Rd BH12 ..88 A2
St Ives CP Sch BH24 .54 B3
St Ives End La BH24 .54 B2
St Ives Gdns BH2 ...121 C3
St Ives Pk BH24 ...54 B3
St Ives Wood BH24 .54 B3
St James DT8 ....204 C4
St James CE Fst Sch SP6 ....42 B3
St James Cl **7** BH15 .119 A1
St James Pk DT6 ...69 A1
St James Rd DT11 ..61 A3
St James St SP7 ...12 C1
St James's **20** BH5 ..122 C2
St James's Pk BH23 .26 C3
St James's Sq BH15 .119 A1
St John's Cl
  5 Salisbury SP1 ...213 C2
  Wimborne Minster BH21 59 B2
St John's Ct **4** BH11 .122 C3
St John's Gdns **3** BH9 .89 C1
St John's Hill
  Shaftesbury SP7 ...12 B1
  Wareham BH20 ...142 C2
  Wimborne Minster BH21 59 B3
St John's Rd
  Bournemouth BH5 .122 C2
  Christchurch BH23 .124 A3
  Poole BH15 ....119 A4
  Yeovil BA21 ....27 C4
St Johns Cl SP1 ...213 C2
St Johns Ct BH21 ..59 B2
  DT4 ....167 C3
St Joseph's RC Comb Sch BH23 ....125 A4
St Joseph's RC Prim Sch BH12 ....120 C4
St Judes Cl SP1 ...213 C4
St Julien Cres DT3 .152 A2
St Julien Rd BH20 .139 B4
St Just Cl BH22 ...61 B2
St Juthware Cl BA22 .193 C3
St Katharine's CE Prim Sch BH6 ....124 A2
St Katherine's Ave BH6 ....124 A2
St Katherine's CE Prim Sch BH6 ....123 A2
St Katherine's Ct BH6 .100 C4
St Lawrence **4** BH16 .128 A4
St Lawrence Cres SP7 .12 C2
St Lawrence Rd DT3 .152 B3
St Ledger's Pl BH1 .122 B3
St Ledger's Rd BH8 .122 B3
St Leonard's Ave BH21 ......212 C2
St Leonard's Rd
  Bournemouth BH8 .122 A3
  Weymouth DT4 ...167 B1
St Leonards City Med Sch DT11 ....212 C2
St Leonards Hospl BH24 ......53 C1
St Leonards Way BH24 .53 C3
St Luke's CE **2** DT6 .100 A4
St Luke's Rd BH3 ..121 C4
St Margaret's Almshouses BH21 ......59 A3
St Margaret's Ave BH23 ....124 A3
St Margaret's Cl **2** SP1 213 C2
St Margaret's Rd
  Bournemouth BH10 .89 B1
  Poole BH15 ......119 B2
St Margarets BH2 ..121 C3
St Margarets Cl BH21 .59 A3
St Margarets Hill BH21 .59 A3
St Mark's Ave SP1 .213 B4
St Mark's CE Prim Sch BH11 ......89 B1
St Mark's Rd
  Bournemouth BH11 .89 A2
  Salisbury SP1 ....213 B3
St Marks CE Jun Sch SP1 ....213 B4
St Martin's CE **1** BH20 .142 C2
St Martin's Cl BH20 .142 C2
St Martin's Rd
  17 Fortuneswell DT5 .186 C4
  Sandford BH20 ...143 A4
  Weymouth DT4 ...180 C4
St Martin's Sq SP8 ..5 C1
St Martins CE Jun Sch SP1 ....213 B2
St Martins Ch* DT1 .212 A2
St Martins Dr DT2 .136 A1

St Martins Field DT2 .133 B4
St Martins Rd BH16 .118 A4
St Martins Sch BH18 .191 E4
St Mary St **8** DT8 ..204 C4
St Mary Well St **1** DT8 204 C4
St Mary's Church (remains of)* SP7 ....24 A1
St Mary's Cl
  Northport BH20 ...142 B3
  Sixpenny Handley SP5 .189 A4
  5 Winterborne Whitchurch DT11 ....210 C3
St Mary's Cres BA21 .27 C2
St Mary's Ct BH6 ..123 C2
St Mary's Ct **3** DT8 .204 C4
St Mary's Maternity Hospl BH15 ....119 B2
St Mary's Mews BH22 .61 B3
St Mary's Rd
  Ferndown BH22 ...61 B3
  Poole BH15 ......119 C2
  Salisbury SP2 ....213 A2
  Sherborne DT9 ...29 C3
St Marys CE Fst Sch BH31 ....135 A4
St Marys CE Mid Sch DT2 ....78 A1
St Marys CE Prim Sch DT6 ....100 B3
St Marys Fst Sch BA22 .52 C2
St Marys Prim Sch DT8 ....204 C4
St Marys RC Sch BH17 .179 A1
St Marys RC Sch BH31 .21 A3
St Marys Sch
  Donhead St Mary SP7 .13 B1
  Thorncombe TA20 .202 E6
St Merrin's Cl BH10 .89 B3
St Michael's **2** BH2 .121 B2
St Michael's Ave BA21 .27 C4
St Michael's CE Mid Sch BH2 ....59 C4
St Michael's CE Prim Sch BH2 ....121 C2
St Michael's La DT6 .100 B3
St Michael's Mews **2** BH2 ....121 C2
St Michael's Pl **18** BH2 .121 C2
St Michael's Rd
  Bournemouth BH2 .121 C1
  1 Wareham BH20 .142 C2
  Yeovil BA21 ....27 C4
St Michael's Trading Est DT6 ....100 B3
St Michaels DT7 ...96 B3
St Nicholas & St Laurence CE Prim Sch DT3 ...152 B1
St Nicholas CE Prim Sch DT11 ....198 C2
St Nicholas Cl
  3 Henstridge BA8 .19 A2
  Yeovil BA20 ......27 B2
St Nicholas Ct **3** DT11 .198 C2
St Nicholas Gdns **2** DT11 ....198 E3
St Nicholas Rd SP1 .213 A4
St Nicholas' St **1** DT7 .96 B4
St Osmond's Sch SP1 .213 B2
St Osmonds Cl **1** DT9 .194 C5
St Osmund's Rd BH14 .120 B3
St Osmunds CE Mid Sch DT1 ....135 A4
St Patrick's Rd BA21 .26 C1
St Patricks Ave SP1 .166 C1
St Paul's Cl DT9 ..30 A4
St Paul's Gn DT9 ..30 A4
St Paul's La BH1 ..122 A3
St Paul's Pl BH1 ..122 A2
St Paul's Rd
  Bournemouth BH1 .122 A2
  1 Fortuneswell DT5 .186 C4
  Salisbury SP2 ....213 A3
St Peter's Abbey* DT3 ....149 A4
St Peter's Cl DT11 .199 D4
St Peter's Cres **32** BH1 .121 C2
St Peter's RC Comb Sch BH6 ....123 C2
St Peter's Rd
  Bournemouth BH1 .122 A2
  Poole BH14 ......120 B3
St Peter's Wlk **33** BH1 .121 C2
St Peters Ct DT11 ..212 A1
St Rayn Hill BA22 ..191 A4
St Richards Cl DT1 .211 F7
St Rumbold's Rd SP7 .12 C1
St Saviors Cl BH7 .123 B4
St Stephen's Ct **6** BH2 .121 C3
St Stephen's Rd BH2 .121 C3
St Stephen's Way **27** BH2 ....121 C2

St Stephens La BH31 ..45 B3
St Swithin's Rd DT9 ..30 B3
St Swithins Ave DT6 .100 B4
St Swithins Cl DT9 ..30 B3
St Swithins Rd DT6 ..100 B4
St Swithun's Rd BH1 .122 A2
St Swithun's Rd S BH1 ....122 A2
St Thomas Cross **1** BA21 ....27 C3
St Thomas Garnet's RC Sch BA21 ....123 A3
St Thomas Rd DT1 .167 B3
St Thomas St DT4 ..167 B1
St Thomas's Cl BH10 .89 C1
St Valerie Rd BH2 ..121 C3
St Vast's Rd BH12 ..121 C3
St Walburga's RC Prim Sch BH9 ....90 A1
St Winifred's Rd BH2 .121 C3
Salerno Pl BH15 ...118 B1
Salisbury & S Wiltshire Mus* SP1 ....213 A2
Salisbury Arts Ctr* SP1 ....213 B3
Salisbury Bsns Pk SP1 ....213 C2
Salisbury Cath* SP1 .213 B2
Salisbury Cath Sch SP1 ....213 B2
Salisbury Coll of Tech SP1 ....213 B2
Salisbury Cres DT11 .212 B3
Salisbury Leisure Ctr SP1 ....213 B2
Salisbury Rd
  Blandford Forum DT11 .212 C3
  Bournemouth BH1 .122 C2
  Burton BH23 ....92 B2
  Donhead St Mary SP7 .13 B1
  Ellingham Harbridge & Ibsley SP6 ....43 B1
  Pimperne DT11 ...199 E4
  Poole BH14 ......120 B3
  Shaftesbury SP7 ..12 C1
  Sopley BH23 ......92 A3
  2 Swanage BH19 .179 B1
  Weymouth DT4 ...167 B2
Salisbury Sch of English SP1 ....213 B2
Salisbury St
  Cranborne BH21 ...40 A3
  Dorchester DT1 ...108 A1
  Marnhull DT10 ....21 A1
  Mere BA12 ....22 C1
  Shaftesbury SP7 ..12 C1
Salisbury Sta SP2 .213 A3
Salisbury Street DT11 .212 B3
Salisbury Swimming Baths SP1 ....213 B3
Sally Kings La SP7 .132 B2
Sally Lovell's La BA8 .18 C4
Salt La SP1 ....213 B3
Salter Rd BH13 ...147 B2
Salterns Ct BH14 ..147 A4
Salterns Point BH14 .147 A4
Salterns Quay BH14 .147 A4
Salterns Rd BH14 ..120 A2
Salterns Way BH14 .147 A4
Salthouse La BA20 ..27 B2
Saltings Rd BH16 ..118 A3
Salway Dr DT6 ....68 A3
Salwayash Prim Sch DT6 ....68 A4
Sammy Miller's Motorcycle Mus* BH25 ....94 C3
Samphire Cl BH14 ..167 B3
Samples Way BH17 .119 C4
Samson Rd BH15 ..118 B1
Samways Cl BA22 ..26 B3
San Remo Twrs **28** BH5 .122 C2
Sancreed Rd BH12 .120 C4
Sancroft BH21 .....60 A1
Sandbanks Bsns Ctr BH13 ....147 A2
Sandbanks Rd BH14 .120 A1
Sandbourne Ave BH11 .178 C3
Sandbourne Cl BH19 .178 C3
Sandbourne Rd
  Bournemouth BH4 .121 B1
  Overcombe/Preston DT3 .168 A4
  Poole BH15 ....120 B2
Sandecotes Rd BH14 .120 B2
Sanderling Cl **6** BH20 .152 B2
Sanderlings **3** BH24 ..55 C3
Sanders Gn **4** DT11 .210 C3
Sandford Cl BH9 ...90 B2
Sandford Dr BH20 .116 A1
Sandford La BH20 ..142 C3
Sandford La Ind Est BH20 ....142 C3
Sandford Mid Sch BH20 ....116 A1
Sandford Orcas Rd
  Castleton DT9 ....15 C2
  Sandford Orcas DT9 .15 C2
Sandford Rd
  Northport BH20 ...142 C3
  Wareham BH20 ...116 A1
Sandford St Martin CE Fst Sch BH20 ....143 A4
Sandford Way BH18 ..86 C1
Sandhills BH17 ....87 B1

Sandhills Cres BH20 .... 139 C1
Sandhurst Dr BH21 .... 53 B4
Sandhurst Rd BA20 .... 27 A1
Sandilands CI SP8 .... 10 C2
Sandleheath Rd SP6 .... 42 A4
Sandlewood CI BA21 .... 28 A4
Sandmartin CI BH25 .... 126 C4
Sandown CI BA20 .... 27 B3
Sandown PI **14** SP2 .... 213 A3
Sandown Rd BH23 .... 124 C3
Sandpiper CI BH17 .... 86 C1
Sandpiper Way DT4 .... 180 B3
Sandpit La BH15 .... 119 B2
Sandringham CI BH9 .... 90 A2
Sandringham Ct
  Bournemouth BH3 .... 122 B3
  1 Dorchester DT1 .... 135 B4
Sandringham Gdns
  BH9 .... 90 A2
Sandringham Rd
  Poole BH14 .... 120 B2
  Yeovil BA21 .... 28 A3
Sandringham Sports Ctr
  DT1 .... 108 A1
Sandroyd Sch SP5 .... 188 C5
Sandsfoot Castle*
  DT4 .... 180 C4
Sandy CI BH21 .... 60 A4
Sandy Hill La BH20 .... 162 A1
Sandy Hole La 191 F8
Sandy La
  Bournemouth BH6 .... 123 A3
  Christchurch BH23 .... 91 C1
  Lytchett Matravers BH16 .... 84 C3
  Minterne Magna DT2 .... 207 C7
  Pamphill BH21 .... 58 A3
  St.Leonards BH24 .... 54 B3
  Upton BH16 .... 118 A3
  Verwood BH21 .... 45 A1
  Whitechurch Canonicorum
  DT6 .... 65 A4
  Wimborne Minster BH21 .... 60 A4
Sandy Mead Rd BH8 .... 90 C1
Sandy Plot BH23 .... 124 B4
Sandy Way BH10 .... 89 C2
Sandyhurst CI BH17 .... 87 B1
Sansome's Hill **5** DT9 .... 17 B1
Santoy BH13 .... 147 B3
Sarah Sands CI BH23 .... 124 B4
Sarah Sands CI BH23 .... 124 B4
Sark Rd BH12 .... 120 B4
Sarum **3** DT9 .... 194 D8
Sarum Ave SP2 .... 53 A2
Sarum Ct SP2 .... 213 A4
Sarum Coll SP1 .... 213 B2
Sarum Ct BH14 .... 120 B2
Sarum St BH15 .... 119 A1
Sarum St Pauls CE Sch
  SP2 .... 213 A3
Saulfland Dr BH23 .... 125 B4
Saulfland House BH23 .... 125 B4
Saulfland PI BH23 .... 125 B4
Saville Ct **9** BH21 .... 59 B2
Sawyers La DT7 .... 106 C4
Saxon Hts BH6 .... 123 C2
Saxon King Gdns BH6 .... 124 A2
Saxon Mead CI SP8 .... 5 C2
Saxon Rd SP2 .... 213 A1
Saxon Rise DT11 .... 210 C7
Saxon Spur SP2 .... 12 C2
Saxon Sq Sh Ctr **2**
  BH23 .... 124 A3
Saxon Way SP6 .... 42 B3
Saxonbury Rd BH6 .... 123 C3
Saxonford Rd BH23 .... 125 B3
Saxonhurst CI BH10 .... 89 C3
Saxonhurst Gdns BH10 .... 89 C2
Saxonhurst Rd BH10 .... 89 C2
Scadden's Cnr DT6 .... 66 A4
Scamell's Rd SP2 .... 213 B3
Scaplen's Ct Mus*
  BH15 .... 119 A1
Scarf Rd BH17 .... 119 C4
Schelin Way **6** DT11 .... 198 B5
School CI
  Chickerell DT3 .... 166 B3
  4 Tarrant Gunville DT11 .... 199 F7
  Verwood BH31 .... 45 B4
School Hill
  Chickerell DT3 .... 166 B3
  Cucklington BA9 .... 4 A2
  Powerstock DT6 .... 70 A3
  South Perrott DT8 .... 192 C1
School House La DT2 .... 103 A1
School La
  Askerswell DT2 .... 102 B4
  4 Blandford Forum DT11 .... 212 B1
  Bournemouth BH1 .... 89 A3
  Broadwindsor DT8 .... 203 B6
  Chetnole DT9 .... 194 D3
  9 Dorchester DT1 .... 107 C1
  Gillingham SP8 .... 6 A1
  4 Pimperne DT11 .... 199 D4
  Poole BH15 .... 119 B3
  Ringwood BH24 .... 55 B4
  St.Leonards BH24 .... 54 B3
  Studland BH19 .... 164 B1
  3 Tarrant Gunville DT11 .... 199 F7
  Toller Porcorum DT2 .... 71 C4
  Verwood BH31 .... 53 A4
  West Lulworth BH20 .... 172 C4
  Wimborne Minster DT2 .... 59 A3
  Winfrith Newburgh DT2 .... 156 C3
  Woodsford DT2 .... 110 B1
School Rd SP8 .... 5 C1

School St **11** DT4 .... 167 B2
Schoolhouse La DT10 .... 21 A1
Scotchey Hill SP8 .... 10 B1
Scotchey La SP8 .... 10 C1
Scots La SP1 .... 213 B3
Scott CI Poole BH12 .... 88 C1
  Stoborough Green BH20 .... 160 C4
Scott Rd BH12 .... 88 C1
Scott's Gn BH23 .... 124 C4
Scott's La DT6 .... 64 A3
Scotter Rd BH7 .... 123 A3
Scotton Way The DT7 .... 137 B3
Scotts Hill La BH23 .... 124 C4
Scotts Way TA18 .... 192 A8
Scouse La BH13 .... 202 B2
Scrubbity Barrows*
  SP5 .... 188 E4
Scutts CI DT4 .... 84 B2
Sea Hall La DT6 .... 99 A3
Sea King Rd BA20 .... 26 C2
Sea Life Pk & Model
  Village* DT4 .... 167 C3
Sea Point **8** BH13 .... 147 C4
Sea Rd
  Barton on Sea BH25 .... 126 C4
  Bournemouth BH5 .... 122 C2
Sea Rd N DT6 .... 100 C4
Sea Rd S DT6 .... 100 B3
Sea View **7** DT5 .... 186 C4
Sea View Rd
  Poole BH12 .... 120 A3
  Upton BH16 .... 118 A4
Sea Vixen Ind Est
  BH23 .... 125 A4
Seabank CI BH16 .... 118 A4
Seaborough View
  TA18 .... 191 F3
Seabourne Pl **12** BH5 .... 123 A3
Seabourne Rd BH5 .... 123 A3
Seacombe Rd BH13 .... 147 A2
Seacroft Ave BH25 .... 126 C4
Seafield CI BH25 .... 126 C4
Seafield Dr BH6 .... 123 C3
Seafield Rd
  Barton on Sea BH25 .... 126 C4
  Bournemouth BH6 .... 123 B2
  Christchurch BH23 .... 125 B4
Seagull Rd BH8 .... 90 B1
Seamoor CI DT3 .... 167 C4
Seamoor La BH4 .... 121 A2
Seamoor Rd BH4 .... 121 A2
Seaton CI BH23 .... 126 A4
Seaton Rd
  Christchurch BH23 .... 126 A4
  Yeovil BA20 .... 27 A2
Seatown CI BH17 .... 88 A1
Seaview Rd
  Barton on Sea BH25 .... 126 B4
  Christchurch BH23 .... 94 B1
Seaward Ave BH25 .... 126 C4
Seaward Gdns DT6 .... 100 B3
Seaward Rd BH19 .... 179 A2
Seaway BH25 .... 127 A4
Seaway Ave BH23 .... 125 B4
Second Cliff Wlk **2**
  DT6 .... 100 A1
Second Marine Ave
  BH25 .... 127 A3
Sedgefield CI DT4 .... 167 B2
Sedgemoor CI BA21 .... 27 C3
Sedgley Rd BH9 .... 121 C4
Seed Warehouse The **15**
  BH15 .... 119 B1
Selby CI BH18 .... 87 A2
Seldown BH15 .... 119 B2
Seldown Bridge BH15 .... 119 B1
Seldown La BH15 .... 119 B2
Seldown Rd BH15 .... 119 A1
Selfridge Ave BH6 .... 124 A2
Selfridge CI BH6 .... 124 A2
Seliot CI BH15 .... 119 B3
Selkirk CI BH21 .... 59 C1
Selle Rd BH20 .... 139 C3
Sellwood Way BH25 .... 126 B4
Selwood CI DT10 .... 35 B1
Selwood Pk BH10 .... 89 B4
Selworthy CI BH14 .... 120 A1
Selwyn CI DT13 .... 119 B2
Senior Dr SP2 .... 213 B1
Sentinal CI BH15 .... 119 C2
Sentry Rd BH19 .... 179 B1
Serpentine Rd BH15 .... 119 B2
Serralls Mead BH19 .... 178 C1
Seth Ward Dr SP1 .... 213 C4
Setley Gdns BH8 .... 90 C2
Seven Acres **9** DT5 .... 186 C1
Seven Acres Rd DT3 .... 153 B2
Seven Ash Comm Rd
  BH20 .... 195 B4
Seven Barrows Rd
  BH20 .... 142 B3
Sevenoaks Dr BH7 .... 123 A4
Severalls Pk Ave **17**
  TA18 .... 191 F4
Severn Rd BH22 .... 62 A3
Seward Ave BH6 .... 123 B2
Sewell Rd BH20 .... 139 B4
Seymer Rd BH19 .... 179 B1
Seymour Rd BH24 .... 47 B4
Shadrack **15** 128 A4
Shadrack St **2** DT8 .... 204 C4
Shady Bower **7** 213 C2
Shaftesbury CI BA21 .... 53 A1
Shaftesbury Fst Sch
  SP7 .... 13 A1
Shaftesbury Mus* SP7 .... 12 C1

Shaftesbury Rd
  Child Okeford DT11 .... 198 C8
  Ferndown BH22 .... 53 A1
  Gillingham SP8 .... 6 A1
  Henstridge BA8 .... 19 B3
  Kington Magna SP8 .... 20 A4
  Mere BA12 .... 3 A2
  Poole BH15 .... 119 B2
Shaftesbury Upper Sch
  SP7 .... 12 C1
Shaftsbury Rd BH8 .... 122 B3
Shakespeare Rd
  Bournemouth BH6 .... 123 B4
  Salisbury SP1 .... 213 A4
  Wimborne Minster BH21 .... 59 B2
Shamrock Ct **2** BH21 .... 59 B2
Shapland Ave DT11 .... 199 D4
Shapwick Rd BH15 .... 119 A1
Shard CI BH31 .... 45 B3
Sharford Bridge*
  BH20 .... 162 A3
Sharlands CI BH18 .... 87 A2
Sharp Rd BH12 .... 121 A4
Shaston CE **10** BH19 .... 178 C1
Shaston Cres DT11 .... 135 A4
Shatcombe La DT2 .... 71 B2
Shatter's Hill BH20 .... 142 C2
Shave Cross DT6 .... 203 C1
Shave Hill SP8 .... 9 A4
Shave La Todber DT10 .... 21 B3
  West Crewkerne TA18 .... 191 E3
Shaves La BH25 .... 95 A3
Shaw CI DT11 .... 212 B3
Shaw Dr BH20 .... 142 C4
Shaw Rd BH20 .... 47 C1
Shawford Gdns BH8 .... 90 B1
Shawford Rd BH8 .... 90 B1
Shear Plot DT6 .... 99 C4
Shears Rd DT4 .... 167 B4
Shearstones DT9 .... 194 D5
Sheasby CI SP5 .... 189 A3
Shedbush La DT6 .... 65 B4
Shedrick Hill TA20 .... 202 E8
Sheep Mkt Hill **4** DT11 .... 212 B1
Sheepcroft La BA21 .... 51 B2
Sheephouse Dro
  BH21 .... 200 E2
Sheeplands La DT9 .... 29 C3
Sheeplands The DT9 .... 29 C4
Sheepspine La TA20 .... 202 C5
Sheepwash La
  Burstock DT8 .... 203 D5
  Tatworth & Forton
  TA20 .... 202 A6
Shelbourne CI BH8 .... 122 B3
Shelbourne Rd BH8 .... 122 A3
Sheldrake Rd BH23 .... 125 A3
Shell Bay Sailing Ctr*
  BH19 .... 147 A1
Shelley CI
  Bournemouth BH1 .... 122 C3
  Christchurch BH23 .... 123 C4
  St.Leonards BH24 .... 53 C3
  Yeovil BA21 .... 26 C3
Shelley Ct BH22 .... 61 B3
Shelley Dr SP1 .... 213 A4
Shelley Gdns BH1 .... 122 C3
Shelley Hamlets BH23 .... 125 B4
Shelley Hill BH23 .... 125 B4
Shelley House **18** BH5 .... 95 A1
Shelley Rd (Bournemouth &
  Poole Coll) BH5 .... 122 C2
Shelley Rd E BH7 .... 122 C3
Shelley Rd W 122 C3
Shelton Rd BH6 .... 123 B3
Shenstone Ct **10** BH25 .... 95 A1
Shepherd CI BH23 .... 93 C1
Shepherd's La*
  BH24 .... 9 B4
Shepherds Croft DT5 .... 187 B3
Shepherds Hill BH24 .... 46 C3
Shepherds La 46 B3
Shepherds Way
  Bournemouth BH7 .... 123 A4
  West Lulworth BH20 .... 172 B3
Sheppards Field **4** BH21 .... 59 A3
Sherborn Cres BH17 .... 88 A1
Sherborne Abbey* DT9 .... 30 A3
Sherborne Castle*
  DT9 .... 30 B3
Sherborne CP Sch DT9 .... 30 B4
Sherborne Cswy SP7 .... 11 C2
Sherborne Dr BH22 .... 61 B2
Sherborne Golf Club
  DT9 .... 16 A2
Sherborne Hill DT9 .... 30 B2
Sherborne Mus* DT9 .... 30 B3
Sherborne Rd
  Henstridge BA8 .... 18 C2
  Milborne Port DT9 .... 17 B1
  Purse Caundle DT10 .... 18 B1
  Yeovil BA21 .... 27 C3
Sherborne Sch DT9 .... 30 A3
Sherborne St DT9 .... 30 A3
Sherborne La **3** DT7 .... 96 B3
Sherborne Old Castle*
  DT9 .... 30 B3
Sherfield CI BH8 .... 90 B1
Sherford Dr BH20 .... 142 B3
Sherford Rd BH20 .... 142 C3
Sheridan CI DT2 .... 73 C2
Sheridan Way **5** BH21 .... 56 B2
Sheringham Rd BH12 .... 120 C3
Sherlands **1** TA16 .... 191 F7
Sherren Ave DT2 .... 75 C1
Sherrin CI BH15 .... 119 B3

Sherwood Ave
  Ferndown BH22 .... 61 B2
  Poole BH14 .... 120 A2
Sherwood Dr BH31 .... 45 B3
Shetland View BH31 .... 45 B3
Shiells La DT9 .... 15 C3
Shillingstone CE Prim Sch
  DT11 .... 198 B6
Shillingstone Dr BH9 .... 90 A2
Shillingstone Gdns
  BH12 .... 120 C4
Shipfield Rd BH6 .... 123 C4
Shillito Rd BH12 .... 120 C3
Ship Knapp DT11 .... 66 A1
Shipney La DT10 .... 19 C1
Shipstal CI BH16 .... 118 B2
Shipstal Nature Trail*
  BH20 .... 144 B2
Shipton La
  Burton Bradstock DT6 .... 101 B1
  Loders DT6 .... 101 C3
Shipton Rd DT6 .... 101 B2
Shirecroft Rd DT4 .... 167 A2
Shiremoor Hill TA16 .... 191 F7
Shires CI BH24 .... 55 B2
Shires Copse BH6 .... 123 C2
Shires Mead BH31 .... 45 B3
Shirley CI
  Ferndown BH22 .... 53 A1
  Swanage BH19 .... 178 C1
Shirley Rd
  Bournemouth BH9 .... 90 A1
  Poole BH12 .... 120 A3
  Upton BH16 .... 118 B4
  Wareham BH20 .... 142 B2
Shoe La DT6 .... 100 C4
Shoot Hill TA17 .... 191 C8
Shop La DT11 .... 150 B1
Shore Ave BH16 .... 118 B3
Shore CI BH16 .... 118 B3
Shore Gdns BH16 .... 118 B3
Shore La BH16 .... 118 B3
Shore Rd Poole BH13 .... 147 B2
  Swanage BH19 .... 179 B2
Shoreacres BH13 .... 147 B2
Shoredown La DT9 .... 17 B3
Short CI BH17 .... 121 A4
Short Cross DT2 .... 206 C6
Short Rd DT4 .... 167 A2
Short's La DT11 .... 212 B2
Shortedge DT10 .... 35 B1
Shortlake La DT3 .... 169 A4
Shortlands DT5 .... 186 C2
Shortlands Rd DT3 .... 152 B3
Shortmarsh La TA18 .... 192 F4
Shorts CI BH21 .... 92 B1
Shorts Gn La SP7 .... 12 A4
Shottsford CI **7** BH19 .... 178 C1
Shottsford Rd BH15 .... 119 B3
Shreen CI SP8 .... 5 C2
Shreen Way SP8 .... 5 C2
Shrubbery La DT4 .... 180 B4
Shute La DT11 .... 37 C1
Shute Lake La **11** TA18 .... 191 F4
Shute's La SP8 .... 9 C4
Sidmouth Rd DT7 .... 96 A3
Sidney Gdns **11** BH9 .... 90 A2
Sidney Smith Ct BH17 .... 87 C1
Sidney St SP2 .... 213 A3
Silchester CI BH17 .... 121 C3
Silk House Barton
  DT10 .... 33 B4
Sillen La SP6 .... 190 B6
Silton Rd SP8 .... 1 C1
Silver Birch CI BH12 .... 121 A2
Silver Bsns Pk BH23 .... 124 C4
Silver St
  Christchurch BH23 .... 124 A3
  Crewkerne TA18 .... 192 B3
  Lyme Regis DT7 .... 96 A3
  Overcombe/Preston
  DT3 .... 153 B2
  Salisbury SP1 .... 213 B2
  4 Stalbridge DT10 .... 33 B4
  Yeovil BA20 .... 27 B3
Silver Way BH23 .... 125 C4
Silverdale BH25 .... 127 A4
Silverdale CI BH18 .... 86 C2
Silverdale Cres SP6 .... 42 B3
Silverwood CI BH21 .... 59 B1
Simmonds CI BH15 .... 119 B3
Simons Rd DT9 .... 30 A4
Sinclair CI **8** BH14 .... 120 A2
Singleton Dr BH20 .... 89 B1
Sir John Colfox Sch
  DT6 .... 68 C1
Sir Richard Hull Rd
  BH20 .... 139 B3
Siskin CI BH22 .... 61 A4
Sitterton CI BH20 .... 81 A2
Six Ways Cross BH21 .... 200 E3
Sixpenny CI BH12 .... 120 C4
Sixpenny Handley Cty Fst Sch
  SP5 .... 189 A4
Skilling Hill Rd DT6 .... 100 B3
Skilling La DT6 .... 100 A3
Skinner St BH15 .... 119 B1
Skipton CI BH18 .... 87 A1
Slade La BA22 .... 15 A3
Slade's La BH10 .... 121 B4
Slades Farm Rd BH10 .... 89 B1
Slades Farm Spec Sch
  BH10 .... 89 B1
Slades Gn DT6 .... 100 C3
Slape Hill DT6 .... 68 B4
Slape Manor* DT6 .... 204 C3
Sleepbrook CI BH31 .... 45 A3
Sleight **1** BA21 .... 26 C3

Sleight La BH21 .... 86 B1
Slepe Cres BH12 .... 120 C2
Slinn Rd BH23 .... 124 C4
Slip Way BH15 .... 119 A1
Slodbrook La SP8 .... 2 B1
Slopers Mead **2** DT11 .... 211 E6
Slough Dro DT2 .... 205 E6
Slough La Horton BH21 .... 44 A4
  Lytchett Minster & Upton
  BH16 .... 117 A4
  Upton BH16 .... 118 A3
  Woodlands BH21 .... 44 A4
Slyer's La
  Puddletown DT2 .... 76 C2
  Stinsford DT2 .... 108 B3
Smacombe La DT6 .... 101 B4
Smallmouth CI DT4 .... 180 B4
Smeaton Rd SP2 .... 213 A4
Smedmore House*
  BH20 .... 175 C1
Smishops La DT6 .... 69 B4
Smith's La TA18 .... 192 B8
Smith's Gn DT2 .... 208 B2
Smith's Terr BA21 .... 27 C2
Smithfield PI BH9 .... 89 C1
Smithson CI BH12 .... 121 B4
Smithy La BH25 .... 94 C1
Smokey Hole La **3** DT1 .... 135 B4
Smugglers La BA21 .... 28 A4
Smugglers La N BH23 .... 93 C1
Smugglers La S BH23 .... 125 C4
Smugglers Reach
  BH23 .... 125 A3
Smugglers Wood Rd
  BH23 .... 93 B1
Smugglers' La
  Colehill BH21 .... 50 C3
  Stourpaine DT11 .... 199 A6
Snag La DT11 .... 150 B1
Snail's La BH24 .... 47 B2
Snails La DT6 .... 47 A3
Snow Down Rd **1** DT11 .... 199 E2
Snow Hill BH20 .... 81 A3
Snow Hill La BH20 .... 81 A4
Snowdon Rd BH4 .... 121 B2
Snowdrop Gdns BH23 .... 93 A1
Soberton Rd BH8 .... 122 B3
Sodern La DT2 .... 107 B4
Sodom La DT10 .... 21 C3
Solar Ct BH13 .... 121 A1
Soldiers Rd BH20 .... 143 B1
Solent Dr BH25 .... 127 A4
Solent Lodge **21** BH25 .... 95 A1
Solent Rd
  Barton on Sea BH25 .... 126 B4
  Bournemouth BH6 .... 124 A2
  Christchurch BH23 .... 94 A1
Solent View BH6 .... 124 A2
Solly CI BH12 .... 120 C4
Solomon Way BH15 .... 118 B1
Someby Rd BH15 .... 119 B3
Somerby Rd BH15 .... 119 B3
Somerfields BH23 .... 96 A3
Somerford Bsns Pk
  BH23 .... 125 A4
Somerford Ct BH23 .... 125 C4
Somerford CI BH23 .... 125 C4
Somerford Cty Inf Sch
  BH23 .... 124 C4
Somerford Cty Jun Sch
  BH23 .... 124 C4
Somerford Rd BH23 .... 124 C3
Somerford Way BH23 .... 124 C4
Somerley View **4** BH24 .... 46 C3
Somerley Rd BH9 .... 122 A4
Somerley View BH24 .... 55 A4
Somers Rd DT7 .... 96 A3
Somerset CI SP8 .... 5 C2
Somerset Rd
  Bournemouth BH7 .... 123 A3
  Salisbury SP1 .... 213 B4
  Weymouth DT4 .... 167 A2
Somerton CI BH25 .... 95 B2
Somerville Dr BH25 .... 94 C2
Somerville Rd
  Bournemouth BH2 .... 121 B2
  Ringwood BH24 .... 55 C4
Sonning Way BH8 .... 90 A1
Soper's La BH23 .... 124 A3
Sopers La BH17 .... 87 A1
Sopley CE Prim Sch
  BH23 .... 126 B4
Sopley Farm Bldgs
  BH23 .... 92 A3
Sopwith CI BH23 .... 125 A3
Sopwith Cres BH21 .... 59 C1
Sorrel CI DT4 .... 167 C3
Sorrel Gdns BH18 .... 86 C1
Sorrel Way BH23 .... 125 A4
Sorrell Ct BH23 .... 125 A4
Sorrell Way DT3 .... 167 B4
South Annings **2** DT8 .... 124 A4
South Ave
  Lyme Regis DT7 .... 96 A3
  New Milton BH25 .... 95 A1
  Swanage DT9 .... 29 C2
South Bridge* BH20 .... 142 C2
South Cliff Rd
  Bournemouth BH2 .... 121 C1
  Swanage BH19 .... 179 B1
South Cross DT9 .... 19 C2
South Cswy DT10 .... 142 C1
South Ct DT9 .... 29 C2
South Dr St.Ave 135 A4
South Dr BH20 .... 206 C2
South Dro DT2 .... 112 B4
South Farm CI DT11 .... 200 A6
South Haven CI BH16 .... 118 A2

South Hill SP6 .... 42 B3
South Holme DT11 .. 198 F4
South Instow DT11 ... 177 C3
South Kinson Dr BH11 ... 89 A2
South Lawns DT6 ... 100 B3
South Mead BH20 ... 81 A1
South Mill La DT6 ... 100 B3
South Par 3 DT4 ... 167 C1
South Pk Rd BH12 ... 121 A4
South Rd
  Bournemouth BH1 ... 122 C3
  Bournemouth BH1 ... 86 C3
  Poole BH15 ... 119 B1
  Swanage BH19 ... 179 A1
  Weymouth DT4 ... 180 B3
South Rd Comb Sch
  BH15 ... 119 B1
South St Arne BH20 ... 142 C2
  Bridport DT6 ... 100 B3
  Corfe Castle BH20 ... 146 C2
  Crewkerne TA18 ... 191 F4
  Dorchester DT1 ... 108 A1
  11 Gillingham SP8 ... 5 C1
  Hinton St George TA17 ... 191 D7
  Kington Magna SP8 ... 9 B1
  Leigh DT9 ... 194 E3
  Milborne Port DT9 ... 17 B1
  13 Sherborne DT9 ... 213 A3
  Sherborne DT9 ... 30 A3
  Yeovil BA20 ... 27 B2
South View
  Bournemouth BH2 ... 121 C3
  Bradford Abbas DT9 ... 28 B1
  Piddletrenthide DT2 ... 208 C1
South View Pl 7 BH2 ... 121 C2
South View Rd
  Christchurch BH23 ... 124 A3
  Milborne Port DT9 ... 17 B1
South Walks Rd DT1 ... 108 A1
South Way DT5 ... 186 B1
South Western Cres
  ... 120 A1
South Western Rd
  SP2 ... 213 A3
South Wilts Gram Sch For
  Girls SP1 ... 213 B4
South Wlk DT6 ... 100 B3
Southampton Rd
  Ringwood BH24 ... 55 A4
  Salisbury SP1 ... 213 C2
Southbourne Coast Rd
  BH6 ... 123 C2
Southbourne Cross Roads 6
  BH6 ... 123 C2
Southbourne Gr BH6 ... 123 B2
Southbourne Overcliff Dr
  BH6 ... 123 B2
Southbourne Rd BH5 ... 123 B2
Southbourne Sands
  BH6 ... 123 B2
Southbrook
  Bere Regis BH20 ... 81 A1
  Mere BA12 ... 3 A2
Southbrook Cl BH17 ... 88 A1
Southbrook Gdns BA12 ... 3 A2
Southcliffe Rd
  Barton on Sea BH25 ... 126 B4
  Christchurch BH23 ... 125 B3
Southcote Rd BH1 ... 122 B2
Southcroft Rd DT4 ... 166 C1
Southdown Ave DT3 ... 167 C4
Southdown Ct 11 BH23 ... 124 C4
Southdown Rd DT4 ... 180 C4
Southern Ave BH12 ... 92 A1
Southern Ave BH22 ... 53 B1
Southern La BH6 ... 126 C4
Southern Oaks ... 94 C1
Southern Rd BH6 ... 123 B2
Southernhay Rd BH31 ... 45 B3
Southey Rd BH23 ... 124 C4
Southfield Ave DT4 ... 167 B3
Southfield Mews 4
  BH24 ... 55 B3
Southill Ave DT12 ... 103 A2
Southill CP Sch DT4 ... 167 A4
Southill Gdn Dr DT4 ... 167 A3
Southill La DT4 ... 167 A3
Southill Rd
  Bournemouth BH9 ... 90 A1
  Poole BH12 ... 120 B4
Southlands Ave
  Bournemouth BH6 ... 123 C2
  Corfe Mullen BH21 ... 86 C3
Southlands Cl DT4 ... 166 C1
Southlands Ct BH18 ... 87 A2
Southlands Rd DT4 ... 166 C1
Southlawns Wlk BH25 ... 94 C1
Southlea Ave BH6 ... 123 C2
Southmead Cres 20
  TA18 ... 191 F4
Southmead La BA8 ... 19 A2
Southover DT6 ... 128 A4
Southover Cl DT11 ... 212 B1
Southover La DT2 ... 79 B1
Southview Rd DT4 ... 167 A2
Southville BA21 ... 27 C3
Southville Rd BH5 ... 123 A3
Southway Cl BA21 ... 27 C3
Southway Cres BA21 ... 27 A3
Southway Dr BA21 ... 27 A4
Southwell Prim Sch
  DT5 ... 186 C1
Southwell Rd
  12 Easton/Weston DT5 ... 186 C1
  Portland DT5 ... 187 A1
Southwick Pl BH6 ... 123 B4
Southwick Rd BH6 ... 123 B3

Southwood Ave
  Bournemouth BH6 ... 123 B2
  Christchurch BH23 ... 94 A1
Southwood Cl
  Christchurch BH23 ... 94 A1
  Ferndown BH22 ... 61 B3
Southwood Ct BH23 ... 94 A1
Southwoods BA20 ... 27 B2
Sovereign Bsns Ctr
  ... 119 A3
Sovereign Cl BH7 ... 122 C4
Sovereign Ct BH7 ... 122 C3
Sovereign Sq 8 BH7 ... 122 C2
Spa Ave DT3 ... 167 B4
Spa Rd DT3 ... 167 A4
Sparacre Gdns DT6 ... 100 B4
Sparkford Cl BH7 ... 123 A4
Sparrow Rd BA21 ... 27 B3
Spearhay La TA20 ... 202 B4
Specket La DT6 ... 203 A5
Speedwell Dr BH23 ... 125 A4
Speke Cl 10 TA16 ... 191 F7
Spence La DT6 ... 64 C3
Spencer Cl 5 BH25 ... 95 A1
Spencer Gdns DT4 ... 198 C5
Spencer Rd
  Bournemouth BH1 ... 122 B2
  New Milton BH25 ... 95 A1
  Poole BH13 ... 147 C4
Spetisbury CE Prim Sch
  DT11 ... 211 D5
Spetisbury Cl BH9 ... 90 A2
Spetisbury Rings* ... 211 E5
Spicer La BH11 ... 88 C3
Spiller Rd DT3 ... 166 B3
Spinacre BH25 ... 95 A1
Spindle Cl BH18 ... 86 C1
Spindlewood Cl 26 BH25 ... 95 A1
Spingfield La BA12 ... 3 A3
Spinners Cl BH22 ... 53 A1
Spinners Way BA12 ... 3 A3
Spinners' La DT6 ... 101 A3
Spinney Cl 3 BA21 ... 53 C2
Spinney The
  Broadmayne DT2 ... 136 A1
  Lytchett Matravers BH16 ... 84 B3
  Radipole DT3 ... 152 A1
  St.Leonards BH24 ... 54 A3
  7 Yeovil BA20 ... 26 C1
Spinney Way BH25 ... 95 A3
Spinneys La BH22 ... 61 B3
Spirite Cl DT2 ... 137 B3
Spittlefields BH24 ... 55 B4
Spittles La DT7 ... 96 B3
Spread Eagle Hill SP7 ... 24 B2
Spring Ave DT4 ... 167 B1
Spring Cl 4 Bridport DT6 ... 68 C2
  Verwood BH31 ... 45 A3
Spring Ct BH12 ... 120 B3
Spring Gdns
  10 Fortuneswell DT5 ... 186 C4
  Mere BA12 ... 3 A2
  West Knighton DT2 ... 136 B2
  Weymouth DT4 ... 167 B1
Spring Gr DT2 ... 196 A1
Spring La
  Longburton DT9 ... 195 B7
  New Milton BH25 ... 95 B1
  Sandford Orcas DT9 ... 15 C3
Spring Rd
  Bournemouth BH1 ... 122 B3
  6 Weymouth DT4 ... 167 B1
Spring St BH20 ... 140 A1
Springbank Rd BH7 ... 122 C4
Springbourne Ct BH1 ... 122 B3
Springbourne Mews
  BH1 ... 122 B3
Springbrook Cl BH20 ... 177 C3
Springdale Ave BH18 ... 86 C3
Springdale Fst Sch
  BH18 ... 86 C2
Springdale Gr BH21 ... 86 C2
Springdale Rd BH18 ... 86 C2
Springfield BH25 ... 95 B1
Springfield
  East Chinnock BA22 ... 192 E8
  Puncknowle DT2 ... 129 C3
Springfield Ave
  Bournemouth BH6 ... 124 A2
  Christchurch BH23 ... 91 B1
Springfield Cl
  2 Shaftesbury SP7 ... 13 A2
  Verwood BH31 ... 45 A3
Springfield Cres
  Poole BH14 ... 120 A2
  Radipole DT3 ... 152 A2
  5 Sherborne DT9 ... 30 A3
Springfield Gdns BH25 ... 95 B1
Springfield Pl BA21 ... 27 A4
Springfield Rd
  Milborne Port DT9 ... 17 B2
  Poole BH14 ... 120 A2
  Radipole DT3 ... 152 A2
  10 Verwood BH31 ... 45 A3
  Verwood BH31 ... 45 A3
  Yeovil BA21 ... 27 A4
Springfields Holt BH21 ... 51 A2
  Stalbridge DT10 ... 33 C4
Springhill Gdns DT7 ... 96 A3
Springvale Ave BH7 ... 123 A4
Springwater Cl BH11 ... 89 A2
Springwater Dr BH23 ... 124 B3
Springwater Rd BH11 ... 89 A2
Springwell Cl BH20 ... 177 C4
Spruce Cl BH17 ... 86 C1
Spur Cl BH21 ... 60 B3
Spur Hill Ave BH14 ... 120 B2

Spur Rd BH14 ... 120 B2
Spurgeon Rd BH7 ... 123 A3
Spy Cl BH16 ... 84 A1
Spyway Rd DT2 ... 102 B4
Square The
  Bournemouth BH2 ... 121 C2
  Cattistock DT2 ... 206 C2
  Corfe Castle BH20 ... 162 A1
  Cranborne BH21 ... 44 A4
  13 Gillingham SP8 ... 5 C1
  Langton Herring DT3 ... 150 B1
  Mere BA12 ... 3 A2
  Milborne St Andrew DT11 ... 79 C4
  Powerstock DT6 ... 70 A2
  Puddletown DT2 ... 78 A1
  Wimborne Minster BH21 ... 59 B3
Squirrel's Cl BH21 ... 91 B1
Squirrel's Cnr BH21 ... 189 D1
Srringfield DT2 ... 207 D4
Stables The BH23 ... 123 C4
Stacey Cl BH12 ... 120 B4
Stacey Gdns BH8 ... 90 C1
Stafford Cl DT2 ... 136 B2
Stafford Gdns DT2 ... 136 A4
Stafford House* DT2 ... 136 A4
Stafford Rd
  Bournemouth BH1 ... 122 A2
  Swanage BH19 ... 179 B1
Stag Cl BH25 ... 94 C2
Stag Gate* DT12 ... 211 F2
Stagswood BH31 ... 45 A4
Stainers Mead SP7 ... 7 A1
Stainforth Cl DT4 ... 166 C2
Stake Ford Cross DT9 ... 194 E4
Staker's Cross TA18 ... 191 B2
Staker's Cross La
  TA18 ... 191 B2
Stakes La DT9 ... 195 E6
Stalbridge CE Prim Sch
  ... 19 B1
Stalbridge Cl DT10 ... 33 B4
Stalbridge Dr BH22 ... 61 B2
Stalbridge La DT10 ... 34 B2
Stalbridge Pk* DT10 ... 19 A1
Stalbridge Rd
  Broadstone BH17 ... 119 A4
  Henstridge BA8 ... 19 A2
  Stalbridge DT10 ... 32 C2
Stalham Rd BH11 ... 120 C3
Stallards La BH24 ... 55 A4
Stamford Rd BH6 ... 123 B3
Stammery Hill EX13 ... 202 A1
Stanbarrow Cl BH20 ... 81 A1
Standpitts La SP8 ... 10 A3
Stanfield Cl BH20 ... 120 B4
Stanfield Rd
  Bournemouth BH9 ... 121 C4
  Ferndown BH22 ... 61 B3
  Poole BH12 ... 120 B3
Stanier Rd DT3 ... 153 A2
Staniforth Ct BH23 ... 124 B3
Stanley Cl BH31 ... 45 B3
Stanley Ct
  Bournemouth BH1 ... 122 B3
  Poole BH15 ... 119 B3
Stanley Gn Cres BH15 ... 119 B3
Stanley Gn Fst Sch
  BH15 ... 119 B3
Stanley Gn Rd BH15 ... 119 B3
Stanley Pearce House
  BH17 ... 87 B1
Stanley Rd
  Bournemouth BH1 ... 122 B3
  Christchurch BH23 ... 126 A4
  Poole BH15 ... 119 B1
Stanley St 5 DT4 ... 167 B1
Stannington Cl BH25 ... 95 A1
Stanpit BH23 ... 124 C3
Stanpit Marsh Nature
  Reserve* BH23 ... 124 B3
Stanstead Rd DT2 ... 73 A4
Stanton Cl DT11 ... 212 B3
Stanton Lacy 17 BH13 ... 147 C4
Stanton Rd BH10 ... 89 B1
Stapehill Cres BH21 ... 60 B3
Stapehill Mus & Gdns*
  ... 60 C2
Stapehill Rd BH21 ... 60 C2
Staple Cl BH25 ... 119 B3
Staple Cross BH23 ... 124 C4
Staplecross La BH23 ... 124 C4
Stapleford Ave BH22 ... 61 C3
Staples Mdw 4 TA20 ... 202 A8
Staples Terr DT7 ... 96 B3
Star Cottage Gdn*
  ... 58 B3
Star La DT6 ... 98 B4
Starlight Farm Cl BH31 ... 45 B4
Stars La BA20 ... 27 B2
Station App
  Branksome BH18 ... 87 A2
  Dorchester DT1 ... 108 A1
Station Pl 1 BH19 ... 179 A1
Station Rd Alderholt SP6 ... 42 A3
  Child Okeford DT11 ... 198 C7
  Christchurch BH23 ... 93 C2
  23 Easton/Weston DT5 ... 187 A2
  Edmondsham BH31 ... 44 C4
  Ferndown BH22 ... 52 C1
  Gillingham SP8 ... 5 C1
  Hamworthy BH15 ... 119 A1
  Henstridge BA8 ... 19 A3
  Holton Heath BH20 ... 116 B2
  Maiden Newton DT2 ... 72 C4
  Milborne Port DT9 ... 17 B2

Station Rd continued
  Misterton TA18 ... 192 A3
  Moreton DT2 ... 138 A4
  New Milton BH25 ... 95 A1
  Poole BH14 ... 120 A2
  Sherborne DT9 ... 30 A3
  2 Shillingstone DT11 ... 198 B6
  Stalbridge DT10 ... 19 B1
  Sturminster Marshall
    BH21 ... 56 B2
  Sturminster Newton DT10 ... 35 A1
  Swanage BH19 ... 179 A1
  Tatworth & Forton
    TA20 ... 202 A8
  Verwood BH31 ... 45 A3
  Wareham St Martin
    BH16 ... 116 B1
  Wimborne Minster BH21 ... 59 B2
  Wool BH20 ... 140 A1
Station Terr
  13 Salisbury SP2 ... 213 A3
  Wimborne Minster BH21 ... 59 B2
Station Yd SP6 ... 42 A3
Staunton BH21 ... 212 C1
Stavordale Rd DT4 ... 167 B2
Stearts La DT10 ... 36 B3
Stedman Rd BH5 ... 123 A3
Steel St BA8 ... 19 A2
Steel's La BA9 ... 1 A2
Steeds La SP6 ... 190 F2
Steep St BA12 ... 3 A3
Steepdene BH14 ... 120 B2
Steeple Cl Poole BH17 ... 87 B2
  Radipole DT3 ... 167 A4
Steepleton Rd BH18 ... 87 B2
Steer Rd BH19 ... 178 C1
Stella Cl 8 BH23 ... 126 A4
Stem La BH25 ... 94 C2
Stenhurst Rd BH15 ... 119 C3
Stephen Langton Dr
  BH11 ... 88 B3
Stephen's Castle (Tumulus)*
  ... 45 B4
Stephens Cl
  Netherbury DT6 ... 204 B1
  1 Salisbury SP2 ... 213 A2
Stephenson Rd SP2 ... 213 A2
Stepleton House*
  ... 198 F6
Stepnell Reach BH16 ... 118 B3
Steppes BH19 ... 178 B3
Steppes Hill BH19 ... 178 B1
Sterte Ave BH15 ... 119 A2
Sterte Ave W BH15 ... 119 A2
Sterte Cl BH15 ... 119 B2
Sterte Ct BH15 ... 119 B2
Sterte Espl BH15 ... 119 A2
Sterte Ind Est BH15 ... 119 A2
Sterte Rd BH15 ... 119 B2
Stevens Cl 2 DT11 ... 212 C3
Stevenson Cres BH14 ... 120 C2
Stevenson Rd BH6 ... 124 A2
Stevensons Cl 8 BH21 ... 59 B3
Steward's La DT11 ... 56 A4
Stewart Cl 5 BH8 ... 122 B3
Stewart Rd BH8 ... 122 B3
Stewarts Way BH22 ... 61 C4
Stibbs La DT11 ... 197 D3
Stiby Rd BA21 ... 27 A4
Stickland Sch DT2 ... 206 A7
Stile La DT7 ... 96 A2
Stile Way DT2 ... 206 E6
Stillam Bank DT11 ... 79 C4
Stillmore Rd BH11 ... 88 C2
Stinford Cl DT10 ... 204 D6
Stinsford Cl BH9 ... 90 A3
Stinsford Hill DT2 ... 108 B2
Stinsford La BH17 ... 119 B4
Stinsford Rd BH17 ... 87 B1
Stinsford View DT1 ... 108 B1
Stirling Cl BH21 ... 95 A2
Stirling Ct
  Bournemouth BH4 ... 121 B1
  New Milton BH25 ... 95 A2
Stirling Rd
  Bournemouth BH3 ... 121 C4
  Radipole DT3 ... 125 A3
Stirling Way DT3 ... 167 A4
  Upton BH16 ... 118 B4
Stirrup Cl Upton BH16 ... 118 B4
  Wimborne Minster BH21 ... 60 B3
Stoborough Cl DT10 ... 33 C4
Stoborough Dr BH18 ... 87 A1
Stoborough Mdw
  BH20 ... 142 C1
Stoborough Sch BH20 ... 142 C1
Stock Hill La DT9 ... 195 F4
Stock La SP8 ... 5 A1
Stockbridge Cl BH17 ... 88 A1
Stockley Rd DT10 ... 32 C1
Stockwood Cl SP1 ... 213 C4
Stoke La
  Mappowder DT10 ... 196 F1
  Stoke Wake DT11 ... 209 A8
Stoke Mill La DT6 ... 67 A2
Stoke Rd
  Beaminster DT8 ... 204 C4
  Weymouth DT4 ... 180 B4
Stoke Wood Rd BH4 ... 121 B2
Stokehouse St DT1 ... 107 C2
Stokes Ave BH15 ... 119 B2
Stokes Cl DT11 ... 212 C1
Stonage La TA18 ... 192 C5
Stone Gdns BH8 ... 91 A1
Stone La
  Wimborne Minster BH21 ... 59 A3
  Yeovil BA21 ... 27 B4
Stone La Ind Est BH21 ... 59 A3

Stonebarrow La
  Charmouth DT6 ... 97 B4
  Hawkchurch EX13 ... 202 C2
  Stanton St Gabriel DT6 ... 97 C4
Stonechat Cl
  Ferndown BH22 ... 61 A4
  8 Radipole DT3 ... 152 A2
Stonechat Cl BH23 ... 124 C4
Stonecrop Cl BH18 ... 86 C1
Stonedene DT9 ... 30 A4
Stoneleigh 18 BH13 ... 147 C4
Stoneleigh Ave SO41 ... 95 C2
Stoney La BA22 ... 193 D6
Stony Lawn DT11 ... 81 B4
Stony Lawn DT11 ... 21 A1
Stony Down La DT6 ... 65 A2
Stony La
  Bishop's Caundle DT9 ... 196 A8
  Burton BH23 ... 92 B1
  Damerham SP6 ... 190 E2
  Holwell DT10 ... 196 C6
Stony La S BH23 ... 124 B3
Stony Weir* BH20 ... 142 B2
Stonyacres DT9 ... 194 C6
Stopples La SO41 ... 95 C2
Story La BH18 ... 87 A2
Stottingway St DT3 ... 152 A3
Stour Cl East Stour SP8 ... 10 B1
  Ferndown BH22 ... 60 B2
  Shillingstone DT11 ... 198 C5
Stour Dr BH20 ... 142 B3
Stour Hill SP8 ... 9 C1
Stour Hill Pk SP8 ... 9 C1
Stour La SP8 ... 21 C4
Stour Mdws SP8 ... 5 C1
Stour Pk BH10 ... 89 C3
Stour Rd
  Blandford Forum DT11 ... 212 C2
  Bournemouth BH8 ... 122 B3
  Christchurch BH23 ... 124 A3
Stour View Cl DT10 ... 35 A1
Stour View Gdns BH21 ... 58 C1
Stour Way BH23 ... 91 B1
Stour Wlk
  Bournemouth BH8 ... 90 B2
  Wimborne Minster BH21 ... 59 B2
Stourbank Rd BH23 ... 124 A3
Stourcliffe Ave BH6 ... 123 C2
Stourcroft Dr BH23 ... 91 C1
Stourfield Fst & Jun Schs
  BH6 ... 123 B3
Stourfield Rd BH5 ... 123 B3
Stourpaine Rd BH17 ... 87 B2
Stourton Cl DT11 ... 121 B2
Stourton Way BA21 ... 26 C4
Stourvale Ave BH23 ... 123 B4
Stourvale Pl 8 BH5 ... 123 B4
Stourvale Rd BH5 ... 123 B3
Stourwood Ave BH6 ... 123 B2
Stourwood Mans 4
  ... 123 B2
Stourwood Rd BH6 ... 123 B2
Stowcastle St DT1 ... 107 B1
Stowell Cres BH20 ... 142 B1
Stowell La 12 TA20 ... 202 C8
Stower Provost CP Sch
  SP8 ... 22 C4
Stowey St DT1 ... 107 B1
Straits DT5 ... 187 A2
Strand St BH15 ... 119 B1
Stratfield Pl BH25 ... 94 C2
Stratford Rd
  Salisbury SP1 ... 213 B4
  Yeovil BA21 ... 27 C3
Strathmore Dr BH31 ... 45 B3
Strathmore Rd BH9 ... 90 A2
Stratton Rd BH9 ... 90 B2
Straw Barrow* DT11 ... 48 B2
Streche Rd
  Swanage BH19 ... 179 B3
  Wareham BH20 ... 142 B2
Street La
  Longburton DT9 ... 195 C6
  Sedgehill and Semley SP7 ... 7 C2
Street The
  Charmouth DT6 ... 97 A4
  Moreton DT2 ... 138 C4
  Motcombe SP7 ... 7 A1
  Sutton Waldron DT11 ... 37 B3
  Winterborne Zelston
    DT11 ... 82 C4
Streets La BH24 ... 55 C2
Streetway La DT7 ... 209 B3
Strete Mount 10 BH23 ... 124 A3
Stretton Ct BH14 ... 120 B2
Stretton Rd BH20 ... 142 B2
Strides La BH24 ... 55 A4
Strode Gdns BH24 ... 54 B3
Strodes La DT2 ... 75 B1
Strongate La DT4 ... 167 A4
Stroud Cl BH21 ... 60 A3
Stroud Gdns 4 BH23 ... 124 C3
Stroud La BH23 ... 124 C3
Stroud Pk Ave BH23 ... 124 B4
Strouden Ave BH8 ... 122 B4
Strouden Rd BH9 ... 90 B1
Stroudley Cres DT3 ... 153 B2
Struan Ct BH24 ... 54 A3
Struan Dr BH24 ... 54 A3
Struan Gdns BH24 ... 54 A3
Stuart Cl BH16 ... 118 A4
Stuart La SP8 ... 5 B1
Stuart Rd BH21 ... 126 A4
Stuart Way DT6 ... 100 C3

Stubhampton Bottom
DT11 ....38 C3
Stuckton Rd SP6 ....43 B4
Student Village BH12 ....121 B4
Studland Heath (National
  Nature Reserve)*
BH19 ....164 A3
Studland Rd BH4 ....121 B1
Studland Way DT11 ....167 A4
Studley Cl BH23 ....126 B4
Studley Ct BH25 ....126 B4
Sturminster Marshall Fst Sch
  BH21 ....56 C2
Sturminster Newton High
  Sch DT10 ....35 A2
Sturminster Newton Leisure
  Ctr DT10 ....35 A2
Sturminster Newton Mill &
  Mus* DT10 ....35 A1
Sturminster Rd 10 BH9 ....90 A2
Sturt La BH20 ....81 B2
Styles Cl 9 DT8 ....204 C4
Styles La DT2 ....78 A1
Sudan Rd DT4 ....180 C4
Suffolk Ave BH23 ....91 C1
Suffolk Cl BH21 ....60 B3
Suffolk Rd
  Bournemouth BH2 ....121 B2
  Salisbury SP2 ....213 A1
Suffolk Rd S BH21 ....121 B2
Sugar Hill
  Bere Regis BH20 ....113 C4
  Bloxworth BH20 ....114 A3
Summer Field Cl BH21 ....60 A2
Summer Fields BH31 ....45 A2
Summer Hill TA17 ....191 D7
Summer House Terr
  BH20 ....27 B2
Summer La
  Evershot DT2 ....206 A7
  Hinton St George TA17 ..191 D8
Summerbee Comp Sch
  BH8 ....90 B1
Summerbee Fst Sch
  BH8 ....90 B1
Summerbee Jun Sch
  BH8 ....90 B1
Summercroft Way
  BH22 ....53 A2
Summerfield Cl BH21 ....92 B1
Summerfields
  Bournemouth BH7 ....122 C4
  Hensridge BA8 ....19 A3
Summerhill Rd DT7 ....96 B3
Summerhouse View
  BA21 ....27 C3
Summerlands
  Ferndown BH22 ....61 B3
  Yeovil BA21 ....27 A3
Summerlands Hospl
  BA21 ....27 A3
Summerlock App 6
  SP2 ....213 B3
Summers Ave BH11 ....89 A3
Summers La BH23 ....92 B1
Summertrees St BH25 .....95 B2
Sun La
  Piddletrenthide DT2 ......208 B1
  Whitechurch Canonicorum
  DT6 ....98 B4
Sunbury Cl BH11 ....89 A3
Sunbury Ct 3 BH21 ....121 C2
Sunderland Dr BH23 ......125 A4
Sundew Cl
  Christchurch BH23 ....93 B1
  New Milton BH25 ....95 B2
  Radipole DT4 ....167 C4
Sundew Rd BH18 ....86 C1
Sunningdale
  Christchurch BH23 ....123 C3
  6 Poole BH15 ....119 C2
Sunningdale Cres BH10 ..89 B2
Sunningdale Gdns
  BH18 ....87 A3
Sunningdale Rd BA21 .....27 C3
Sunny Hill Ct BH12 ....120 B3
Sunny Hill Rd BH12 ....120 B3
Sunnybank Dr BH21 ....60 A3
Sunnybank Rd BH21 ....60 A3
Sunnybank Way BH21 .....60 A3
Sunnyfield Rd BH25 ......127 A4
Sunnyhelds DT3 ....153 B2
Sunnyhill Rd
  Bournemouth BH6 ....123 B3
  Salisbury SP1 ....213 B4
Sunnylands Ave BH11 ...123 C2
Sunnymoor Rd BH11 ......89 A1
Sunnyside Ridge BH20 ...143 A1
  West Lulworth BH20 ......172 B3
Sunnyside Rd
  Poole BH12 ....120 B3
  Weymouth DT4 ....180 B4
Sunridge Cl
  Poole BH12 ....121 A3
  Swanage BH19 ....179 A1
Sunrise Bsns Pk DT11 ...212 C4
Sunrise Ct BH22 ....61 B3
Sunset Lodge BH13 ......121 A1
Surrey Cl
  Christchurch BH23 ....91 C1
  Weymouth DT4 ....166 C2
Surrey Gdns BH4 ....121 B2
Surrey Rd BH4 ....121 A2
Surrey Rd S BH4 ....121 B2

Sussex Cl BH9 ....90 A2
Sussex Farm Way 8
  DT9 ....194 C5
Sussex Rd
  Salisbury SP2 ....213 A1
  Weymouth DT4 ....167 A2
Sutcliffe Ave DT4 ....167 A3
Sutherland Ave BH18 ......86 C3
Sutton Cl 4 Gillingham SP8 ..5 C1
  Overcombe/Preston
  DT3 ....153 B2
  Poole BH11 ....88 A1
Sutton Ct Lawns DT3 .....153 B2
Sutton Grange BA21 ....26 C3
Sutton Hill BA22 ....193 D6
Sutton Pk DT3 ....153 B2
Sutton Rd
  Bournemouth BH9 ....90 A1
  Overcombe/Preston
  DT3 ....153 B2
Swaffield Gdns 5 BH4 ...180 B4
Swainson Rd DT1 ....199 E4
Swallow Cl BH17 ....118 C4
Swallow Way BH21 ....60 A4
Swallowcliffe Gdns
  BA20 ....27 B3
Swallowfields 15 SP8 ......5 C1
Swallowmead 2 SP2 .....213 B1
Swan Cl SP2 ....213 B1
Swan Gn 3 BH23 ....124 A3
Swan Hill TA18 ....192 B5
Swan La DT2 ....208 B1
Swan Mead BH24 ....55 C3
Swan St BH21 ....40 A4
Swanage Cty Mid Sch
  BH19 ....178 C2
Swanage Her Ctr*
  BH19 ....179 A1
Swanage Hospl BH19 ....179 A1
Swanage Rd BH19 ....164 B1
Swanage Rly* BH20 ......177 B3
Swanmore Cl BH7 ....123 A4
Swanmore Rd BH7 ....123 A4
Swansbury Dr BH8 ....106 B3
Swary Gdns BH8 ....90 B1
Sway Rd BH25 ....95 B3
Swaynes Cl 3 SP1 ....213 B3
Sweep The BH24 ....55 A4
Sweet Hill La DT5 ....186 C1
Sweet Hill Rd DT5 ....186 C1
Sweetmans Rd SP7 ....12 C2
Swift Cl BH17 ....118 C4
Swiftdown 6 SP2 ....213 B1
Swilletts La DT6 ....203 D4
Swinton Ave BH20 ....139 B4
Swordfish Dr BH23 ....125 A4
Swyre Rd DT2 ....129 C1
Sycamore Ave BH20 ......116 A2
Sycamore Cl
  Broadstone BH17 ....86 C1
  Christchurch BH23 ....123 B4
  Sandford BH20 ....143 A4
  Sixpenny Handley SP5 ..189 A4
Sycamore Dr
  6 Crewkerne TA18 ....191 F5
  Yeovil BA20 ....27 A1
Sycamore Pl BH21 ....60 B3
Sycamore Rd
  Hordle SO41 ....95 C2
  Radipole DT4 ....167 A3
Sycamore Way SP8 ....5 B1
Sydenham Cres BH20 ...139 C1
Sydenham Rd BH19 ......178 C1
Sydenham Way 17 DT1 ..108 A1
Sydling Cl BH17 ....88 A1
Sydling Rd
  Cerne Abbas DT2 ....207 C3
  Yeovil BA21 ....27 C3
Sydney Pl 3 SP8 ....5 C1
Sydney Rd
  Broadstone BH18 ....87 A2
  Christchurch BH23 ....91 C1
Sydney St DT4 ....167 A2
Sylmor Gdns BH9 ....90 A2
Sylvan Cl 4 Gillingham SP8 ..5 C2
  St.Leonards BH24 ....53 C2
Sylvan Fst Sch BH12 .....120 A3
Sylvan Rd BH12 ....120 A3
Sylvan Way SP8 ....5 C2
Symes Cl TA18 ....192 C4
Symes Rd BH15 ....118 C2
Symonds Cl DT3 ....167 B4
Symondsbury Prim Sch
  DT6 ....99 C4
Syward Cl DT1 ....108 B1
Syward Rd DT1 ....108 B1

T

Tabbit's Hill La BH20 .....177 C3
Tabernacle La 6 BA20 ....27 B2
Tadden Cotts BH21 ....58 B4
Tadden Wlk BH18 ....86 C1
Tadnoll Barrow* DT2 ....138 B2
Tait Hill TA16 ....191 F7
Tait Cl BH17 ....119 C4
Talbot Ave BH3 ....121 C4
Talbot Cl SP1 ....213 C4
Talbot Comb Sch
  BH12 ....121 A4
Talbot Ct BH9 ....89 C1
Talbot Dr
  Christchurch BH23 ....93 C1
  Poole BH12 ....121 A4
Talbot Heath Sch BH4 ...121 B3
Talbot Hill Rd BH12 ......121 B4

Talbot House Prep Sch
  BH9 ....121 C4
Talbot Manor BH3 ....121 B4
Talbot Mews BH12 ....121 A4
Talbot Mews BH10 ....89 A1
Talbot Rd
  Bournemouth BH9 ....121 C4
  Lyme Regis DT7 ....98 A4
Talbot Rise BH10 ....89 B1
Talbothays Rd DT1 ....135 A4
Tall Trees BH14 ....120 A3
Tallidge Cl DT3 ....168 B4
Tamar Cl BH22 ....62 A3
Tamlin St BH20 ....143 A4
Tamworth Rd BH7 ....122 C3
Tan Howse Cl BH7 ....123 A4
Tan La SP8 ....2 A1
Tanglewood Cl 11 BH25 ..95 A2
Tanglewood Lodge
  BH17 ....118 C4
Tangmere Cl BH23 ....125 A3
Tangmere Pl BH17 ....119 C4
Tanner's La 10 BH20 .....142 C2
Tannery Rd DT6 ....100 B3
Tansee Hill TA20 ....202 E6
Tantinoby La BH20 ....142 B3
Tanyard DT2 ....206 A7
Tanyard La SP7 ....12 B1
Tanzey La DT10 ....21 A2
Taphouse La DT6 ....66 B4
Tapper Ct SP2 ....59 C2
Tark's Hill DT9 ....194 C5
Tarn Dr BH17 ....118 C4
Tarrant Abbey House*
  DT11 ....211 F6
Tarrant Cl BH17 ....87 C1
Tarrant Dr BH20 ....142 B3
Tarrant Rd BH9 ....90 A2
Tarratt La BA20 ....27 A1
Tarratt Rd BA20 ....27 A1
Tasman Cl BH23 ....123 C4
Tatnam Rd BH15 ....119 B2
Tattershall Gdns 4 BH21 ..56 B2
Tatum Cres BH15 ....119 B2
Taunton Rd BH19 ....179 B1
Taverner Cl BH15 ....119 B1
Taylor Dr BH8 ....90 B2
Taylor Way BH31 ....45 B3
Taylor's Bldgs 2 BH15 ..119 B1
Taylor's La
  Mappowder DT10 ....196 E1
  Whitchurch Canonicorum
  DT6 ....66 A1
Teal Ave DT3 ....166 B3
Teasel Way BH22 ....53 A1
Tecan Way DT4 ....166 C2
Technology Rd BH17 .....119 A4
Tedder Cl BH11 ....89 A2
Tedder Gdns BH11 ....89 A2
Tedder Rd BH11 ....89 A2
Teeling Rd DT3 ....166 B3
Telegraph St BH21 ....198 EB
Telford Cl DT1 ....168 A4
Telford Rd
  Ferndown BH22 ....61 A4
  Salisbury SP2 ....213 A2
Temple Cl DT11 ....134 C4
Temple La BA8 ....8 A1
Temple Mews BH1 ....122 B3
Templecombe La 2 BA8 ..8 C3
Tender Cl BH11 ....88 C1
Ten Acres SP7 ....12 C2
Tennyson Rd
  Bournemouth BH9 ....89 C1
  1 Poole BH14 ....120 A2
  Weymouth DT4 ....167 B1
  Wimborne Minster BH21 ..59 B3
Tensing Rd BH23 ....124 C4
Terence Ave BH17 ....87 B1
Terence Rd BH17 ....86 B3
Termare Cl BA22 ....26 B3
Terminus St 3 DT4 ....167 B2
Tern Ct BH1 ....123 B3
Terrace Rd BH2 ....121 C2
Terrington Ave BH23 ......93 C1
Tewkesbury St BA21 ......26 C3
Thames Alley 18 BH15 ..119 A1
Thames Cl BH22 ....62 A3
Thames Mews 12 BH15 ..119 A1
Thames St BH15 ....119 A1
Thatcham Cl BA21 ....27 A4
Thatcham Pk Cl BA21 ....27 A4
Thatcham Rd BA21 ....27 A4
Theobald Rd BH3 ....93 A4
Thessaly St 17 BH5 ....122 C2
Thetchers Cl BH25 ....95 A3
Thetford Rd BH12 ....120 C3
Thickthorn Cross
  BH21 ....200 D7
Thickthorn La DT10 ....197 A2
Third Cliff Wlk 8 DT6 ....100 A1
Thistlebarrow Rd
  Bournemouth BH7 ....122 C3
  Salisbury SP1 ....213 B4
Thomas Hardy Cl DT10 ..35 A1
Thomas Hardy Dr SP7 ..13 A2
Thomas Hardye Leisure Ctr
  DT1 ....134 C4
Thomas Hardye Sch
  DT1 ....134 C4
Thomas's London Day Schs
  BA8 ....55 A4
Thompson Cl
  Briford SP2 ....213 A1
  Puddletown DT2 ....78 A1
Thomson Dr 10 TA18 ....191 F4
Thoresby Cl BH25 ....94 C2
Thorn Rd BH17 ....87 B2

Thornbury 15 BH4 ....121 B2
Thornbury Rd BH6 ....124 A2
Thorncombe Beacon*
  DT6 ....99 B2
Thorncombe Cl
  Bournemouth BH9 ....90 A2
  Poole BH17 ....87 C1
Thorne Cl BH31 ....45 A4
Thorne Gdns BA21 ....26 C4
Thorne La
  Brympton BA22 ....26 C4
  Yeovil BA21 ....27 A4
Thorners CE Prim Sch
  DT2 ....103 B1
Thornfield Dr BH23 ....93 C1
Thornford CE Prim Sch
  DT9 ....194 DB
Thornford Rd DT9 ....194 C6
Thornford Sta DT9 ....194 C7
Thornham Rd BH25 ....95 B2
Thornhill Cl DT1 ....134 C4
Thornhill Cres BH24 ......167 B2
Thornhill Rd DT10 ....33 B4
Thornicks DT11 ....156 C3
Thornley Rd BH10 ....89 B2
Thornlow Prep Sch
  DT4 ....167 B1
Thornton Cl BH21 ....86 B3
Thornton Rd BA21 ....26 C4
Thorny La BA22 ....14 B4
Thorogood Ct 4 BH15 ...119 C2
Thrasher's La BH20 ....162 A2
Three Acre Dr BH25 .....126 C4
Three Acre La BH19 ....178 B1
Three Acres DT2 ....207 A2
Three Barrows*
  BH20 ....161 A3
Three Cnr Mead 5 BA21 ..26 C3
Three Cross Rd BH21 .....53 A3
Three Legged Cross Fst Sch
  BH21 ....45 A1
Three Lions Cl 12 BH21 ..59 A3
Three Lords' Barrow*
  BH20 ....160 B3
Three Yards Cl DT5 ......186 C1
Thrift Cl DT10 ....33 C4
Throop Cl BH8 ....91 A1
Throop Hollow DT2 ....112 B3
Throop Rd
  Abbas & Templecombe
  BA8 ....8 A2
  Bournemouth BH8 ....90 C2
Throopside Ave BH9 ....90 B2
Thrush Rd BH12 ....88 B1
Thursby Rd BH23 ....93 C1
Thwaite Rd BH12 ....121 A3
Tidemill Ct BH23 ....124 A4
Tiffany Cl SO41 ....95 C2
Tilburg Rd BH23 ....124 B4
Tilbury Mead BH20 ....177 A4
Tilley Knap DT2 ....207 EB
Tilly Whim Caves*
  BH19 ....185 B3
Tilly Whim La DT2 ....106 C2
Tillycombe Rd DT5 ....187 A4
Timber Hill DT7 ....96 B4
Timothy Cl BH10 ....89 B3
Tin Pot La DT11 ....212 B3
Tincleton Cross DT2 .....110 B3
Tincleton Gdns BH9 ....90 A2
Tinker's Barrow*
  DT2 ....137 C2
Tinker's La
  Cucklington BA9 ....4 A3
  Wareham Town BH20 ...142 C2
Tinneys La DT9 ....30 B3
Tintagel Rd BA21 ....26 C4
Tintern BA21 ....26 C3
Tintinhull Rd
  Yeovil Without BA21 ......26 C4
Tiptoe Prim Sch SO41 ...95 B4
Tithe Barn Children's Farm*
  DT3 ....149 B4
Tithe Barn Mus*
  BH19 ....179 A1
Tiverton Cl 24 BH4 ....121 B2
Tizard's Knap DT6 ....66 A1
Toby's Cl DT5 ....186 C2
Tobys Ct SP7 ....12 C2
Todber Cl BH11 ....88 C2
Tollard Cl BH12 ....120 C4
Toller La DT2 ....72 A4
Tollerdown Rd 4 DT4 ....166 C1
Tollerford Rd BH17 ....87 B1
Tollgate Pk SP7 ....12 C3
Tollgate Rd SP1 ....213 B2
Tolpuddle Gdns BH9 ......90 A2
Tolstoi Rd BH14 ....120 A3
Tomlins La SP5 ....5 C1
Toms Field Rd BH19 .....178 A1
Tonge Rd BH11 ....89 A3
Toose The BA21 ....26 C3
Top La Ringwood BH24 ...55 B4
  Stourton with Gasper BA12 ..1 B4
Torbay Rd BH14 ....120 B2
Torre The BA21 ....26 C3
Totnel Rd BH17 ....88 A1
Tourney Rd BH17 ....88 C3
Tout Hill
  East Stoke BH20 ....140 A2
  Shaftesbury SP7 ....12 B2
Tout La DT2 ....104 C3
Tout Quarry Nature
  Reserve* DT5 ....186 C3
Tout Quarry Sculpture Pk*
  DT5 ....186 C3
Towans The BH13 ....147 B2

Tower Cl 1 BH21 ....201 D1
Tower Ct BH21 ....121 C1
Tower Hill
  Bere Regis BH20 ....81 A1
  Iwerne Minster DT11 .....37 C1
  Netherbury DT6 ....204 B2
Tower Hill Rd 6 TA18 ...191 E4
Tower La DT6 ....59 B3
Tower Mews SP1 ....213 B3
Tower Rd
  Bournemouth BH1 ....122 C3
  Poole BH13 ....121 A1
  Yeovil BA21 ....27 B4
Tower Rd W BH13 ....121 A1
Towers Farm BH21 ....86 B4
Towers Way BH21 ....86 B4
Town Farm Pl SP5 ....189 B4
Town Hall La BH19 ....179 A1
Town Path SP2 ....213 A2
Towngate Bridge
  BH15 ....119 B2
Towngate Sh Ctr 1
  BH15 ....119 B1
Townsend BH21 ....56 B2
Townsend Cl
  Bournemouth BH11 ....89 A3
  Mere BA12 ....2 C3
Townsend Gn BA8 ....19 A2
Townsend La SP6 ....190 A6
Townsend Mead
  BH20 ....177 A4
Townsend Orch TA16 ...191 F8
Townsend Prim & Com Sch
  BH8 ....91 A1
Townsend Rd
  Corfe Castle BH20 ....177 A4
  Swanage BH19 ....179 A1
Townsend Way DT6 ....68 C1
Townsville Rd BH9 ....90 A1
Tozer Cl BH11 ....88 C1
Tracey Cl BH23 ....126 A4
Tradecroft DT5 ....186 C3
Trafalgar Ct BH23 ....124 C3
Trafalgar Rd BH9 ....121 C4
Tree Hamlets BH16 ....118 B3
Treebys Cl BH23 ....92 B1
Treeside BH23 ....93 B1
Treetops 9 BH13 ....147 C4
Trefoil Way BH31 ....45 B3
Tregonwell Rd BH2 ....121 C1
Trellech St 3 BA22 ....26 C3
Treloen Ct 3 BH4 ....122 A3
Trenchard Mdw BH16 ....84 B2
Trenchard Way DT3 ....166 B3
Trendle St DT9 ....30 A3
Trent Cl Tolpuddle DT2 ..79 B1
  Yeovil BA21 ....28 A4
Trent Dr BH20 ....142 B3
Trent Path La DT9 ....29 C3
Trent Way BA21 ....62 A3
Trent Youngs CE Prim Sch
  DT9 ....14 C1
Trentham Ave BH7 ....123 A4
Trentham Ct BH7 ....123 A4
Tresco Spinney BA21 ....26 C3
Tresillian Cl BH23 ....94 A1
Tresillian Way BH23 ......94 A1
Treves Rd DT1 ....134 C4
Trevone 18 BH25 ....95 A2
Triangle The
  Bournemouth BH2 ....121 C2
  Upton BH16 ....118 A4
Tricketts La BH22 ....61 C3
Trigon Rd BH15 ....119 B4
Trill La DT9 ....194 B7
Trinidad Cres DT4 ....120 B4
Trinidad Fst Sch DT4 ....120 B4
Trinidad House BH12 ....120 B4
Trinity 2 BH1 ....122 A2
Trinity Ind Est BH21 ......59 C2
Trinity La BH20 ....142 C2
Trinity Rd
  Bournemouth BH1 ....122 A2
  Weymouth DT4 ....167 B1
Trinity St
  Dorchester DT1 ....108 A1
  Salisbury DT1 ....213 B2
  7 Weymouth DT4 ....167 B1
Trinity Terr DT4 ....167 B1
Trinity Way DT6 ....68 C1
Troak Cl BH23 ....124 C4
Troon Rd BH18 ....87 A3
Trotters La BH21 ....60 A3
Truman Rd BH10 ....89 A3
Truscott Ave BH9 ....122 A4
Trusthams DT8 ....203 E5
Trustin Cl 6 DT6 ....100 B4
Trystworthy 20 BH21 ....121 B2
Tuckers La BH15 ....118 C1
Tuckers Mill Cl BH20 ....160 C4
Tucks Cl BH23 ....93 A4
Tuckton Cl BH6 ....123 B2
Tuckton Rd BH6 ....123 C2
Tudor Cl SP6 ....42 B3
Tudor Ct
  Bournemouth BH1 ....122 C3
  Poole BH15 ....119 C3
Tudor Gdns DT11 ....212 C3
Tudor Rd BH18 ....87 A2
Tulse Hill 2eale BA22 ....2 A2
  Zennor BA21 ....1 C2
Tuncombe La TA18 ......191 F4
Tunnel Rd DT8 ....204 C5
Turbary Cl
  Bournemouth BH21 ....89 A1
  Ferndown BH22 ....61 C3
  Upton BH16 ....118 B4
Turbary Hts BH11 ....88 C1

rbary Pk Ave BH11 ...89 A1
rbary Rd BH22 ...61 C3
rbary Ret Pk BH1 ...88 C2
rberville Rd BH20 ...81 A1
rbetts Cl BH16 ...84 B2
rbury Cl DT2 ...120 B4
rbury Rd DT2 ...120 B4
rf Croft Ct BH23 ...94 A1
rk's La BH14 ...120 C1
rlin Moor Fst Sch
BH16 ...118 B2
rlin Moor Mid Sch
BH16 ...118 B2
rnberry Cl BH23 ...123 C3
rner Cl 2 SP2 ...213 A2
rner's La
  Marshwood DT6 ...202 E2
  Tarrant Monkton DT11 ...200 B4
rners La
  Turners La SP8 ...7 C1
rnpike TA18 ...192 B3
rnpike Rd 3 TA18 ...192 B3
rnstone Cl DT3 ...152 B2
rnworth Cl BH18 ...87 B2
rton St 3 DT4 ...167 B2
rut Hill DT9 ...31 C1
weedale Rd ...90 B2
wemlow Ave BH14 ...119 C2
wo Oaks Cl BH18 ...87 A2
winways La DT6 ...69 A4
wo Droves DT2 ...109 C4
wo Elms BA22 ...14 B4
wo Riversmeet Leisure Ctr
BH23 ...124 B3
wo Twr La BA20 ...27 B1
wyford Cl BH8 ...90 B2
wyford Way BH17 ...88 A1
wynham Ave BH23 ...124 A4
wynham Sch BH23 ...124 A3
ynedale Cl BH9 ...90 A2
yneham Ave BH12 ...120 B4
yneham Cl
  Radipole DT3 ...167 A4
  Sandford BH20 ...143 A4
yneham House (remains
of)* BH20 ...174 B3
yneham Mus* BH20 ...174 B3
yrrell Gdns BH8 ...91 A1
ytherley Gn BH8 ...90 B1

U

Jbsdell Cl BH25 ...95 A2
Jddens Dr
  Ferndown Town BH21 ...51 C1
  Wimborne Minster BH21 ...60 B4
Jddens Trad Est BH21 ...60 C3
Jllswater Cres DT3 ...167 A4
Jllswater Rd BH21 ...59 B1
Jlwell Rd BH19 ...179 A3
Jmbers Hill SP7 ...12 B1
Jndercliff Dr BH1 ...122 B1
Jndercliff Rd BH5 ...122 C2
Jnderdown Hollow
DT9 ...28 B2
Jnderhedge Gdns
DT5 ...186 C1
Jnderhill Mere BA12 ...2 C3
  Pen Selwood BA9 ...1 A1
Jnderhill Jun Sch
DT5 ...186 C4
Jnderwood Cl BH17 ...87 A1
Jnion St 2 BA20 ...27 B2
Jnity La 2 TA18 ...192 A3
Jpland Cl DT10 ...197 D7
Uplands
  Bothenhampton DT6 ...101 A3
  Yetminster DT9 ...194 C5
Jplands Ave BH25 ...127 A4
Jplands Cl BH22 ...62 A4
Uplands Rd
  Bournemouth BH8 ...90 B1
  Ferndown BH22 ...53 A1
Jplands Sch BH14 ...120 B2
Jplyme Cl BH17 ...88 A1
Jplyme Rd DT7 ...96 A3
Upper Fairfield Rd
  2 Dorchester DT1 ...107 C1
  2 Dorchester DT1 ...108 A1
Jpper Golf Links Rd
BH18 ...88 B1
Jpper Gordon Rd BH23 ...94 A1
Upper Hinton Rd BH1 ...121 C2
Jpper Linhay SP7 ...205 A8
Jpper N Rd SP5 ...188 C5
Upper Norwich Rd 16
BH2 ...121 C2
Jpper Rd BH12 ...120 B3
Jpper Sch La DT11 ...212 B3
Jpper St 3 DT1 ...198 C7
Jpper Terr Rd BH2 ...121 C2
Jpper Westhill Rd DT7 ...96 A3
Upper Wr St BA12 ...3 C1
Jppington Cl BH21 ...120 B3
Jppleby Rd BH17 ...87 C1
Jpton Cl BH16 ...118 A4
Upton Cross Mobile Home Pk
BH16 ...118 B4
Jpton Ctry Pk* BH17 ...118 C3
Jpton Heath Est BH16 ...118 B4
Upton Ind Est BH16 ...116 B3
Upton Inf Sch BH16 ...118 A4
Upton Jun Sch BH16 ...118 A4

Upton Rd
  Broadstone BH17 ...119 A4
  Poole BH17 ...118 C4
Upton Way BH18 ...86 C2
Upway St 2 DT4 ...167 B2
Upwey Ave BH15 ...118 C2
Upwey Dr DT3 ...152 B2
Utrecht Ct BH24 ...124 B4

V

Vaggs La SO41 ...95 C3
Vale Cl
  4 Crewkerne TA18 ...191 F3
  Poole BH14 ...120 C2
Vale Lodge BH1 ...122 B3
Vale Mans 4 BH1 ...122 B2
Vale Pk BH1 ...212 B1
Vale Rd
  Bournemouth BH1 ...122 B2
  Poole BH14 ...120 C2
  Stalbridge DT10 ...33 A2
  West Lulworth BH20 ...172 C3
  Yeovil BA21 ...28 A3
Vale St BA8 ...19 A2
Vale View Pk SO41 ...95 C4
Valencia Cl BH23 ...91 B2
Valette Rd BH9 ...90 A2
Valiant Way BH23 ...125 A4
Valley Bladen DT2 ...112 A4
Valley Cl
  Christchurch BH23 ...91 C2
  Poole BH14 ...120 B4
Valley Rd
  Blandford Camp DT11 ...199 E3
  Bournemouth BH8 ...90 C2
  Bridport DT6 ...100 B2
  Langton Matravers
  BH19 ...178 A3
  Worth Matravers BH20 ...177 B3
Valley View
Vallis Cl BH15 ...119 B1
Vanessa Ave SP1 ...213 C3
Vanguard Ave DT4 ...166 C1
Vanguard Rd
  Bournemouth BH8 ...90 C1
  Poole BH15 ...35 A3
Veals La DT10 ...35 A3
Vearse Ct DT6 ...100 A3
Vecta Cl BH23 ...125 B3
Vectis Rd BH23 ...126 B4
Velvet Lawn Rd BH25 ...94 C2
Venator Pl BH1 ...213 C3
Venn Hill TA20 ...202 F6
Venn La Chideock DT6 ...86 C1
  Stoke Abbott DT6 ...203 D2
Venn The SP7 ...12 C2
Venning Ave BH11 ...88 C3
Ventnor Rd DT5 ...186 C4
Ventry Cl Poole BH13 ...120 C2
  2 Salisbury SP1 ...213 B3
Ventry Pl The 1 SP1 ...213 B3
Ventura Ctr The BH16 ...118 B3
Ventura Pl BH16 ...118 B3
Verity Cres BH17 ...88 A1
Verlands Rd DT3 ...153 B2
Vermin La BH20 ...83 A4
Vernalls Cl BH10 ...89 B3
Vernalls Ct BH25 ...95 B3
Vernalls Gdns BH10 ...89 B3
Vernalls Rd DT9 ...30 A4
Verne Cl DT4 ...167 B1
Verne Comm Rd DT5 ...186 C4
Verne Hill Rd DT5 ...187 A4
Verne Rd Verwood BH31 ...45 B3
  Weymouth DT4 ...167 B1
Verne Way DT4 ...167 B1
Verney Cl BH11 ...89 A2
Verney Rd BH11 ...89 A2
Verno La BH23 ...93 B1
Verona Ave BH23 ...123 B3
Verona Rd SP1 ...213 A4
Verriott's La DT6 ...66 B1
Verulam Rd 4 BH1 ...121 C2
Verulam Rd BH14 ...119 C2
Verwood CE Fst Sch
BH31 ...45 A3
Verwood Cres BH6 ...124 A2
Verwood Ind Est BH31 ...45 B3
Verwood Leisure Ctr
BH31 ...45 A3
Verwood Rd
  Ellingham Harbridge & Ibsley
  BH24 ...49 A3
  St Leonards & St Ives
  BH24 ...54 C4
  Three Legged Cross BH21 ...45 A1
  Verwood BH31 ...53 A4
  Woodlands BH21 ...44 B4
Verwood Sports Ctr
BH31 ...45 B3
Vespasian Way DT1 ...134 C4
Vetch Cl BH23 ...125 B4
Vian Cl BH25 ...94 C2
Vicarage Cl 3 BH20 ...140 A1
Vicarage Cots BH6 ...90 C2
Vicarage Ct 4 DT6 ...100 B4
Vicarage La DT7 ...107 C3
Vicarage Rd
  Bournemouth BH9 ...89 C1
  Poole BH15 ...119 B3
  Verwood BH31 ...45 A3
Vicarage St 9 BA20 ...27 B2
Vickers Cl BH8 ...91 A1
Vickery Way BH23 ...124 B4

Victoria Ave
  Bournemouth BH9 ...89 C1
  Radipole DT3 ...152 A3
  1 Swanage BH19 ...178 C1
Victoria Ave Ind Est
BH19 ...178 C2
Victoria Cl
  Corfe Mullen BH21 ...86 B3
  Wool BH20 ...139 B3
  Yeovil BA21 ...27 C3
Victoria Cres BH12 ...120 B3
Victoria Ct SP1 ...213 B4
Victoria Gdns
  Ferndown BH22 ...61 B3
  Ringwood BH24 ...55 B3
Victoria Gr DT6 ...100 B4
Victoria Hospl BH21 ...59 A3
Victoria Pl BH9 ...89 C1
Victoria Pl
  Bournemouth BH1 ...122 B3
  Easton/Weston DT5 ...187 A3
  Wimborne Minster BH21 ...59 A3
Victoria Rd
  Blandford Forum DT11 ...212 B2
  Dorchester DT1 ...107 C1
  Christchurch BH23 ...124 C3
  Dorchester DT1 ...107 C1
  Easton/Weston DT5 ...187 A3
  Ferndown BH22 ...61 B3
  Gillingham SP8 ...6 A1
  Poole BH12 ...120 B3
  Salisbury SP1 ...213 B3
  Swanage BH19 ...179 A1
  Wimborne Minster BH21 ...59 A3
  Yeovil BA21 ...27 C3
Victoria Sq DT5 ...186 C4
Victoria St
  Radipole DT4 ...167 C2
  Shaftesbury SP7 ...12 C2
Victory Cl 2 DT3 ...53 B3
Victory Rd DT5 ...186 C4
View Rd DT7 ...96 A3
Viewside Cl BH23 ...91 C1
Viking Cl BH6 ...124 A2
Viking Way
  Bournemouth BH6 ...124 A2
  Christchurch BH23 ...125 A3
  Salisbury SP2 ...213 B1
Village Rd DT6 ...68 C1
Villette Cl DT4 ...167 B2
Vince Cl BH11 ...89 A3
Vincent Cl 2 BH25 ...95 A4
Vincent Rd 2 BH25 ...95 A4
Vincents Cl DT9 ...31 A1
Vine Cl BH7 ...123 A4
Vine Farm Cl BH12 ...120 B4
Vine Farm Rd BH12 ...120 B4
Vine Hill BH21 ...58 C3
Vineries Cl BH21 ...59 C3
Vineries The BH21 ...59 C3
Vinery The BH25 ...95 A1
Vineyard Cl BH16 ...84 B1
Vinney Cross DT6 ...102 A3
Vinneys Cl BH23 ...92 B1
Violet Farm Cl BH21 ...84 B1
Violet La BH25 ...95 A2
Virginia Cl
  1 Henstridge BA8 ...19 A2
  Poole BH12 ...120 B4
Viscount Cl BH11 ...88 B3
Viscount Dr BH23 ...125 A3
Viscount Rd DT4 ...180 C4
Viscount Wlk BH11 ...88 B3
Vista Marina BH14 ...147 B3
Vivian Pk BH19 ...179 A2
Vixen Wlk BH25 ...95 A3
Voss's La DT2 ...206 B3
Vulcan Cl DT4 ...166 C1
Vulcan Way BH23 ...125 A4

W

W Burton Medieval Village
of* DT2 ...139 B1
Waddock Dro DT2 ...111 C2
Waddon Hill (Roman Fort)*
DT6 ...203 F4
Waddon House* DT3 ...150 C4
Waddon Way DT3 ...69 B1
Wadham Com Sch
TA18 ...191 F5
Wadmore La BH19 ...146 C4
Wagtail Dr BH25 ...94 C1
Wain Rd BH20 ...139 B4
Wain-a-long Rd SP1 ...213 C3
Wainwright Cl DT3 ...153 A2
Wakefield Ave BH10 ...89 C2
Wakefield Rd BH20 ...187 A2
Wakely Gdns BH11 ...89 A3
Wakely Rd BH11 ...89 A3
Walchren Pl BH15 ...118 B2
Walcott Ave BH23 ...91 C1
Waldich Gdns BH17 ...87 C1
Waldich Rd DT6 ...100 C3
Waldren Cl BH15 ...119 C1
Waldrons The 5 DT9 ...194 D8
Walford Cl BH21 ...59 B3
Walford Gdns BH21 ...59 B3
Walford Mill Craft Ctr*
BH21 ...59 A3
Walker Cres DT4 ...180 B3
Walkford Cl BH25 ...94 B2
Walkford Rd BH23 ...94 B1
Walkford Way BH23 ...94 A1
Walkingfield La BH15 ...119 B1

Walkwood Ave BH7 ...123 A4
Wall La DT6 ...203 D4
Wallace Rd BH18 ...87 A2
Wallis Rd BH10 ...89 A1
Walliscott Rd BH11 ...89 A1
Wallisdown Rd BH10 ...121 B4
Walls View Rd BH21 ...142 B3
Walsend Cl 3 DT5 ...186 C1
Walnut Ave BH11 ...212 A3
Walnut Cl DT5 ...94 C2
Walnut Orch 3 DT3 ...180 A4
Walpole Rd BH1 ...122 C3
Walpole St DT4 ...167 B2
Walrond Rd BH19 ...179 A2
Walsford Rd BH4 ...121 B3
Walsingham Dene
BH7 ...122 C4
Walters Dr 16 DT11 ...199 D4
Waltham Rd BH7 ...123 A3
Walton Elm Hill DT10 ...35 A4
Walton Rd
  Bournemouth BH10 ...89 B1
  Poole BH15 ...120 C3
Wanchard La DT2 ...107 B4
Wanderwell DT6 ...100 B2
Wanderwell Farm La
DT6 ...100 B2
Wanstead Cl BH24 ...47 B1
Warbler Cl BH18 ...118 A4
Warburton Rd BH17 ...119 C4
Wardcliffe Rd DT4 ...167 B2
Wardstone Barrow*
DT2 ...171 B4
Ware La DT7 ...96 A2
Wareham Ct BH7 ...123 A3
Wareham Golf Club
DT2 ...142 C3
Wareham Hospl BH20 ...142 B2
Wareham Lady St Mary CE
Fst Sch BH20 ...142 C2
Wareham Mid Sch
BH20 ...142 B2
Wareham Mus* DT2 ...142 C2
Wareham Rd
  Corfe Mullen BH21 ...86 B3
  Hawkchurch EX13 ...202 B2
  Lytchett Matravers BH16 ...84 B1
  Lytchett Minster & Upton
  BH16 ...116 A3
  Overmoigne DT2 ...155 C4
Wareham St Martin
BH16 ...116 B2
  Warmwell DT2 ...155 A4
Wareham Sta BH20 ...142 B3
Wares Cl 5 DT11 ...81 C4
Warland Rd BH21 ...86 C4
Warmwell Cl
  9 Bournemouth BH9 ...90 A2
  Poole BH17 ...87 C1
Warmwell Dro DT2 ...154 C4
Warmwell House*
DT2 ...155 A4
Warmwell Hill DT6 ...100 C4
Warnford Rd BH6 ...123 B4
Warren Ave BH23 ...124 C3
Warren Cl
  St.Leonards BH24 ...54 C3
  Weymouth DT4 ...166 C1
Warren Dr BH24 ...54 C3
Warren Edge Cl BH6 ...123 C2
Warren Edge Ct BH6 ...123 C2
Warren Edge Rd BH6 ...123 C2
Warren Hill DT2 ...78 B4
Warren La BH24 ...54 C3
Warren Rd
  Bere Regis BH20 ...113 B2
  Bournemouth BH4 ...121 A3
  Poole BH14 ...120 B2
  Puddletown DT2 ...78 A3
Warren Way BH16 ...116 B1
Warren Wlk BH22 ...61 A4
Warwick Ave BH25 ...95 A2
Warwick Cl SP1 ...213 A4
Warwick Ct 14 BH5 ...122 C2
Warwick Pl BH7 ...123 A3
Warwick Rd
  Bournemouth BH7 ...123 A3
  Poole BH14 ...120 B2
Washington Ave BH1 ...122 B3
Washpond La BH19 ...178 C3
Watchcombe Cl DT3 ...150 B4
Watcombe Hts BA20 ...26 C1
Watercombe La BA20 ...26 C2
Watercombe Pk BA20 ...26 C2
Waterditch Rd BH23 ...93 A2
Waterford Cl BH14 ...120 A1
Waterford Gdns BH23 ...91 A4
Waterford Lodge
BH23 ...125 A3
Waterford Pl BH23 ...126 A4

Waterford Rd
  Christchurch BH23 ...126 A3
  New Milton BH25 ...95 B2
Waterfront Mus*
BH15 ...119 A1
Watergates La DT2 ...136 B2
Waterlake Rd TA20 ...202 B8
Waterloo House BH17 ...87 A1
Waterloo La Silton SP8 ...5 A4
  Stourton Caundle DT10 ...33 A1
Waterloo Rd
  Bournemouth BH9 ...121 C4
  Broadstone BH17 ...119 B4
  Corfe Mullen BH21 ...86 A3
  Salisbury SP1 ...213 C2
Waterloo Way 3 BH24 ...55 C3
Watermead
  1 Tatworth TA20 ...202 A8
Watermill Rd BH23 ...124 A4
Waterpot Hill DT6 ...204 C2
Waters Edge BH13 ...147 B3
Waters Rd SP1 ...213 C4
Watership Dr BH24 ...55 C3
Waterside BH23 ...124 C2
Waterside BH24 ...47 B1
Watersmeet Rd SP2 ...213 B1
Waterston Cl DT7 ...87 B1
Waterston La DT2 ...77 B2
Waterston Manor*
DT2 ...77 B2
Watery La
  Christchurch BH23 ...125 A4
  Donhead St Mary SP7 ...24 C4
  Halstock BA22 ...193 D2
  Iwerne Minster DT11 ...37 C1
  Lytchett Minster & Upton
  BH16 ...
  Radipole DT3 ...152 A2
  Shaftesbury SP7 ...12 C1
  Studland BH19 ...164 B1
  Tincleton DT2 ...110 B2
  Upton BH16 ...118 A4
  West Crewkerne TA18 ...191 D2
Watford La DT6 ...68 C1
Watkin Rd 15 BH5 ...122 C2
Watton Cl BH8 ...91 A1
Watton Cross DT6 ...100 A3
Watton Gdns DT6 ...100 A3
Watton La DT6 ...100 A3
Watton Pk DT6 ...100 A3
Wavell Ave BH17 ...87 C1
Wavell Rd
  Bournemouth BH11 ...89 A2
  Salisbury SP2 ...213 B1
Wavendon Ave BH25 ...126 C4
Wavering La SP8 ...5 A2
Waverley Cres BH15 ...119 B3
Waverley House 12 BH25 ...95 A1
Waverley Rd
  New Milton BH25 ...95 A1
  Radipole DT3 ...167 B3
Wayclose La
  Buckhorn Weston SP8 ...4 A1
  Cucklington SP8 ...4 A1
Wayford Hill BH18 ...191 B1
Wayground Rd BH24 ...58 C1
Wayman Rd BH21 ...86 C3
Wayne Rd BH12 ...120 A3
Wayside Rd
  Bournemouth BH6 ...123 C2
  St Leonards BH24 ...54 C1
  St.Leonards BH24 ...53 C1
Waytown Cl BH17 ...87 B2
Weare Cl DT5 ...186 C4
Weatherbury Way
DT1 ...135 A4
Weatherby Castle (Fort)*
BH20 ...79 C3
Weavers Cl
  Crewkerne TA18 ...191 F4
  Ferndown BH22 ...53 A1
Webb La DT10 ...196 E8
Webb's Way BH11 ...89 A3
Webbers La BH20 ...176 C4
Webbers Piece DT2 ...206 C1
Webbs Cl BH24 ...55 C3
Webster Rd BH9 ...90 A2
Wedgwood Dr BH14 ...120 A1
Weiner Cl DT1 ...199 E2
Weir The DT3 ...153 B2
Weir View DT2 ...107 B3
Welbeck Rd BA21 ...28 A4
Welch Cl BH11 ...88 C3
Well Cl
  Bradford Abbas DT9 ...28 B1
  New Milton BH25 ...94 C1
Well La Poole BH15 ...119 B2
  Powerstock DT6 ...70 A2
  Shaftesbury SP7 ...12 B2
Well Plot DT6 ...101 B4
Welland Rd
  Wimborne Minster BH21 ...59 B2
  Yeovil BA21 ...27 C4
Wellbridge Cl DT1 ...135 A4
Wellesley Ave BH23 ...123 C4
Wellhayes EX13 ...202 E2
Wellfields Dr DT6 ...100 C4
Wellington Ave BH23 ...125 B4
Wellington Ct
  Bournemouth BH8 ...122 A3
  New Milton BH25 ...95 A2
Wellington Rd
  Bournemouth BH1 ...122 A3
  Poole BH14 ...120 B2

Wellstead Rd BH20 ....142 B3
Wendover Cl BH25 ....94 C1
Wendy Cres BH22 ....61 C2
Wenlock Ct BH23 ....124 C4
Wentwood Gdns BH25 ....95 B1
Wentworth BH14 ....147 B4
Wentworth Ave BH5 ....123 A2
Wentworth Cl
  Bournemouth BH5 ....123 A2
  Radipole DT3 ....152 C1
Wentworth Coll BH5 ....123 A2
Wentworth Dr
  Broadstone BH18 ....87 A3
  Christchurch BH23 ....123 C3
Wentworth Rd BA21 ....28 A4
Wescott Way BH11 ....88 C2
Wesley Cl
  6 Bournemouth BH8 ....122 B3
  Charmouth DT6 ....97 A4
Wesley Grange **33** BH4 ....121 B2
Wesley Rd Poole BH12 ....120 B3
  Wimborne Minster BH21 ....59 C3
Wessex Ave
  New Milton BH25 ....95 A1
  Shillingstone DT11 ....198 B5
Wessex Cl BH23 ....125 B4
Wessex Dr DT9 ....28 B1
Wessex Est BH24 ....55 B4
Wessex Gate Ret Pk
  BH17 ....120 A4
Wessex Oval DT10 ....142 B3
Wessex Rd
  Dorchester DT1 ....107 B1
  Poole BH14 ....120 A2
  Ringwood BH24 ....55 B4
  Salisbury SP1 ....213 C3
  Stalbridge DT10 ....33 B4
  Weymouth DT4 ....167 A2
  Yeovil BA21 ....26 C4
Wessex Trad Ctr
  BH12 ....120 A4
Wessex Way
  Bournemouth BH8 ....122 B3
  Dorchester DT1 ....107 B1
  Gillingham SP8 ....5 C2
  Swanage BH19 ....179 A2
West Allington DT6 ....100 A4
West Ave BH21 ....53 A4
West Bay Cres DT4 ....180 B4
West Bay Rd DT6 ....100 B2
West Borough BH21 ....59 A3
West Bourton Rd SP8 ....1 A1
West Brook BA21 ....26 C3
West Butts St **1** BH11 ....59 A3
West Chinnock Prim Sch
  TA18 ....192 B8
West Cl Chickerell DT3 ....166 B3
  Verwood BH31 ....44 C3
West Cl Ct BH6 ....124 A2
West Cl House BH4 ....124 A2
West Cliff Cotts BH2 ....121 C1
West Cliff Gdns BH2 ....121 C1
West Cliff Mews BH2 ....121 C1
West Cliff Rd
  Bournemouth BH2 ....121 B1
  Bridport DT6 ....100 A1
West Coker Rd
  East Coker BA20 ....26 C1
  Yeovil BA20 ....27 A1
West Coker VC Prim Sch
  BA22 ....193 A8
West Dr **3** BH19 ....179 A1
West Durlston Ct
  BH19 ....179 A1
West End DT2 ....206 B3
West Gables Cl BH6 ....100 A4
West Hall* DT9 ....195 C7
West Hendford DT1 ....27 A2
West Hill
  Charminster DT2 ....107 B3
  Portland DT5 ....205 F7
  Milborne Port DT9 ....17 B1
West Hill Pl **10** BH2 ....121 C2
West Hill Rd
  Bournemouth BH2 ....121 C1
  Lyme Regis DT7 ....96 A3
West Hill Rd BH11 ....89 A2
West Hove Ind Est
  BH11 ....88 C2
West La Arne Ind Est BH20 ....142 C1
  Hazelbury Bryan DT10 ....196 E4
  Melbury Abbas SP7 ....24 A3
  Mosterton DT8 ....203 F8
  North Wootton DT9 ....30 C1
West Lulworth CE Fst Sch
  BH20 ....172 C3
West Mans **8** BH4 ....121 B2
West Mead DT6 ....100 A4
West Mill Cres BH20 ....142 B3
West Mill La
  Castleton DT9 ....30 A2
  Stalbridge DT10 ....20 A2
West Mills Rd DT1 ....107 C2
West Moors Mid Sch
  BH22 ....53 A1
West Moors Rd
  Ferndown BH22 ....61 B4
  Three Legged Cross BH21 ....53 A4
  West Moors BH22 ....53 A4
West Overcliff Dr BH4 ....121 B1
West Pk BH20 ....27 A3
West Pk Dr SP6 ....190 F3
West Pk La SP6 ....190 F3
West Quay Rd BH15 ....119 A1

West Rd
  Bournemouth BH5 ....123 A2
  Bransgore BH23 ....93 A4
  Symondsbury DT6 ....99 B3
  West Lulworth BH20 ....172 B3
West Row BH21 ....59 A2
West Row Mews BH21 ....59 A2
West St
  Abbotsbury DT3 ....149 A4
  Bere Regis BH20 ....81 A2
  Blandford Forum DT11 ....212 B2
  Bridport DT6 ....100 B3
  Broadwindsor DT8 ....203 E5
  Chickerell DT3 ....166 B3
  Corfe Castle BH20 ....162 A1
  Crewkerne TA18 ....191 E4
  Fontmell Magna SP7 ....37 C3
  Hinton St George TA17 ....191 C7
  Kington Magna SP8 ....9 B1
  Poole BH15 ....119 A1
  Radipole DT4 ....167 B1
  Ringwood BH24 ....55 A4
  Salisbury SP2 ....213 A3
  Shapwick DT11 ....56 A4
  Templecombe BA8 ....18 B4
  Wareham BH20 ....142 C2
  Wimborne Minster BH21 ....59 A3
  Winterborne Kingston
  DT11 ....81 B4
  Winterborne Stickland
  DT11 ....210 C7
  Yeovil BA20 ....27 A2
West St Ct **11** BH21 ....59 A3
West Sta Terr BH4 ....121 B2
West View SP7 ....37 C4
West View Rd
  Christchurch BH23 ....124 C3
  Poole BH15 ....119 B2
West Walks Rd **8** DT1 ....108 A1
West Walls BH20 ....142 C2
West Way
  Bournemouth BH9 ....90 A1
  Broadstone BH18 ....87 A2
  Easton/Weston DT5 ....186 C1
  Winterborne Abbas
  DT2 ....105 B1
West Way Cl BH9 ....90 A1
West Ways BA22 ....192 D8
West Wlk Bridport DT6 ....100 A1
  Salisbury SP1 ....213 B2
West Wools SP6 ....186 C1
Westbourne Cl
  Bournemouth BH4 ....121 B2
  Salisbury SP1 ....213 A2
  Yeovil BA20 ....27 A3
Westbourne Gr BA20 ....27 A3
Westbourne Pk Rd
  BH4 ....121 A1
Westbourne Rd DT4 ....167 B3
Westbridge Pk DT9 ....29 C2
Westbrook Cl BH31 ....89 B1
Westbrook Sp SP8 ....5 A1
Westbury
  Bradford Abbas DT9 ....28 B1
  Sherborne DT9 ....30 A2
Westbury Ct
  Barton on Sea BH23 ....127 A4
  Bransgore BH23 ....93 A4
Westbury Ct **10** BH24 ....120 A2
Westbury Rd BA20 ....55 B4
Westby Rd BH5 ....122 C2
Westcliff
  Charmouth DT6 ....96 C4
  Easton/Weston DT5 ....95 A1
Westcroft Par **21** BH25 ....95 A1
Westcroft Pk BH18 ....87 B2
Westdown Rd BH11 ....89 A3
Westdowne Cl DT4 ....167 A1
Westerhall Rd DT4 ....167 C3
Westerham Rd BH4 ....121 A2
Westerleigh BH4 ....121 B1
Western Ave
  Barton on Sea BH25 ....126 B4
  Bournemouth BH10 ....89 B2
  Poole BH13 ....120 C1
  Yeovil BA22 ....26 B4
Western Cl BH10 ....89 B2
Western Downland Prim Sch
  SP6 ....190 F2
Western Rd BH13 ....121 A1
Western St DT9 ....28 B4
Westerngate BH13 ....121 A2
Westfield
  2 Portesham DT3 ....150 A4
  Sherborne DT9 ....29 C2
  5 Wimborne Minster BH21 ....59 A3
Westfield Ave BA21 ....27 A3
Westfield Cl BH21 ....59 A3
Westfield Com Sch
  BA21 ....27 A3
Westfield Cres BA21 ....27 A3
Westfield Est BA12 ....1 C2
Westfield Gdns BA21 ....27 A3
Westfield Gr BA21 ....27 A4
Westfield Inf Sch BA21 ....27 A3
Westfield Pl BA21 ....27 A4
Westfield Rd
  Bournemouth BH6 ....123 C2
  Yeovil BA21 ....27 A3
Westfield Sch DT3 ....153 A2
Westgate Pk BH14 ....121 A2
Westham Cl BH17 ....87 C2
Westham Rd DT4 ....167 B2
Westhaven DT4 ....167 A1
Westhaven Cty Inf Sch
  DT4 ....167 A2
Westhaven Cty Jun Sch
  DT4 ....167 A2

Westhaven Hospl DT4 ....167 A2
Westhill Cl **14** BH14 ....180 A4
Westhill Cl **8** DT4 ....180 A4
Westhill Rd DT4 ....180 B4
Westlake Cl DT3 ....152 A2
Westland Rd BA20 ....27 A2
Westlands Ct BH23 ....93 A4
Westlands Dr BH13 ....147 C4
Westleaze DT2 ....107 C3
Westleaze Cl DT2 ....107 C3
Westminster BA22 ....26 B3
Westminster Cl **10** SP7 ....12 C2
Westminster Ct BH25 ....126 C4
Westminster Meml Hospl
  SP7 ....12 C1
Westminster Rd
  Bournemouth BH20 ....142 B3
  Poole BH13 ....121 A1
  Salisbury SP2 ....213 A3
Westminster Rd E
  BH13 ....121 A1
Westminster St **10** BA20 ....27 B2
Westmoreland Ct SO41 ....95 C2
Weston Cl BA22 ....192 E8
Weston Dr BH1 ....122 A2
Weston Hill SP8 ....9 A3
Weston La
  Closworth BA22 ....193 E5
  Corscombe DT2 ....192 F1
  Ryewood BA20 ....27 A2
Weston Rd
  Easton/Weston DT5 ....186 C2
  Easton/Weston DT5 ....167 B1
  Wimborne Minster BH21 ....59 A2
  Worth Matravers BH19 ....183 B4
Weston St
  East Chinnock BA22 ....192 E8
  Easton/Weston DT5 ....187 A1
Westons La **6** BH15 ....119 B1
Westover Hill DT6 ....64 C1
Westover La BA22 ....54 C3
Westover Rd
  Bournemouth BH1 ....121 C2
  10 Dorchester DT1 ....107 C1
Westport Rd BH20 ....142 B2
Westray Hall BH4 ....121 B1
Westridge **6** DT9 ....30 A3
Westville BA21 ....27 C3
Westwey Rd DT4 ....167 B1
Westwood Ave BH7 ....123 A3
Westwoods & Glendene Pk
  BH25 ....94 B3
Wet La BA12 ....3 B1
Wetherbury Ct DT11 ....212 C3
Wetherby Cl
  Broadstone BH18 ....87 A1
  Milborne St Andrew DT11 ....79 C4
Wey Valley Sch The
Weyman's Ave BH10 ....89 B3
Weymans Dr BH10 ....89 B3
Weymouth & Portland Sailing
  Acad* DT5 ....181 A1
Weymouth Ave
  16 Dorchester DT1 ....108 A1
  Dorchester DT1 ....134 C4
Weymouth Bay Ave
  DT4 ....167 B4
Weymouth Coll
  Dorchester DT1 ....107 B1
  Radipole DT4 ....167 C3
Weymouth Com Hospl
  DT4 ....167 A2
Weymouth Golf Club
  DT4 ....167 A2
Weymouth Mus* DT4 ....167 C1
Weymouth Rd
  Dorchester DT1 ....134 C4
  Poole BH14 ....120 B3
  Winterborne Monkton
  DT2 ....134 C3
Weymouth Rugby Football
  Club DT3 ....167 A4
Weymouth Sports Club
  DT3 ....152 A1
Weymouth Sta DT4 ....167 B2
Weymouth Way DT4 ....167 A3
Weyview Cres DT3 ....152 A2
Wharf Cl BH12 ....120 C3
Wharfdale Rd
  Bournemouth BH4 ....121 B2
  Poole BH12 ....120 C3
Wharncliffe Ct BH23 ....125 C4
Wharncliffe Gdns
  BH23 ....126 A4
Wharncliffe Rd
  Bournemouth BH22 ....122 B2
  Christchurch BH23 ....126 A4
Whatcombe Rd DT11 ....210 D4
Whatleigh Cl BH15 ....119 B1
Whatley Rd DT6 ....86 B2
Whatley La TA20 ....202 C8
Wheat Cl **1** DT10 ....197 A4
Wheat Farland DT3 ....166 B3
Wheatear Cl **4** DT4 ....152 B2
Wheathill La DT7 ....17 B1
Wheathill Way DT7 ....17 B1
Wheatlands DT5 ....186 C1
Wheaton Grange BH4 ....121 B2
Wheaton Rd BH7 ....123 B2
Wheatplot Pk Homes **2**
  BH10 ....89 C2
Wheel House La TA20 ....202 E7
Wheelers La BH11 ....88 B3
Wheelwright's Cl SP5 ....189 A4
Whetham Mill La DT8 ....203 C6
Whetland's La DT6 ....99 B1

Whimbrel Ct BH23 ....125 A3
Whincroft Cl BH22 ....61 C4
Whincroft Dr BH22 ....61 C3
Whitby Ave BH18 ....87 A1
Whitby Cl BH23 ....91 A2
Whitby Cres BH18 ....87 A1
Whitchurch Ave BH18 ....87 A2
Whitchurch La BA8 ....19 A3
Whitcombe Rd DT8 ....204 D3
Whitcross **9** BA22 ....193 F8
White Cl **1** Bridport DT6 ....68 C1
  Poole BH15 ....120 A4
White Cliff DT11 ....212 B2
White Farm Cl BH10 ....121 B4
White Hart Ct DT10 ....196 D5
White Hart La SP7 ....12 C2
White Hill
  5 Puddletown DT2 ....78 A1
  Tolpuddle DT2 ....79 B1
White Hill La DT2 ....79 B1
White Horse Dr
  Overcombe/Preston
  DT3 ....153 B2
  Poole BH15 ....119 B3
White Horse La
  Hinton St Mary DT10 ....35 A3
  Overcombe/Preston
  DT3 ....153 B2
White Horse Mews
  DT2 ....72 C4
White Horses BH25 ....126 C4
White House La DT9 ....195 A4
White Knights BH25 ....126 C4
White La DT2 ....205 C8
White Lodge BH15 ....119 C2
White Lovington BH20 ....81 A1
White Mead BA21 ....26 C3
White Mill Bridge* 56 C3
White Pit DT10 ....198 B5
White Pit La SP7 ....24 B2
White Rd BA12 ....3 A3
White Way
  Buckland Newton DT2 ....208 B6
  Lifton Cheney DT3 ....103 B2
White Way La DT10 ....21 C1
Whitebeam Way BH31 ....45 B3
Whitebridge Rd SP1 ....213 C3
Whitecliff Cres BH14 ....120 A1
Whitecliff Gdns BH14 ....120 A1
Whitecliff Rd
  Poole BH14 ....119 C1
  Swanage BH19 ....179 A3
Whitecross Cl BH17 ....87 C2
Whitecross Dr DT4 ....180 A4
Whitefield Dr SP8 ....10 B2
Whitefield Lodge **1**
  BH25 ....95 A2
Whitefield Rd
  New Milton BH25 ....95 A1
  Poole BH14 ....120 A1
Whitefriars Rd **6** SP1 ....213 B2
Whitehall BH23 ....124 A3
Whitehall St **3** TA18 ....191 F5
Whitehart Fields **1**
  BH24 ....55 C4
Whiteheads Cl BH23 ....92 B1
Whiteheyes Rd BH23 ....92 B1
Whitehead Dr DT4 ....180 B3
Whitehouse Rd BH21 ....59 C3
Whiteleap Way BH10 ....89 C3
Whitemarsh BA12 ....3 A2
Whites Cl DT2 ....76 C4
Whiteway Hill BH21 ....201 B4
Whiteways BH21 ....59 C3
Whitfield Pk BH24 ....54 B3
Whitfield Rd DT11 ....107 B1
Whithay La DT4 ....68 A4
Whitingham Ct **8** BH25 ....123 A3
Whitley Way BH25 ....95 A3
Whitmore La BH21 ....201 A4
Whitsbury Cl BH8 ....90 B1
Whittle Rd BH21 ....60 C4
Whittles Way BH15 ....119 A1
Whynot Way DT3 ....166 B2
Wick 1 Ind Est BH25 ....94 C1
Wick 2 Ind Est BH25 ....94 C1
Wick Cl BH25 ....94 C1
Wick Dr BH25 ....94 C1
Wick Farm BH6 ....124 A3
Wick Hill DT9 ....17 A3
Wick La BH6 ....124 A3
Wick Rd DT9 ....17 B2
Wicket Rd BH10 ....89 B3
Wicketsbeer Rd BA22 ....193 C6
Wickfield Ave BH23 ....124 A3
Wickfield Cl BH23 ....124 A3
Wickford House BH13 ....124 A3
Wickham Cl BH21 ....61 C3
Wickham Dr BH21 ....86 B2
Wickham Rd BH7 ....123 A3
Wicklea Rd BH6 ....124 A2
Wickmeads Rd BH6 ....124 A2
Widdicombe Ave
  BH14 ....120 C1
Wide St DT5 ....186 C3
Widget Cl BH11 ....89 A4
Widworthy Dr BH18 ....86 C3
Wight Wlk BH21 ....61 C1
Wightman's Orch DT2 ....208 B2
Wilderness The DT9 ....30 B3
Wilderton Rd BH13 ....120 C2
Wilderton Rd W BH13 ....121 A2
Wildfell Cl BH23 ....92 A1
Wildown Gdns BH6 ....124 A2
Wildown Rd BH6 ....124 A2
Wilfred Rd BH5 ....122 C2

Wilkins Way BH15 ....119 A
Wilkinson Dr BH8 ....91 A
Willett Rd BH21 ....59 A
William Barnes CP Sch
  DT10 ....197 C
William Cl
  Christchurch BH23 ....94 A
  Laverstock SP1 ....213 C
William Cl **17** BH23 ....126 A
William Rd BH7 ....122 C
William St DT4 ....167 C
William's Ind Pk BH25 ....94 C
Williams Ave DT4 ....180 B
Williams' Ave DT4 ....180 B
Williford La DT7 ....195 C
Willis Way BH15 ....119 A
Willis's La TA18 ....192 B
Willoughby Cl **3** DT2 ....78 A
Willow Cl
  Bournemouth BH4 ....121 A
  Salisbury SP1 ....213 C
  St.Leonards BH24 ....53 C
  Upton BH16 ....118 B
Willow Cres
  Holton Heath BH20 ....116 A
  Overcombe/Preston
  DT3 ....168 A
Willow Ct BH7 ....123 B
Willow Dr
  Christchurch BH23 ....124 A
  Ringwood BH24 ....55 B
  Wimborne Minster BH21 ....60 B
Willow Farm **11** DT9 ....194 C
Willow Gr **6** DT6 ....204 D
Willow Lodge **1** BH11 ....122 B
Willow Lodge Montessori
  Sch BH11 ....122 B
Willow Mead BH8 ....90 B
Willow Pk BH14 ....120 A
Willow Pl BH23 ....124 B
Willow Rd BH24 ....53 C
Willow Tree Rise BH11 ....89 A
Willow View BH16 ....118 B
Willow Way
  Bridport DT6 ....100 C
  Christchurch BH23 ....124 A
  Ferndown BH22 ....61 A
  Motcombe SP7 ....12 A
  Northport BH20 ....142 B
Willow Wlk BH25 ....127 A
Willowdene Cl BH25 ....95 B
Willows The BH25 ....127 A
Wills Cl BH21 ....86 B
Wills La DT2 ....207 D
Wills Rd Poole BH12 ....120 C
  Swanage BH19 ....178 C
Wilman Way SP2 ....213 A
Wilmslow Rd DT3 ....166 B
Wilmur Cres BH15 ....119 C
Wilson Pk DT11 ....212 C
Wilson Rd
  Bournemouth BH1 ....122 C
  Dorchester DT1 ....108 B
  Poole BH14 ....120 B
Wilton Cl BH23 ....91 B
Wilton Dr DT4 ....167 A
Wilton Gdns BH25 ....94 C
Wilton Rd
  Bournemouth BH7 ....122 C
  Salisbury SP2 ....213 A
  Yeovil BA21 ....28 A
Wiltshire Ave DT4 ....167 A
Wiltshire Cl SP8 ....5 C
Wiltshire Gdns BH23 ....92 C
Wiltshire
  Bransgore BH23 ....92 C
  Salisbury SP2 ....213 A
Wilverley Ave BH8 ....90 C
Wilverley Rd BH23 ....125 A
Wilverly Gdns DT11 ....212 C
Wimborne Fst Sch
  BH21 ....59 A
Wimborne Minst Model Town
  & Gdns* BH21 ....59 A
Wimborne Rd
  Blandford Forum DT11 ....212 C
  Bournemouth BH10 ....89 B
  Broadstone BH21 ....58 C
  Lytchett Matravers BH16 ....84 C
  Poole BH15 ....119 B
  Tarrant Keyneston DT11 ....211 E
  Tarrant Rushton DT11 ....48 A
  Wimborne Minster BH21 ....59 A
Wimborne Rd E BH22 ....61 B
Wimborne Rd W BH21 ....60 B
Wimborne St BH21 ....40 A
Wimborne St Giles CE Fst
  Sch BH21 ....201 E
Wimborough La BA22 ....192 F
Win Gn View SP7 ....13 A
Winbrook Fold DT2 ....156 C
Winchelsea Sch BH12 ....88 B
Winchester Cl DT4 ....166 C
Winchester Gdns BA21 ....27 C
Winchester Pl **3** BH15 ....119 B
Winchester Rd BH15 ....95 B
Winchester St SP1 ....213 B
Wincombe Bsns Pk
  SP7 ....13 A
Wincombe Cl BH22 ....61 B
Wincombe Dr BH22 ....61 B
Wincombe La SP7 ....12 C
Wind Whistle Farm **3**
  DT11 ....81 C
Windermere Cl BA20 ....27 A

Win - Zoa 243

indermere Cres
)T3 167 A3
indermere Rd BH3 122 A4
indgreen Est BH21 86 C4
indham Mews BH1 122 B3
indham Rd BH1 122 B3
indlesham Rd SP1 213 B4
indmill Barrow*
3H21 84 A4
indmill Cl
haftesbury SP7 12 C2
t.Leonards BH24 54 C2
indmill La
t Leonards & St Ives
3H24 55 A2
t.Leonards BH24 54 C2
indmill Rd DT11 212 C2
indmill Rise 6 TA18 191 F5
indsor Cl
ovington Camp BH20 139 C3
lordle SO41 95 C2
1 Mosterton DT8 204 A7
t.Leonards BH24 54 A3
indsor Ct
5 Christchurch BH23 126 A4
oole BH14 120 A2
indsor La SP8 5 B1
indsor Rd
ournemouth BH5 122 C2
hristchurch BH23 123 C4
orchester DT1 107 C1
oole BH14 120 A2
adipole DT3 152 A2
2 Salisbury SP2 213 A3
indsor St 11 SP2 213 A3
indsor Way SP6 42 B3
indwhistle Cnr SP7 13 C2
indy Cnr DT11 200 C1
indy Ridge DT8 204 C4
ine St 1 BA20 27 B2
infrith Cres BH12 120 C4
infrith Dro
West Lulworth BH20 172 C4
infrith Newburgh DT2 156 C3
infrith Newburgh CE Fst
Sch DT2 156 C3
infrith Tech Ctr DT2 139 A1
ingate Ave BA21 27 C4
ingfield Ave
hristchurch BH23 93 B1
oole BH15 119 B3
ingfield Ct BH1 122 B2
ingfield Rd DT9 30 A3
ingreen Cl 3 DT3 168 A4
inifred Rd BH15 119 C3
inkelbury Hill (Hill Fort)*
SP7 188 C8
inkton Cl BH23 92 B2
inkton House BH23 92 B2
innards Cl BH22 61 C1
inniford Cl DT6 99 A4
insford Cl BH23 93 B1
insley Ave BH6 123 B2
inslow Rd DT3 153 B2
inspit Cl BH15 118 C2
inspit Rd BH19 183 B4
inston Ave BH12 121 A3
inston Ct
1 Christchurch BH23 124 A4
20 New Milton BH25 95 A1
inston Dr BA21 27 A4
inston Gdns BH12 121 A3
inston Par 22 BH25 95 A1
inston Pk BH12 121 A3
inston Rd BH9 90 A2
inston Way BH24 55 B4
inter La DT9 15 C3
inter's La DT3 150 B4
interborne La BH20 82 C3
interborne Cl
BH15 119 B2
interborne Copse
DT4 180 B4
interborne Faringdon
Village* DT2 135 A3
interborne Hospl
DT1 134 C4

Winterbourne Rd
BH15 119 B3
Winterbourne Valley CE Fst
Sch DT2 105 B1
Winterhayes Cl BH17 87 C2
Winters Cl 6 DT3 150 A4
Winton (Boys) Sch
BH10 89 B1
Winton Prim Sch BH9 89 C1
Winton Way
Bournemouth BH10 89 B1
New Milton BH25 95 A3
Winyards View TA18 191 F3
Wisbech Way SO41 95 C2
Wishart Gdns BH9 90 A3
Wishay St 2 DT1 107 B1
Wistaria Ho 7 BH10 89 C2
Wisteria Cl BA22 26 B3
Wisteria Dr BH31 45 C2
Witch Cl SP8 10 B2
Witch La SP8 10 B2
Witcham La DT2 205 F5
Witchampton CE Fst Sch
BH21 200 F1
Witchampton La
Hinton Martell BH21 50 A4
Witchampton BH21 201 A1
Witchampton Rd BH18 86 C1
Withermoor Rd BH9 121 C4
Withies Croft DT5 187 B3
Withingham Rd BH13 120 C2
Withybed La BA9 4 B2
Witley BH14 147 B4
Witney Rd BH17 87 B1
Wittey's La TA20 202 E6
Woburn Rd BA21 28 A4
Woking Rd BH14 120 B2
Wolfe Cl BH23 124 B4
Wolfeton House*
DT2 107 B3
Wollaston Rd
Bournemouth BH6 123 C2
Dorchester DT1 108 A1
Wollaton Cres BH22 61 B2
Wollaton Rd BH22 61 B2
Wollstonecraft Rd 25
BH5 122 C2
Wolseley Rd BH12 120 B3
Wolterton Rd BH12 121 A3
Wolverley Ct 16 BH4 121 B2
Wolverton Rd BH7 122 C3
Wonderholm Par BH11 89 A1
Wood Cl La TA17 191 A8
Wood Fold View DT2 205 B8
Wood La
Bournemouth BH11 88 C3
Broadwindsor DT8 203 B7
Hinton St Mary DT10 35 A2
Stalbridge DT10 33 B4
Symondsbury DT6 67 B3
Wood Lawn Cl BH25 126 C4
Wood Row BH9 90 C2
Wood View BH21 60 A4
Woodacre Gdns BH22 61 C2
Wood's La DT8 204 B3
Woodbury BH1 122 A1
Woodbury Ave BH8 90 C1
Woodbury Cl BH23 91 C2
Woodbury Dro DT2 137 B3
Woodbury Gdns SP2 213 B1
Woodbury Hill (Fort)*
BH20 81 B1
Woodcocks Cres BH7 123 A4
Woodcote 2 BA20 26 C1
Woodcote Dr BH16 118 A3
Woodcutts La BH21 50 B4
Woodend Rd BH9 121 C4
Woodfield Gdns BH23 93 B1
Woodfield Rd BH11 89 A3
Woodford Cl BH24 55 B4
Woodford Rd BH1 122 B2
Woodgreen Dr BH11 88 B2
Woodhayes BA8 19 A2
Woodhayes Ave BH23 93 C1
Woodhenge BA22 26 B3
Woodhouse Cross SP8 4 C2
Woodhouse La EX13 202 A1
Woodhouse Rd EX13 202 A1

Woodlake Cl BH17 87 B1
Woodland Ave BH5 123 A2
Woodland Cl BH31 45 A4
Woodland Ct BH7 122 C3
Woodland Gr 12 BA20 27 B2
Woodland Mans BH14 120 A3
Woodland Way BH23 125 B4
Woodland Wlk
Bournemouth BH5 123 A2
Ferndown BH22 61 C4
Woodlands DT2 136 A1
Woodlands Ave BH15 118 C2
Woodlands Cl BH23 93 A4
Woodlands Cres BH15 118 C2
Woodlands Dr BH20 116 A1
Woodlands Manor*
BA12 3 A2
Woodlands Mead DT10 20 C2
Woodlands Rd
Barton on Sea BH25 126 C4
Mere BA12 3 A1
Woodlands Way
New Milton BH25 95 A3
St.Leonards BH24 54 A2
Woodleaze Cl BH18 87 A3
Woodlinken Cl BH31 45 B2
Woodlinken Dr BH31 45 B2
Woodlinken Way BH31 45 C2
Woodmead Rd DT7 96 A3
Woodpecker Cl BH31 45 A3
Woodpecker Dr BH17 118 C4
Woodpeckers The
DT3 152 B2
Woodrising BH13 147 A2
Woodrisings The BH2 121 B2
Woodroffe Sch DT7 96 A3
Woodruff Cl BH23 125 B4
Woods View Rd BH9 121 B4
Woodsage Dr SP8 5 B1
Woodsford Castle*
DT2 110 A1
Woodsford Cl DT2 137 B3
Woodsford House Sch
DT2 110 B1
Woodsford La DT2 138 A4
Woodsford Rd DT2 137 B4
Woodside Cl BH22 61 C3
Woodside Rd
Bournemouth BH5 123 A2
Ferndown BH22 52 C2
Poole BH14 120 B2
Woodstock Cl BH14 120 A1
Woodstock Ct BH22 61 C2
Woodstock La BH24 55 B4
Woodstock Rd
Burton BH23 92 B1
Poole BH14 120 A1
Salisbury SP1 213 B3
Yeovil BA21 27 C4
Woodswater La 5 DT8 204 D4
Woodvale Gdns BH25 95 B2
Woodvill Rd SP1 213 C4
Wool Bridge* BH20 140 A2
Wool CE Fst Sch
BH20 140 A1
Wool Rd BH12 120 A4
Wool Sta BH20 140 A1
Woolland Gdns DT4 180 B4
Woolands La SP7 12 B2
Woolcombe Rd DT5 186 C2
Woolcott La SP8 1 B1
Woolmer La BH24 47 B1
Woolsbarrow (Fort)*
BH20 114 C3
Woolsbridge Ind Est
BH21 53 B3
Woolsbridge Rd BH24 54 A2
Woolslope Cl BH22 53 A1
Woolslope Gdns BH22 53 A1
Woolslope Rd BH22 53 A1
Woolven Cl BH14 120 A3
Wooperton St 9 DT4 167 B2
Wootton Cross DT6 65 B2
Wootton Gdns BH1 122 A2
Wootton Gr DT9 30 A4
Wootton La DT6 65 A2
Wootton Mount BH1 122 A2
Wootton Rd BH25 95 B4

Wootton Rough BH25 95 A4
Wor Barrow (Long Barrow)*
SP5 189 C4
Worbarrow Gdns
BH12 120 B4
Wordsworth Ave BH8 90 C1
Wordsworth Rd SP1 213 B3
Worgret Hill BH20 141 C1
Worgret Rd
Poole BH15 119 B4
Wareham BH20 142 B2
Worrell Dr BH12 120 B4
Worthington Cres
BH14 120 A2
Worthy Rd BH25 95 A1
Wortley Rd BH23 126 A4
Wrackle Cl DT2 106 C4
Wraxall Cl BH17 87 B1
Wraxall La DT2 206 B2
Wraxhill Rd BA20 27 A1
Wren Cl
Christchurch BH23 125 A3
New Milton BH25 94 C1
Ringwood BH24 55 C3
Wren Cres BH12 121 A3
Wren Gdns SP6 42 B3
Wrenscroft 9 SP2 213 B1
Wriggle River La DT2 194 E1
Writh Rd DT9 31 B1
Wroxham Rd BH12 120 C3
Wyatt's La BH20 142 C2
Wyatts Cl BH21 86 B3
Wyatts La BH21 86 B3
Wych Hill DT6 100 B2
Wych Ridge DT6 100 B2
Wychwood Cl BH2 121 C2
Wychwood Dr BH2 121 C2
Wychwood Grange 1
BH2 121 C2
Wycliffe Rd BH9 121 C4
Wydford Cl DT9 29 C3
Wyelands Ave BH21 60 B3
Wyke CP Sch SP8 5 B1
Wyke Oliver Rd DT3 168 A4
Wyke Rd Gillingham SP8 5 C1
Weymouth DT4 167 A1
Wyke Regis CE Jun Sch
DT4 180 B4
Wyke Regis Com & Sports Ctr
DT4 180 B3
Wyke Regis Inf Sch
DT4 180 B4
Wykeham Cl BH17 119 C4
Wykeham Lodge
BH13 147 C3
Wynchard Bank 1
DT11 198 E3
Wyncombe Rd BH5 123 A3
Wyndham Cl BH23 94 A1
Wyndham Pk Sch SP1 213 B4
Wyndham Rd
Christchurch BH23 94 A1
Poole BH14 120 A2
Salisbury SP1 213 B3
Wyndham St 5 BA20 27 C3
Wyndham Terr SP1 213 B3
Wyndham View BA21 27 C3
Wynford Rd
Bournemouth BH9 90 A2
Poole BH14 120 B2
Wynne Cl BH18 86 C2
Wynnes Cl 4 DT9 30 A3
Wynnes Rise DT9 30 A3
Wynter Cl BH7 122 C4
Wytch Pas BH20 162 B4
Wyvern Cl
East Coker BA20 26 C1
Poole BH12 120 B4
Wyvern Ct 24 TA18 191 F4
Wyvern Rd 1 DT1 107 C1

Y

Yalbury La DT2 137 B3
Yard La
Marshwood DT6 203 D2
Rampisham DT2 205 E6

Yarde Farm 5 DT11 199 D3
Yarmouth Cl BH12 121 A3
Yarmouth Rd BH12 120 C3
Yarn Barton
10 Beaminster DT8 204 D4
18 Yeovil BA20 27 B2
Yarnbarton DT8 203 E5
Yarrells Cl BH16 118 B3
Yarrells Dr BH16 118 A4
Yarrells La BH16 118 B3
Yarrells Sch BH16 118 A4
Yarrow Cl BH23 125 A4
Yarrow Ct 1 SP8 5 B1
Yarrow Rd BH12 120 A4
Yearlings' Dro BH20 113 A4
Yeates Rd DT5 186 C3
Yeatman Hospl The
DT9 30 A3
Yeatmans Cl SP7 12 B2
Yeatmans La SP7 12 B2
Yeatminster Rd BH17 87 C1
Yellow La DT6 69 B1
Yellowham Hill DT2 109 B4
Yelverton Rd 33 BH1 121 C2
Yenston Hill BA8 18 C4
Yeolands Rd 7 DT5 186 C2
Yeomans Ind Pk BH8 90 C1
Yeomans Rd BH8 90 C2
Yeomans Way BH8 90 C1
Yeovil Coll BA22 26 B4
Yeovil Coll IT Ctr BA20 27 C2
Yeovil Golf Club BA21 28 A2
Yeovil Junc Sta BA22 28 A1
Yeovil Pen Mill Sta
BA21 28 A3
Yeovil Rd
Crewkerne TA18 191 F4
Halstock BA22 193 D3
Sherborne DT9 29 C3
Yeovil BA20 27 A1
Yeovil Ski Activity Ctr
BA20 27 C2
Yeovil Sports Club
BA21 27 A4
Yerville Gdns SO41 95 C2
Yetminster Sta DT9 194 C5
Yew La BH25 95 B2
Yew Tree Cl
Wimborne Minster BH21 59 B3
Yeovil BA20 27 A1
Yew Tree Ct 30 BH25 95 A1
Yew Tree Farm DT2 205 A8
Yew Tree La DT2 106 C3
Yews The BA12 3 A3
Yewstock Sch DT10 35 A1
York Ave BH25 95 A2
York Cl Broadstone BH18 87 A1
Charminster DT2 107 C3
Christchurch BH23 123 C4
York Pl
Bournemouth BH7 123 A3
17 New Milton BH25 95 A2
Yeovil BA20 27 B3
York Rd
Bournemouth BH1 122 A2
Broadstone BH18 87 A1
Dorchester DT1 108 A1
Salisbury SP2 213 A3
Youngs Rd BH11 89 A3

Z

Zamek Cl BH11 89 A3
Zeals Fst Sch BA12 2 A2
Zeals Gn Dr BA12 2 A2
Zeals Rise BA12 1 C2
Zetland Ct BH4 121 A1
Zig Zag Hill SP7 24 C3
Zinnia Cl BH10 89 C1
Zoar La DT10 197 B4